Social Studies in Elementary Education

Social Studies in Elementary Education

Sixth Edition

John Jarolimek
University of Washington, Seattle

Macmillan Publishing Co., Inc.
NEW YORK

Collier Macmillan Publishers
LONDON

Macmillan Publishing Co., Inc.
866 Third Avenue, New York, New York 10022

Collier Macmillan Canada, Inc.

Library of Congress Cataloging in Publication Data

Jarolimek, John.
  Social studies in elementary education.

  Includes bibliographies and index.
  1. Social sciences—Study and teaching (Elementary)
I. Title.
LB1584.J3 1982   372.8'3'044   81-1346
ISBN 0-02-360440-9   AACR2

Printing: 1 2 3 4 5 6 7 8   Year: 0 1 2 3 4 5 6 7 8

Every now and then an event occurs that rekindles the flame of patriotism in the hearts of most Americans. The landing of the men on the moon was such an event, as were the Bicentennial celebration and the release and return of the hostages from Iran. It is at such times that Americans are reminded that they really have a unique national character and that it means something special to be a citizen of this nation. It is at such times, too, that America shows the world that its enduring strength is to be found in the history of its people. People whose forebears from all over the globe, from all walks of life, of every religious and political persuasion, of all ethnic, racial, and cultural groups came to this part of North America—this favored land—and created a nation based on principles of freedom, human dignity, social justice, and equality.

To build a nation based on such values under the conditions of the 18th century was indeed a remarkable achievement in itself. But to have it survive for over 200 years is a record unmatched in modern history. The republic has not only preserved those democratic values on which it was founded, but has extended them to increasingly greater numbers of individuals and groups. The significant question today is whether or not those who follow will be able to make this same claim a decade from now, or at the turn of the century, or in the year 2076 when the nation celebrates its Tricentennial.

We have no way of forecasting accurately what lies ahead for our nation, but if we are to be optimistic about the future, we know that teachers in the decades to come will have to be attentive to the citizenship education of young children. This speaks to the importance of social studies in the elementary school curriculum because much of citizenship education, as well as what we refer to as the mainstream culture, is embodied in social studies. The nation's future depends on the civic and political competence of its citizens, and much of the responsibility for building such competence rests in the hands of those teachers who work with children in the elementary school grades.

This text is intended to facilitate teaching social studies in the elementary school. The content and methods presented in this edition have been thoroughly updated in terms of current and emerging educational trends and priorities. A conscientious effort has been made to preserve those features that teachers have found attractive, practical, and useful in earlier editions. It remains a balanced, comprehensive treatment of social studies in elementary education, written in a style intended to communicate clearly to the reader.

Learning *about* teaching should never be too far removed from the actual practice of teaching. Thus, the study aids at the ends of chapters have been expanded in this edition and focus directly on classroom situations. In nearly all cases, the suggested activities require the student to apply what is being studied by developing a product that could be useful in a practical classroom setting.

Many attempts have been made to institutionalize new organizational structures for the elementary school. Most of those efforts have been less than successful, and the self-contained classroom remains the predominantly preferred arrangement. Such classrooms are supposed to educate "all the children of all the people" and, as such, provide numerous opportunities for good teaching of values associated with citizenship. The so-called "pull-out model" for teaching exceptional children is still widely applied, although the trend is clearly toward mainstreamed instruction. This means that pupil populations are even more diverse than they have been in the past. Social studies instruction that is properly planned and implemented can be used to accommodate this wide range of individual pupil differences. Moreover, social studies units of instruction can be helpful in teaching basic skills such as reading, writing, arithmetic, speaking, and listening in settings where they can be used and applied. The social studies can serve as a mechanism for integrating the total curriculum of the classroom. This edition stresses the mutual benefits that result when social studies is related to other school subjects and skills, and vice versa. Many suggestions are provided in the text for putting such practices into operation.

The author acknowledges assistance from and expresses thanks and appreciation to the following individuals and school districts, all of Washington State, for contributing photographs and artwork for this edition: Kay Franks-Englesen, Tacoma School District; Gene Gesley, Editor, *Bremerton Sun*; James Hawkins, Kathy Rockwell, and Faith Beatty, Seattle Public Schools; Jane Hartnett and Christine E. Meyers, Design Artists; Robert Knorr and Hisako Funai, Northshore School District; Terri Malinowski, *The Northshore Citizen*; Marilyn J. Church, Clover Park School District; Barbara Ryan, Lake Washington School District; and Barbara J. Scott and Lowell R. Jackson, Shoreline School District.

The author also wishes to express sincere thanks and appreciation to his wife, Mildred Fleming Jarolimek, for her expert technical assistance in the preparation of the manuscript and in the production of the book.

John Jarolimek

CONTENTS

Contents

▌▌ SOURCES OF CONTENT

PROCESSES AND SKILLS

Contents

IV EVALUATION

1

PLANNING for Teaching

1

ORIENTATION TO the Social Studies Curriculum

An analysis of the contemporary lives of young people of high school and college age provides confusing and contradictory findings. On the one hand, there is much evidence that millions of young people are thoughtful and responsible persons of good character who will doubtless carry these qualities into their adult lives. At the same time, there is a growing number who are showing serious signs of psychological disturbance and anti-social and self-destructive behavior. One is left with an uneasy feeling about the future of this society when one reviews current data relating to homicides, suicides, drug and alcohol use, illegitimate births, venereal disease, larceny, and rape among adolescent youth. The data show all of these on the rise, and dramatically so, among this particular age group.[1] Moreover, the data show that it is adolescents themselves who are most often victimized by the anti-social and destructive behavior of other adolescents.

Are these alarming statistics causing a ground swell of concern throughout the nation, demanding that families, communities, and schools marshal their resources to stem this growing tide of destruction of our young people? Hardly so. We find, rather, parents, teachers, school officials, and legislators obsessed with raising the achievement levels of children in the basic skills of reading, writing, and arithmetic! Some have seriously proposed doing away with social studies altogether in the primary grades in order to provide more time to teach "the basics."

An index that can be used to assess the exercise of citizenship responsibilities is to check whether or not an individual votes. Voting is one of the least demanding and easiest ways to participate in civic affairs. It is completely private. Additionally, there is a considerable amount of social approval that goes along with voting. One would think that those who are just completing their elementary and secondary education—society's training ground for citizenship competence—would be the group most persuaded of the power of the ballot box

[1] Edward A. Wynne, "Facts about the Character of Young Americans," *Character* 1 (November 1979), pp. 1–7.

and would turn out on Election Day in great numbers. The facts are that the number of 18- to 21-year-olds who have bothered to vote since the voting age was lowered to 18 years by Constitutional amendment in 1971 has been so low as to be a national embarrassment.

The reality of the present situation is simply that America has become careless in the citizenship education of its children and youth. What is most astonishing is that the groups who should be most active in reversing this trend—parents, teachers, and legislators—seem to find it impossible to convert their concerns into positive action. Perhaps they are overwhelmed by the magnitude of the problem and feel helpless to do anything about it. Be that as it may, it is imperative that school programs, whose mission it is to build civic competence—meaning social studies education—be revitalized, and soon. It is difficult to know how America will be able to sustain its more than 200-year tradition as a strong and free nation unless there is a turnabout in the half-hearted efforts at citizenship education that now prevail in many schools.

All of education, and most especially social studies education, concerns itself with social continuity. The young are socialized and educated to follow in the footsteps of their forebears to perpetuate and improve the social life of the group—to carry on its traditions and values, to educate its young, to maintain the political and legal systems, to develop loyalty and fidelity to the society, and so on. This accumulated wisdom and skill is passed on from one generation to the next, and if the society defaults in this responsibility, its culture cannot survive. All societies provide for this type of socialization, which in a broad sense might be thought of as citizenship education.

Basically, social studies education deals with knowledge, skills, attitudes, and values that make it possible to participate in group life. The arena of this participation extends outward from the self, first to primary groups of the family and school, to secondary groups in the larger community, then to state and national groups and ultimately encompassing the global community. Because social studies is so directly related to citizenship competence, it is worthy of the highest priority in the school curriculum. Furthermore, the evidence is overwhelming that socialization into group life takes place early in the child's life. Thus, social studies programs in all grades of the elementary school are critical to the entire citizenship education effort.

What kind of a teacher will it take to inspire young children with the ideals that helped to shape this nation: a teacher who will be able to help children make sense out of the world in which they live and who will help them learn to lead productive, happy lives in it; one who will help pupils develop knowledge and skills that allow them to deal with—and to some extent manage—the physical and social forces of the world in which they live? What kind of teacher will it take to instill in children a realistic hope in the future and confidence in their ability to solve social problems? Of course, it will take a caring, competent, dedicated teacher to achieve such goals. But more than that,

Why is it important that pupils engage in exercises such as this that symbolize patriotism? What values do such activities promote? What other activities or symbolic gestures are used in schools—and in society—to inspire feelings of patriotism? In order that such symbolic exercises are kept in proper perspective, provide a few guidelines that could be used to ensure appropriate use of them.

". . . it will take a teacher who sees the future in the children he or she teaches."[2]

GOALS FOR THE SOCIAL STUDIES

There are numerous goal statements for social studies education. The National Council for the Social Studies (NCSS), a professional asso-

[2]Nan Bowman, student, Cascade High School, Everett, Washington, in a presentation to the Washington State Council for the Social Studies, Seattle, May 10, 1980.

ciation, has issued statements dealing with the role of the social studies, as have many school districts and state departments of education. Nearly all of the fifty states require the teaching of certain elements of social studies. The following are typical examples of what is expected of social studies education:

Knowledge and information goals

Learning about
1. the world, its people, and their cultures.
2. the settlement, growth, history, and development of the United States.
3. the neighborhood, community, and home state; how people live and work there; how they meet their basic needs of life; how they interact and depend on each other.
4. the legal and political systems of the local community, the state, and the nation.
5. the world of work and an orientation to various careers.
6. basic human institutions, such as the family.
7. how people use and misuse the earth.
8. the problems and challenges that confront people today in the realm of social living and human relations in the local, state, national, and international arenas.
9. the basic social functions that characterize all societies such as producing, transporting, distributing, and consuming goods and services; providing for education, recreation, and government; protecting and conserving human and natural resources; expressing esthetic and religious drives; communicating with others.

Attitude and value goals
1. knowing the common values of this society as defined in the historical documents of the republic, by laws of the land, by court decisions, and by the religious heritages of this country.
2. being able to make decisions that involve choices between competing values.
3. knowing the basic human rights guaranteed to all citizens.
4. developing a reasoned loyalty to this country.
5. developing a sense of respect for the ideals, the heritages, and the institutions of this nation.
6. developing a feeling of kinship toward human beings everywhere.

Skills goals
Social skills
1. living and working together; taking turns; respecting the rights of others; being socially sensitive.
2. learning self-control and self-direction.
3. sharing ideas and experiences with others.

What clues in these photographs suggest that this child has been socialized into American mainstream culture? What values are there in providing experiences of this type in the social studies curriculum?

Study skills and work habits

1. locating and gathering information from books, the library, and from a variety of other sources and special references.
2. making reports; speaking before a group; listening when others are reporting; listening to and following directions.
3. reading social studies materials for a variety of purposes, e.g., to get the main idea; to locate a particular point or fact; to predict outcomes; to detect author bias; to compare and contrast.
4. using maps, globes, charts, graphs, and other graphic and pictorial materials.
5. organizing information into usable structures such as outlining; making charts; making time lines; classifying pictures or data; arranging ideas, events, or facts in a sequence; taking notes; keeping records; and preparing summaries.
6. conducting an inquiry on a problem of interest.

Group work skills

1. working together on committees and assuming various roles in small groups such as being chairperson, secretary, or group member.
2. participating in a group discussion; leading a discussion.
3. participating in group decision-making.

Intellectual skills

1. defining and identifying problems; relating prior experiences to a present inquiry.
2. forming and testing hypotheses; drawing conclusions based on information.
3. analyzing and synthesizing data.
4. distinguishing between fact and opinion; learning to separate relevant from irrelevant information and to recognize bias in persuasive materials such as advertising, political statements, and propaganda.
5. sensing cause-and-effect relationships.
6. comparing and contrasting differing points of view.
7. recognizing the value components in decision-making.

Some goals are achieved through the encounters with subject matter, whereas others are achieved through the *process* of the study itself. For example, to learn about the history of their country or the geography of the home state, or of life in another culture, pupils must deal with the subject matter appropriate to those topics. On the other hand, to learn the skill of using the encyclopedia, the pupil must be involved in the use of that reference. Similarly, to learn to inquire, the pupil must engage in investigative searches. To learn group-work skills, pupils must be involved in group-work processes. Soundly based social studies programs build content and process

Chart 1 Characteristics of Less Desirable and More Desirable Social Studies Programs

Less Desirable	More Desirable
1. Sole reliance on history and geography as basic subject matter.	1. Subject matter drawn from a broad range of social sciences; the humanities; and the experiences of pupils.
2. Emphasis on Western culture, ignoring large parts of the world.	2. A global view with attention to non-Western, non-Christian cultures as well as to those of the West.
3. Rigid and formal programs; recitation procedures common.	3. Greater informality; more discussion; more pupil participation.
4. Much textbook teaching; fact-oriented.	4. Use of multiple resources with an emphasis on concept development.
5. Tendency to cover large areas and topics as in a survey.	5. More use of in-depth studies as cases and examples; learnings generalized and transferred to other situations.
6. Little relationship between in-school program and out-of-school behavior.	6. Application of learnings to out-of-school settings through social action.
7. Little emphasis on thinking as a major outcome of social studies.	7. Thinking emphasized as a major concern of social studies; inquiry strategies encouraged to develop reflective processes.
8. Emphasis on melting-pot idea.	8. Emphasis on pluralism and the contributions of many cultures.
9. Values taught through exhortative procedures and by indoctrination.	9. Value clarification and a rational approach to value education.
10. Distorted pictures of social reality; failure to recognize the impact of science and technology; a largely rural focus; emphasis on the past.	10. Truthful pictures of social reality; greater urban focus; more attention to changes due to science and technology; speculation on the future.
11. Finding the *right* answers; memorization of answers.	11. Use of open-ended approaches to problem resolution; thoughtful responses to questions.
12. Little if any attention to racial and sex-role stereotyping.	12. Concern with racism, sexism, and racial and sex-role stereotyping.
13. Few options available to the teacher in terms of program design, teaching materials, and teaching strategies.	13. Many options available to the teacher in terms of various programs, texts, materials, and teaching strategies.
14. Reward of pupil behavior that is obedient, unquestioning; few pupil decisions required or expected.	14. Reward of pupil behavior that is inquiring; expects and requires pupil to make choices and decisions; requires reasoned obedience; helps pupil learn how to learn.

9

learnings simultaneously. Much of social studies teaching is directed toward the achievement of multiple objectives.

There is good teaching and poor teaching of social studies today, just as there always has been. A social studies program can be no better than the teacher who implements it. Nevertheless, it is possible to look at programs in terms of practices and procedures that have proven to be effective and are recommended by specialists in the field. Several contrasts between less desirable and more desirable programs are summarized in Chart 1.

CURRICULUM ORGANIZATION

Although most schools include the social science disciplines in their elementary school social studies program, they do not ordinarily conduct special courses in geography, history, economics, political science, or the other disciplines. The usual organizational format is one that combines components from more than a single discipline to form an interdisciplinary study around some topic of interest. For example, a sixth-grade class might study the topic "Crossroads of Three Continents—The Middle East." In such a study, geography would be essential, as would be history, economics, and government. Doubtless, too, religious concepts would be included because this area of the world was the birthplace of three of the world's major religions.

Let us look at an example from the primary grades. Here there may be no concern about having the children identify the contributing disciplines, but when children are studying the local landscape, they are dealing in a simple way with geography. When they learn about the need for rules and laws, they are beginning to understand ideas from political science, and when they study about life in early times, they are having their first brush with history. Most schools are introducing basic concepts from the social sciences and related disciplines in the early years of the elementary school, although they may not always be labeled as such.

It is not the purpose of the elementary school to teach the social science disciplines apart from their relevance to social reality. They should be taught in ways that will help children build an understanding of the social and physical world in which they live. Unless children are able to understand the connection between what they are studying as history, geography, and so on, and something in their real world, the subject matter cannot make much sense to them. Meaningful teaching that relates what is studied to actual experiences helps build awareness of the potential explanatory power of the subject matter and will do much to intercept an undue emphasis on memorizing inconsequential information.

The young children in this photograph were part of a first grade class housed temporarily in a junior high school. The photograph reminds us of the perspective from which young children view the world. Their junior high school counterparts on the right look like giants to these first graders. Notice the look of apprehension on the faces of these young children! Suggest classroom practices in social studies that would take into account the eye-level from which young children perceive their surroundings.

CURRICULUM CONTENT AND SEQUENCE

Children learn a great deal about social studies in their life experiences outside of school through travel, television, and contact with adults. This applies not only to informational aspects of social studies but to other dimensions as well. They learn values and skills from their families and from contact with other persons in their social worlds. Consequently, hardly anything encountered in the social studies program will be totally new to all children, perhaps not even to *any* children in some classrooms.

The social studies program should be built on what the child already knows. This means that in introducing topics or units for study the teacher will need to explore with the children the extent of their prior experiences with the subject. Social studies programs are then planned to build learnings sequentially year by year, as each teacher assumes some responsibility for maintaining continuity in learning.

Each year there will be study units and topics that are consistent with the emphasis suggested by the district curriculum for that year. Ordinarily, topics that are physically close to the child such as the school, family, neighborhood, and community are placed in the primary grades. Topics that are more remote in space and time, such as the home state, the nation, and foreign cultures, appear in the middle and upper grades. It should be noted, however, that newer programs expand the world of the child early and rapidly. For example, even in the primary grades it is not unusual to find children studying family living as it takes place in many parts of the world. Teachers often begin a study by focusing on aspects of a topic that are familiar to the children, such as their own homes, schools, and families; then the study is expanded to include these same institutions in other cultures. The movement from things that are close to those that are far away and back again is common in social studies programs today.

The content and sequence of social studies programs vary from place to place. Nevertheless, some common elements can be found in most elementary school social studies programs. Here are a few:

1. Almost everywhere some attention is given to the study of the home state. Often this comes in grade four, but it is also found in grades six and seven.
2. Commonly, grades five and eight deal with the growth and development of the United States.
3. Exposure to the world beyond the immediate environment comes early in most programs and continues throughout the grades, with some apparent emphasis on the non-Western, non-Christian world.
4. Most programs incorporate aspects of current affairs, holiday observances, and local issues.
5. Many schools include topics of contemporary interest in their curriculum, such as law-related education; the world of work; envi-

ronmental education; drugs and dangerous substances; energy; or economic education.

6. Most programs reflect an awareness of racism, sexism, and racial and sex-role stereotyping.
7. Greater numbers of schools are allowing and encouraging teachers to explore alternatives and options to the regular program.

Several national surveys have been conducted in recent years to find out what is being taught in the social studies curriculum at the various grade levels. The results of these surveys are summarized in an article in the May 1980 issue of *Social Education*. According to data reported there, the dominant themes in the social studies curriculum are these:

K — Self; School; Community; Home
1 — Families
2 — Neighborhoods
3 — Communities
4 — State History; Geographic Regions
5 — U.S. History
6 — World Cultures; Western Hemisphere
7 — World Geography or History
8 — American History
9 — Civics or World Cultures
10 — World History
11 — American History
12 — American Government[3]

What follows provides descriptive information that is accurate in a general way, but the teacher will need to consult local curriculum sources to find out precisely what is required. The following examples should not be construed as a model curriculum pattern; they are simply representative examples of topics and units that can be found at the levels indicated in programs across the nation.

EXAMPLES OF UNIT TOPICS FOR EACH GRADE LEVEL

Kindergarten

Kindergarten programs ordinarily deal with topics that help to familiarize the children with their immediate surroundings. The home and school provide the setting for these studies. With some kindergarten children it is possible to include, in a simple way, references to the world beyond the immediate environment.
Learning About Myself
Rules for Safe Living
Learning How My Family Buys Goods and Services
Working Together at School

---

[3] Douglas P. Superka, Sharryl Hawke, and Irving Morrissett, "The Current and Future Status of the Social Studies," *Social Education* 44 (May 1980), p. 365.

Continents and the Globe
People Change the Earth

Grade One

Grade-one studies are based in the local area, such as the neighborhood, but provision is often made to associate the local area with the larger world. A major criticism of first-grade units in particular and primary units in general has been that they have tended to be too confining and that their content has been thin and inconsequential. Units should provide for easy transition from the near-at-hand to the faraway and back again at frequent intervals—when it is established that the backgrounds of pupils warrant such movement. Neighborhood and community services can be stressed in this grade.

The Shopping Center
Families at Work
Great Americans
A Japanese Family (comparative study)
Scarcity and Demand
Families: Size and Structure
Families and Their Needs
Dividing the Work

Grade Two

The grade-two program provides for frequent and systematic contact with the world beyond the neighborhood. Through the study of transportation, communication, food distribution, and travel, the children begin to learn how their part of the world is connected to other places on earth.

Suburban Neighborhoods
Transportation and Communication
Rural and Urban Communities
Where and How We Get Our Food
People Working Together
How Neighborhoods Change

Grade Three

The grade-three program often emphasizes the larger community concept: what a community is, types of communities, why some communities grow while others do not, how communities provide for basic needs. Many programs include an outside community for purposes of comparison. Schools are giving a great deal of attention to the large, urban community at this grade level.

Our City's Government
Food for the Community
Keeping Cities up-to-date—Change
Communities at Home and Abroad (comparative cultures study)
Life in Early American Settlements
Why a City Is Where It Is
The Parts of a City
Natural Surroundings and People's Actions
The Person: Wants, Actions, Feelings

Grade Four

In grade four the world as the home of people, showing various geographical features of the earth along with variety in ways of living, is often stressed. These studies help pupils understand some of the adaptive and innovative qualities of human beings. Home-state studies are popular in grade four; often they are included to meet legislative requirements. Comparative studies are commonly recommended.

Historical Growth and Change of the State
The Beef State (state study)
The Pacific Northwest (regional study)
The Story of Agriculture in the Midwest
Others Who Share Our World (comparative cultures study)
The Story of Industry
India, a Society in Transition (comparative study)
Different Cultures of the World

Grade Five

Almost everywhere the fifth-grade program includes the geography, history, early development, and growth of the United States. The program may focus on the United States alone or on the United States and Canada or on the United States, Canada, and Latin America. The latter option makes the fifth-grade program a very heavy one. The fifth-grade emphasis should be coordinated with the eighth and eleventh grades in order to avoid repetitive treatments.

Founding of the New World
The Native Americans
The Making of Our Nation
The War Between the States
An Early American Mining Community
History of the Great Plains
Completion of National Expansion
One Nation; Many Heritages

Grade Six

The sixth-grade program may include the study of Latin America and Canada or of cultures of the Eastern Hemisphere. Both of these patterns are in common use. A major limitation of sixth-grade programs is that they attempt to deal with too many topics. Often this results in a smattering of exposures without the pupils' developing significant depth of understanding. The same criticism applies to the seventh grade. Stronger programs emerge where teachers carefully select a few units that are representative of basic concepts having wide and broad applicability. For example, a class need not study all of the Third World nations to develop some understanding of the problems of newly developing countries.

Western Hemisphere Emphasis

Cooperation in the Americas
The Prairie Provinces
Three Inca Countries
The Saint Lawrence Seaway and Its Effect on Canadian Growth
The Organization of American States

Eastern Hemisphere Emphasis

Ancient, Classical, and Medieval Civilizations
The Birthplace of Three Religions
The U.S.S.R. and Eastern Europe in Recent Times
Great Discoveries

The Renaissance and Reformation
Empires and Revolutions
The People's Republic of China

Grade Seven

The nature of the seventh-grade program depends on the content of grade six. Either Latin America or culture regions of the Eastern Hemisphere are popular choices for this grade. Some schools are developing exciting programs in anthropology in grade seven. World geography is also included in some districts as are studies of the home state.

Rise of Modern Civilization
Africa: Yesterday, Today, and Tomorrow
The Home State
Challenges of our Times
World Resources: Who Has Them? Who Uses Them?
The Age of Technology—Its Effects on People
Environmental Problems
Principles of Geography
A Look at Tomorrow: The Future

Grade Eight

The study of the United States and of the American heritage is widespread in grade eight. The program usually stresses the development of American political institutions and the development of nationality. The approach typically consists of a series of units arranged chronologically. The fifth and eleventh grades also include elements of American history. Defining the emphasis for each of these grades and differentiating appropriately among them in terms of content and approach is necessary in order to avoid unwarranted duplication in the three grades.

Old Nations in the New World
A Free and Independent Nation
A Strong and Expanding Nation
A Divided Nation
Birth of an Industrial Giant
A World Power in a Time of Unrest

SOCIAL STUDIES AND BASIC EDUCATION

As the nationwide concern for accountability grew in recent years, a great deal has been made of teaching "the basics." Loud voices have admonished the schools to "go back to the basics." Used in this way, the term *basics* is taken to mean fundamental literacy skills—reading, writing, and arithmetic. The call for a "return to the basics" is based on the assumption that the job of teaching such basics is being done less well today than it was at some earlier time. The concern for basics also assumes that an overwhelming number of American children are deficient in these areas. There are reasons to believe that both of these assumptions are of questionable validity. The highly respected scholar and educator, Ralph W. Tyler, expresses a contrary view on this subject in this excerpt:

The American public has given strong support to a Back-to-Basics movement in which the Basics are usually defined very narrowly to include literacy and arithmetic. Yet, the vast majority of American children are not illiterate. The National Assessment of Educational Progress reports that more than 80 per cent of 17-year-old youth can comprehend the reading materials commonly used by adults. In arithmetic, more than 90 per cent can add, subtract, multiply and divide accurately with whole numbers although less than half that proportion are able to use their computations properly in solving the problems adults commonly encounter in making purchases, figuring tax liabilities, and the like.

In the International Evaluation of Educational Achievement, the average test score in reading comprehension of American 14-year-old children was exceeded only by those of Finland and New Zealand, small countries with a relatively homogeneous population. The problems of student learning in reading and arithmetic are serious only with a small fraction of American children, mostly those who are economically and socially disadvantaged. *Where American students are more widely lacking is in civic education.*[4] (Italics added.)

When something in the school curriculum is *basic*, it must be regarded as fundamental or essential. Learnings that are considered basic must be common to all, and everyone must be able to demonstrate that he or she has learned them at an acceptable level of proficiency. Our concern here is whether or not there are elements of the social studies curriculum that can be considered basic.

As has already been noted, the social studies curriculum is related directly to civic and citizenship education. Such education is almost always thought to be concerned with learning about components of the common culture that constitute the social and cultural heritage of this nation. It is these learnings that give our people a sense of identity as a free nation. In this context, social studies can be considered *the most* basic of all school subjects. If we cannot sustain ourselves as a strong and free people, little else is of much consequence.

DISCUSSION QUESTIONS AND SUGGESTED ACTIVITIES

1. Try to recall two or three specific things you learned as an elementary school pupil that would fit in each of the three sets of goals presented in this chapter. Are these things still worth learning by pupils who are in school today? Why or why not?
2. Using the list of goals in this chapter, write a one-sentence explanation of the purposes of elementary school social studies.

[4] Ralph W. Tyler, "The Needs of Elementary and Secondary Education for the 1980's," *Needs of Elementary and Secondary Education in the 1980's: A Compendium of Policy Papers.* Committee on Education and Labor, House of Representatives, Carl D. Perkins, Chairman. Washington, D.C.: U.S. Government Printing Office, 1980, pp. 78–79.

3. Describe what is meant by the phrase "multiple objectives in the social studies." Then select *two* grade levels in which you have a special interest. Provide a brief explanation of how the units listed below for those grades could be used to achieve multiple objectives concurrently. Check your responses with your instructor.
   a. All About Me (kindergarten).
   b. Families Near and Far (first grade).
   c. People Need People (second grade, emphasis on interdependence).
   d. Getting It from Here to There (third grade, transportation).
   e. Boom-Town Economics (fourth grade, early history of home state).
   f. What Right Do You Have to . . . (fifth grade, rights and responsibilities).
   g. Your Culture Is Showing (sixth grade, effect of culture on the individual).
4. The education codes of most states stipulate the amount of time that is to be spent on social studies each week. This might be expressed in clock hours per day, per week, days per week or term, or some other standard unit of measure. These minimum time requirements are usually different for primary, intermediate, and upper grades. Check local sources to find out if there are such requirements, and if so, what they are.
5. Decide when in the day's schedule you would prefer to teach social studies and provide a rationale for your choice.
6. Examine the list of skills on pages 6–8. Which of these skills are also included in other areas of the elementary school curriculum and which ones fall entirely within the social studies? Suggest ways that social studies and other curriculum areas might be combined for purposes of instruction in skills.
7. Visit the educational materials collection in your campus library and examine a few social studies curriculum guides from school systems throughout the country. Include the curriculum guides for your state and community. Indicate the extent to which these documents incorporate ideas discussed in this chapter.
8. Study the scope and sequence of a major publishing company's social studies textbook series. To what extent does the program reflect the "more desirable" characteristics identified in Chart 1?
9. Become familiar with the magazines *Social Education, Instructor, Learning, Early Years*, and *Teacher*. Learn what they have to offer the elementary teacher in the social studies. Locate one or more teaching ideas from these journals and make plans to apply them in an elementary school classroom.
10. Talk to your instructor and/or your supervising teacher about local and state councils for social studies. Arrange to attend one of their meetings.

SELECTED REFERENCES

Allen, Jack et al. *Social Studies for the 80's*. Washington, D.C.: National Education Association, 1980.

Association for Supervision and Curriculum Development. "Citizenship Education," *Educational Leadership*, 38 (October 1980), pp. 6–71. (Several authors contribute to eighteen articles on citizenship in this issue.)

Gross, Richard E. "The Status of the Social Studies in the Public Schools of the United States: Facts and Impressions from a National Survey," *Social Education*, 40 (March 1977), pp. 194–200+.

Jarolimek, John. "The Social Studies: An Overview," Chapter 1. NSSE Yearbook on the Social Studies. Howard D. Mehlinger and O. L. Davis, Jr., eds. Chicago: University of Chicago Press, 1980.

Jarolimek, John and others. "The Status of Social Studies Education: Six Case Studies," *Social Education*, 41 (November–December 1977), pp. 574–601.

Mehlinger, Howard D. "The NAEP Report on Changes in Political Knowledge and Attitudes, 1969–1976," *Phi Delta Kappan*, 59 (June 1978), pp. 676–678.

Michaelis, John U. *Social Studies for Children*, 7th edition. Englewood Cliffs, N.J.: Prentice-Hall, Inc., 1980. Chapter 1.

National Council for the Social Studies Positon Statement. "Essentials of the Social Studies," *Social Education*, 45 (March 1981), pp. 162–164.

National Council for the Social Studies Position Statement. "Revision of the NCSS Social Studies Curriculum Guidelines" *and* "How to Use the Guidelines for Social Studies Needs Assessment," *Social Education*, 43 (April 1979), pp. 261–278.

Pigano, Alicia L., ed. *Social Studies in Early Childhood: An Interactionist Point of View*. Bulletin 38. Washington, D.C.: National Council for the Social Studies, 1978.

Ponder, Gerald. "The More Things Change . . . : The Status of Social Studies," *Educational Leadership*, 36 (April 1979), pp. 515–518.

Schneider, Donald O. and Ronald L. Van Sickle. "The Status of the Social Studies: The Publishers' Perspective," *Social Education*, 43 (October 1979), pp. 461–465.

Shaver, James P., O. L. Davis, Jr., and Suzanne Helburn. "The Status of Social Studies Education: Impressions from Three NSF Studies," *Social Education*, 43 (February 1979), pp. 150–153.

Superka, Douglas P., Sharryl Hawke, and Irving Morrissett. "The Current and Future Status of the Social Studies," *Social Education*, 44 (May 1980), pp. 362–369.

Walsh, Huber M. *Introducing the Young Child to the Social World*. New York: Macmillan Publishing Company, Inc., 1980. Chapters 1 and 2.

2

Planning for Teaching the Social Studies

Public concern over the quality of education received by the nation's children has required schools to provide much more documented evidence of pupil achievement than has been the case in the past. The best example of the consequences of public concern over accountability is the widespread use of minimum competency testing in a growing number of states. Increased public concern for pupil achievement has also resulted in "precision teaching," meaning teaching targeted on the achievement of specifically defined objectives. This latter trend is illustrated in the use of the Individualized Education Program (IEP) with handicapped learners and in the increasing required use of pre-stated Student Learning Objectives (SLOs) with all learners. These developments are having important implications for the planning that must go into teaching. Teachers are being required to be precise in defining what pupils are expected to learn. The planning process itself has become more technical than it once was.

LEVELS OF INFLUENCE IN PLANNING AND TEACHING

Few teachers can plan and teach social studies completely on their own, unencumbered by forces beyond their own specific situation. In most cases, planning and teaching are influenced by a variety of factors, agencies, and organizations at the national, state, and local levels.

In the United States, education is legally under the jurisdiction of the various states. School programs, therefore, are not subject to the scrutiny and supervision of the federal government. Nonetheless, social studies education is influenced at the national level by federal social and/or fiscal legislation, by projects funded by the Department of Education that may encourage certain procedures or emphases, by textbook and standardized test authors and their publishers who sell to a national market, by national lay organizations whose special interests are aligned with social studies education, and by national professional associations.

21

The largest and most significant professional association for social studies is the National Council for the Social Studies. This organization has given leadership and direction to social studies planning at the national level. Its several committees study problems relating to the social studies on a continuing basis. Its monthly journal, *Social Education*, and its numerous other publications have been widely circulated and have proven to be valuable aids to teachers and curriculum planners. Membership in the National Council for the Social Studies is open to anyone who has an interest in any of the facets of the social studies at any teaching level.

State governments have the legal responsibility for directing educational programs of public schools. Typically, one finds certain curricular requirements relating to social studies in state education codes. These range from mandating the teaching of United States history and the Constitution to requiring the observance of state Admission Day. State education agencies often have a state framework for social studies that provides guidance to local districts in developing a philosophy and rationale, selecting subject matter for various grade levels (scope and sequence), recommending teaching strategies, and selecting instructional materials. In practice, state agencies have delegated much of their responsibility for education to local school districts.

Much choice making in curriculum is left to local districts. The feeling that the schools belong to the people of the local community and that schools should serve local needs has long been fundamental to educational planning in this country. Social studies programs must be tailored to the experience and background of children who live in a specific attendance area. State and national influences presumably ensure attention to common societal goals that are necessary for national unity; local influences should ensure that the pupils living in the area are well served by the social studies program.

As teachers design social studies programs, they should not be unmindful of the influences at the national, state, and local levels. It is helpful, for example, for the teacher to be familiar with the social studies guidelines published by the National Council for the Social Studies. Likewise, the teacher ought to know what is required by the state framework for social studies. The teacher should consult the local curriculum guide before the planning process begins.

TYPES OF PLANS

Thorough planning will not ensure successful teaching, but it will do much to give the teacher a margin of confidence that will enhance the possibility of more effective teaching. Many experienced teachers make use of three types of plans for the social studies: (1) unit plans;

(2) short-range plans focused on a single topic, main idea, or skill; and (3) daily plans. The long-range plan, usually referred to as a *unit* or a *unit of work*, covers a period of six to ten weeks during which time the class studies some broad topic on an ongoing basis. The unit plan is a way of organizing materials and activities for such an extended study. A unit might be thought of as a *depth study*. The following are examples of topics that would be suitable for parcels of work called units:

Living in Our Community
Families Around the World
The Exciting World of Lewis and Clark
The World of the Big City
Life in Early America
The Middle East—Crossroads of Cultures

Not all social studies instruction needs to be organized around comprehensive units of the type described. Many topics can be dealt with in a time span of no more than a week or two. These can often be sandwiched in between the larger units. Such topics, calling for short-range plans, might be organized around subject matter that is timely or is of especial relevance to a class. They might consist of unconventional subjects or topics on which there is not an abundance of learning resources for pupil use. The following are examples of topics suitable for such shorter blocks of work:

Winners and Losers in the Election
Danger Spots in Our Home
Caring for Pets
Getting Information from Maps
Workers and Their Wages
Getting Your Money's Worth
Who Is the Me I See?

It is also possible, of course, to plan a large unit of work in a series of sequentially related miniunits of the type described here. When this is done, however, the teacher will want to provide some ongoing activities in order to give continuity to the larger study.

The third type of teaching plan is that which the teacher takes to the classroom to give direction to the lesson. It is what is usually called a "daily lesson plan." Such plans should extend and continue the instruction from one class session to the next. Naturally, these specific teaching plans are based on the more extended unit of study. Separate and discrete plans that do not tie into some larger framework are not recommended because of the resulting fragmentation of the topics studied. Plans should move the process of learning sequentially and continuously over a period of time.

23

Textbook-Based Plans

A textbook-based plan is one that is developed in advance by the teacher, who often relies on the textbook or other curriculum documents in determining the nature and content of the program. If pupils help in the planning, they do so minimally and usually in matters that do not alter the basic content and emphasis. That is, they might exercise some choice concerning individual activities to be performed but would not suggest alternative topics to be studied. Reliance on the textbook as the prime data source is complete. Variations in requirements to accommodate pupil differences would include varying the lengths of assignments or varying the amount of time needed to complete them. All pupils deal with the same basic subject matter.

If we follow a teacher through the steps in planning and teaching social studies in this way, we would observe the following:

The teacher

1. Surveys the text to find out which units are included and decides how to apportion the amount of time available to each one. The recommendations of the textbook authors may be used in making these decisions.
2. Studies the teacher's guide accompanying the text to find out how the program is organized and what major goals and objectives are stressed. These goals and objectives may be accepted as appropriate for the program.
3. Uses the teacher's guide for teaching plans and pupil activities.
4. Uses additional resources and activities for enrichment, extension of learning, and for individualizing learning. Some of these are suggested by the teacher's guide, including those provided by the publisher of the text series as satellite materials.
5. Evaluates learnings as suggested by the text and teacher's guide, focusing mainly on informational learnings, basic concepts, and related skills.
6. Uses formal teaching procedures consisting mainly of question and answer, some discussion, an occasional pupil report, and map making; there is infrequent use of drama, art, music, or construction activities.

Topic or Subject-Oriented Plans

A planning approach based on a topic or subject has some of the same characteristics as the one just discussed, but the reliance on the text is not as complete, more of the teacher's personality is apparent, and it is not so thoroughly preplanned and teacher-directed. Pupils are more involved in planning and there is greater use of a wide range of instructional materials and activities. The formality that characterizes the textbook-based approach is missing. Pupils feel freer to voice their own opinions and views on issues. Interactions are more along the lines of true discussion as opposed to question-and-answer procedures. The teacher is sensitive to pupil individuality and provides for pupil variations in ability and motivation. Pupils may be involved in expressive activities such as construction, art, music, role playing, and simulation games. This is not a completely pupil-centered approach, yet it is not one that is wholly teacher-directed either.

If we follow a teacher through the steps in planning and teaching in this way, we would observe the following:

The teacher

1. Examines the curriculum guide and the textbook to find out what topics and units are expected to be included in the program.
2. Establishes broad goals and objectives for the year. Takes into consideration those suggested by the curriculum guide and textbook teacher's guide, but makes his or her own.
3. Tentatively selects topics to be studied; consults teacher's guide and curriculum guide in this process, selects some that are suggested, omits others, and adds some. These topics may be modified as the program develops and as pupil interests and capabilities are better known.
4. Decides on sequence of units selected, time allotment for each, taking into account holidays, seasons of the year, and so forth.
5. Uses some teaching suggestions from the teacher's guide and curriculum guide but develops many of his or her own ideas for activities and strategies.
6. Develops and uses learning packets, self-paced materials, learning centers, and pupil contracts; also, individualizes learning through use of small groups.
7. Plans for and uses many instructional resources in addition to the textbook. This includes pictures, packets, library books, films, filmstrips, recordings, and artifacts.
8. Uses a variety of informal evaluative techniques and devices such as discussion, observation, pupil conferences, teacher-made tests, checklists, and experience summaries.
9. Maintains a relaxed instructional pace but stays close to teacher–pupil planned treatment of the unit topic.

Informal Pupil-Centered Plans

Some teachers find open education to be an attractive setting in which to teach social studies. Although it requires considerable pre-planning by the teacher, the program itself is not structured in advance, as are the other two approaches that have been discussed. Study units and pupil experiences are planned jointly by the teacher and pupils in terms of the interests, backgrounds, and needs of the pupils. Thus, the unit emerges under the guidance of the teacher, who relies on pupil initiative and interest. Children help decide what they will study. They raise questions about the information they are interested in getting and search out relevant sources. They plan ways of working, activities in which they will engage, and ways of sharing ideas with one another. Pupils are encouraged to become involved in assuming responsibility for what they are to learn and how they will go about learning it. The boundaries between the various disciplines contributing to social studies education are blurred; indeed, the social studies units often incorporate learnings from the total elementary school curriculum.

If we follow a teacher through the steps in planning and teaching in this way, we will observe the following:

The teacher

1. Formulates broad goals and objectives for the year in terms of anticipated social and intellectual growth of the pupils.
2. Studies pupil backgrounds; develops an awareness of the social milieu from which pupils come.
3. Prepares motivating or facilitating questions dealing with social issues and topics to arouse pupil interest.
4. Provides books, artifacts, displays, visuals, construction materials, and other items to motivate pupil interest and curiosity.
5. Encourages pupils to suggest topics for study and to suggest possible questions and problems for exploration.
6. Guides pupils in exploratory information searches.
7. Assists pupils in developing an in-depth study of topics and problems selected; plans are refined and/or modified as the study progresses.
8. Individualizes the program in accordance with pupil interest and need using interest centers, individual study contracts, individual study materials, projects, and activities.
9. Closely relates social studies work to reading, language arts, mathematics, science, art, music, and drama.

PLANNING INSTRUCTIONAL UNITS

One must conclude from the foregoing discussion that the way units are planned and taught varies greatly from one teacher to another. For one, the unit may be no more than a chapter or a section of the textbook that deals with a single topic. For another teacher, the unit may be a comprehensive study that incorporates learnings and activities from all the rest of the school curriculum. One teacher may structure the unit in advance by thorough preplanning; another may plan the unit as the study evolves. Two teachers working on an identical topic at the same grade level may have their classes deal quite differently with it. The same teacher might handle the same topic differently with different groups of children. What follows is a description of the essential components of a comprehensive unit plan. The reader should understand, however, that a great deal of individual teacher judgment and decision-making go into the planning and teaching of social studies units.

Selecting a Unit Topic

In most instances, the school district will supply a curriculum guide, a list of suggested topics, a curriculum framework, a textbook, or some directive that provides the teacher with guidance as to which topics and/or units are to be included in the curriculum. Often, teachers can exercise some choices within the established guidelines. It is not uncommon to find some units required, some optional, and perhaps some free choice. A teacher must know district policy in order to plan appropriately. Having selected the unit topic, or at least establishing what it is to be, the teacher proceeds with the planning process.

Making A Survey of Available Learning Resources

If a school district includes particular topics in the social studies curriculum, it will ordinarily provide the necessary instructional resources. The amount of such resources that are available will vary, however, from no more than a basic textbook to a generous amount and variety of multimedia. As an initial step in planning, the teacher should inventory the availability and the adequacy of learning resources for the unit to be studied. What the teacher finds will have a direct bearing on how the unit will be planned. Whereas instructional materials should not dictate the nature of the social studies program, the availability of essential learning resources necessarily affects the teacher's planning.

Much difficulty is avoided in securing and using instructional materials when teachers plan well in advance what they will need. Books, recordings, pictures, films, and filmstrips must be requested early enough to ensure their arrival at the time they are needed. Usually, instructional resources must be ordered, reserved, or even secured before the unit begins.

Establishing Objectives

Social studies instruction is almost always concerned with the attainment of multiple objectives. Facts, concepts, generalizations, principles, and general knowledge are derived from the encounter with the subject matter. Skills are learned during the process of study, including many of those discussed on pages 6–8 in Chapter 1. Affective outcomes deal with attitudes, values, and feelings that are

27

"Consideration for others" is a human value that can be promoted through a food drive for the needy, such as the one shown in this photograph. But many other learner outcomes relevant to social studies can result through pupil involvement in such projects. Name a few subject matter and skill objectives that might be achieved while engaging in this activity.

important learnings in most social studies units. It is not likely that all of the outcomes of a study will be formally defined by the teacher. Many outcomes are realized as side effects, or what might be called "fall-out," meaning fortuitous learnings or unpredicted extensions of learnings associated with the unit.

We restrict our attention here to those few objectives that the teacher singles out for special attention. These are objectives that the teacher perceives to be the major purposes of the study. Our concern is not with those serendipitous outcomes that emerge as children read, interact with their teachers and with each other, prepare and give reports, and engage in various other activities. This is not to say that these latter outcomes are not important, only that it is not possible to know what they are to be in advance of the study.

Instructional objectives should be stated in ways that make clear what pupils are supposed to *learn*. This will enable the teacher and the pupils to see more clearly how instructional activities relate to the purposes of the study. Insufficient clarity of objectives is likely to lead to the performance of activities that have neither purpose nor meaning. It makes little sense for teachers and pupils to try to solve a problem when no one seems to know what the problem is.

28

Objectives may be framed as broad, general statements that describe what it is the pupils are expected to learn. The following are examples, selected from several different units, of such descriptive objectives:

As a result of a study of this unit the pupil will

- learn the use of simple research skills associated with gathering information.
- understand that certain basic needs must be satisfied if human life is to be sustained.
- realize that decisions are based on one's value orientation.
- learn to work in small groups, respecting the rights and feelings of others.
- understand the interdependent relationship between regions.
- develop the skill of orienting a map to directions.
- gain a knowledge of vocabulary associated with the legal system.
- learn how advertising aids both the consumer and the producer.
- learn to formulate and test causal hypotheses relating to community development.

These examples would provide purpose and direction for a study. Many teachers are comfortable with descriptive objectives of this type. Although they are general, they are, nonetheless, specific enough to communicate what the main concerns of the study are to be. Such objectives obviously need further clarification, but most teachers prefer to make these statements more specific and explicit at the time the material is actually taught.

Another way to state objectives is in terms of specific observable learner behavior. Such statements are referred to as *behavioral objectives*. Prior to the time the instruction takes place, the teacher frames statements of expected pupil performances that are predicted to occur as a result of the learning experience. These predicted performances are so precisely stated that their achievement could readily be assessed by an objective observer.

In order to achieve this degree of precision, it is necessary to use language that leaves no doubt as to what is wanted. Verbals such as "to comprehend," "to know," "to realize" are not well suited for this purpose because they do not specify what the pupils are *doing* that would convince an impartial observer that the pupils do, indeed, "comprehend," "know," or "realize." Stems that are more suitable for behavioral objectives are these:

to name	to explain why
to choose	to identify
to illustrate	to cite
to provide examples	to define
to write	to locate
to place in order	to use

Examples of behavioral objectives are these:

As a result of a study of this unit the pupil will be able to

- identify four different types of structures people use for homes.
- provide five examples of consumer fraud.
- locate a specific reference book in the library.
- list the main ideas in a passage of social studies prose.
- show that he or she knows how to use the index to find factual material in the textbook.
- match causes and effects in an exercise relating to labor-management conflicts in the textbook.
- define the essential characteristics of the concept *region*.

The use of behavioral objectives has accompanied the growing concern for accountability in education. Advocates of behavioral objectives claim that such objectives encourage precision in teaching and learning by focusing on observable pupil performance. They would argue that unless the pupil can actually do something to show what has been learned, that one can only speculate about whether or not learning has taken place. They argue, further, that unless the teacher can define what is to be learned in terms of the pupil's intellectual or physical behavior, it cannot be assumed that learning has actually occurred. The issue boils down to the question, "What can the pupil *do* that he or she could not do prior to the instruction?" In this framework, it is pupil behavior that provides convincing evidence that intended learning has or has not taken place.

Those who do not favor the use of behavioral objectives say that many significant outcomes of social studies instruction, or any instruction, for that matter, do not lend themselves well to behavioral definition. For example, who can say precisely what happens to a child while reading an exciting account of life on the frontier? How does one define such learning behaviorally? Should it be the same for all learners? Besides, there is the value question of whether or not such a degree of precision serves any useful purpose. Another argument against the use of behavioral objectives is that the practice encourages the narrowing of the instruction to those objectives that can easily be defined behaviorally, thereby neglecting other important learnings that cannot be so defined or that are difficult to manage in behavioral terms. Additionally, opponents claim that the use of behavioral objectives tends to fragment the social studies curriculum into bits and pieces of content and skills rather than to encourage the integration of learnings into larger wholes.

Perhaps there is a midposition that suggests a limited use of behavioral objectives for those components of social studies that lend themselves well to definition in terms of observable pupil performance. For example, certain work–study skills would be of this type—reading maps, using references, gathering data, interpreting graphs and charts, reading for a specific purpose. Some content-related objectives can also be stated behaviorally, such as arranging events in a sequence, relating effects to causes, drawing a conclusion based on data, providing examples and nonexamples of concepts, and so on. In the case of social, intellectual, and/or affective learnings that cannot be easily defined behaviorally, the teacher may want to state instructional objectives in descriptive terms as illustrated by the examples on page 29. The types of objectives used will depend on local requirements and on teacher preference. Because there are philosophical differences among competent professionals as to the appropriateness of behavioral objectives, this is an issue that individual teachers will need to resolve for themselves.

Whatever form the teacher uses to state objectives, it is important to stress that the objectives should indicate clearly what it is the pupils are *expected to learn*, not what they will do. For example, the following are *not* appropriate instructional objectives because they simply describe procedures and activities that will be used by the pupils presumably to learn something that remains undefined:

The pupils will view a film.
The class will work in small committees.
The pupils will draw a map of the local area.
The class will discuss individual projects.
Pupils will make a model of a harbor.
Pupils will role-play workers in a shopping center.

Organizing the Subject Matter

When teachers are asked what they are doing in social studies, they often respond by naming the title of the unit or topic under study, as for example, "We are studying Japan (or Canada, Mexico, the Community, and so forth)." The presumption is that this response will communicate the nature of the study. The fact is, however, that the title or topic of a unit tells us little about the focus of the study, the concepts being developed, the relationships being established, or the conclusions reached, if any. Any topic can be studied from several different perspectives. Part of the task of organizing subject matter, therefore, deals with establishing the focus of the study and determining which particular main ideas and concepts will receive priority.

Many social studies programs and most of the modern textbook series organize subject matter around basic ideas from the various social science disciplines. These are usually called major generalizations, basic concepts, key ideas, or other similar designations, depending on the preference of the district. Examples of such ideas are listed in various parts of this text where the disciplines are discussed.

There is some variation in school district policies, but typically elementary school teachers do not have a great deal of choice about subjects and topics to be included in the social studies curriculum.

31

These are either designated by the school district curriculum guide or the district has adopted a textbook series that pretty much determines the units and topics to be included. Teachers do, however, have a considerable amount of latitude in deciding how those topics will be developed and what ideas will be singled out for emphasis. It is those ideas that really determine the specific subject matter. An example will illustrate how this comes about.

Let us say that the fifth-grade curriculum guide calls for a unit on Canada. The guide also indicates what the emphasis is to be and the major generalizations that are to provide a focus for this unit:

Canada: Land Giant of the Western Hemisphere

This unit should provide pupils with a comprehensive view of Canada as it is today. This does not mean that historical information will be excluded, but simply that the stress is to be interdisciplinary with an emphasis on contemporary life. The unit should treat Canada as a whole rather than focus on a particular small sample of Canadian life and culture. Whereas the similarities between the United States and Canada should be studied, it is important to present Canada as a nation distinguished by its own nationality and culture. Some emphasis must be placed on how it is different from the United States. The long-standing tradition of cordial relations between the United States and Canada also should be stressed. The following generalizations should emerge as a result of the study of Canada:

1. The physical features of an area influence settlement patterns and transportation routes. (Geography)
2. Maintaining an ethnic identity is important to most members of a cultural group. (Anthropology)
3. The use of available resources depends on the nature of the economic system, the values of people, and their level of technology. (Economics)
4. The early history of a country has a definite bearing on the present culture of its people. (History)

How does the teacher go about selecting subject matter about Canada that will be in accord with the focus suggested by the curriculum guide?

One option available to the teacher, obviously, is simply to teach whatever is included in the children's textbook. If the textbook treatment is in harmony with the focus suggested and the teacher makes enlightened use of the books, this is not an altogether undesirable procedure. We would like to think, however, that the teacher will be able to develop a more imaginative approach and, in the process, make better use of the text and other learning resources that are available.

The basic question here is this: What is it that the pupils are expected to learn about Canada that is consistent with the suggested emphasis? Or, what are the main ideas about Canada that will receive attention in this unit?

In order to respond to this question, the teacher should do some self-study with the thought of selecting six to eight major ideas to be included in the unit. The public library, *The World Almanac*, encyclopedias, and the pupil materials in the classroom can be used for this purpose. Let us assume that the teacher has done this research and decides that the following *main ideas* will be developed in the unit:

1. Canada is a country with a unique northern geographic location.
2. Canada is a large, regionally divided and diverse country.
3. Canada is a highly industrialized and technologically advanced country.
4. Canada is an urbanized country, rapidly becoming a nation of city-dwellers.
5. Canada is an exposed country, open to a multitude of external cultural, economic, and political influences.
6. Canada is a multi-ethnic country with two predominant linguistic groups.[1]

After the teacher has selected the main ideas, such as those listed here, it is possible to identify the essential related concepts and the specific subject matter, as shown by Chart 2.

Thus far we have discussed subject matter selection only in terms of informational outcomes—that is, cognitive objectives. But what about skills, attitudes, and values? How do they fit into the picture? Objectives that deal with skills, attitudes, and values are structured around the subject matter, too, and are developed concurrently with informational objectives. Unless the curriculum guide specifically indicates which skills, attitudes, and values are to receive attention—and usually it does not—the matter is left to the judgment of the teacher.

In the example of Canada, it is reasonable that map and globe skills would be a necessary part of main ideas numbers 1 and 2. All of the main ideas will require information searches that will provide a way to teach and apply research and inquiry skills. The teacher will doubtless plan activities that require the children to use group-work skills. Attitudinal outcomes can hardly be ignored because the curriculum guide states explicitly, "The long-standing tradition of cordial relations between the United States and Canada also should be stressed." Values will come into the study as pupils begin to examine the trade-offs involved in Canada's becoming an urbanized country, exploiting its resources, assimilating its native people, and maintaining an official bicultural position.

These suggestions provide some possibilities for the coordination of information, skills, attitudes, and values objectives. The essential point is that it is around the basic subject matter that all of these objectives are achieved.

[1]CONTACT, Number 5, Canada Studies Foundation, 252 Bloor Street West, Toronto, Ontario M5S IV5, September 1974.

Chart 2   Essential Cognitive Elements of a Unit on Canada

Main Ideas	Essential Concepts	Subject Matter Synopsis
1. Canada is a country with a unique northern geographic location.	Arctic Latitude Coastline Heartland Natural boundary Political boundary	Location and size of Canada along with its dominant physical features, unique natural regions, and climatic characteristics; population distribution; location in terms of other nations of the Northern Hemisphere.
2. Canada is a large, regionally divided and diverse country.	Regionalism Prairie Maritime Offshore Province	Brief history of Canadian development; political and natural regions; occupations of its people; regionalism as a social, economic, and political factor in Canadian life.
3. Canada is a highly industrialized and technologically advanced country.	Natural resources Minerals Raw materials Technological change	Development of Canadian resources for export and domestic use; rise of Canadian industry; transportation and communication systems in Canada.
4. Canada is an urbanized country, rapidly becoming a nation of city dwellers.	Metropolitan area Trading center Manufacturing center Urban environment	Move toward urbanism with cities gaining in their influence over the lives of all Canadians; problems associated with urban sprawl and urban renewal: Toronto, a case study.
5. Canada is an exposed country, open to a multitude of external cultural, economic, and political influences	Foreign investment Nationalism Cultural influnece	Influence of foreign investments in Canadian industry and agriculture; the American presence; cultural influences from the States; influence of immigration on Canadian development.
6. Canada is a multiethnic country with two predominant linguistic groups.	Ethnic group Bilingual Bicultural Heritage Minority Cultural mosaic	Historical background of Canadian bilingualism; effect of bicultural life on social, political, and economic decision-making; status of native people in Canada.

Beginning the Study

Building and sustaining the interest of children in a topic is, of course, a continuing responsibility of the teacher, but is especially important when beginning a new unit of study. This involves more than simply getting started. It requires arousing the curiosity of the youngsters, exploring some of the possibilities for study presented by the topic, and, in general, setting the stage for learning to take place. In advance of the time the unit is actually undertaken, the teacher should post material in the room that will arouse interest in the anticipated study, and the relationship of the new topic to previous work

SOCIAL STUDIES UNIT PLANNING

Unit Title _____   Date _____

Main Idea to Be Developed:	Related Skills:	Related Attitudes and Values:	Questions to Stimulate Reflective Thinking:
Key Concepts and Terms:			
Text References:	Oral and Written Language Activities:	Dramatic Activities:	Construction Activities:
Supplementary References:			
Audiovisual Resources:			
Community Resources:	Related Curriculum Activities (Science, Math, Art, Music):		

FIGURE 1. This form can be used in developing unit plans. Notice that it consists of three components: (1) the learnings to be achieved; (2) the references and resources to be used; and (3) the activities to be performed. A plan such as this should be developed for each Main Idea included in the unit.

35

should be indicated. There should be books and other appropriate materials in the room through which the youngsters may browse. Materials can be brought to class that stimulate the thinking of the children. All these activities and others, which the imaginative teacher will use, serve to create interest and will help cause the children to want to learn more about the topic. Through procedures such as these, the children have an opportunity to discover the new material gradually and will be ready to engage in teacher-guided pupil planning.

Some teachers use dramatic representation successfully in the initial stages of the unit. Let us assume that a primary class is beginning a unit on transportation. The teacher interests the pupils in having them show through creative dramatics what the workers at an airline terminal do. The children become excited about this and want to start immediately, which the teacher allows. Under the teacher's guidance they begin to plan and to play the representation, but they soon discover that they do not really know enough about the situation to present it accurately. They do not know who the workers are at the terminal, let alone what each worker does. Now they have identified a problem they can understand and can go about their research and problem-solving with genuine purpose. This situation also demonstrates the difference between pupil purposes and teacher purposes. Although the example given applies to a primary grade, the procedure can be used at any level.

Other activities can be used in a similar fashion to motivate work, to develop purposes, and to give pupils reasons for doing the things they do. The projects are important in that they provide a child-oriented vehicle for learning. Construction activities are often used in this way. If individual pupils or a class is to build something, they have to learn what goes into it, how it functions, and how it is or was used. One has to be careful, of course, to make certain the time taken in such endeavors is justified by the learnings that result.

Properly understood, this phase of unit development consists of a *group* or *series* of experiences rather than a single experience. Sometimes teachers plan to initiate a unit through the viewing of a film. A film may be used in the introductory stages of a unit, but this experience should be supported by many others of the type previously described. In one sense, this unfolding process is continued throughout the unit in that each new learning is a readiness for the next.

Developing the Study: Problems, Experiences, or Activities

A distinguishing characteristic of a good elementary schoolteacher is the ability to engage pupils in an interested way in activities that help them achieve important learnings. One unfortunate practice in elementary social studies is using pupil activities without relating them to social studies purposes. This applies to traditional activities such as reading textbook assignments and giving reports, as it does to the more informal activities such as committee work or some type of expressive experience. Activities are means to ends—they are used to help pupils learn something. It is thus imperative that the teacher sets purposes and knows clearly what the pupils are supposed to learn *before* deciding what activities are to be used.

Good unit development always makes provision for pupil involvement in the planning of instructional activities. Having pupils participate in planning can to much to overcome the feeling that they are only "doing assignments for the teacher." Such participation assists in clarifying goals of learning for the children and allows them to identify psychologically with the unit activities. The many values of teacher-guided pupil planning have been well documented and it is now generally recognized as sound teaching procedure by good teachers everywhere.

Teachers should plan with pupils many of the specific learning tasks undertaken in the unit: listing questions on which information is desired; making charts of what to do; finding and listing sources of information; appointing committees; reporting progress; pooling suggestions; and making plans for a construction activity. A fifth-grade teacher and the pupils summarized their plans for work on a part of a unit on New England on a chart as shown on this page.

JOBS IN A COLONIAL NEW ENGLAND TOWN

Each of us will select a different job from New England town life.
Each of us will find out what skills and responsibilities each person has.
Each of us will share our role with the others in the class by dressing up like the person, showing something one might have created or used, making a bulletin board or diorama, or preparing a dramatization.

Some of the jobs in a colonial New England town are:

candlemaker	homemaker/mother
blacksmith	merchant
weaver	shipbuilder
farmer	minister
schoolteacher	fisherman
miller	barrister
carpenter	tanner
slave	doctor
watchman	innkeeper
printer	cooper

WHAT WE WILL WANT TO FIND OUT ABOUT OUR JOBS

1. What skills did the person need?
2. What training was necessary to do the job?
3. How much money did the person make?
4. How was the person paid?
5. How many people will need the services?
6. How does the job relate to other jobs in the community?
7. What special equipment or resources did the people use in their job?
8. Would you like to have done this job or performed this service?

In general, the development of a unit consists of a sequence of procedures, each one emerging from the preceding one. In its simplest form, this pattern might be described as follows:

1. *problem identification* and related information getting; problem-solving activities such as reading, interviewing, listening, viewing, collecting, using references, doing mapwork.

2. *application* through expressive activities such as discussing, illustrating, exhibiting, dramatizing, constructing, drawing, and writing.

3. *summarizing*, *generalizing*, and *transferring* to new situations resulting in identification of new problems of a more complex nature; the cycle is then repeated.

This procedure includes both intake and outgo activities. Pupils not only take in knowledge but also must act on knowledge so obtained. Moreover, they must generalize and apply their knowledge to new problems and situations.

As the unit moves into the development phase, each class period should provide for three instructional operations: (1) readiness, (2) work–study, and (3) summary and evaluation. Teachers usually begin the social studies instructional period with the entire class in one group. At this time the previous day's progress is reviewed, plans for the day's work are outlined, and work goals are clarified. The children then turn to their various tasks while the teacher moves from one child to the next or from one group to another, guiding, helping, clarifying, encouraging, and suggesting. The teacher will terminate the work period sufficiently early to assemble the entire group once again to discuss progress, to evaluate work, and to identify tasks left undone that must be continued the next day. As the children complete their various work projects and are ready to share them with the class, time will be arranged for them to do so. On some days the children may spend the entire period sharing, presenting reports, discussing, and planning. Other days may be spent entirely in reading and research or on work sheets the teacher has prepared because of a special need of the class. And on other days part of the group may be reading while others are preparing a mural and still others are planning a report.

The need to take time at the end of the work period to summarize what has been learned or to review work that has been accomplished should be underscored. Having a clear understanding of the goal or purpose of a learning activity and having knowledge of the progress made in the direction of that goal go hand in hand. Unless the teacher spends some time crystallizing what has been accomplished or learned, the children may work for days without feeling that they have learned anything or that they are getting anywhere. Some teachers find it worthwhile to place these daily summaries on charts that serve as a log of the unit work as it progresses. Such logs are helpful in the culmination and may also be useful in evaluation activities associated with the unit.

The work–study or problem-solving phase of the unit is handled somewhat differently in the primary grades than it is in the middle and upper grades. Although children of all ages need many first-hand experiences to extend their understanding of social studies concepts, the older child has a greater familiarity with the world of things and people and can, therefore, profit from vicarious experiences to a much greater extent than the primary-grade child. Furthermore, the older child can make use of reading as a tool for learning in the social studies, whereas the young child is less able to do so. The physiological and psychological makeup of the primary-grade child makes necessary the use of learning activities that involve the child actively on a firsthand experience basis. (See Chart 3.)

Chart 3   Learning Activities for Social Studies

Type of Learning Activity	Examples	Purposes Served
Research	Reading Writing Interviewing Note-taking Collecting Map work Reporting Using references	To 　Gather data 　Practice data-gathering skills 　Answer questions
Presentation	Telling Demonstrating Illustrating Dramatizing Exhibiting Announcing Giving directions Pantomiming Relating events	To 　Share ideas with others 　Practice communication skills 　Clarify ideas 　Encourage initiative 　Apply information
Creative experiences	Writing Sketching Illustrating Sewing Soap carving Manipulating Comparing Drawing Modeling Painting Constructing Singing Dramatizing Imagining	To 　Express ideas creatively 　Encourage creative abilities 　Stimulate interest 　Extend and/or enrich learning

Chart 3 *(Continued)*

Type of Learning Activity	Examples	Purposes Served
Appreciation	Listening Viewing Describing Reading	To Develop attitudes and feelings Provide valuing experiences Extend and/or enrich learning
Observation or listening	Observing Visiting places of interest Viewing pictures or films Listening to recordings	To Gather information Build observation and perceptual skills Compare and constrast
Group cooperation	Discussing Sharing Helping one another Doing committee work Conversing Asking questions	To Develop group-work skills Use socialization skills Engage in larger projects
Experimentation	Measuring Demonstrating Conducting experiments Collecting	To Clarify complex procedures Develop inquiry skills Gather information
Organization	Planning Outlining Holding meetings Discussing Summarizing	To Clarify relationships Prepare a plan of action Organize ideas
Evaluation	Summarizing Criticizing Asking questions Reviewing	To Clarify direction and purpose Assess progress toward goals Modify plans

The following are a few examples of learning activities for all grade levels:

Sharing

Mr. Johnson's second-graders were studying their seashore community. Using a sandbox and things that each of them had gathered or collected with their families, they created a model of a seashore. The boys and girls talked about what they had brought and where their items had come from. They discussed whether or not the items were natural or artifically constructed.

Construction

Ms. Smather's class studied early people and constructed tools and weapons with sticks, rocks, and vines they gathered in nearby wooded areas. Each child demonstrated the use of the implement.

Experimenting

Miss Womble secured samples of various grains—oats, corn, barley, wheat—while studying agriculture with her class. The children compared the appearance and taste of each type of grain and then planted some to compare germinating time and appearance of the first shoots.

Listening

In Mr. Potts' class, the focus of study was the American Indian. In motivating the unit Mr. Potts read the children an Indian legend and asked them to decide what the Indians valued in their lives, using the legend as a clue to their value system.

Discussion

Ms. Perkle's sixth-grade class had a current events time, and a child brought an article from the evening paper telling about the sale of United States grain to China. A discussion that weighed the advantages and disadvantages of this action to the American people followed.

Written Language Experience

Miss Thomas's class had written letters to their grandparents asking them to share their recollections of earlier schooldays. Those grandparents who lived nearby were asked to visit Miss Thomas's classroom.

Dramatic Activities

During their study of Indonesia, each of the pupils in Miss Monroe's class created a shadow puppet. In small groups they dramatized situations from Indonesian life.

Art Experience

In a first-grade class the pupils made a trip to a farm. On their return they painted a mural showing the animals, equipment, people, and buildings they had observed.

Field Trip

A day was spent at a fair during the study of the state. The children noticed what products were displayed and what their region of the state had contributed.

Processing

During a study of colonial history the class divided into groups to make soap, dip candles, bake bread, churn butter, make dyes, and weave.

Some of the unit activities will involve the entire group, whereas others will be individual and/or small-group endeavors. In carrying out this part of the unit, the teacher should make certain that each child knows what is expected. Classrooms operating in this way are places where children are doing things; consequently, they will be moving about, asking questions, and communicating with one another, and a generally informal but task-oriented atmosphere will prevail.

Unfortunately, not all social studies learning experiences are able to produce the high level of affect displayed by the boys in these two photographs. But when teachers use activities of this type in combination with necessary but less exciting modes of learning, pupils develop long-lasting, positive attitudes toward social studies and learn subject matter and skills, too.

Evaluating Learning

Throughout the study the teacher and the pupils should make frequent evaluations of how well the unit is progressing. Much of this formative evaluation is, and ought to be, informal. The teacher sees children working well or poorly and adjusts the instruction accordingly. The teacher can also sense whether or not pupils are interested in what they are doing. Through observation and feedback from pupils, the teacher can gauge the extent to which progress is being made toward the achievement of objectives. An appropriate short teacher-made test can be used to check on pupil progress in specific areas of content and skills. Much of the informal evaluation that takes place on a day-to-day basis involves the children themselves. Pupils should be encouraged through discussion to take stock of their work individually and as a group. Evaluation of learnings, therefore, should not be associated only with the conclusion of a unit, but should be an important part of the ongoing instruction. Of course, the end of a unit provides a time to examine the extent to which the overall objectives have been achieved. Both informal and formal evaluation procedures are appropriate for this purpose.

Concluding the Study

As pupils near the end of a unit, the teacher should plan a series of activities that encourages them to summarize what they have learned. This might involve opportunities to show what they have done or to share interesting things they have learned with other classes in the school or with their parents. The trend in recent years, however, has been away from elaborate exhibits and performances for the benefit of others. What is important about closing a unit of study is the opportunity to discuss conclusions, evaluate what has been learned, identify what pupils found to be of especial interest to them, and to identify areas where additional study is needed. Concluding activities should include a suggestion of various interesting facets of the topic that were left unexplored and about which the children may wish to read and study independently. Concluding activities can and should serve as bridges to new intellectual pursuits.

PLANNING SHORTER INSTRUCTIONAL SEQUENCES

Thus far our discussion has concerned itself only with planning a unit—a parcel of work that might take several weeks to complete. In order to implement such a plan, it is necessary for the teacher to extract from the unit plan ideas that can be converted into shorter instructional sequences that may last anywhere from a single day to a

43

week or more. Sometimes these are called daily lesson plans, although there is some objection to that term because it suggests—and may lead to—fragmentation, rigidity, and old-fashioned teaching procedures. Social studies learning is, or ought to be, continuous from one day to the next. Pupils simply pick up where they left off in their study the day before. Lesson plans should be consistent with this continuous flow of learning. Short-range plans are a teaching trip-map that the teacher has in hand and uses at the time the teaching is done. Because the teacher relies on these plans to implement the instruction, they must be complete in every detail, correctly sequenced, contingencies anticipated and accounted for, with as little as possible left to chance. As the teacher prepares such plans, it is helpful to rehearse mentally how the lesson is expected to proceed, step by step. This will help reduce the possibility of encountering surprises while the lesson is in progress.

There are five essential components of plans of this type. These are: (1) the purpose or objective that identifies what pupils will *learn;* (2) the readiness or interest-building procedures that indicate how the sequence is to *begin;* (3) pupil work–study activities that indicate what pupils will *do* to help them learn; (4) summary and evaluation that indicate how the sequence will *close;* and (5) a list of the instructional materials and resources needed to teach the sequence. The following examples show how these plans can be constructed.

TOPIC:	The Japanese Meal
GRADE:	Two
OBJECTIVE:	Pupils will become acquainted with Japanese food, utensils, and method of eating, and will compare these with their own culture.
INTEREST BUILDING:	The teacher will have a sample of Japanese eating and cooking utensils and Japanese food items. These items will be shown to the children who will try to determine what they are and how they are used.
ACTIVITIES:	View films and filmstrips of Japanese life. Take a field trip to a Japanese restaurant and/or an Asian food store. Invite a resource person to class. Practice using chopsticks for eating. Draw and label pictures of Japanese food and utensils.

SUMMARY: In small groups have the children assist an adult in preparing a Japanese dish to be shared with the class for lunch.

Discuss: How did this compare with the meals you have at home? Do you think Japanese children would enjoy American food? Why are tastes different?

MATERIALS:

teapot	filmstrips
teacups	rice
chopsticks	tea
rice bowls	assorted Japanese vegetables
wok	soy sauce
pictures	Japanese cookies and crackers
films	Mandarin oranges

TOPIC: Futuring

GRADE: Six

OBJECTIVE: Pupils will be able to identify present trends and to project the consequence of a specific trend.

INTEREST BUILDING: Suggest that the class has gathered together in the year 2025 for a reunion. Have them speculate on what their lives will be like then. Define *trends* and have the pupils list current trends such as more mechanization in our daily lives or the increased use of computers.

ACTIVITIES: With the pupils working in groups of three, have them choose one of the current trends and brainstorm all of the consequences of that trend, such as more leisure time in the case of the mechanization trend, which leads to more recreation needs, which means an increase in the use of state parks and the like.

Ask the pupils to organize their ideas for sharing with their classmates.

SUMMARY: In the next class period have each group identify consequences that seem to be negative.

Ask them to develop an ideal plan that could make this consequence beneficial to people in the future.

45

MATERIALS:	None necessary, but outside sources have commercial materials on this topic. Two possible references are:
	The Center for Curriculum Design 823 Foster Street Evanston, Illinois 60204
	Science Fiction Research Association Box 3186 The College of Wooster Wooster, Ohio 44691

JUDGING THE ADEQUACY OF A LESSON PLAN

A teacher is never as well prepared as he or she *might* have been, given more time and more resources. Lesson planning is an open-ended process that can go on endlessly. Many teachers can recall, as student teachers, staying up half the night preparing a half-hour lesson to be taught the next day. Although such effort is commendable, it cannot be sustained for any length of time. At some point, the teacher must decide that the lesson is well enough planned and then be able to turn to other matters with a clear conscience.

It is not always easy, especially for the beginning teacher, to know when one has reached the point of diminishing returns in lesson planning. The checklist that follows can be useful in deciding whether or not all important aspects of the lesson have been given appropriate attention in the planning process.

Lesson Plan Checklist

1. Do the lesson objectives state clearly what it is that the pupils are expected to *learn* during the lesson?
2. Do the pupil activities for the lesson relate in a direct way to the stated objectives? That is, will the pupils learn what they are supposed to learn by doing the things they are asked to do in the lesson?
3. Do you know how the lesson is to begin? What is the very first thing you will do? Say? What next? What third?
4. Have you written down the questions you plan to ask? Do you have them in the order you plan to ask them?
5. Do you have all the needed instructional material? Equipment? If you are planning to use a machine, have you arranged to get

it? Do you know where the electrical outlets are in the room? Will you need an extension cord? Screen?

6. Are there specific directions you are planning to give the pupils regarding what they are to do? If so, do you know what they are?

7. If you are going to group the pupils, do you have productive work planned for *all* the groups, *all* of the time?

8. Do you know how much time will be needed for each component of your lesson?

9. Have you provided for differences in rate and level of learning among pupils? Do you have productive work–study activities planned for those pupils who complete their assignments quickly? Have you provided additional help for the slower learners? Do you have appropriate learning activities planned for any children with handicapping conditions?

10. Have you considered whether or not the lesson will require changes in the room environment, movement of furniture, and so forth?

11. Do you know exactly how the lesson is to close—that is: What you will do? What you will say? What you expect the pupils to do?

12. Have you planned for any follow-up activity?

13. Have you taken into account how pupil learning is to be evaluated?

14. Should the lesson be completed more quickly than you have planned, do you have some "back-up" activities ready that can be used during the extra time?

DISCUSSION QUESTIONS AND SUGGESTED ACTIVITIES

1. Select a unit topic that would be appropriate for a grade of your choice and identify six to eight main ideas that could be developed in such a unit. State these as declarative sentences (generalizations). Arrange them in the order in which they would be presented in the unit.

2. Select one of the main ideas you identified in your response to question 1. Develop it into a teaching plan using the format suggested by Figure 1 on page 35.

3. Using the ideas you developed in your answer to question 2, prepare a teaching sequence (lesson plan) using the form suggested on pages 44–46.

4. Write behavioral objectives for a unit such as the one you identified in responding to question 1.

5. Suggest social studies learnings that lend themselves especially well to the use of behavioral objectives and some that do not.

How would the teacher evaluate pupil achievement of objectives that are not stated behaviorally?

6. Discuss teaching plans and how to prepare them with your supervising teacher or with some other inservice teacher you know. If possible, bring to class a sample of the format for social studies planning used by that teacher. Compare plans brought to class in terms of similarities in the items included.

7. Prepare a list of decisions that could be made in your classroom in which pupils could legitimately participate. Also, make a list of decisions in which pupils would not participate. What guidelines can you suggest regarding the involvement of pupils in classroom decision-making?

8. Suppose as a teacher you were assigned to a school that had no social studies curriculum guide or any type of a planned social studies program. How would you go about planning the social studies program for your class?

9. Identify a few events, decisions, or actions that occurred at the national level that have had an impact on social studies education at the local level.

10. Prepare a lesson plan just as you would teach it to a grade of your choice. Apply the checklist on pages 46–47 to test for its completeness. Have the plan critiqued by a practicing teacher.

SELECTED REFERENCES

Ellis, Arthur K. *Teaching and Learning Elementary Social Studies*, Second Edition. Boston: Allyn & Bacon, Inc., 1981. Chapter 2.

Gronlund, Norman E. *Stating Objectives for Classroom Instruction*, 2nd ed. New York: Macmillan Publishing Company, Inc., 1978.

Hunter, Madeline. "Diagnostic Teaching," *The Elementary School Journal*, 79 (September 1979), pp. 8–18.

Jarolimek, John and Clifford D. Foster. *Teaching and Learning in the Elementary School*, 2nd ed. New York: Macmillan Publishing Company, Inc., 1981. Chapters 5, 6, and 7.

McKenzie, Gary R. "The Importance of Teaching Facts in Elementary Social Studies," *Social Education*, 44 (October 1980), pp. 494–498.

Orlich, Donald C. *et al. Teaching Strategies: A Guide to Better Instruction.* Lexington, Massachusetts: D.C. Heath and Company, 1980. Chapter 5.

Ryan, Frank L. *The Social Studies Sourcebook: Ideas for Teaching in the Elementary and Middle School.* Boston: Allyn & Bacon, Inc., 1980.

Seif, Elliott. *Teaching Significant Social Studies in the Elementary School.* Chicago: Rand McNally College Publishing Company, 1977. Chapter 9.

Skeel, Dorothy J. *The Challenge of Teaching Social Studies in the Elementary School*, 3rd ed. Santa Monica, CA.: Goodyear Publishing Company, Inc., 1979. Chapters 3 and 6.

3

Social Studies Teaching
Techniques and Strategies

Teaching looks deceptively easy when one observes a master doing it. Everything seems to happen in an unhurried, deliberate way. The transactions between teacher and pupils exude a feeling of confidence and assurance. Watching such a teacher, the observer might think, "Anyone could do that!" And, interestingly enough, the more skillful the teacher, the easier the process appears to be. It is only when the beginner attempts to emulate the teaching behavior of the master teacher that the complexity of teaching becomes apparent.

How one goes about teaching should have something to do with the nature of what is to be learned. For instance, many skills require the pupil to participate actively on a firsthand basis in the process of learning them. Group work skills are of this type; no amount of reading about group work skills or listening to someone explain them will make the learner proficient in their use. On the other hand, if one wants to learn about European settlements in the New World, reading might be the best way to achieve that goal.

How one goes about teaching should also have something to do with the characteristics of the person doing the learning. A well-presented series of technical, lengthy lectures on the Westward Movement, for example, might be wholly appropriate for a college course in American history. But no matter how well they are presented, such lectures would be inappropriate for fifth-graders studying the same topic; we can do some things with some groups that we cannot do with others.

The techniques and strategies used in teaching social studies, therefore, have to be considered in terms of the goals of the program, the objectives to be achieved, and the maturity of the learners. If we want children to gain information, this can be achieved through reading, viewing, discussing, and other procedures that involve the transmission of informational messages. These are referred to as *expository* teaching strategies. If we want children to develop critical habits of thought, to search for data independently, to be able to form hypotheses and test them, we use *inquiry* teaching strategies. If we want children to learn to work with each other, to plan together, or to apply what they are learning as they are learning it, we would use *activity* teaching strategies. *Demonstration* strategies can be a part

49

of any of the others and would be used to improve the communication process through showing, doing, and telling. What is called discovery learning is a variation of inquiry. These modes of teaching—expository, inquiry, activity, and demonstration—are discussed in detail in other sources.[1]

Beginning teachers are usually most comfortable starting with an expository strategy. The teaching situation can be controlled sufficiently well to reduce management concerns to a minimum, the objectives can be made specific, the pupils' study materials can be preselected by the teacher, and the process can be entirely teacher-directed. First encounters with teaching social studies should be short—20 to 30-minute episodes—and involve teaching a simple concept or skill. This initial teaching experience might be based on the textbook, with heavy reliance on the suggestions presented in the teacher's manual that accompanies the book. After a few experiences of this type, the novice will have gained some confidence in the teaching role, will know how to gauge pupil responses, and can begin to add variations, such as increased use of visual material, discussion questions, and pupil follow-up activities.

Having achieved a backlog of success experiences in the expository mode, the teacher might plan a demonstration. Some aspects of map or globe use would serve well for this purpose. Pupil follow-up work to the demonstration might be individualized, perhaps giving individual pupils some choice in what they will do. This can be succeeded by a class discussion of the individual follow-up activities.

While doing this type of rather formal teacher-directed expository teaching, the questions asked by the teacher will be informational, requiring the pupils to do little more than recall what they have read or observed. The teacher is not concerned with much beyond the literal comprehension of what has been taught. With increased experience and confidence, the teacher should begin asking some questions that require other intellectual operations, such as interpretation, analysis, synthesis, or application. These reflective questions should not be ones that can be answered by recalling factual information but should require pupils to respond to such queries as "Why?" "How do you know?" "If that happened, how do you explain . . . ?" "Can you summarize . . . ?" "What conclusion can we come to?" "What other problems does that raise?"

These questions will gradually lead the teacher and the class away from exposition and in the direction of inquiry. In time, pupils will be raising questions and problems themselves and will speculate about their solutions. These hunches will be converted into hypotheses that result in pupil searches for data, which will necessitate the wide use of resources, individualized assignments, and a variety of interesting pupil activities. At this stage the teacher is well on the way to devel-

[1]John Jarolimek and Clifford D. Foster, *Teaching and Learning in the Elementary School*, 2nd ed. New York: Macmillan Publishing Co., Inc., 1981, pp. 109-131.

oping professional maturity in the use of teaching techniques and strategies in social studies.

TEACHING CONCEPTS AND GENERALIZATIONS

In everyday parlance, the term *concept* is used to mean *idea*, as when someone says, "My concept of leisure is not the same as yours." In social studies, a concept may also be thought of as an idea expressed as a word, term, or phrase. Social studies concepts often embody an extensive meaning that develops with experience and learning over a period of years. Let us explore in some detail the meaning and implications of concepts for teaching and learning social studies.

The Nature of Concepts

If asked to tell what a village is, most adults would probably say something along this line: "A village consists of a group of persons living in a rural area in a cluster of homes smaller than a city or a town." For most purposes this is an adequate definition to make communication possible. But *village* had a much more elaborate meaning for the Indians of British Columbia, as explained in Margaret Craven's novel *I Heard the Owl Call My Name*. On the boat trip north, the young priest, Mark Brian, recalls what his bishop had told him about the village:

> The Indian knows his village and feels for his village as no white man for his country, his town, or even for his own bit of land. His village is not the strip of land four miles long and three miles wide that is his as long as the sun rises and the moon sets. The myths are the village and the winds and the rains. The river is the village, and the black and white killer whales that herd the fish to the end of the inlet the better to gobble them. The village is the salmon who comes up the river to spawn, the seal who follows the salmon and bites off his head, the bluejay whose name is like the sound he makes—"Kwiss-kwiss." The village is the talking bird, the owl, who calls the name of the man who is going to die, and the silver-tipped grizzly who ambles into the village, and the little white speck that is the mountain goat on Whoop-Szo.
>
> The fifty-foot totem by the church is the village, and the Cedar-man who stands at the bottom holding up the eagle, the wolf and the raven! And a voice said to the great cedar tree in Bond Sound, "Come forth, Tzakamayi and be a man," and he came forth to be the Cedar-man, the first man-god of the people and more powerful than all other.[2]

This is a superb example of a concept because it illustrates so well the richness and depth of meaning that can inhere in a single word label. It also illustrates how vital experience is in developing such

[2] From *I Heard the Owl Call My Name*, Copyright © 1973 by Margaret Craven. Reprinted by permission by Doubleday & Company, Inc., and George G. Harrap & Company.

meanings. It is doubtful if anyone who did not actually grow up in the village culture of these Indians could understand and appreciate the full meaning of *village* as they conceptualize it. Yet the novelist does very well in conveying the meaning by skillfully building word images for us of things that are familiar because they come out of our own background of experience.

Concepts are sometimes described as abstract categories of meanings. They are abstract because they are removed from specific instances. For example, *island* is the word label for a geographic phenomenon consisting of land completely surrounded by water. Kauai is one specific example of such a set of conditions. There are thousands of other specific examples of the concept *island*. But to know that Kauai is an island (that is, a body of land completely surrounded by water) is not to know very much about that beautiful outcropping of land in the Pacific. To early Hawaiians, Kauai had a meaning closely akin to that of village to the Pacific Northwest Indians described earlier. Concept definitions, therefore, tell us only about those qualities or attributes that a class or group of examples *have in common*. They do not tell us about the unique features of particular examples.

The human intellect makes use of this system of classifying, categorizing, and organizing the vast amount of specific knowledge with which it deals. Trees having certain attributes are *evergreen*, others having other attributes are *deciduous*. Some groups of animals are known as *mammals*, others *reptiles*, and others *birds*. A certain form of government is called a *democracy*, another an *autocracy*. This ability and inclination to classify perceptions of reality into groups having common qualities is what is meant by conceptual thought. Conceptual thought makes it possible to manipulate reality intellectually, i.e., one can figure out complex problems "in one's head." This is a distinctly human quality.

Concepts *always* have to do with meanings; words are simply their labels. Animals can be taught to respond to words and some can be taught to speak words. But they can never conceptualize the meanings for which the word is a referent. Concepts may deal with concrete places, objects, institutions, or events such as these:

mountain	flood	valley
plateau	dairy	ocean
home	island	Chinese
country	famine	harbor
state	community helpers	desert
producer	political party	consumer goods

Concepts may also be more or less abstract ways of thinking, feeling, and behaving, such as these:

adaptation	freedom	responsibility
democracy	justice	cooperation

tolerance	fairness	rights
honesty	liberty	equality
loyalty	interdependence	conflict
culture	free enterprise	legal system

The meanings of these concepts can be developed by description or by definition, providing the descriptions and/or definitions are rooted in the experiences of the learner—that is, in something that is already known. This means that if we are to develop new concepts or extend the meanings of those partially understood, it is critical to link them to prior experience and knowledge.

Social studies material is literally loaded with concepts. The following paragraph was selected from a fifth-grade social studies textbook. The concepts have been italicized here to call attention to them:

In the *Chicago area* many *foodstuffs* are prepared for *market*. Corn is made into all kinds of *corn products*. Chicago is the *center* of this *industry*. It is also a busy *grain market*. Chicago leads all of our *cities* in the *manufacture* of *farm machinery*. It is also an important *iron and steel center*. Chicago's position on the Great Lakes provides cheap *transportation* for bringing *raw materials* into its *factories*. The *finished products* can also be shipped out cheaply to all parts of the world.[3]

If one tries to simplify this paragraph by substituting alternate words for those that are italicized, one finds that it cannot be done and still convey the same meaning. This example illustrates that concepts carry much of the meaning of social studies.

The Nature of Generalizations

Let us return to the village concept cited earlier and ask the question: What can we say about the relationship between the village and the people who live there? Several things could be said, of course, but the following will serve our purpose:

The village embraces the total culture of traditional Pacific Northwest Indians.

This statement expresses a relationship between the concepts *village* and *culture*. Such relationships are called *generalizations* and are expressed as declarative statements. Because generalizations are relationships between two or more concepts, they are summarizing statements that have wide applicability. They can be transferred to many situations. For example, the generalization cited does not apply only to one village but to *all* villages of traditional Pacific Northwest Indians. That is what makes it a generalization. The generalization

<hr>

[3] Allen Y. King, Ida Dennis, and Florence Potter. *The United States and the other Americas.* New York: Macmillan Publishing Company, Inc., 1982, p. 263.

53

"All human societies have a culture" has even broader applicability. It would apply to *any* human society, anywhere in the world.

Generalizations are similar to concepts in that they, too, help the individual order the physical and social environments. Rather than being represented by a single word or expression, however, generalizations are usually expressed as declarative statements. The following are examples of generalizations often found in social studies. Notice how each expresses a relationship between concepts embedded in the statement.

1. New inventions lead to changes in ways of living.
2. Human beings change (adapt) their living to existing conditions.
3. Peoples of the world are interdependent.
4. Members of families help one another.
5. People influence their environment and are influenced by it.
6. Many people have contributed to our present civilization.
7. Basically, all people are very much alike, although they differ in their ways of living because of geographical and historical factors.
8. People live in a continually changing world.
9. Workers in our neighborhood help one another.

Converting Concepts Into Thought Forms Appropriate for Elementary Schoolchildren

Social studies concepts and topics can be studied at various levels of complexity. Kindergarteners and first graders often study the family and family life. Yet a graduate student working on a doctor's degree in sociology or anthropology might take an advanced seminar on the same subject. The United States Supreme Court struggles with the meaning of justice in a complex case, yet children in the elementary school learn about the meaning of "liberty and justice for all." How does a teacher go about setting the complexity of subject matter, concepts, and generalizations and present them in ways that make sense to children? The following are suggested:

1. Define concepts and key ideas in child-oriented terms. For example:

Concept	For a Young Child This Means
Justice	Being or playing fair
Laws	Rules
Equality of opportunity	Seeing that everyone gets a turn
Cooperation	Working with others
Responsibility	Doing your part or doing your duty

2. Select subject matter with which pupils can identify. This does not mean that topics selected for study must in all cases be physically close to the children. The usual assumption is that things that are physically close to children will be more familiar than

those far away. This is not always the case. Children can study about things far away that are psychologically close to them. On the other hand, things that are physically close may be psychologically remote. The lifestyles of families who live across town, for example, may be as unfamiliar to a child as those of people halfway around the world.

3. Develop ideas only to the point where children can apply them to reality. It takes time for children to learn concepts. They acquire a grasp of ideas cumulatively over several years. Do not expect children to learn complex concepts to completion in the early grades. The tendency is to try to teach children more than they want or need to know about a concept or a subject at a particular time.

4. Rely heavily on diagnostic approaches to teaching. Find out how much pupils already know. This can usually be accomplished through informal class discussions in which children respond to open-ended questions the teacher has prepared in advance. Observe how well they use new terms and concepts naturally and easily. Be aware of the level of interest in what is being studied. Draw on the experiences of pupils in planning and teaching social studies. Encourage children to talk about what is studied as it relates to their lives.

Concept Development: Three Strategies

In order to have meaning, concepts must be anchored in the experience of an individual. Such experience may be direct or vicarious, real or simulated, but one way or another, new ideas *must* be linked to prior experience. Concepts that are not or that cannot be associated with life experiences will, almost without exception, seem irrelevant to the learners. For this reason, it is hopeless to attempt to teach complex social studies concepts to pupils who have impoverished life experiences. This is why real objects, models, illustrations, pictures, field trips, films, and vivid examples are essential to concept learning.

In general, concepts are learned by *citing an example* (Denver is an example of a *city*); by *describing the concept* (a *city* has a high population density); or by *defining the concept* (a *city* is an incorporated municipality whose boundaries and governmental powers are authorized and defined in a charter from the state in which it is located). The teaching strategies used in developing social studies concepts often incorporate all three of these ways of learning concepts.

Strategy One: Listing, Grouping, Labeling.

Imagine a primary grade class that has just returned from a field trip to a supermarket. Now back in the classroom, the teacher asks the pupils to list as many things as they can remember having seen in

55

the supermarket. As the children name items they saw, the teacher writes them on the chalkboard—e.g., eggs, bread, beans, meat, butter, checkout person, stock clerk, watermelons, candy, store manager, dog food, ice cream and so on.

After completing the process of listing what they saw, the teacher asks the pupils to examine their list to see if certain things on the list seem to go together. That is, can these items be put together in groups that have something in common, as, for example, milk, butter, cheese, cream, and yogurt? The pupils catch on to this activity quickly, and soon they are suggesting which items can be placed in the same group. Having placed items that seem to go together in the same group, the pupils are then asked to think of names or labels for these groups. In the foregoing example, a name for that group would probably be "dairy products." The pupils should develop a name or label for each of the groups.

This listing–grouping–labeling strategy was developed by the late Hilda Taba and her associates. It can be used in many ways to teach concepts in social studies. Here are a few additional examples:

1. Suppose a visitor from another country spent a day at our school; what would he see?
2. What did you see on the walk through the neighborhood?
3. What are all the ways goods and people can be moved from one place to another?
4. How many things can you list that are manufactured in our city (or state)?
5. What items are sold in a department store?

This strategy is particularly useful in situations where learners have made a great number of observations or perceptions in a short period of time and need to sort out what they experienced into meaningful categories.

Strategy Two: Experiencing, Hypothesizing, Testing.

An intermediate-grade class is studying the concept *advertising*. The teacher begins the study by having the pupils search for as many different examples of advertising as they can find. This search uncovers newspaper and magazine advertisements, classified ads, radio and television commercials, billboards, signs on transit buses, signs in public buildings, direct mailers, catalogs, and others. These various methods of advertising are discussed in terms of their purpose; the audience to which they are directed; the extent to which they are local, regional, or national; and the nature of the appeal. This leads the class to speculate on the value of advertising. Who benefits from advertising and how do they benefit? Out of this discussion the pupils develop the following hypotheses:

1. Advertising helps consumers because it informs them about new products and their prices.

2. Effective advertising tries to create wants for products whether they are needed or not.
3. Local advertising has a more direct effect on sales in local stores than does national advertising.

The pupils begin searching for information that would support or refute these hypotheses. Much of their information gathering was done outside of school by interviewing consumers, local merchants, and representatives of advertising agencies. This process forced the pupils to explore further such related subconcepts as needs and wants, promotion, audience, client, account, market, layout, impact, theme, and sales appeal. In time they were able to form some tentative conclusions relating to their hypotheses, but their searches suggested other hypotheses that needed exploration. The entire process provided the pupils with a thorough familiarity with the concept of advertising from several different perspectives.

In one form or another, the procedure just described is frequently used in teaching social studies concepts. What takes place is the following:

1. Pupils are provided with extended, direct, firsthand exploratory experiences.
2. Terms and subconcepts related to the main concept are explained and their meanings are developed as a natural extension of the study.
3. Pupils discuss ideas relating to the main concept and are encouraged to speculate about explanations of perceived relationships. These speculative statements become hypotheses to be tested.
4. A data search is made to test the hypotheses.
5. Tentative conclusions are drawn, which give rise to other hypotheses and the search continues.
6. Through extended study and firsthand experiences, the meaning of the main concept is extended and refined.

This strategy is particularly useful in teaching such concepts as *culture, justice, conflict, democracy, equality,* and many others in social studies that do not lend themselves well to easy definition. In fact, there is not even consensus among experts on the exact meaning of many of these concepts. They are understood by being subjected to extended exposure in many different settings over a long period of time.

Strategy Three: Recognizing Examples and Nonexamples.

A sixth-grade class has been studying emerging nations of the Third World. The teacher wants to develop the concept *modernization* and does so in the following way. She writes on the chalkboard:

Modernization involves

1. the application of technology to the control of nature's resources.
2. the use of inanimate sources of power and energy.

57

3. the use of tools to multiply the effects of human energy expended.
4. a high per capita production output.

She then explains the meaning of each of the four attributes by using large pictures. That is, she shows the pupils specific examples of modernization—situations in which technology is applied to the control of resources, where inanimate power and energy sources are used, where tools multiply human energy, and where the per capita production is high. As pupils raise questions, these are discussed and issues clarified. The teacher then provides the pupils with a series of pictures in which modernization, as defined by the particular attributes, is *not* evident. Again, these are explained and discussed, and questions raised by pupils are answered.

Having satisfied herself that the pupils understand the attributes that indicate modernization, the teacher presents the class with another set of pictures, but this time the *pupils* must identify examples and nonexamples of modernization and tell why or why not each is an example. These pictures are discussed in detail. The teacher then provides the pupils with back issues of the *National Geographic* and asks them to find picture examples and nonexamples of modernization and to tell why each is or is not an example. Finally, the teacher evaluates the pupils' ability to understand the concept by having them identify examples and nonexamples from a new set of pictures.

This strategy is less inquiry-oriented than the other two, but it does, nonetheless, present opportunities for search and discovery. In this case, the teacher provided the attributes of the concept in advance, rather than having pupils define them in the process of study. In summary, the teacher did the following:

1. She identified the label for the concept (modernization).
2. She provided the major attributes (or critical properties) of the concept.
3. She provided examples that illustrated the presence of the attributes.
4. She provided nonexamples in which the attributes were missing.
5. She presented examples and nonexamples and had the pupils identify the attributes and had them tell why or why not each was an example.
6. She had pupils find examples and nonexamples on their own.
7. She evaluated their ability to use the attributes in identifying examples and nonexamples.

Many social studies concepts can be developed in this way. This strategy is most useful for those concepts where there is reasonable agreement among experts on the attributes that define the concept. A few other examples are *island*, *desert*, *metropolitan region*, *industrial park*, *market*, *erosion*, and *capital*.

Developing Generalizations

Generalizations are relationships between two or more concepts that are usually expressed as declarative statements. Four different types of generalizations are relevant to social studies education:

1. A supermarket sells all food products needed by consumers.

This is a *descriptive* generalization. It could have evolved in the study of the children using the first strategy in the prior section on concept development. It describes in summary form the relationship between the supermarket and the food needs of consumers.

2. Advertising the price of merchandise results in more comparative shopping by consumers.

This is a *cause-and-effect* generalization. It might have been developed by the class studying advertising in the second strategy under concept development in the prior section. "If-then" statements are usually generalizations of this type.

3. Misleading or false advertising takes unfair advantage of consumers and is illegal.

This generalization is a statement of a *value principle*. It, too, might have evolved in the study of advertising described earlier. Generalizations of this type constitute the guidelines by which individuals govern their actions, and many have been handed down through the ages in the form of proverbs or wise statements for good living.

4. The capacity of a nation to modernize depends on its natural resource base, the quantity and quality of its labor force, the amount and kinds of capital available to its industry and agriculture, and the institutions, attitudes, values, and habits that determine the effectiveness with which these economic resources are used.

This generalization is a *universal law* or *principle* and is highly abstract. These generalizations are often used as the organizing frameworks for the social sciences and for social studies curricula. Such a generalization may have been the focus of the study of modernization discussed in the prior section under concept development. The possibility of the children arriving at such a generalization themselves is, indeed, remote, and it is probably inappropriate to expect them to do so.

It should be clear that generalizations are expressed as summarizing statements. That means that they will usually come near the ends of study sequences. For example, in the strategies for concept development described earlier, the children should be involved in stating generalizations that illustrate relationships between concepts. When generalizations are introduced at the beginning of a study sequence, they should be used as hypotheses to be confirmed or rejected in the process of study. This might occur in the following way:

The teacher says, "Many people believe in the law of supply and demand, which states that 'Scarcity of goods results in higher prices, whereas an oversupply of goods drives prices down.' How might we go about finding out whether or not this is true of the things we and our families buy on an everyday basis?"

At this point the search begins in order to test the validity of the generalization the teacher has provided as a working hypothesis.

Generalizations, like concepts, have to be developed out of the experiences of pupils. It is essential that pupils understand the concepts in the generalizations in order to grasp the meaning of the relationship being expressed. For this reason, it is not appropriate for pupils to simply memorize generalizations. Generalizations that are memorized but not understood are of no value in gaining meaning from new situations where the relationships expressed in the generalization apply.

If we are to teach for generalized knowledge that can be useful in new situations, pupils must be given as many broad and varied experiences with ideas as is possible. They need to view the ideas in a variety of contexts. Citing single examples should be avoided whenever possible, because this presents too narrow an experience for the pupil. When pictures or illustrations are used, several should be presented. Tests of understandings should not be cast in the exact context as presented in the instruction but should be placed in new settings. The teacher needs to ask frequently such questions as these: "Where else do we see this happening?" "How is this like or different from the problem we discussed at newstime?" "Can you give another example of that?"

It cannot be assumed that pupils will apply knowledge from one situation to another if left unaided by the teacher. A skillful teacher will pave the way for transfer to take place and, in so doing, will be teaching understandings with wide application. In teaching concepts and generalizations, the need is not to repeat, drill, and practice. Rather, it is to enable the pupil to encounter the idea in many settings, each slightly different from the other.

TEACHING SOCIAL STUDIES SKILLS

The systematic and sequential development of skills is of utmost importance to children because skills are the tools with which they continue their learning. Consequently, inadequately developed skills tend to retard learning and growth in many areas of the elementary school curriculum, particularly in the social studies. Inadequate achievement in the social studies can, in most cases, be traced to poorly developed reading skills, inability to handle the vocabulary of the social studies, inability to read maps and globes, poor work-study skills, inability to use reference materials, or retarded language skills. Therefore, a well-balanced program in the social studies needs to provide for systematic and planned instruction to ensure the development of these skills.

Skill implies proficiency, the capability of doing something well. To have a skill is ordinarily taken to mean that a person is able to respond more or less habitually in an efficient manner. Skills are commonly classified as motor, intellectual, and social.

All skills have two characteristics in common: they are developmental and they require practice if they are to be mastered. To speak of skills as being developmental means that they are learned gradually over a period of years. They are never really learned to completion, although there usually comes a time when the learner has mastered them sufficiently for most purposes. However, one could continue refining these skills throughout one's lifetime. Thus, teachers should not assume that skills are taught and learned only once in some particular grade. All teachers need to assume some responsibility for the teaching and maintenance of social studies skills.

No amount of explanation or meaningful teaching will make pupils proficient in skills. They must practice and use the skills they have learned in order to build facility in them. This does not mean repetition or drill in the traditional sense, where a response was repeated over and over in exactly the same way. Instead, it is hoped that pupils will practice skills with the intention of improving. This also does not mean that skills would be practiced wholly out of their functional setting, although there might be occasions when this would be necessary. In the ordinary study of a topic, there will be numerous opportunities to practice skills in the daily work–study activities of the class. In this way, the children improve their skills as they develop understandings. Skills are learned more effectively when they are closely related to actual situations in which they will be used.

Procedures in skills teaching are fairly clear-cut. The pupils should first understand what is involved in the skill, how it is used, and what it means. Providing a good model of its use is helpful at this point. Second, the pupils need to work through a simple use of the skill under careful teacher guidance. This is essential to verify that they understand what is involved and are making a correct response. Third, they need additional practice in increasingly complex variations of the skill, applied in functional settings. Pupils need to use it in solving problems, thus demonstating its value as a learning tool. Finally, they need continued practice in its use over an extended period of time to maintain and improve facility with the skill.

Teachers who hope to help children develop skills do not depend entirely on incidental teaching of them. Rather, the skills are carefully

61

Chart 4   Example of Steps in Skills Teaching Strategy

Skill: Using the directory of a newspaper to find needed information.

Skills Teaching Strategy

Directions:

Step 1. Make sure pupils understand what is involved in performing the skill. Show them how it is used. Provide the children with a good model of the skill in operation.

Step 2. Break the skill into components and arrange them sequentially. Develop the teaching sequence step by step, having the children do each component as it is presented and explained. Supervise carefully to make sure children's responses are correct.

Step 3. Have the pupils perform a simple variation of the skill under your close supervision. This is to ensure that the pupils are performing the skill correctly.

Step 4. After it is established that the pupils are performing the skill correctly, provide for supervised practice, using simple variations that ensure pupil success.

Step 5. Gradually increase the complexity of the variation of the skill and begin having pupils apply the skill in situations in which it is useful. Continue this procedure until the desired level of proficiency is achieved.

Step 6. Continue to practice the skill at regular intervals, largely through functional application, in order to maintain and improve performance.

identified, systematically taught, thoroughly practiced, and widely used. This principle applies to such intellectual skills as critical and reflective thinking, coming to valid conclusions based on evidence, evaluating sources of information, and interpreting data as well as to work–study and group-process skills. (See Chart 4.)

TEACHING VALUES AND ATTITUDES

Adults most often remember from their elementary school social studies program experiences that were distinctively affective—a skit

1. Secure a newspaper, preferably a Sunday edition, and show how difficult and time-consuming it is to find some bit of information if one has to leaf through the entire paper to find it. Have pupils try their hand at finding items without using the newspaper directory. Show how easily one can find information with the aid of the directory.

2. a. Make sure pupils know how to use the dictionary and the encyclopedia prior to teaching this skill.
   b. Acquaint pupils with various sections of the newspaper: general news, classified ads, sports, editorials, weather, and so on.
   c. Teach pupils the specialized vocabulary associated with the newspaper: vital statistics, obituaries, market quotations, masthead, dateline, syndicated, and so on.
   d. Teach pupils what items are included in the various categories listed in the directory, and how they are arranged. For example, what is included in the Arts and Entertainment section; how are the classifieds organized; and how does one find out what arrangement is used?
   e. Provide a newspaper for each member of the class and have the pupils locate easy items using the directory such as the television schedule, sports, and the comics. Supervise to make sure everyone is performing the skill correctly.

3. Follow Step 2 immediately with an exercise requiring pupils to locate items making use of the directory. Supervise and assist as needed. Check responses.

4. Assign pupils to find information in the next day's newspaper. This should be done on their own without teacher supervision. Check responses.

5. Bring to class copies of a different newspaper from the one used thus far in which a slightly different directory format appears. Assign pupils to find information in this paper without your assistance, to see if they can transfer and modify their skill from one situation to another. Check responses.

6. From time to time have pupils make use of the directory to locate needed information. Observe the accuracy and extensiveness of use of the directory.

on George Washington's birthday in one of the primary grades, a play about the Pilgrims and the first Thanksgiving in the fourth grade, a pageant depicting highlights of our country's history in the fifth grade, or those moving stories of courage and bravery that some teacher used to read to the class. These experiences are important for young children not necessarily because they will remember them but because these are ways children become acquainted with those common values, attitudes, and ideals that go into the making of our national character. The attachment to and internalization of common core values by individual members is an essential requirement for stable social life in a society. It is critical, therefore, that the process of socialization of young children attends to this important dimension of social education. The process begins, of course, in the home but is continued and extended in the school, particularly in social studies education. Concern for values and the valuing process obviously relates to the moral development of children.[4]

Values education is concerned with both *general* values and *personal* values. Such values as liberty, justice, equality, honesty, consideration for others, individualism, human dignity, responsibility, and truthfulness are examples of general values on which there is concensus. This does not mean that everyone has the same values or interprets them in the same way. But there is general agreement that such values reflect the basic orientation of the society. These values are a part of our political and religious heritages. They are incorporated in our great historical documents and in our legal and judicial systems. They are apparent in our folklore and in our literature. Individuals who lead exemplary lives that reflect such general values are extolled as national heroes.

USING SYMBOLS TO REPRESENT VALUES

Topic: Symbolic messages.

Objectives: Pupils will deduce certain information about a country from symbols placed on its coins.
Pupils will relate the symbols to basic values of their country.

Resources: At least one coin for each child, preferably coins or facsimiles of coins, from several different nations.

Procedure: Teacher: Boys and girls, for the past few days we have been studying the use of signs and symbols. At the close of our discussion yesterday we came to an important conclusion. What was it?

Pupil: We said that we could tell what people considered to be important to them by the symbols and signs they use on their buildings.

Teacher: Yes. Now today you will have a chance to test that idea in a slightly different way. Each of you will be given a coin to use. Study the coin carefully and see how many things you can tell about the country just from what you see on the coin.

Coins are distributed to the pupils. After they have had time to make their observations, ask the children what they have concluded. As these are presented, write them on the chalkboard. Have each pupil tell *why* the con-

[4] For a discussion of recent research on moral development in children, see "The Cognitive-Developmental Approach to Moral Education," Edwin Fenton, Guest Editor, *Social Education*, 40 (April 1976). This special section includes an introduction, four articles, and a selected bibliography of materials about moral education based on the research of Lawrence Kohlberg. Jack R. Fraenkel provides a critique of the theory of moral stages and the moral reasoning approach to values education in this same issue of *Social Education*.

clusion was made. Pass the coins about for other children to inspect. Items such as the following may surface in this discussion:

These people believe in God.
They want (or believe in) liberty.
They are able to read their language.
Men must be more important than women in this country.
They construct large buildings.
They speak more than one language.
It is an old country.
They have a queen (or king).
They are a peace-loving people.
They are proud of their wars and war heroes.
They want people to be courageous.

Follow-up: Imagine that the United States is planning to issue a new coin and there is a contest to get the best design. You decide to enter the contest. The rules are these:

    1. Write down two ideas that best describe what people in our country think are important to them.
    2. Think of and draw symbols that could be used on a coin to show these two qualities.

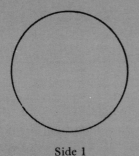 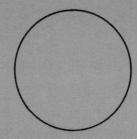

      Side 1   Side 2

If children are to be socialized in accordance with these general values of society, they must be provided with examples of behavior that illustrate these values in action. That is, young people need to have encounters with idealized types—persons who illustrate by their way of life the values that society rewards and likes to see in its citizens. It is because these general values are internalized by the majority of citizens that orderly social life can take place. We expect our fellow citizens to behave in ways that are predictable and consistent with the basic premises inherent in those values on which there is general consensus. Law enforcement agencies are provided to protect society from the minority of persons who cannot or will not live in accordance with the general values embraced by the majority. But no police force could possibly monitor the behavior of all citizens if they were not willing to comply voluntarily with the accepted rules of the society. We are able to enjoy social order because a large majority of citizens have internalized general values on which there is accordance.

The lesson plan dealing with symbolic values provides a good example of a lesson based on general values. General values are promoted through social studies in the following ways:

1. daily life in the classroom that stresses consideration for others, freedom and equality, independence of thought, individual responsibility for one's actions, and the dignity of individual human beings.
2. the study of the history and development of this country stressing the ideals that inspired it and showing that a continuing effort is needed to move reality closer to those ideals.
3. the study of biographies of individuals whose lives reflect the general values of the nation.
4. the study of the law and the legal and justice systems.
5. the celebration of holidays that reinforce values and ideals associated with the holiday.
6. thoughtful analysis of the meaning of such statements as the Pledge of Allegiance, the Preamble to the Constitution, and the Bill of Rights.
7. building awareness to situations that are not in accord with values to which this society is committed.
8. cross-cultural studies to illustrate differences in values from one society to another.

As we move from general values to *personal* values, the role of social studies becomes considerably different, and to some extent, less clear. Personal values are those values that affect the decision-making of individuals in their own personal lives. To some extent they represent individual interpretations of general values, i.e., the operationalizing of general values in the personal life of each individual.

Modern life involves an incredible amount of choice-making. How to spend our time; what career to choose; what clothes to buy and to wear; where to live; what brand products to buy; what hobbies and leisure-time activities to pursue; how to spend our money. The list could go on and on to include literally every facet of our lives. In each of these decisions there are probably no absolutely right and wrong choices in the sense that basic general values are being compromised by either choice. Rather, these decisions are expressions of individual preferences. As a transportation piece, one person buys a blue Ford sedan, another a yellow Chevrolet stationwagon, and a third a red Plymouth coupe. To ask which is *right* is inappropriate because right and wrong in the absolute sense is not an issue in such choice-making. This is really what personal values are all about—choice-making concerning our personal lives.

It should be obvious that the social studies program cannot promote personal values in the same way that it can promote general values. What social studies *can* do is to help pupils think about the choices they make in terms of a values framework. This is often referred to in current literature as "values clarification" or the "process of valuing." Raths, Harmin, and Simon suggest that if adults seek to help children in the process of valuing, they should:

1. Encourage children to make more choices, and to make them freely.
2. Help them discover alternatives when faced with choices.
3. Help children weigh alternatives thoughtfully, reflecting on the consequences of each.
4. Encourage children to consider what it is that they prize and cherish.
5. Give them opportunities to affirm their choices.
6. Encourage them to act, behave, live in accordance with their choices.
7. Help them be aware of repeated behaviors or patterns in their life.[5]

Value clarification exercises are one means of helping pupils gain insight into questions of value. Such an exercise presents the pupil with a situation in which there is a conflict of values, both of which are attractive, but a choice has to be made between them. These choices are between or among "goods" rather than between or among something that is desirable and something that is not. Similarly, the choice is *not* between options that are illegal, unethical, or contrary to social norms. Good sources of value clarification exercises are available to the teacher.[6]

Almost any subject, topic, situation, or picture can be used to explore values. Questions of this type are suggested to elicit value responses for discussion:

1. If you returned someone's lost billfold, do you think you deserve a reward?
2. Do you think you would like a job like that?
3. How would you like to live in such a place?
4. If you won a cash prize of $100, what would you do with it?
5. How did you feel when you read that paragraph?
6. If you could change *one* thing about this community in order to make it a better place to live, what would you change?
7. If the principal dismissed everyone at noon today and you could do anything you wanted this afternoon, what would you choose to do?

[5]Louis E. Raths, Merrill Harmin, and Sidney B. Simon, *Values and Teaching: Working with Values in the Classroom*, 2nd ed. Columbus, Ohio: Charles E. Merrill Publishing Co., 1978, p. 38.

[6]Sidney B. Simon, Leland Howe, and Howard Kirschenbaum, *Values Clarification: A Handbook of Practical Strategies for Teachers and Students*, New York: Hart Publishing Company, Inc., 1972.

8. What do you think are the three most important qualities of a person who is President of the United States?
9. Can you name three decisions about which you think you ought to have something to say? Why do you think you should have something to say about these decisions?
10. Can you think of some person you really admire? Why do you admire that person?

There is nothing mysterious about the process of valuing. Everyone makes choices based on values several times each day. Valuing exercises and value clarification simply build an awareness of the value dimension of the choices we make. In the day-to-day work of the class, the teacher can use many situations to build such a consciousness of values, and thereby get pupils to think more deeply about what is important to them.

DEVELOPING INQUIRY AND THINKING ABILITIES

The major goal of inquiry-oriented teaching is to develop in pupils those attitudes and skills that enable them to be independent problem solvers. This means, among other things, that pupils need to develop a healthy skepticism about things and events in the world. Good problem solvers have a curiosity about what they see going on around them. They develop a questioning attitude. It is perhaps this element of inquiry that makes some parents have reservations about its use with young children. They would prefer to have their children accept certain beliefs and ideas as basic truths that are not to be questioned. The religious concept of faith is an example. Because of these conflicts, it is important for the teacher to know that inquiry, based on scientific problem-solving procedures, is only one of several ways of knowing things to be true. Unfortunately, in school we sometimes teach as though this were the only way of knowing, and as a consequence we alienate those who do not share this view.

Ways of Knowing

Perhaps the most common way of knowing something is by relying on an authoritative source. Our first and best teachers are our parents. As young children we perceive our parents as authoritative sources of knowledge. They protect and shelter us. They answer our questions about how things work. Because they seem to know so much and seem usually to be right in what they tell us, we learn to accept their explanations as true. As we grow older, we rely on other authorities—our teachers, scientists, books, doctors, historians, and so on. We simply do not have time to rediscover everything for ourselves, and even if we did, this would be an extremely inefficient use of our time. We can, we do, and indeed, we must rely on authorities for much of what we know about social and natural phenomena because we have no other way of getting such information.

The problem with the use of authority as a way of knowing is, of course, the credibility of the authority. We have to know enough about medicine, for example, to be able to differentiate between the wisdom of a competent physician and that of one less capable. Sooner or later all of us discover that our parents are not a reliable source of information on all subjects. We also learn that not everything we read in books can be accepted as true, either—we need to know something about the credentials of the author before we can evaluate the validity of the account.

It should be apparent that the potential for conflict between inquiry as a way of knowing and the use of authority is great. Parents are understandably concerned if the school undermines their child's perception of them as authoritative sources of information. The conflict becomes even greater if parents perceive the school's teaching as jeopardizing the child's belief in God as the ultimate authority. This is most likely to happen in cases where the family accepts the meaning of the Bible literally. This issue surfaces even at the college level in connection with courses entitled "The Bible as Literature." If one regards the Bible as the literal word of God, treating it simply as a piece of literature would be disrespectful at least and possibly even blasphemous.

Teachers cannot ignore the fact that a large segment of our population believes that revealed truth is a legitimate way of knowing— that is, that God revealed truth to human beings either through written accounts (such as the Bible or the Koran) or through holy persons who were especially commissioned to make these truths known to others. It does not matter in the slightest what the teacher's personal views on this matter are; the fact is that seated in the public school classrooms of this nation are hundreds of thousands, perhaps millions, of children who, to some extent, are taught the validity of revealed truth, and to fail to take this into account in school instruction is a mistake.

Personal knowledge is still another way of knowing. We know something to be true simply because we believe it to be so. What we believe to be true may seem preposterous to someone else—we have no way of "proving" it in the scientific sense—yet we know it is true. Such beliefs may even be regarded as superstitions by others, and, therefore, such truths may not be shared except with intimates, if at all. Premonitions, extrasensory experiences, and clairvoyance are examples of personal knowledge regarded as true by the participants in such experiences.

We come finally to scientific problem solving as still another way of knowing. When this procedure is explained, it is usually presented as a five-step operation involving (1) problem identification; (2) hypothesis formation; (3) data gathering; (4) testing hypotheses in terms of evidence (or data); and (5) drawing conclusions based on the evidence. The process should not be conceptualized as a series of steps, however, but as a way of thinking that requires hard evidence or observable events to associate causes with effects. Conclusions based on scientific problem solving are accepted tentatively, based on information available at the time. This leaves the door open to the further refinement of explanations and conclusions—or even different explanations or conclusions—at a later time when more information may become available. This procedure stresses the *probability* of something's being true in terms of evidence rather than being true in the *absolute*, unchanging sense. This means that there are no areas closed to further investigation, obviously another point of conflict with those who embrace other ways of knowing.

Scientific problem-solving procedures are exceedingly powerful weapons in the battle against ignorance. It is no exaggeration to say that knowledge breakthroughs that have made possible modern science, technology, and medicine can be attributed to this system of thinking. So spectacular have been the achievements of scientific problem solving that critics suggest that science itself has become a god in the modern world. As a result, in recent years, the plea has been heard more frequently that more attention should be given to other ways of knowing. The demand for equal time by those who espouse the creation theory and oppose the evolution theory provides an example of this issue.

The purpose of this discussion of knowledge and knowing, although admittedly brief and incomplete, is to alert the teacher to some of the complex issues surrounding inquiry teaching. Although this section is intended to promote inquiry procedures in the classroom, this is not to deny that there are other legitimate ways of learning. It is the responsibility of public school teachers to help children develop ways of thinking that characterize an educated rational citizenry. At the same time, teachers must be sensitive to the fact that there is so much about which we know so little; for many people, ways of knowing other than scientific problem solving appear to be more appropriate in dealing with those unknowns. The individual's right to embrace other ways of thinking must be respected.

Teaching Thinking Abilities Through Inquiry

In statements of educational goals and objectives, it is quite common to find the development of thinking abilities being given a high priority. Similarly, it is rare to find a teacher who does not claim to teach pupils to think. The problem, of course, is that there is often a big gap between intent and performance, resulting partly from a failure to understand how thinking skills are taught and learned. To admonish someone to think is of no value except as a way of telling the individual to pay attention and concentrate on the task at hand.

In this popular activity, pupils can see first hand that butter actually does come from the churning of cream. Suggest how a teacher might use the centuries-old process of butter making to foster inquiry in social studies.

More appropriate strategies for teaching those thinking skills that are associated with problem solving are those we call inquiry- or investigation-oriented.

The usual assumption is that the development of thinking skills flows naturally as a result of the acquisition of knowledge. The belief

71

is widespread that if one is well-informed, the application of that knowledge to the solution of problems will pretty much take care of itself. Consequently, educational programs often emphasize the accumulation of information rather than a concern with its application. If there is a concern for application at all, the feeling is that it should come later, after there has been a period of knowledge accumulation, in high school or college or as an adult. Research indicates that this procedure is based on faulty assumptions and that knowledge accumulation and knowledge application go hand in hand and are part of the same process we call thinking.

The process of thinking consists of a series of subskills, and like any other skills, they must be practiced if they are to be applied with any degree of proficiency. These subskills can be identified as follows:

1. Identifying problems and questions for study.
2. Making inferences and drawing conclusions from data.
3. Making comparisons.
4. Developing hypotheses.
5. Using evidence to test hypotheses.
6. Planning how to study a question or a problem.
7. Getting data from a variety of sources.
8. Predicting possible outcomes.
9. Deciding what evidence is needed in studying a problem.
10. Deciding what evidence is relevant to the study.

These skills must be incorporated in the on-going work of the class if pupils are to develop proficiency in their use. Occasional special lessons on inquiry are not in themselves adequate for building competence. Of course, not all of these subskills will appear in social studies lessons every day. During a period of a few weeks, however, one should see balanced and systematic attention being given to them.

Special instructional materials that are inquiry-based are helpful, but not essential, to engaging children in inquiry. Any of the standard materials can be used as sources of information, including textbooks. What is different about inquiry, however, is the way these materials are used. The usual assumption regarding instructional material is that it includes essential information that must be learned by the pupils. Nowhere is this more evident than in the use of textbooks. Textbook content often *becomes* the curriculum. In inquiry teaching, the textbook is a data or information *source*, and it should be used along with other data sources.

Not all social studies teaching need be, nor even should be, inquiry-oriented. The teaching mode selected must be consistent with the objectives to be achieved. If the purpose is to convey information to pupils or to teach a skill, exposition and demonstration are often more effective and efficient teaching modes than is inquiry. If the purpose is to teach thinking and problem-solving skills, however, an inquiry strategy should be used.

AN INQUIRY

Problem-Solving Behavior

Miss Carroll's class is discussing the concept of problem solving in relation to their study of early societies. To further increase their understanding of this concept, she divides the class into groups of four and gives each group a kiwi fruit (any food that is very uncommon—jicama, plantain, and so on, would do).

Miss Carroll: Pretend you are an early person and you have just found one of these fruits while food gathering. You do not know what it is because you have never seen one like it before. You are not sure whether or not you can safely eat it. In your group, discuss what decisions you can make concerning this "find" and the consequences of each decision.

The groups discuss this question, and then Miss Carroll has each group present its decisions to the class. They conclude there are three options, and Miss Carroll writes them on the chalkboard.

Decision	Consequence
1. do nothing; pass it by	1. might lose a good and needed food source
2. test it by eating it	2. could become sick or could even die if it is poisonous; *or* could be a tasty nutritious food
3. develop some way of testing it before eating it	3. would take time, but would be safe

Miss Carroll then continues: Suppose you made decision no. 3. In your group develop a plan of action you could use to test whether or not you could safely eat the new-found fruit.

The pupils developed plans that involved testing the food on non-human subjects. These plans were discussed and compared with modern-day practices in testing food products, new drugs, and medical practices. This discussion raised many issues related to the use of human subjects for experimental purposes.

Miss Carrol concluded the inquiry by asking the pupils to speculate on:

1. the risks of trial-and-error behavior.
2. how such risks can be reduced.
3. alternatives to trial-and-error problem-solving procedures.

Almost any topic can be shaped to meet the requirements of an inquiry episode. However, topics that are to some extent controversial and problematic are best because they are consistent with the nature of inquiry. That is, there is clearly something to inquire about and the outcome may still be in doubt. Subject matter and topics relating to current affairs, law and justice, the environment, energy, intergroup relations, economics, and geography are a few that lend themselves well to inquiry. As an example, the following case could be used as the basis for an inquiry into certain aspects of the legal and justice systems:

Farmer Indicted in Elk-Killing Case

Kenneth Reed was indicted in Sheridan District Court Tuesday on five counts of killing elk, a protected species in this state. Reed, a local farmer, did not deny killing the elk, but said they were damaging the grain crop he needed to feed his dairy herd.

Reed said that the animals began damaging his crop in midsummer and that he had repeatedly asked the Fish and Game Department to do something about it. Through his attorney, Reed said that he had contacted the department "at least a dozen times" by telephone. He also said that he sent three letters to the department warning that if something were not done, he would shoot the animals. Reed insists that he was justified in killing the elk to protect his property.

It is expected that the case will come to trial this fall. If found guilty, Reed could be sentenced to one year in jail and fined $1,000 on each of the five counts.[7]

This case raises some interesting legal questions relating to the right to protect one's property. Because television programs often show individuals using firearms to protect their property or themselves, children may have distorted ideas about the legal aspects of protecting one's self or one's property. Some of the issues raised by this case are these:

1. Why might the person be found not guilty in this case even though the specific action—that is, killing the elk—is clearly against the law in that state? Why should such a finding *in one case* not be interpreted by citizens as encouragement to break the law any time they think it is unfair or does not apply to them?
2. How does the fact that Reed had contacted the Fish and Game Department several times, without any apparent results, have any bearing on the outcome of the case?
3. Do individuals have the right to "take the law into their own hands" when appropriate officials refuse to or are unable to take corrective action?
4. Would the outcome of this case most likely be different if the trespassers were people instead of elk?

Inquiry episodes can be generated from situations such as the following:

1. Inquiry based on an *artifact*.
   The lesson using coins on pages 64–65 illustrates an inquiry of this type.
2. Inquiry based on a *problem situation* that needs to be resolved.

[7]This is a fictitious case, although in 1975, in a case much like this one, a Minnesota farmer was found not guilty by a district court jury.

The assistance of the local police officers was enlisted in this unit on safety. Identify knowledge, skill, and attitude objectives that might be developed in a unit such as this.

See the kiwi fruit lesson on page 73 for an example of this type of inquiry.
3. Inquiry based on a *controversial issue* or on a *current event*.
   The elk story, above, and the homeowners' concern for noise lesson pages 213–216 illustrates this type of inquiry.
4. Inquiry based on *concepts encountered in the study*.
   The lesson based on culture borrowing on page 169 illustrates this type of inquiry.
5. Inquiry based on a *photograph* or *illustration*.
   See the list of questions on page 240 for use in inquiry episodes based on a photograph.

EFFECTIVE QUESTIONING PROCEDURES

Questioning is a commonly used teaching technique that serves a variety of purposes. For example, many questions deal simply with procedural matters: Is everyone ready to move to the next step? How much longer do you think you will need in order to finish that project? What should you do after you get your materials? Such questions are important but do not deal directly with the substantive materials under study. The teacher uses them to clarify procedures, to

75

determine whether pupils understand what they are to do, to find out whether additional explanation is required, to get feedback on the effectiveness of a demonstration or explanation, and so on.

Questions may also be used to check the child's comprehension of concepts, generalizations, or subject matter. Often such questions require the pupil to reproduce or recall information that has been read or discussed in class. Research of classroom–teacher behavior through the years shows that teachers use a high percentage of questions of this type. These questions are sometimes referred to as "low level" because they involve simple recall and memory rather than higher-order mental operations such as application, analysis, synthesis, interpretation, sensing cause and effect, or evaluation. These questions can be easily identified because they usually begin with who, what, when, and where. These questions are important, especially in checking comprehension or to ascertain that pupils are familiar with facts essential to the topic. The problem is that there is a tendency to overuse them, with a corresponding lessened use of other questions that do require higher-order thought processes. In terms of inquiry the most important questions to ask are those that require elaborative reflective responses. These higher-level questions often begin, "Why . . . " "How . . . " "How do we know . . . " "Show that . . . " "If that is true, then . . . ".

These higher-level questions serve two general purposes relating to inquiry. One is that they trigger mental operations that are in accord with a problem-solving discovery learning format. For example, what mental operations are involved if the teacher asks the question: What is the most important reason for a small population in the area? Before responding, the child has to (1) analyze the situation, (2) consider all of the reasons that might apply, (3) evaluate each in terms of its importance, and then (4) select the one considered to be most important. Mental operations of this type characterize higher-level, or reflective, questions. Simply recalling a "correct" response is not adequate—the information has to be processed intellectually: analyzed, synthesized, applied, interpreted, evaluated, and so on. Thus, appropriate questions are essential in building reflective habits of thought.

These questions also serve the purpose of teaching the child improved habits of study. If the only kinds of questions encountered are based on recall of factual information, the child learns to study in terms of such objectives. The child may not learn how to apply information or even to process it in terms of broader intellectual outcomes. For example, without such experience, a child may attach the same degree of importance to a trivial incident as to a major concept or a profound generalization. Also, problem solving requires the ability *to ask* appropriate questions, and pupils cannot develop this skill unless they encounter such questions in their study.

For what purposes are questions used in social studies? Here are examples of some of the more common ones:

1. To establish procedures. Examples:
   a. Does everyone have a copy of the map?
   b. Are you looking at the lower part of the picture?
2. To analyze component elements. Examples:
   a. How many steps are involved in the process?
   b. What land features are most important to the occupations of the people who live there?
3. To check comprehension or general understanding. Examples:
   a. Where was the first settlement made?
   b. What were the reasons for moving to a new location?
4. To interpret data. Examples:
   a. Why is there such a difference in climate between Rome and Boston even though they are on about the same parallel of latitude?
   b. Which income groups are hardest hit by a sales tax on foods? Why?
5. To predict outcomes. Examples:
   a. What other products are likely to be affected by increased prices of steel?
   b. If everyone worked only four days a week, what businesses might be expected to grow?
6. To probe for additional information. Examples:
   a. Who can tell a little more about why the law was passed?
   b. Does this mean that one could not enter that country without a visa?
7. To clarify meanings of pupil responses. Examples:
   a. Who can give an example of how daylight saving time benefits people?
   b. I am still not sure I understand your explanation of "duty free." Is "duty free" the same as tax free?
8. To explain something. Examples:
   a. How might a winter frost in Florida affect the lives of people in northern cities such as Minneapolis, Milwaukee, Detroit, and Cleveland?
   b. If farmers make greater use of machinery and there is less need for farm hands, where do people in the rural areas find jobs?
9. To describe something. Examples:
   a. What was life like for an immigrant family from Eastern Europe living in Chicago at the turn of the century?
   b. Your book tells how the people felt when they arrived at their destination after traveling for several weeks in the wagon train. What were their feelings?
10. To verify statements or conclusions. Examples:
    a. Which paragraph tells exactly why environmental impact statements are required?
    b. That figure seems low to me. Would you mind locating the source of these figures and rechecking that second amount?

11. To guide independent study. Examples:
    a. What advantages does the author give for the use of checks instead of coins and currency?
    b. What reasons are given on pages 81–87 for our strong ties with Japan?
12. To diagnose learning difficulties. Examples:
    a. How would you find something about the cotton gin in this book?
    b. What is the main idea in the third paragraph on page 153?
13. To summarize ideas or to draw conclusions. Examples:
    a. Based on what we have learned thus far, what conclusions might we make about life in these early settlements?
    b. What is the relationship between the availability of a product and its price?

It is apparent that there is overlap among some of these categories. For instance, a question for independent study might also be used to check comprehension, to analyze component elements, or to draw conclusions. The object of these examples is to show that questions can be used for many different purposes, not that the categories are mutually exclusive.

In order to improve questioning techniques, the following suggestions are provided:

1. Consciously reduce the number of factual recall questions asked. These are usually questions that begin with "Who?" "What?" "Where?" and "When?" Replace these with questions that require elaborative, reflective responses, e.g., "Why?" "How?" "How do we know?"
2. Match the type of question with the purpose it is to serve. Questions that call for yes–no responses are not appropriate to stimulate a discussion. Reflective or discussion questions should not be used for homework or independent study.
3. State questions in ways that communicate precisely what is being asked. Sometimes pupils cannot respond to questions not because they do not know the material but because the question is ambiguous or otherwise poorly framed. The vocabulary level must be consistent with the age and maturity of the pupils. Although this may seem to be a trite reminder, it does constitute a problem for adults who have not been closely associated with children. Beginning teachers should write out in advance the main questions they plan to use.
4. Provide adequate time for the pupils to respond. Ask the question *before* calling on a specific respondent. This requires all pupils to form their own response intellectually.
5. Vary the way you acknowledge pupil responses. In addition to "uh-huh," "all right," and "O.K.," which are commonly overused by teachers, try asking another question such as a probing or clari-

fying question. Avoid *always* acknowledging pupil responses with evaluative comments such as "right," "yes," or "that's good," although these should be used from time to time to encourage pupil participation.

DISCUSSION QUESTIONS AND SUGGESTED ACTIVITIES

1. Select three unit topics from the following list and provide examples of five concepts that might be included in such units. Then, using two or more of the concepts you have identified, write a generalization that expresses a valid relationship between them that is relevant to each of the topics you have selected.
    People Change the Earth (K-8)
    School Living (K)
    Families and Their Needs (1)
    The Shopping Center (2)
    Life in the City (3)
    Our Home State (4)
    The Westward Movement (5)
    Crossroads of the World: The Middle East (6–7)
    Colonial America (8)
2. Interview individually four or five children from a grade in which you have a special interest to determine their understanding of selected social studies concepts. Use a straightforward procedure and everyday concepts. For example, you might say, "What does the term *family* mean to you? What is a family anyway?" (or use *community*, *city*, *park*, and so on.) When the child responds, probe to get an elaboration of what the concept means to the youngster. You might vary the procedure by including abstract concepts such as *justice* and *freedom*, or quantitative concepts such as *several years later* or *long ago*. These experiences will provide you with firsthand knowledge of what it means to convert subject matter into thought forms appropriate for elementary schoolchildren. Report your findings to the class.
3. Select a grade of your choice. Suggest situations for that grade that would make use of the three strategies for concept development discussed in this chapter.
4. What are the essential differences between how one teaches concepts and how one teaches skills?
5. Select a nontext children's book that might be especially useful in illustrating a general value. Explain why you selected the one you did.
6. Why do you think parents often react negatively when the school deals with the development of personal values in children? Suggest guidelines that a teacher can use in order to handle personal values in ways that are educationally and ethically acceptable.

79

7. Develop an appropriate values clarification exercise for a grade of your choice.
8. Develop a short inquiry exercise as suggested on pages 74–75.
9. In assigning questions for independent study or homework, why is it important that the pupil be able to get the answers from the available books and resources?
10. Do you think the kinds of questions a teacher asks reflect the major objectives the teacher has in mind for the lesson? *Should* they? Explain your response.

SELECTED REFERENCES

Armstrong, David G., John J. Denton, and Tom V. Savage, Jr. *Instructional Skills Handbook*. Englewood Cliffs, N.J.: Educational Technology Publications, Inc., 1978.

Chapin, June R. and Richard E. Gross. *Teaching Social Studies Skills*. Boston: Little, Brown and Company, 1973.

Cogan, John J. and Wayne Paulson. "Values Clarification and the Primary Child," *The Social Studies*, 69 (January–February 1978), pp. 20–24.

Davis, Hilarie Bryce. "Kids Have the Answers: Do You Have the Questions?" *Instructor*, 90 (November 1980), pp. 64–68.

Fraenkel, Jack. *How To Teach About Values: An Analytic Approach*. Englewood Cliffs, N.J.: Prentice-Hall, Inc., 1977.

Fraenkel, Jack R. "Now is *Not* the Time to Set Aside Values Education," *Social Education*, 45 (February 1981), pp. 101–107.

Hunkins, Francis P. *Involving Students in Questioning*. Boston: Allyn & Bacon, Inc., 1976.

Hunkins, Francis P. *Questioning Strategies and Techniques*. Boston: Allyn & Bacon, Inc., 1972.

Joyce, William W., ed. "Moral Education in the Elementary School: A Neglected Responsibility?" *Social Education*, 39 (January 1975), pp. 23–39. (Elementary education supplement of five articles.)

Kaltsounis, Theodore. "Developing Concepts and Generalizations Through Inquiry," Chapter 4 of *Teaching Social Studies in the Elementary School*. Englewood Cliffs, N.J.: Prentice-Hall, Inc., 1979.

Kohlberg, Lawrence. "The Cognitive-Developmental Approach to Moral Education," *Phi Delta Kappan*, 56 (June 1975), pp. 670–677.

Kurfman, Dana G., ed. *Developing Decision Making Skills*, 47th Yearbook. National Council for the Social Studies. Washington, D.C.: The Council, 1977.

Leming, James S. "Research in Social Studies Education: Implications for Teaching Values," *Social Education*, 43 (November–December 1979), pp. 597–601.

Martorella, Peter H. "Research in Social Studies Education: Implications for Teaching in the Cognitive Domain," *Social Education*, 43 (November–December 1979), pp. 599–601.

Massialas, Byron G. and Joseph B. Hurst. *Social Studies in a New Era: The Elementary School as a Laboratory*. New York: Longman, Inc., 1978.

McKenzie, Gary R. "The Importance of Teaching Facts in Elementary Social Studies," *Social Education*, 44 (October 1980), pp. 494–498.

Raths, Louis E., Merrill Harmin, and Sidney B. Simon. *Values and Teaching*, 2nd ed. Columbus, Ohio: Charles E. Merrill Publishing Company, 1978.

Ross, John A. "Selecting a Values Education Framework," *The History and Social Science Teacher*, 15 (Fall 1979), pp. 17–25.

Samples, Bob, Cheryl Charles, and Dick Barnhart. *The Wholeschool Book*. Reading, Massachusetts: Addison-Wesley Publishing Co., 1977.

Shaver, James P. *Facing Value Decisions: Rationale Building for Teachers*. Belmont, California: Wadsworth Publishing Company, Inc., 1976.

Simon, Sidney B., Leland Howe, and Howard Kirschenbaum. *Values Clarification: A Handbook of Practical Strategies for Teachers and Students*. New York: Hart Publishing Company, Inc., 1972.

Williams, David M. and Ian Wright. "Values and Moral Education: Analyzing Curriculum Materials," *The Social Studies*, 67 (July–August 1977), pp. 166–172.

4

Selecting and Using Resources for Teaching and Learning

A generous supply of learning resources and instructional media will do much to ensure a good social studies program. If nothing more is provided than a basic textbook, a set of encyclopedias, a handful of additional references, and some audiovisual materials to be shared with other rooms, it becomes easy for the teacher to fall victim to textbook teaching, thereby ignoring individual differences in children and making social studies teaching dull, uninteresting, and largely ineffectual. But a large amount of materials will not in and of itself assure good teaching. This can be achieved only when instructional resources are used skillfully by an inspired and creative teacher.

The availability of instructional media is not the problem that it once was. The teacher of today who accepts a position in a school district of average or even modest means will find a supply of instructional resources that would have been found only in the best school districts just a few years ago. This does not mean that all of the available instructional material is of good quality and is up-to-date. Neither does it mean that the teacher is relieved of the responsibility of searching for and evaluating learning resources that are best suited for classroom use. Although the emphasis is on the use of multimedia in modern social studies programs, the busy teacher may not have the time and energy to locate, evaluate, and arrange for the use of a wide array of instructional media. Consequently, the teacher comes to rely on a few with which he or she is familiar and that are conveniently available in the classroom. This explains, in part, the frequent overuse of such resources as the textbook and the encyclopedia.

Learning materials and resources for the social studies can be grouped into two categories: (1) reading materials and resources (textbooks, encyclopedias, references, magazines, pamphlets, newspaper clippings, travel folders, classroom periodicals, and similar printed material) and (2) nonreading materials and resources (pictures, films, filmstrips, recordings, field trips, maps, globes, and community resources of all types). Together they provide the data sources for a good social studies program.

In the selection of any instructional resource, the objectives to be achieved should be uppermost in the mind of the teacher. The par-

83

ticular resource or material selected should be the one that will move the pupils most effectively in the direction of those objectives. In short, instructional aids, materials, and resources are used to achieve specific purposes. The teacher is encouraged to use a wide range of instructional media for any or all of the following reasons:

1. Not all pupils learn in the same way; different media are able to appeal to the learning styles of different learners.
2. The reading ranges among children who are randomly selected to form elementary classrooms are great, averaging three to five years in the lower grades and five to ten years in the middle and upper grades.
3. Each of the media has peculiar strengths and limitations in the way it conveys messages.
4. The impact of a message is likely to be stronger if more than one sensory system is involved in receiving it.
5. Material to be learned varies greatly in its abstractness and complexity.
6. The use of a variety of media has motivating and interest-generating qualities.

A woman from the community discusses her album of travel photos as part of a "Senior Share" project developed by pupils. Senior citizens are often excellent resource persons because of the wisdom they have accumulated through life experiences. Besides, they often have the time to give their service and many love the contact with schoolchildren. Identify two or three individuals in your community who could be invited to participate in a "Senior Share" program.

7. Inquiry-oriented teaching modes require extensive information searches and sources.
8. Different sources may provide different insights on the same subject; there may be discrepancies or inaccuracies that go undetected if a single source is used.

Instructional materials need to be carefully evaluated before, during, and after they have been used. It is not a good policy to use any and all materials simply because they are available. The quality of the material or resource should be a primary consideration in deciding on its use. Maps that are out-of-date, films that are of poor quality, pictures that are inaccurate, or field trips that are poorly guided, for example, might better not be used at all.

The maximum value of any instructional resource requires skillful use on the part of the teacher. No instructional material is entirely self-teaching—all require a teacher to set the stage for learning to take place. A first-rate textbook in the hands of an unimaginative teacher can be devastating to the social studies program. The same book used by another teacher can become one of the most valuable resources available to the class. Materials of instruction can be no better than the teachers who use them.

READING MATERIALS

Textbooks

If properly used, the textbook can be a valuable aid to learning. On the other hand, the misuse of textbooks is fairly common. Attention is called particularly to the practice of expecting children who are known to vary markedly in their reading and intellectual abilities to use identical textbooks for identical purposes. In spite of all of the criticism leveled against the use of textbooks, a weekend visitor to middle-grade classrooms is still likely to find in the desks of almost all the children the same basic textbook in social studies. In some areas, schools must provide each pupil with the same basic textbook because of local school policy or state law. Basic textbooks in the social studies are likely to be widely used for years to come; thus, the teacher should know how to make the best use of them.

The publishers of children's textbooks have not been unmindful of current efforts to revise and reform curriculum and teaching methods. Textbook development has tended to be consistent with these changes. Modern textbooks are attractive, inviting, a pleasure to look at and read. There is better use of maps and visual materials; some social studies textbooks for elementary grades boast of at least one illustration on every page, many of the illustrations in color. Multiple

85

authorship is common, with at least one author being a specialist in elementary education. This has served to retain high scholarly accuracy as well as to refine and improve the format and reading level of the books. Significant changes are apparent in the treatment of racial and ethnic groups and of women. In general, there has been substantial headway in presenting social reality more accurately in modern social studies textbooks.

Social studies textbooks almost always present problems of reading difficulty even though they are written at a level that is suitable for the average reader. The reason for this is that these books are designed to deal with substantive content, and this means that the terms and concepts relating to that content must be used in explaining the ideas presented. For example, a book may be treating a topic such as *trade and commerce*. This subject cannot be meaningfully presented without including at least some of the following concepts and terms: *cargo, tariff, import, duty, international markets, ports, interdependence, hold, tonnage, trade, freight, shipping, stevedore, merchant, commercial, barge.* If these terms are eliminated from the selection in order to simplify the reading task, it is no longer an essay on trade and commerce. It is the complexity and frequency of concepts that often make reading social studies textbooks difficult, and there is no way this problem can be overcome entirely. An easy-to-read textbook is probably not a good social studies text because its purpose should be to provide information rather than being a simple storybook.

Textbook authors assume that the teacher will guide and direct the pupils in their use of the book. Textbooks are highly condensed and factual presentations and are written with the thought that teachers will supplement and enrich the textbook presentation through the use of other materials. Moreover, texts are not meant to be entirely self-instructing, and if children use them without guidance from the teacher, much of their value may be lost. This is especially true of accompanying visual material in the form of pictures, maps, charts, cartoons, graphs, and study helps.

Textbooks are written to be used as source books and are not intended to become the social studies curriculum. They can be used in a variety of ways, and individual children may make different uses of the same book. For one child it may constitute a reading resource, for another child the illustrations may be more valuable, for a third child the map materials may be needed, and for a fourth child it may be a source of ideas for additional study. Similarly, different teachers may choose to make different uses of the same book, depending on their skill, experience, or method of teaching. Teachers are encouraged to make such differential use of textbooks rather than uniformly "cover" the content and require all children to "master" the facts presented.

If the teacher keeps in mind that no single book can meet adequately the reading needs of all children in the class, the textbook can be a useful tool in teaching social studies. Four of the most common uses of the textbook are for (1) exploratory reading; (2) securing facts related to the study; (3) map, chart, graph, or picture study; and (4) summarization of learning.

Exploratory Reading

The textbook can be used as a point of departure in the early stages of a new unit to help the children find out what the unit is about and to establish a common background of basic information for all pupils. In this way, the textbook can be used to introduce the pupils to some of the key ideas of the unit, acquaint them with vocabulary, and help them learn enough about the topic to be able to proceed intelligently with further teacher-pupil planning of other activities. When texts are used for this purpose, the teacher should

1. Build readiness for the material to be read by a proper introduction of the content through the use of pictures, maps, reference to current affairs, a community problem, a historical event, or other similar and appropriate introductory activities.
2. Identify for the children some of the purposes for which they are to read the material. These purposes could be written on the chalkboard. When pupils are instructed to "read to find out . . . ," the reading is likely to be more productive than if they are simply told to "read pages 55 to 60 in the book." In exploratory reading the purposes should be general rather than detailed or highly specific.
3. Anticipate vocabulary difficulties and develop the meaning of key new words prior to the reading. Consideration of a new topic commonly introduces new words.
4. Call attention to important pictures, illustrations, maps, or charts included in the material. This is especially necessary when some element of an illustration is critical to the understanding of the text but might be overlooked by the child.
5. Have some type of follow-up performed by the children individually. This should include an activity dealing with the purposes established for the reading.
6. Take the children aside who are low in reading ability and assist them with the material. For this directed study the teacher should choose *selected short passages* along with the visual material presented in the text. An "around the circle" oral reading approach should *not* be used. Instead, the teacher can call the children's attention to a passage, a picture caption, a picture, a chart, or a map or diagram; discuss it with them; and ask them to see if they can find out various facts or sense implications from the material presented in the text. If the teacher cannot give this close supervision and help to the children of low reading ability, other more simple material should be found for them, or the teacher should re-write certain passages at a level they are capable of handling.

87

7. Provide additional, more difficult books to which the more skill-ful readers can turn for extended exploratory reading when they have completed the text. These could be other textbooks, ency-clopedias, magazines, or supplementary books.

Securing Facts Related to the Study

When the unit is underway, it is often necessary to have pupils obtain factual information. The textbook can serve as an excellent source of such information. When the text is used for this purpose, the teacher should

1. Help the children identify precisely what factual information is wanted. This can take the form of finding answers to specific questions such as: "What pieces of furniture might one find in a pioneer home?" "What steps are involved in getting a letter from the sender to the receiver?" "How does geography affect the way people live in Mexico?" "What hardships were encountered by a group of early settlers in Wisconsin?" "What crops are grown in the southeastern section of the United States?" When used on a class basis, the factual material to be obtained can be decided on by the teacher, by the pupils, or by both.
2. Teach children how to use the index, table of contents, glossary, and list of illustrations to help them develop independence in locating information in the text.
3. Have children consult other sources to confirm factual informa-tion presented in the text. This procedure helps overcome the feeling that the textbook is a sufficient source book on any topic.

Map, Chart, Graph, or Picture Study

Modern textbooks provide an abundance of visual materials that can be used profitably by the teacher in short directed-study situa-tions. In map study, for example, the text provides all children with a well-produced map. In the study of a chart, the children can follow along in their books as the teacher explains its makeup and meaning. If children are asked to point to the elements of the chart being dis-cussed, the teacher can tell at a glance which children are following accurately and which ones are not. Likewise, pictures can be used more effectively when all children have one in their hands than would be possible by passing a single print around the classroom or posting one on the bulletin board. Textbooks are, therefore, *more* than reading books and should be used in ways other than as readers.

Summarization of Learning

Textbooks can be used profitably near the conclusion of a sub-topic of a study to summarize and pull together learning that has taken place through other activities. The text is presented to the children at a time when they have already built a background of information related to the topic. They are familiar with the vocabulary and concepts and are psychologically ready to take full advantage of the factual presentation of the text. The textbook, therefore, not only may serve as a point of departure for a study but also may be a frequent port of call and a point of return. When the text is used for the purpose of summarization, the teacher should

1. Establish readiness by discussing material previously studied and establish definite purposes for reading the text. This, again, should take the form of "reading to find out. . . . " Purposes for this use of the text should be detailed and specific as contrasted with the general purposes discussed in connection with exploratory reading.
2. Clarify any vocabulary difficulties the children may encounter.
3. Follow the same procedure with slower and more rapid readers as was explained in the section dealing with exploratory reading.
4. Have definite follow-up activities planned that will allow the children to apply information obtained in the reading.
5. Allow for a thorough discussion of the major ideas presented. These should be summarized in writing and perhaps placed on the chalkboard or in the individual child's notebook or folder.

What does a teacher look for in selecting a textbook? From the teacher's point of view, the most important criterion would seem to be *usability*. The book has to fit the teacher's style of teaching if it is to be used well. This means that the text has to be constructed in such a way that it lends itself to flexible use. A book that can be used in only one teaching mode, or stresses only one approach to social studies, is generally less useful than one that can be adapted to a variety of teaching modes. Readability always has to be an important consideration, and it is significant that one of the most frequent criticisms of social studies texts is that they are hard for the pupils to read. Good social studies texts include study aids; such study aids should facilitate learning the content and skills, and at the same time, encourage good study habits.

Many good social studies textbooks are available today. Some are better suited for certain purposes than others. Some more accurately reflect current curriculum developments than do others. Those who are charged with the responsibility of making the selection should develop their own criteria for evaluating textbooks in social studies, but they will probably want to look critically at the following points:

1. *Authorship*—to ensure scholarly accuracy as well as suitability for use with elementary schoolchildren in terms of interest and appeal, reading gradation, and curricular consideration. How is the author identified with elementary social studies?
2. *Treatment of Content*—to ensure adequate treatment of important concepts in sufficient depth as opposed to highly descriptive factual accounts or storybook approaches to significant content.

89

Does the book focus on relevant, key concepts? Does the book deal with ethnic minorities and women in a realistic way? Is there evidence of stereotyping and/or tokenism in illustrations?

3. *Format and General Appearance*—to ensure an interesting and appealing book, proper size, good-quality binding, suitable type size. Are illustrations functional or simply decorative?

4. *Organization*—to ensure its harmony with the existing curricular pattern and that it meets the needs of the instructional program within which it will be used. Is the book organized in a way to encourage pupil inquiry?

5. *Visual Materials*—to ensure colorful, accurate illustrations of sufficient number and size. Are these related to the text or included only to enhance the attractiveness of the book?

6. *Instructional Aids*—to ensure their being an integral part of the text itself and of such nature as to be genuinely helpful to the teacher. Do study aids help explain and extend the meaning of important ideas?

Encyclopedias

In the middle and upper grades, all classrooms should have at least one and preferably two sets of encyclopedias suitable for children. Even in the primary grades encyclopedias can be used to good advantage from time to time, and many schools are placing them in first, second, and third grades. Much of what was said in connection with the improvement of textbooks could also be said concerning encyclopedias.

The value of an encyclopedia lies in the easy, quick manner in which factual material can be obtained on a multitude of topics. It is, like the textbook, an important source of information and one that will be referred to many times in the course of social studies units. When encyclopedias are available in the primary grades, the teacher will find the pictures and illustrations helpful in social studies instruction. Selected short portions of content may be read to the children from time to time, and some children at these early levels will be able to read portions of the encyclopedia independently. Perhaps the chief value of an encyclopedia in the primary grades is the contribution it can make to building positive attitudes toward the use of reference materials. Children learn fairly early that in the encyclopedia one can find answers to most questions on many topics. In this sense, early contact with this reference serves as a readiness for its more organized use at the upper levels. In the middle and upper grades the encyclopedia is a constant source of factual information. Remember, however, that articles in an encyclopedia are highly condensed presentations. This suggests that there is need for additional references—ones that may give interesting sidelights on the problems not ordinarily included in encyclopedia coverage.

The teacher should guard against the misuse of the encyclopedia.

Pupils need to learn that the encyclopedia is only one source, and in some cases may not even be the best source, of information. A children's biography, for instance, of Babe Didrikson Zaharias or Amelia Earhart might be more informative and more engaging for a 12-year-old than a factual, encyclopedia account of these women's lives. Pupils often become too dependent on the encyclopedia at the expense of not learning the value of other resources available to them. Thus pupils may copy written reports verbatim from the encyclopedia or make oral reports based on encyclopedia accounts that are memorized but not understood. The difficulty, of course, lies not with the encyclopedia but with the way it is being used. The teacher needs to make a conscious effort to discourage such flagrant misuse of this instructional resource.

Supplementary References

In addition to textbooks and encyclopedias, there is a need for an abundance of supplementary books. Some of these may be other textbooks, although the need is not so much for additional textbooks as it is for nontext material on a variety of topics. We are referring here specifically to "trade books"—books about Indians, airplanes, urban life, space travel, national parks, biographies of famous Americans, life in other lands, communities at work, and similar topics. Many contemporary children's books are not only informative but represent good children's literature. They have exceptional artwork and maintain high standards of literary quality.

Literary works useful for social studies instruction may be classified as (1) *informative accounts*—works that simply convey specific information in literary form on topics studied, such as books about trucks, trains, countries, printing, communication, homes around the world; (2) *informative fiction*—reconstruction of historical events that are built around a fictionalized plot or story; (3) *biographies*; (4) *nonfiction history*; (5) *poems*; (6) *locally produced materials*—consisting possibly of works falling in any of the preceding five categories.

Literature and literary materials should play an important part in social studies instruction because they convey so well the affective dimension of human experience. The realism that is achieved through vivid portrayals in works of literature stirs the imagination of the young reader and helps develop a feeling for and identification with the topic being studied. The relationship between literature and some of the subjects included in the social studies—particularly history—has been noted by numerous writers. Some great works of literature are also considered important historical documents, and the reverse is also true.

One reason that literary materials are so important is that they provide rich detail that is impossible to get in even a well-designed text or an encyclopedia. A textbook, for example, may make little mention of women who spearheaded the movement to gain equal rights for their sex, such as Susan B. Anthony, Elizabeth Stanton Cady, Lucretia C. Mott, and Julia Ward Howe. However, the child can learn much about these courageous and determined Americans by reading children's biographies of their lives. Here the pupil can get a vivid word picture of the times in which these women lived. Such supporting details add richness and meaning to an understanding of the historical period studied.

For factual information there is also need for atlases, the *World Almanac*, and the state legislative manuals. Many local communities and cities also publish brochures, handbooks, and pamphlets. Local and state historical societies, museums, and art galleries may make available publications that are valuable for classroom work. These sources provide a storehouse of information, but children of elementary school age need a considerable amount of guidance and help from the teacher in their use.

Free and Inexpensive Materials

Free and inexpensive materials have become valuable resources in teaching social studies. There is a wealth of material in the form of posters, charts, bulletins, folders, booklets, films, filmstrips, and travel folders available free on request. In addition to the free material, an abundance of similar resources can be obtained at small cost. Much of the material available today is well prepared and useful for classroom work, but it does need to be examined carefully to ascertain whether or not is is suitable. Just because the material is available and free is no assurance that it is of value. Items such as these should be considered in evaluating free and inexpensive material:

1. Is the material produced by a socially responsible organization?
2. Does the presence of advertising make the material unsuitable for use? A piece may or may not be rejected on this point, but it should, in any case, be considered.
3. Is the material honestly and objectively presented? Is it consistent with democratic values and ideals? Is it free of racial and sex bias?
4. Is the material suitable in terms of readability, maturity of the pupils, technical qualities, and the topic under study?
5. Is the material up-to-date?
6. Are the sources of information given?
7. Does use of the materials carry any obligations with it?
8. In whose interest was the material prepared? Who benefits from its use in the classroom?

The teacher should not overlook the diplomatic offices of foreign countries based in the United States as a source of free material. In most cases, the best place to direct inquiries concerning the availability of such material is the embassy of the country in Washington, D.C. Some countries (for example, Japan) have excellent instructional packets available for school use.

Because the demand for free and inexpensive material is great and the quantity usually limited, the teacher is advised to use an up-to-date list of sources. Professional journals carry lists in almost every issue. In addition, there are compilations of sources of free and inexpensive material that can be purchased.

NONREADING MATERIALS AND RESOURCES

The term *nonreading material* is a broad classification to indicate the materials that depend more heavily on sight and sound to convey meaning than on the interpretation of printed words. In the strictest sense, most learning materials depend on reading to some extent—charts and maps have titles and legends, filmstrips have captions, even films contain some print. For the most part, however, these learning devices use symbols other than print as the primary method of conveying meaning.

An extensive treatment of certain nonreading instructional materials is unnecessary because other sources discuss this topic in depth. The teacher should become familiar with the general nature of various nonreading materials and gain an understanding of the general principles under which they should be used. What follows is a brief summary of the ways some of these materials can be used in social studies.

Pictures, Photographs, Illustrations

The most widely used of all visual aids are pictures, photographs, and illustrations. These are used to obtain realism, to clarify ideas, to recall the real object, and, in short, to give meaning to learning. It is well known that words cannot convey meanings as accurately, vividly, or quickly as pictures. Pictures can also be helpful in promoting inquiry skills. For this reason some textbooks now use questions for captions instead of a description of the content of the picture or illustration.

What makes a picture, photograph, or illustration suitable for instructional purposes in social studies? Certainly, the most important consideration is accuracy of the portrayal. The fundamental purpose of any learning aid is to convey accurate meaning, and if this is lacking the picture, photograph, or illustration must be rejected unless, of course, it is being used to illustrate inaccuracy. Other factors that should be considered are that it be of sufficient size for the purpose it is to serve, appropriate to the age children with which it is to be used, of good artistic quality, impressive, of easy interpretation, and that it have a definite center of interest that is not subordinated by a great many details.

93

Films

Many 16 mm sound motion pictures are available dealing with social studies topics. Ordinarily, these films are secured on a rental basis and must be booked several weeks in advance of their anticipated use. Larger school districts usually have their own film libraries from which the teacher can obtain films.

Films have much to contribute to social studies teaching. In a film, the children can traverse great distances and move through centuries of time, having before them a picture of places, persons, and processes that would be impossible to obtain in other ways. In many respects, the film has advantages over field trips because it singles out the most important aspects of a situation and eliminates the nonessentials. It is more selective in what it allows the viewer to see than is the human eye. It is a demanding medium and holds the attention of the viewer to a greater extent than do most other learning aids. A film can telescope great lengths of time into minutes, making it possible to observe a timeless process in a single class period. Its greatest asset, of course, is that it depicts motion; and the best use can be made of films showing situations involving motion. If motion is not a factor, a good photograph, a slide, or a filmstrip may be equally effective.

In social studies, films may be appropriate at a variety of stages. They are often used at the beginning of a unit to build a common background of experience or to arouse interest. They may be used during the work stages to add meaning to material that is being read, or they may be used at the final stages of the study in order to summarize and reinforce ideas that have been developed. They should serve as a stimulus for discussion and further study.

Filmstrips

When motion is not essential in pictures, the filmstrip may be used as effectively as a motion picture. Filmstrips offer advantages over motion pictures in terms of cost, availability, and use. Because of the relatively low cost, schools ordinarily maintain their own filmstrip library, and they are immediately available, therefore, when needed. A good instructional feature of the filmstrip is that it is possible to discuss its content as it is being shown. If it becomes necessary to refer to a picture previously shown, the filmstrip can be turned back to the picture in question. Filmstrips are easy to catalog and store and are simple to show. In this respect, they have many advantages over slides.

Filmstrips may be used to achieve a number of purposes in the social studies unit. A filmstrip on the New England States, for example, gives a clear picture of the physical features of this area and thereby assists in understanding map symbols and serves as a good readiness for map reading. It may serve to introduce children to other countries of the world, showing how people in other lands live, work, and play. Filmstrips are useful in presenting material that follows a definite sequence—how a letter gets from sender to receiver; the steps in the production of milk; the history, growth, and development of an area; the course of soil erosion; or the steps to be followed in the event of some emergency such as a fire, drowning, an accident, or a hurricane. The nature of the content of the filmstrip will determine how and when it can be used most effectively.

Slides

Photographic slides have been used in schools for many years. They may be purchased from commerical agencies or produced by the teachers and children. They have the same instructional use as pictures but have the advantage of being able to be viewed by the entire class at one time. Many teachers use their own 35 mm cameras with color film and have excellent personal collections of slides. Because the filmstrip has advantages over slides in terms of maintaining a permanent sequence, cost, and storage, there are many more filmstrips available commercially than slides.

The globe, the recording, and the print material symbolize the type of multimedia that can be used to enrich social studies learning. Many of the media are self-operated; thus, as is illustrated in this photograph, they are well suited for individualizing learning. If you visited an elementary school classroom, what would you look for as evidence of the frequent use of multimedia?

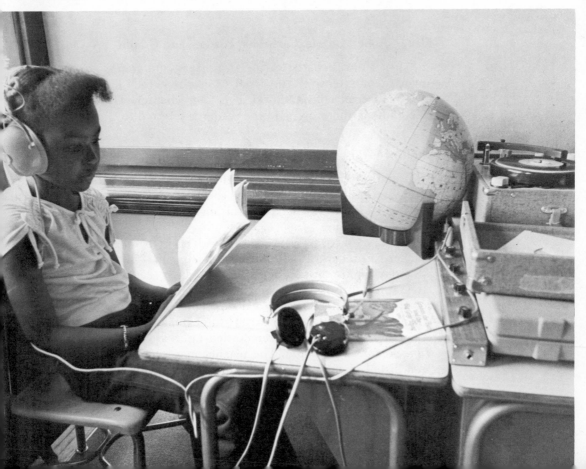

Overhead Projector

One of the most valuable and popular instructional aids is the overhead projector. This device is versatile and easy to use. With it the teacher may use a 10″ × 10″ prepared transparent acetate slide or may use a blank sheet of acetate and write directly on it with a grease pencil, a felt pen, or a slide marker. This device can be used for some of the same purposes as a conventional chalkboard yet has some advantages over the chalkboard. For example, the slides or drawings can be used repeatedly; the illuminated platform is easier to write on than is a chalkboard; there is no chalk dust with the overhead projector. It does not require a totally darkened room. Semidarkness is almost always satisfactory for overhead projector use, and in some cases no darkening at all is needed. It is not possible to project photographs or other nontransparent illustrations on the overhead projector. Hence, these slides are referred to as "transparencies." Because they are transparent, one transparency can be placed on top of another in the cumulative development of an idea. The use of these overlays is helpful in developing ideas that follow a sequential pattern.

Teachers often make their own transparencies for use in the social studies. Commercially prepared transparencies are also available through instructional resources outlets. These are usually advertised in journals such as *Instructor, Learning, Teacher,* and *Social Education.*

Maps, Globes, Charts, Cartoons, Posters, and Graphs

Maps, globes, charts, cartoons, posters, and graphs are items that are used so extensively in social studies that they have been singled out for special consideration in a later chapter. They are not considered here, therefore, and the reader is referred to Chapter 10.

Auditory Aids

In addition to visual material, the teacher will find the use of auditory media helpful in teaching social studies. This material most often is in the form of tape recordings, disc recordings, and to a limited extent, radio.

The tape recorder is versatile and easy to operate. With it the teacher can record a radio broadcast any time—in the evening or on a Sunday afternoon—and play it for the class several weeks or months later at the precise time it will be of most use to the class in their social studies unit. Prerecorded tapes on a variety of topics, many of which are relevant to the social studies, may be obtained. The programs available through prerecorded tapes are listed in the *National Tape Recording Catalog.* The teacher may obtain a copy of any program listed in the catalog by sending a blank tape to National Center for Audio Tapes, Stadium Building 348, University of Colorado,

Boulder, Colorado 80302. The catalog costs $4.50, but an annual supplement is available free of charge. Tape charges are made according to running time.

The tape recorder has many other uses. It can be used, for example, to record travel talks by teachers or other adults in the community who cannot visit the class in person. The lecture of a classroom visitor also may be recorded for replaying and study at a later time. Some teachers have had children write and record commentaries to accompany filmstrips to be shared with the remainder of the class, other classes, or classroom guests. Pupils may record their class discussions in order to note progress, to evaluate their work, or to use for future reference. They can also record dramatic presentations, news broadcasts, or make "on-the-spot" recordings. They can prepare a bulletin board display and record an explanation of the material posted that can be listened to as the display is viewed.

Pupils may wish to exchange 15-minute tapes with youngsters in other countries. This can be arranged through Ruth Y. Terry, Director and Publisher, International Tape Exchange, 834 Ruddiman Avenue, North Muskegan, Michigan 49445.

Conventional disc recordings dealing with various aspects of American history are available through commercial sources and can do much to make history come alive for children. These recordings are coordinated on occasion with filmstrip presentations in a sight and sound format. Disc recordings are also helpful for music and dance activities related to social studies.

Television

Research on the television-viewing habits of children during out-of-school hours indicates that television-viewing is a well-established pastime of nearly all American schoolchildren. Studies consistently have shown that pupils view television from two to four or more hours each day during the week with some increase in this amount on weekends. The pupil in school, therefore, is well acquainted with this medium and is accustomed to viewing professionally produced programs even if the substance of such programs is not always of high quality.

There is an inclination to use instructional television in the same way a "live" teacher is used. This practice works to the disadvantage of television because the unique characteristics of the television medium are lost in the process. If television has instructional value, it is because it can do something more effectively than other media or because it can do some things that other media cannot do at all. Educational television can be of tremendous assistance to the elementary schoolteacher in enriching and vitalizing social studies providing it is used to achieve purposes the teacher cannot accomplish at least as well through the use of books and other conventional learning resources.

One valuable contribution television can make to social studies instruction is to motivate pupils. The television program has the total resources of the world outside the classroom to use in constructing programs that are highly interesting and motivating. Television can span both time and space in bringing relevant events into the classroom in capsule form. Television can visually transport pupils to the areas they are studying. It can also show them details they would probably miss if they were actually there. The most eminent authorities and world leaders can be their teachers through television. The dramatic capabilities of good television production can be used in making a subject alive and exciting for pupils.

A second contribution television can make is to provide information not available through other sources. Some of these possibilities were suggested in the previous paragraph. No other medium can make it possible for a child to witness the inauguration of the president taking place a thousand miles away. A young man from Africa cannot visit all fourth-grade classrooms in a large city and tell the pupils interesting things about his homeland. But he can share his ideas with these pupils via television. A major strength of television is that it can assemble and distribute information widely and quickly.

A third contribution of television to social studies is to clarify, elaborate, interpret, and enrich information that may be available through other sources. For example, a museum curator may be able to explain the religious significance of certain artifacts of early Indians who lived in the region. An authority or a traveler might be able to provide interesting details to help pupils understand why people of another culture do some particular thing the way they do. Television is an excellent medium for vitalizing knowledge because it can provide intimate, personal details that are not readily available to the children.

Unless the classroom has a video recording and playback capability—and some do have—television use demands even more careful planning than other media. For example, programs are presented at specific times on specific days and are presented in a specified sequence. This means that the classroom instructional program must be planned in accordance with the scheduled television programs if they are to be used profitably. Proper planning for television use calls for preparation by the teacher and pupils prior to the program and a satisfactory follow-up after the viewing. In most cases the value of the viewing depends almost entirely on what the class has done to prepare itself for the program and what the pupils will do after they have watched it. Usually, educational television stations provide the teacher with a manual or a teaching guide that will be of assistance in planning for the viewing and in providing relevant follow-up activities.

Room Environment

A frequently overlooked learning resource is the classroom environment itself. A well-planned and stimulating classroom arrangement can do much to arouse and sustain interest as well as to provide the child with many avenues for learning. This is especially true in the primary grades. The primary grade classroom needs a "home" corner where children can play the roles of various members of the family, set the table, do the dishes, run the vacuum cleaner, dress and undress "baby," and so on. They need large blocks and manipulative material with which they can build the post office or the airlines terminal. They need building tools with which they can construct boats, airplanes, farm buildings, trucks, cars, and trains. They need a generous supply of art mediums—paints, easels, chalk, crayons, finger paint, clay, colored paper, paste—to allow them to express their ideas and feelings through creative expression. Similarly, in a middle- or

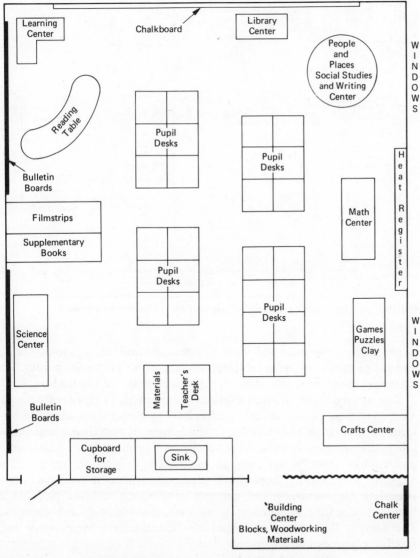

FIGURE 2. One possible classroom arrangement for the primary grades.

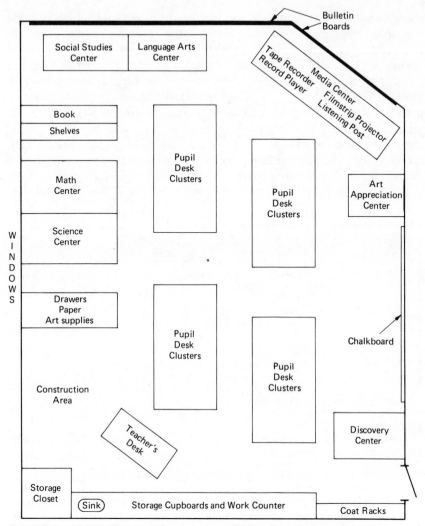

FIGURE 3.   One possible classroom arrangement for the intermediate grades.

upper-grade classroom one would expect to find many books, maps, globes, pictures, models, exhibits, children's work, tools, paints, art materials, costumes, and attractive and informative bulletin boards.

The arrangement of the room environment also helps create an atmosphere that can serve either to enhance or retard learning. On entering a classroom one should get the feeling of orderliness and flexibility. Elementary classrooms generally, and primary-grade classrooms particularly, must be arranged so as to allow children to feel psychologically at home in them. Such classrooms provide materials that stimulate the curiosity and interest of growing children and place them in a setting suggestive of warmth, friendliness, and security. The sample floor plans on pages 99–100 illustrate imaginative and flexible classroom arrangements.

Bulletin Boards

Modern and well-designed elementary school classrooms provide generously for stationary wall-type bulletin boards. In addition, many schools provide various types of portable bulletin boards. In the primary grades, children can suggest some of the material to be placed on the bulletin boards, but the actual display will have to be handled almost entirely by the teacher. As children move into the middle and upper grades, they are able to assume more of the responsibility for posting material themselves.

In order for the bulletin board display to be effective, certain elements in its preparation and use should be observed by the teacher. The following are suggested:

1. Use captivating captions of one type and color. Letters for captions might be made from dark construction paper, corrugated paper, cardboard, yarn, aluminum foil, or material that has a related design such as discarded book jackets, newspaper, or woodgrain.
2. Use sound principles of design, balance, order, and color. Too much material carelessly displayed gives a cluttered effect. Adapt the display to the physical makeup of the room. Take into consideration door and window heights, other displays, lighting, and the location of the display in terms of its basic purpose. Secure an organized effect by developing continuity in the display. Anchor material squarely and securely on all four corners.
3. Change the displays frequently and use variety in the material posted. There should be a purpose for posting any material, and after it has served its purpose it should be removed.
4. Take time to discuss the material on the bulletin boards; call the attention of the children to new material posted; teach directly from the bulletin board from time to time.
5. Encourage children to bring or prepare material suitable for bulletin board display. As soon as the children are sufficiently mature, involve them in the planning and preparation of some of the displays.

COMMUNITY RESOURCES

It is in the local community that the teacher should sow the seeds of a lifetime study of human society. Here the social processes that function a thousand times over in communities around the world may be observed firsthand. In the local community, the child is introduced to geographical concepts, to the problems of group living, to government in operation, to the production and distribution of goods and services, and to the rich historical heritage of the nation.

In most American communities the child can see evidence that it is possible for persons of varied backgrounds, nationalities, religious faiths, and races to live and work harmoniously together.

The teacher may make use of the local community in two basic ways. One is to bring some portion of the community to the classroom; the other is to take the class out of the school to some place or person of importance in the community. As a matter of principle, it is advisable to take elementary schoolchildren into the community only for the experiences that cannot be duplicated in the classroom. For example, it is usually better to arrange to have a person bring photographs of early life in the community to the school and to speak to the children there than it is to take the class of 30 children to a home. On the other hand, the process involved in canning tuna fish or cranberries cannot be observed in the classroom; the children must be taken to the cannery if this process is to be observed first-hand. Teachers make use of community resources when children bring materials from home for the bulletin boards, the "market," or the "dry dock;" when parents are asked to assist in any way; when books are obtained from the public library; when the local newspaper is used; or when children bring items from home to share with others in "show and tell." The personal experiences children have in the com-

The local community is an essential information source for pupils engaged in social studies. Here members of the local fire department brought their equipment to the school site to demonstrate and explain how they make use of the equipment in responding to emergency calls.

munity and share with the class are likewise a common use of community resources.

The teacher must always select with care the persons who are invited to spend time with the class for instructional purposes. Some people should not be asked to speak to children, because they are not able to make themselves understood, they lack an understanding of children, they freely hold and express attitudes or beliefs that may be offensive to members of the group, or they fail to grasp the significance of their visit to the class. The teacher should plan to spend some time with the visitor sufficiently far enough in advance to brief the guest on the activities of the class, the purpose of the visit, and the points to be discussed and stressed. Likewise, the children must be prepared for the visitor, listing questions they should like to ask, and general courtesies extended to classroom guests. Handled in this way, persons from the community can make a positive contribution to the instructional program in the social studies. Those who might be used either for the purposes of interview or as classroom resource visitors might include

County agent
County commissioner
Members of the Federal Conservation Service, the Farm Bureau, the
    Izaak Walton League, local conservation groups, Future Farmers
    of America
4-H club leaders
Old inhabitants of the community
Professional persons: ministers, doctors, lawyers
Judges
Legislators
Local officials
Representatives of local industries
Travelers
Recent immigrants or other newcomers to the community
Authors
Persons with special skills: weavers, pottery makers, jewelry makers
Armed forces personnel
Exchange students
Persons with interesting hobbies
Community helpers
Members of the local historical society
Newspaper reporters
Members of service organizations

Whenever children are taken off the school site, the teacher must attend to a number of exceedingly important details. Adequate planning will help the teacher anticipate some of the problems that may arise in connection with the field trip and will help make the trip educationally worthwhile. Poorly planned field trips are worse than none at all, for they lack purpose, may jeopardize the safety of the children, may cause poor public relations between the school and community, and can break down learnings the teacher should have been trying to build in the classroom. Although the field trip should be pleasant for everyone including the teacher, it is first of all an educational experience, and its primary objective is not that everyone have a joyous outing. Good planning will ensure that the trip will be both a pleasant as well as an educational experience. The following suggestions will be helpful in achieving that goal:

FIELD TRIPS

Preparing for the Trip

1. Clearly establish the purposes of the trip and make certain that the children understand the purposes, too. The excursion should provide opportunities for learning that are not possible in the classroom.
2. Obtain administrative permission for the field trip and make arrangements for transportation. As a matter of policy, it is better to use a public conveyance or a school bus than it is to use private automobiles. In using private cars the teacher is never sure if the driver is properly insured, is competent behind the wheel, or even if the driver has a valid operator's license.
3. Make all necessary preliminary arrangements at the place of the visit. This should include the time for the group to arrive, where the children are to go, who will guide them, and so forth. It is recommended that the teacher make the excursion prior to the time the children are taken. This will alert the teacher to circumstances and situations that should be discussed with the children before leaving the classroom. Make sure that the field trip guide is aware of the purposes of the field trip.
4. Study the literature on the subject. No teacher should approach a field trip unprepared. This knowledge will later be valuable in helping prepare pupils for the field trip and in initiating follow-up and study activities.
5. Obtain written permission from each parent for the child to go on the trip and do not take children who cannot or do not return signed permission slips. Although this action does not in itself absolve the teacher of responsibility or liability in the event of an accident, it indicates to the teacher that the parent knows of the field trip and approves of the child's going. Most schools have forms for this purpose that are filled out by the teacher and sent home with each child for the parent's signature.
6. Prepare the class for the field trip. "What is it that we wish to find out? What things in particular do we want to look for? What questions do we want to ask the guide?" Through careful planning and preparation the teacher helps children to be more observant and makes a geniune research activity out of the field trip. The children probably will be taken to places to which many of them have been before. Most of them have seen trains, many have been to the airport, some have been to the harbor, and all have been to a filling station. Why, then, should the school take children to such places on field trips? The answer is that different purposes exist for the field trip than for incidental visits. The children are prepared to look for things they would not otherwise see.

The class should set up standards of conduct for the trip before leaving the school. Children are quick to accept the challenge that the responsibility for a good trip rests personally with each member of the group. Time spent on this part of the preparation for the excursion will pay dividends when the trip is underway. Nothing is more embarrassing for the teacher, more damaging to school-community relations, or more devastating to the educational purposes of the field trip than a group or rude and unruly children. This often happens when the children have been inadequately prepared for the trip.

7. If the trip is to be long, make arrangements for lunchroom and restroom facilities. Take along a first-aid kit.

8. Have an alternate plan in case the weather turns bad or something interferes with your plans.

Conducting the Trip

9. Take roll before leaving the school grounds and "count noses" frequently during the trip to make sure that some of the children have not become lost or left in some restroom along the way. With young children it is a good idea to place them in pairs, because a child will know and report immediately the absence of a partner. To assist with supervision of the children and to help ensure a safe trip, the teacher should arrange for other adults to accompany the group. Teachers can usually count on parents to assist in this way but should plan to meet with them prior to the trip and explain the purposes, standards of behavior, the route to be followed, and other important details. The adults accompanying the children must be prepared for the excursion just as the children.

10. Arrive at the designated place on time and have children ready for the guide. Be sure to introduce the guide to the class. Supervise children closely during the tour to prevent accidents or injury. Before leaving, check again to make sure all children are with the group.

11. Make sure that time is allowed for the answering of pupil questions so that individual differences can be met on the trip.

12. Make sure that each pupil can see and hear adequately. Be sure that a summarization is made before the trip is concluded.

Evaluating the Trip

13. Engage the class in appropriate follow-up activities. This should include writing a thank-you note to the firm and to the adults who accompanied the class. In the primary grades, the children should dictate such a letter to the teacher who writes it on the chalkboard or chart. Individual children then copy the letter and one may be selected to be sent or, in some cases, they may all be sent. The teacher and children will also want to evaluate carefully the extent to which the purposes of the trip have been achieved. "Did we accomplish what we set out to do? Did we get the answers to our questions? What did we learn that we didn't know before? What are some other things we will want to find out?" Finally, the teacher and children will want to evaluate the conduct of the class in terms of the standards set up before the trip was made. This evaluation should always include some favorable reactions as well as ways in which the group might improve on subsequent trips. A list might be made of these suggestions for improvement to be saved for review just before the next trip is undertaken.

14. Discuss work and study projects in which pupils may engage for fur-

ther study. Such projects may include construction activities, original stories, reports, dramatic plays, and diaries. Survey other resources available in the community for study.

15. Use opportunities to draw upon data and experiences from the field trip in other subjects taught in the classroom.

Field trips to the state capitol are always exciting and can also be informative. What special preparation is required if such a trip is to be instructive as well as being a pleasant outing?

Every community has places that can be visited by classes and thereby can contribute to the enrichment of learning in the social studies. These will differ from place to place but any of the following could be used:

State historical society displays
Historical sites, monuments
Flood plain, eroded areas, dam
   sites
Razing of a building
Hospitals
Weather bureau
Warehouses
Airports
Railway station
Assembly plants
Post office
Broadcasting or telecasting
   station
Courthouse
Factories
Farms
Urban planning commission
Docks

Aquarium
Library
Refinery
Fish hatchery
Museum
Public health department
Local stores
Legislative bodies in session
Art galleries
Fire station
Newspaper printing facilities
Bakery
Observatory
Canal locks
The harbor
Police station
Zoo
Parks
Shopping centers

AN EXAMPLE OF A PRIMARY GRADE UNIT USING MULTIMEDIA

In studying an apple-growing community, Mr. Orlik's third-grade class used the following materials and activities:

Materials

Textbook: An Apple Growing Community—Yakima (Allyn & Bacon, Inc.)
Encyclopedia: The World Book
Supplementary References:
   Picture Book of Washington, B. Bailey,
   Apple Orchard; I. Eberle,
   The Story of Johnny Appleseed; Alike
Free and Inexpensive Materials: Yakima, Washington, Chamber of Commerce materials on fruit growing
Nonreading Materials and Resources:
   Individual road maps of the State of Washington
   Wall map of the state
Field Trips:
   Western Washington State Fair at Puyallup
   Local fruit orchards
Films:
   "The Apples"
   "Washington State Appleland" (Washington State Apple Commission)

"Washington and Its Natural Resources"
"Mount Rainier Wonderland"
Filmstrips: "How Apples Grow" (National Apple Institute)
Slides: Personal slide collection on the fruit-growing industry of the state
Overhead Projector: Transparencies made from *Washington Colorfun Book*,
  Metropolitan Press, Seattle
Posters, Graphs, Cartoons: Secured from the Yakima Chamber of Commerce
Auditory Aids: Record of "Johnny Appleseed"

Activities

1. Reviewed basic map skills.
2. Made a Washington State map using proportional drawing; made a key; colored main physical features.
3. Viewed personal slide collection of fruit-growing operations.
4. Used job-card activities involving research for individualizing learning.
5. Made dioramas depicting scenes from the apple-growing industry.
6. Created and presented a puppet show on Johnny Appleseed.
7. Displayed varieties of apples.
8. Dissected an apple to learn its various parts.
9. Designed a mural showing the growing and harvesting of apples.
10. Brought apple sauce, apple cookies, apple cake, apple bread, and apple juice from home for tasting.

AN EXAMPLE OF INTERMEDIATE GRADE UNIT USING MULTIMEDIA

In a unit entitled "The Challenge of Change" a fourth- and fifth-grade class used the following resources and activities that were in an activity packet:

1. Write a diary pretending you are in a Conestoga Wagon going from Independence, Missouri, to the Oregon Territory; have at least five entries. Then write a similar diary for a trip in the present day. Again include five entries telling of things that you have seen and have done.

2. Research one of the following inventions or choose a scientific discovery of your own. Be sure to include a discussion of how the invention changed the lives of the people at the time of the invention and how it affects our lives today.

a. cotton jenny	h. phonograph
b. cotton gin	i. telephone
c. steam engine	j. electric lamp
d. steam boat	k. streetcar
e. locomotive	l. motor car
f. telegraph	m. airplane
g. reaper	n. television

3. Make a booklet of tools and utensils used by the pioneers; in a second part include tools and utensils that might be used in the daily lives of people today.

4. Interview someone who has immigrated to the United States. Try to find out what changes this made in the person's life. Decide on several (three to six) questions you wish to ask the person and show them to your teacher prior to the interview.

5. Collect cartoons that deal with people making changes in some way. Perhaps the change might come as the result of some conflict or disagreement, or it might show the results of a changed attitude.

6. Make a collage showing change. Have a theme such as:

   a. Changes in My Life
   b. Changes in Our Natural Environment
   c. Inventions That Change Lives
   d. Human Equality
   e. Changes in Recreation

7. Collect newspaper articles that deal with changes. These could be changes in government or in local affairs such as schools or city planning. Display these articles in some way. You might even choose a theme around which to build your collection.

8. Create a map that shows the places where several (three to six) of your classmates have lived during their lives. Be sure to have a key so you can clearly show which moves were made by which classmate. Your teacher has an outline map for you to use.

   Or take a poll to find out how many times each person in your class has moved. Compile your results and show them on a graph.

9. Make a photographic essay showing changes in your community. This could show natural changes or those made by people.

10. Watch one of the films listed as resources in your packet. Create a poster or a five- or six-frame filmstrip showing the main ideas of the film.

11. Read a fiction book that deals with the changes in the lives of people your own age. Create a way to share your book with the rest of the class. Check the Reading Center for ideas. You might look for one of the following books:

    Courage of Sarah Noble, A. Dalgliesh. A true story of a brave girl who in 1707 went with her father into the wilds of Connecticut.
    Edge of Two Worlds, W. Jones. Sequoyah, an aging Cherokee leader, and fifteen-year-old Calvin, lone survivor of a Comanche raid, journey across the wilderness.
    The Empty Schoolhouse, N. S. Carlson. A ten-year-old black girl in a small Louisiana town endures loneliness and abuse as the first to integrate her school.
    Blue Willow, D. Gates. Janey is a child of migrant workers in the San Joaquin Valley in California whose greatest desire is a permanent home.

RESOURCES

Textbooks:

The United States and the Other Americas, Macmillan Publishing Co., Inc.
Forming a New Nation, American Book Company
The United States of America, Prentice-Hall, Inc.

Resource books available in our library (only a few are listed):

The New Land, P. Viereck
Frontier Living, E. Tunis

Pioneer Children of America, C. D. Emerson et al.
Sweet Land, Sweet Liberty, based on A. Landsburg television series *The American Idea*.

Films:

"Age of the Buffalo"
"Inventions in American Growth: 1750–1850"
"Inventions in American Growth: 1850–1910"
"Factory: How a Product is Made"
"Maps for a Changing World"
"American Road"
"Our Changing Way of Life: Cattleman"
"Prairie"
"Good Morning Freedom"
"Ways to Settle Disputes"
"Understanding Stresses and Strains"

Filmstrips:

"America's First Factory"
"How Farming Has Changed"
"The Story of Alexander Graham Bell"
"From Kitty Hawk to Canaveral"
"How Automation Affects Your Life"
"Blazing the Oregon Trail"

Slides:

Early Hometown (Compiled by the local school district)

Study Prints:

Transportation—Includes photographs that tell the story of transportation from Indian canoes to airplanes.
Jamestown, Virginia—Color photographs of seventeenth-century people in authentic costumes.
Historic Williamsburg—Color photographs showing the social, political, economic, and family life of the Virginia colonists in the eighteenth century.

Minifield Trips: (Small groups accompanied by adult)

Bell Telephone Center
Safeway Food Distribution Center
State Historical Society
Museum of History and Industry
American Bakeries Co./Langendorf Division

Current Newspapers and News Magazines.

DISCUSSION QUESTIONS AND SUGGESTED ACTIVITIES

1. What reasons can you suggest that would justify the expense and additional professional time involved in using a multimedia approach to social studies?

2. Select three or four textbooks that are designed for a grade in which you have a special interest. Evaluate these texts in terms of their potential usefulness to you as a teacher, using the criteria listed on pages 89–90.
3. How might a classroom teacher get help from the school librarian in improving social studies learning for children?
4. Find a photograph that would be suitable for teaching social studies in a grade of your choice. Develop questions based on the photograph that require interpretation and analysis as described on pages 238–239 in Chapter 9.
5. Prepare and display a bulletin board for the class and show how it might be used as an instructional aid.
6. Who should select social studies learning resources for a class? The teacher? Parents? The principal? Explain.
7. How can a teacher keep himself or herself up-to-date on new learning resources for social studies?
8. Visit your local curriculum library or a district instructional materials center and examine on a firsthand basis some of the various learning resources available for social studies.
9. Develop a lesson that will provide your pupils with experience in evaluating information sources. If you are working with primary-grade pupils, this might take the form of evaluating the credibility of a popular television commercial with which they are familiar. With older youngsters you might develop an exercise to sensitize them to bias in printed material. Discuss your ideas in class, and if possible, teach the lesson to a group of elementary school pupils.
10. Do you think parents have the right to censor textbooks used by their children? Would the words "review" or "screen" be more acceptable than "censor"? What guidelines would you propose to accommodate the legitimate and understandable concerns of parents about textbook content, while at the same time not allowing pressure groups to force a distortion of text narratives in accordance with their beliefs and biases?

SELECTED REFERENCES

Banks, James A. *Teaching Strategies for Ethnic Studies*, 2nd ed. Boston: Allyn & Bacon Books, Inc., 1979. (Provides numerous sources of instructional material relevant to multiethnic education.)

Cox, C. Benjamin. *The Censorship Game and How to Play It*, Bulletin 50. National Council for the Social Studies. Washington, D.C.: The Council, 1977. (Includes seven National Council for the Social Studies Statements on Academic Freedom, Controversial Issues, and Civil Rights issued between 1951–1974.)

Educators Progress Service. *Educators Guide to Free Social Studies Materials: A Multi-Media Guide*. Randolph, Wisconsin: Educators Progress Service. Revised annually.

Garcia, Jesus and Ricardo Garcia. "Selecting Ethnic Materials for the Elementary School," *Social Education*, 44 (March 1980), pp. 232-236.

Haley, Frances and Regina McCormick. *Directory of Social Studies/Social Science Service Organizations*. Boulder, Colorado: Social Science Education Consortium, 1976.

Kaltsounis, Theodore, ed. "The Community: Laboratory for Social Learnings," *Social Education*, 40 (March 1976), pp. 158-171. (Six authors contribute articles dealing with the use of the local community in teaching social studies.)

Metcalf, Fay, guest ed. "The Textbook as a Teaching Tool," *Social Education*, 44, (February 1980), pp. 84-114. (Five articles discuss textbooks as teaching tools.)

Miller, Jack W. and Edward V. Johnson. "Library Resources to Support Curriculum Improvement," *Social Studies Curriculum Improvement*, Bulletin 55. Raymond H. Muessig, ed. Washington, D.C.: National Council for the Social Studies, 1978. (Lists many sources of instructional materials.)

National Council for the Social Studies. "Notable Children's Trade Books in the Field of Social Studies," *Social Education*, 43 (April 1979), pp. 298-303, and *Social Education*, 44 (April 1980), pp. 292-297.

National Council for the Social Studies. *How to Do It Series*. Several pamphlets discuss practical applications of instructional resources: "Effective Use of Films in Social Studies Classrooms," 1977; "Reach for a Picture," 1977; "Architecture as a Primary Source for Social Studies," 1978; "Using Popular Culture in the Social Studies," 1979. Washington, D.C.: The Council.

Ochoa, Anna S. "Censorship: Does Anybody Care?" *Social Education*, 43 (April 1979), pp. 304-309.

O'Toole, Dennis. "Field Trips Are *Basic*," *Social Education*, 45 (January 1981), pp. 63-65.

Patton, William E., ed. *Improving the Use of Social Studies Textbooks*, Bulletin 63. National Council for the Social Studies. Washington, D.C.: The Council, 1980.

Social Science Education Consortium. *Social Studies Curriculum Materials Data Book*. Boulder, Colorado: Social Science Education Consortium. (Provides analyses of new curriculum and learning materials.)

Welton, David A. and John T. Mallan. *Children and their World: Teaching Elementary Social Studies*. Chicago: Rand McNally College Publishing Co., Inc., 1976. Chapter 13.

5

Individualizing Teaching and Learning in the Social Studies

The practice of moving handicapped pupils out of segregated educational settings and into regular classrooms has had the effect of sensitizing teachers to individual differences between and among *all* children. If the teacher is required to prepare an Individualized Education Program for a handicapped child, it is likely that the teacher will be more observant of the individual learning needs of the child's non-handicapped peers as well. Much of the educational literature published in this century deals with pupil variation and its effect on school achievement. Pupils differ one from another in their capacity to learn; in the rate at which they can learn; in their learning styles; in their methods of work; in their socio-ethnic, home, and family backgrounds; in their motivation to learn; in their physical fitness; and, indeed, on almost any variable we choose to examine. Some variations are obviously more critical to school achievement than are others, but the evidence is overwhelming that individual differences among pupils are so extensive and so pervasive that a group cannot be taught effectively as if it were a single pupil. The alternative to group instruction is, of course, some form of individualized teaching.

WHAT IT MEANS TO INDIVIDUALIZE INSTRUCTION

To individualize instruction means that each pupil is provided with learning experiences that are suitable to his or her capabilities and that are personally meaningful, thereby enabling the learner to move in the direction of goals that are believed to be important. *Individualizing instruction does not mean that the teacher always works with individual children in a one-on-one tutorial setting.* Even if the teacher could work with children in a one-to-one relationship, this would not necessarily result in individualized instruction as we are defining it. Unless the teacher is sensitive to the unique learning requirements of each child, tutorial instruction can be just as impersonal and meaningless as whole-class instruction.

Individualization of instruction stresses independence and self-

113

direction on the part of learners. This means that a key element in the process is flexibility. Much of the instruction will, of necessity, take place in group settings. But membership in learning groups does not take the form of a permanent placement. Pupils are moved from one group to another as is needed to help them learn in their own best way. There is no standard instructional format for individualizing instruction. However, a teacher's attitude of sensitivity to and caring about the idiosyncrasies and optimum learning modalities of individual pupils is critical.

The teacher who individualizes instruction sees individual pupils rather than the class. He or she places heavy emphasis on diagnosis to ascertain the level at which a pupil is functioning. The program requirements are open-ended. Pupils are neither restricted by so-called grade level content nor are they required to achieve grade level standards. Achievement is assessed in terms of gains made by each individual. Pupil interests and preferences are respected and, insofar as is feasible, are accommodated. Uniform assignments and uniform requirements for the entire class are, as a rule, avoided. Pupil initiative and self-direction are generously rewarded.

Because of the flexibility that should characterize much of individualized instruction, it is easy for the teacher to become careless in setting requirements and standards. Levels of achievement expectations have to be set in terms of their appropriateness for individual pupils and, once set, pupils must be held to them. Records of pupil progress must be kept if judgments are to be made of achievement. Also, a knowledge of one's status and progress is a powerful force in motivating improved performance. It is significant that there is hardly any game that human beings play that does not require keeping score. Games in which no score is kept are frequently played carelessly and are less interesting to the players. And although school is not a game, the same principles apply. Teachers will usually get the level of performance they require and expect of pupils.

OBSTACLES TO INDIVIDUALIZING INSTRUCTION

If individualization is so important to good instruction, why don't more teachers do more of it? The answer to this question is not hard to find. Perhaps most important is the long tradition of whole-group instruction that is reinforced in many practices even today. The way children are grouped in schools often obscures important differences among them. Also, the belief is widely held that if pupils would just work harder, they could all achieve at the level required. Grade standards tend to be applied as minimum learnings that all pupils must achieve. Sometimes administrative and supervisory policies discourage individualization of instruction by requiring teachers to cover speci-

114

fied required material. Misuse of textbooks and standarized tests also work against individualizing instruction.

At a more subtle level, we find that the reality of individual differences runs contrary to our social philosophy of equality, i.e., the conflict between a recognition of obvious differences between individuals on the one hand and the desire to provide for equality of opportunity on the other. These represent conflicting values, both of which are embraced by this society, and no doubt by a large number of teachers. We sense a basic unfairness about setting different standards or requirements for different children. Yet we know that unless we do, some children cannot possibly succeed whereas others succeed too easily. Some believe that schools serve a sorting function and that individualization of instruction confounds this process. Others believe that schools *should* teach pupils how they compare in achievement with their classmates, and this can be accomplished by using the achievement of the group as a norm.

There are other practical obstacles to individualization of instruction. There is no doubt it is demanding of teacher time. It necessitates a considerable amount of record-keeping, requires a skillful teacher to manage it well, and also requires a considerable amount of learning resources. Some teachers are not able to cope with the flexibility it demands.

These obstacles to individualization of instruction cannot be swept aside as being unimportant. Teachers need to think about how they stand on these issues. Although we strongly urge the use of individualized teaching strategies, we are not unmindful of the problems this creates for the teacher. Perhaps most teachers feel comfortable at some midway point on a continuum of differentiated teaching. Consequently, we would expect all teachers to do as much as they are able to do in reaching each child in the social studies.

APPROACHES TO INDIVIDUALIZATION

Because teachers have their own particular styles and preferences, each teacher will develop ways of individualizing instruction that seem to work best for him or her. Most teachers, however, will find it necessary to use a combination of procedures in order to attend to the learning needs of individual pupils.

Management Approaches

Management and instruction are the two basic components of teaching. Consequently, the management aspects of a classroom have a great deal to do with the individualization of instruction. This becomes most apparent in such areas as the room environment, schedul-

115

ing, the extent of "openness," and the amount and nature of teacher supervision.

Room Environment

If we visit a classroom where learning is individualized, we are struck by the variety of interesting things children can do there that promote their opportunity to learn. The classroom is a storehouse of learning resources (see pages 98–100). We see areas of the room arranged for independent, quiet study. Other areas are planned for small group interaction. We see interesting displays where pupils can handle and manipulate materials. There are learning centers where children can work at their own pace. There is easy access to books and other media that can be used as needed. There are work areas where the pupil will find art materials, tools of various types, paper, boxes, and other raw materials needed to make things. The room is characterized by disciplined freedom where children can explore intellectually and move about physically. The environment is greatly varied in its appeal to children.

Learner Groups

In social studies, most groups should be temporary task-oriented clusters of pupils. Often these groups are formed on the basis of a common interest, as, for example, a group working together on a display, a report, or a small construction project. Other groups are formed on the basis of a common need. For instance, the teacher may work with a small group in reading their text, developing a map skill, or showing them how to use the learning center materials, while other pupils work independently. With the class arranged in this way, it will be possible to group children in many different configurations in accordance with individual needs. What should be avoided are fixed groups that separate children into fast-, medium-, and slow-achieving clusters on a more or less permanent basis.

Scheduling

In traditional instruction, time is usually thought of as a constant fixed amount that applies to everyone. Assignments are given on a specific day, and the completed work is due on a specific day. Because individual pupils work at different rates, individualized approaches make time a variable rather than a constant. Within reasonable limits, pupils are allowed to work at their own pace. This obviously requires careful supervision. Left entirely on their own, some would not make good use of their time, and this would work to the detriment of their learning. Nonetheless, the principle of providing for varying rates of learning is sound. This speaks against the use of rigid time schedules that apply to all, with penalties for "late" work.

Extent of Openness

We use the term *openness* to mean both intellectual and physical freedom to learn. It suggests an absence of unnecessary and artifically imposed restrictions on what pupils learn and how they go about learning it. Regimented management procedures, whole class teaching, and the use of strict *grading* practices tend to reduce the extent of openness in social studies.

The term *grading* has two meanings. The first has to do with placing children in groups called *grades*, usually on the basis of common age, e.g., most six-year-olds are in the first *grade*. The second meaning of grades has to do with the awarding of letters or numerical scores to represent a child's level of achievement, e.g., an A, B, or C *grade*. The grade concept is often associated with certain curriculum requirements, hence the common expression "first-grade work," "second-grade work," and so on. There is not now, nor has there ever been, a consensus among teachers and educators as to precisely what constitutes "first-grade, second-grade, or third-grade" work. Nonetheless, it is usually interpreted to mean the average achievement of a child of average intelligence and motivation to do the work prescribed by the curriculum for that grade.

When grade standards are rigidly applied, as they often are, this practice has the effect of restricting learning opportunities. Pupils who are capable of doing so are discouraged from proceeding beyond what is specified because this would infringe on the curriculum content of the next grade. Meanwhile, the teacher intensifies efforts to get the slower-learning children up to the grade level standard. Thus, by placing a lid on learning for some pupils, and by requiring unattainable standards for others, the grade standard concept is clearly incompatible with individualized instruction.

These conventional ideas about grades and grade standards must be revised if we are to have the extent of openness needed to individualize instruction. The term *grade* should simply mean the group in which the child is placed and should be disassociated from an expected standard of achievement. That is, to say that a child is in the "third-grade" should mean that he or she is in the third year of school along with other eight-year-old children—and no more. What each child knows or "should" know depends on the individual child. Some will know a great deal; others very little. Once the issue of grade-level standards is set aside, the teacher can begin looking at the achievement levels of individual children and can set realistic levels of expectation for them.

Teacher Supervision and Guidance of Learning

Fairly early in the school year the teacher will be able to identify the children who are well on the way to self-direction in their study habits, those who need a moderate amount of supervision and guidance, and those who will need to be monitored almost continuously.

117

In the primary grades there will be a greater dependence on the teacher than at upper-grade levels because young children have not yet attained sufficient maturity to be capable of lengthy periods of self-direction. But even at the early levels there will be big differences in the degree of individual responsibility manifested by children. In building study habits, the teacher must, on the one hand, remain close enough to the situation to lend direction and support, yet, on the other hand, be far enough away to allow the child to experiment with independence. When five or six first-graders are operating the "store" in one corner of the classroom while the teacher is helping four or five others with a mural in another part of the room, it can be expected that help will be needed occasionally in the store to iron out minor problems. The same group as sixth-graders could be expected to work through the entire period without help if their goals were well defined.

Children need supervision and guidance from the teacher in a great variety of ways. In every class some will need special help with reading. These children may be taken singly or in a small group, while the remainder reads independently. In this reading-study situation the teacher helps the children with word difficulties, helps them get meaning from visual material, calls their attention to picture captions and discusses the pictures, selects certain key passages and singles those out for special teaching, reads to the children short selections of special significance, and tries to build independence in reading. The teacher, through careful guidance, must help children make the best use of reading resources. This type of guidance is not limited to the primary grades but persists throughout the elementary school.

In most classes, too, there will be another group of children who can go much beyond the remainder of the class in their depth of understanding of the topics studied. With these children, the teacher points out possibilities for additional study, challenges them with provocative problems, suggests topics for additional research, helps them secure appropriate reading material, teaches them how to organize their ideas, and gives similar guidance. The teacher can be of most help to these children by suggesting, challenging, and holding them to high standards of achievement and yet expecting much of their study to be done independently.

For most children the teacher will be expected to lead the way, show them how to do what is expected, and get them started. From then on, occasional help and well-placed suggestions will be adequate. It is not uncommon to find teachers who are so interested in a social studies activity that they have to guard against doing the work for the pupils. This is most likely to happen in construction, processing, or dramatic activities.

The teacher's role in guiding and supervising social studies activities may be described, therefore, as a function of the needs of individual children. Children should not be supervised so closely as to discourage independent habits of work. But neither should the teacher fail to offer the kind of constructive help and guidance growing children need. The teacher should be actively involved during the social studies period—moving from group to group and child to child assisting, encouraging, suggesting, and doing whatever else is needed to help children move in the direction of desired learning goals.

Multimedia Approaches

The intake of new information is, of course, an essential requirement of social studies education, and the conventional data sources for pupils have been the textbook and the teacher. For years teachers have been urged to expand these classroom data sources to include the many newer learning resources that have become available in modern times. The planned use of a generous and varied offering of learning resources greatly enhances the possibility of individualized learning. What is sought is the use of several different learning resources in combination, which is essentially what a multimedia approach does. Providing variation in the data sources available to children is one of the easiest first steps a teacher can take in individualizing the social studies program. Several of the available resources are discussed in this section.

Reading Materials

The differences in reading ability among pupils are apparent early in the grades and become greater as the children move through school. By the time they are in the fifth and sixth grades, the difference between the least capable and the most capable readers is often as much as six to eight years. Accommodating these variations in reading ability is, therefore, basic to individualized instruction.

Usually the teacher will have little problem in securing appropriate reading material for the more capable readers. Given a minimum of direction, they will be able to handle the textbook on their own. They can then be guided to other sources of information, most of which can be geared to their individual interests related to a topic under study or to individual or small group research projects. School and public libraries provide good selections of books that are relevant to many social studies topics. Additionally, the better readers can make use of special references, pamphlets, newspapers, and magazines. The teacher's role is not so much to assist these children with the reading task itself but to provide stimulating and challenging guidance that will motivate them to do the reading. The reading should help pupils develop advanced skills related to information gathering and processing.

With the less capable readers, the teacher will need to (1) provide direct assistance with the reading, and (2) make available less difficult materials that deal with the topic under study. A third option is to provide ways for these pupils to get information and/or data

119

through listening, viewing, direct experience, or some other nonreading resource. In using nonreading resources, however, the teacher must recognize that this further reduces the opportunity for the child to learn how to read.

When working with less capable readers, either in small groups or individually, the teacher will want to select only those passages or graphic material that are particularly vital to the topic. The meanings of essential terms and concepts included in the passage should be developed prior to the reading. Carefully structured guide questions should be used in order to ensure that the reading is done with purpose. That is, pupils are reading to find out specific information. Have pupils confirm their responses to literal questions by reading orally the sentence that provides the answer. These reading-study sessions should be kept short (15 to 20 minutes) and highly motivated. Additional suggestions relating to reading social studies content are provided in Chapter 9.

As one moves lower in the elementary grades, it becomes more difficult to secure simplified reading materials for social studies. There comes a point beyond which it is impossible to simplify the reading task and still have the narrative provide significant informational content. The teacher can rewrite some passages or create original selections for the slower readers. Because this is time-consuming and often difficult, the amount of such original material a teacher can produce is necessarily limited.

Often overlooked as valuable reading sources for social studies are trade books and literary works. Trade books are what children call "library books." Ordinarily such books can be secured from the school library or from the district instructional resources center. Pupils will use trade books as sources of information as well as reading them for enjoyment. In the middle and upper grades, simplified nontext books are available on many social studies topics.

In addition to making these books available to pupils, the teacher must structure the learning environment in ways that will ensure that the children and books are brought together. This can be done by making the books an integral part of a learning center. Although some use can be made of book reports, this procedure can easily become routine, uninteresting, and self-defeating. Teachers can prevent this from happening by devising imaginative ways for children to share what they have read with each other. For example, teachers have had pupils engage in follow-up activities such as these: (1) evaluate the books they have read in terms of specific criteria (What did you like or dislike about the book? What is especially good about the book? What information does it provide? Would you recommend it to a friend? and so forth); (2) make an illustration that conveys some interesting feature of the book; (3) tape-record a short review of the book; (4) persuade a classmate to read a book found to be especially interesting or useful; (5) read orally to the class selected passages thought to be particularly relevant to the topic.

Learning Kits and Packages

A learning kit or package is a small collection of relevant materials that pupils can use on their own in studying a topic, concept, or skill. It will ordinarily contain instructions to the pupils, data source materials (reprints, maps, pictures, pamphlets, or other appropriate re-

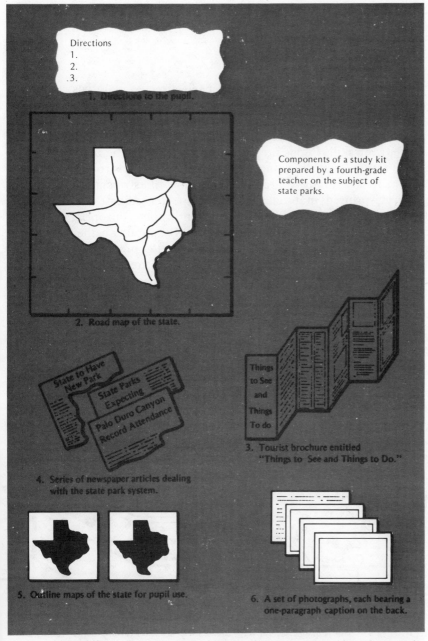

Directions
1.
2.
3.

1. Directions to the pupil.

Components of a study kit prepared by a fourth-grade teacher on the subject of state parks.

2. Road map of the state.

State to Have New Park
State Parks Expecting
Palo Duro Canyon Record Attendance

Things to See and Things To do

3. Tourist brochure entitled "Things to See and Things to Do."

4. Series of newspaper articles dealing with the state park system.

5. Outline maps of the state for pupil use.

6. A set of photographs, each bearing a one-paragraph caption on the back.

FIGURE 4. Components of a Learning Kit based on the subject of state parks.

121

sources), along with study guide questions, self-correcting work sheets, and/or other pupil response formats. Directions must be clear enough to allow the pupil to use the kit or package independently. Learning kits vary in the extent to which they can be used without teacher assistance, but insofar as possible, the kit or package is self-selected by the pupil, self-directed, self-paced, and self-corrected. Ordinarily such a kit could be contained in a file-size envelope or box. It can be constructed by the teacher or can be purchased from commercial sources. An example of a teacher-prepared self-directed study packet is provided on page 121.

Learning Centers

Learning kits, packages, and other self-directed materials can be assembled for pupil use in a designated place in the classroom. Such areas have come to be called *learning centers*. Usually a learning center will contain multimedia materials focused on a specific topic, concept, or skill. Pupils are expected to work in the learning center itself, rather than checking out materials that are to be used elsewhere. In a learning center one may find filmstrips and projectors, pictures, printed materials, cassette tape recordings, cartridge-type films, books, learning packets, maps, and other appropriate learning resources. They are designed to be used by pupils on their own as a means of (1) obtaining basic information; (2) practicing a skill; (3) following up on something taught to the entire class; (4) enriching and extending basic instruction.

The Big "E" Learning Center

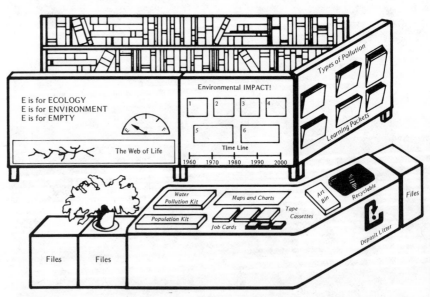

FIGURE 5. This is one of several ways that a social studies Learning Center can be arranged. Artwork by Jane Hartnett.

Learning center activities and materials must provide the pupil with specific and precise directions because they are intended to be used with a minimum of teacher direction and supervision. If this is to happen, pupils will also have to be instructed on how to use the learning center. If learning is to be individualized in a learning center, pupils must be provided with some choice in what is to be done, and they should be allowed to work at their own pace. More than one pupil should be able to work in the center at the same time, and in some cases may work cooperatively on the same activity. A classroom might have more than one learning center in operation concurrently. An example of a learning center design is included on page 122.

It is important to emphasize that the learning center, as a collection of relevant learning resources, is an integral part of the total resources used by the class in studying a topic. *All* pupils can and should be expected to make some use of it. The learning center should not be perceived only as a "fun" place for those pupils who complete their regular assignment quickly—as a reward for good work. Such restricted use limits the value of the learning center and denies its use to precisely those pupils who could benefit most from it.

Performance-Based Approaches

In using performance-based approaches to individualizing instruction, careful attention must be given to the specific objectives to be achieved by each pupil. For example, it is clear that ideas and skills can be handled at varying levels of complexity. Likewise, pupils vary in their ability to deal with complex ideas. In performance-based teaching, the teacher attempts to match the level of complexity of the objectives with the pupil's ability to achieve them. This can be done by using behavioral objectives that are geared to various levels of difficulty, by using programmed material that is self-paced, or by using individual contracts with pupils.

A *pupil contract* is defined as a cooperatively developed agreement between an individual pupil and the teacher. The contract specifies precisely what the pupil will do and when the work is to be completed. Because contracts are individually negotiated, the nature and extent of the work to be completed can be well suited to the ability level and the interests of the pupil. Some teachers develop and use a contract form that gives the agreement an official appearance. Contracts are signed by both the pupil and the teacher. Examples of contract forms are provided on pages 124-125.

The use of contracts has educational values for pupils beyond being an interesting assignment format. The pupils should learn what is involved in a contractual agreement and that there usually are adverse consequences when contracts are not completed as specified. Therefore, it is important that pupils know what it is they are agree-

A Contract

I Do Hereby Agree to Do the Following Activities in Social Studies.

1. _____

2. _____

3. _____

4. _____

Pupil's signature _____

Teacher's signature _____

Today's Date _____

Date Due _____

A sample Pupil Contract format.

ing to do and what penalties may be attached to the failure to fulfill the conditions of the contract.

Performance-based strategies require a close working relationship between individual pupils and the teacher. This means frequent pupil conferences in order to monitor the pupil's performance and progress toward specific objectives. An assessment of the pupil's status is essential if an individual study program is to be planned. Thus, a system for the diagnosis of pupil needs is an essential component of performance-based programs. Much of this can be done informally as the teacher observes the work of individual children. In the middle and upper grades the teacher can make use of diagnostic tests to help identify pupil needs.

It is important to stress that independent study, as characterized by performance-based strategies, is not the same as individualized

124

AN AGREEMENT

As my contribution to the unit, OUR TOWN, I agree to do the project or projects checked:

_____ 1. Interview a person who has lived here a long time.

_____ 2. Conduct a survey of old buildings in our town.

_____ 3. Write a true story about our town.

_____ 4. Write a short play about our town.

_____ 5. Work on a mural with _____ .
(Name other pupils)

_____ 6. Paint a picture of something in our town.

_____ 7. Prepare a TV program script about our town.

_____ 8. Do an original activity of my own: _____

_____ .

Today's date: _____   _____
Pupil

Due date: _____   _____
Teacher

INDIVIDUAL STUDY PLAN

I contract to do the following activities that are described on pages 157–158 of our text, to be completed by November 15:

(Check *two*)

_____ Using A Time Line   _____ Making History Real

_____ Building Ideas from Words   _____ Interesting Things To Do
and Pictures
_____ Things to Think About
_____ Making an Outline   (Write out your answers)

_____ Making a Chart

Date: _____   _____
Pupil

_____
Teacher

Other Variations of Pupil Study Contracts

learning. Individualized learning can and often does take place in group settings. Good social studies programs will not result if pupils constantly work by themselves without the opportunity to interact with others. Some provision must be made for small and large group activities during which time the results of individual study are shared, ideas are discussed, group activities are planned, and new areas of study are explored. This will ensure that the social dimensions of social studies education are not being overlooked.

125

Creative or Activity-Based Approaches

Much can be done to individualize social studies learning by encouraging children to imagine, to wonder, to act out feelings, to create, and to express their ideas and feelings through art forms and similar creative and/or activity modes. These approaches must be used in combination with some of the other approaches suggested in this chapter. The difference between this approach and the others is that it individualizes learning at the outgo or expressive level, whereas all of the others vary the ways children receive ideas or data. The use of creative and expressive activities is discussed in detail in Chapter 12.

Social studies activities should be sufficiently varied to appeal to the broad range of interests and capabilities of pupils. Some activities such as oral and written reports tend to be overused. Activities that are highly correlated with the usual academic skills and abilities are useful, of course, but other options should also be available. Not all children are able to perform these activities well, and consequently their involvement in the social studies program is limited. Most social studies teaching would be improved through the use of a wide range of activities, especially those that require the pupil to use creative imagination. The chart on pages 39–40 suggests the types of learning activities that should at one time or another be included in social studies instruction.

This chapter has emphasized the need for taking a broad view of individualizing social studies instruction. Too frequently, individualizing instruction is understood to mean "doing something for the gifted" or "doing something for the slow learners." The fact is that every child presents the teacher with the challenge of individual differences. The teacher who accepts this broader concept of individual differences will take into account not only the child's IQ but also the other factors that influence the child's growth in social studies learnings. This will ensure that some adjustments will be made in the program for the unique needs of every child irrespective of his or her mental ability. But because the problem of providing for exceptional children is a matter of special concern to many teachers, the next section addresses that subject.

INDIVIDUALIZING FOR EXCEPTIONALITY

The Congress of the United States enacted two pieces of legislation during the decade of the 1970s that had a profound effect on the education of persons with handicapping conditions. The first of these was Section 504 of the Vocational Rehabilitation Act of 1973. This law deals largely with the removal of discriminatory practices against the handicapped. Although it is basically a law that protects the civil

Handicapped pupils have become a part of the regular classroom because of federal and state mandates and because of changing attitudes toward individual human variations. Why does the social studies program have especially significant responsibilities for providing education in the least restrictive environment for handicapped learners?

rights of handicapped persons, it has a number of implications for education. It guarantees that an individual may not be denied access to education solely on the basis of a handicapping condition. As a result, Section 504 brought some greater extension of employment, training, and promotion opportunities to handicapped individuals.

Perhaps the most important contribution of Section 504 was its mandate to remove barriers in architecture and in transportation. The law requires that all *activities* (not all areas or spaces) must be accessible to physically handicapped participants and spectators. This meant that substantial structural modifications in existing school buildings had to be made in order to bring them into compliance. New structures must make provisions for these antidiscriminatory requirements in their design. Section 504 was instrumental in establishing "barrier-free" environments in schools.

In 1975 two Congressional Subcommittees held hearings in various parts of the country to determine what, if any, additional legislation was needed to accommodate the educational needs of the handicapped. Some of the findings of these hearings were astounding: Over 1.75 million children with handicaps were being excluded *entirely* from receiving a public education solely on the basis of their handicap. Over half of the estimated 8 million children were not receiving appropriate services. Many children with handicaps were being placed

127

in inappropriate educational environments because their handicaps had not been detected. As a result of these findings and as a result of concurrent judicial intervention, the 142nd piece of legislation passed by the 94th Congress was the Education for All Handicapped Children Act, otherwise known as PL94-142. It passed both Houses of Congress by very wide margins—probably because the issue had already been settled by the courts. The Bill was signed into law by President Gerald Ford on November 29, 1975, to go into effect in 1977, with no expiration date.

PL94-142 is one of the most lengthy and complex pieces of legislation ever enacted by Congress. Its main points, however, are easily summarized. The law requires

(1) the availability of a free appropriate public education for all handicapped children between the ages of three and 21, unless inconsistent with state laws; school districts are obliged to search and identify handicapped children;
(2) the maintenance of an Individualized Education Program (IEP) for all handicapped children, prepared in cooperation with the parent or guardian, the teacher, and the school principal;
(3) the guarantee of complete due process procedures;
(4) the provision of special education and related services as needed in the "least restrictive" environment;
(5) the non-discriminatory testing, evaluation, and placement; and
(6) the placement in regular public school settings with non-handicapped peers to the maximum extent appropriate and feasible.

PL94-142 is based on a philosophy of *inclusion*, rather than *exclusion*. It embraces the "zero-reject" principle. It frowns on the segregation and labeling of human beings. It shatters long-held assumptions about who is educable.

Teaching Handicapped Pupils in Social Studies

Traditionally, elementary school teachers dealt with handicapped pupils by referring them to special education classes. As we have seen, this type of arbitrary exclusion is no longer socially or legally acceptable. Today the teacher can expect one or more children with varying types of handicapping conditions to be present in most elementary school classrooms. This practice, known popularly as "mainstreaming," is the school's response to the mandate that children must be educated with their non-handicapped peers to the maximum extent appropriate.

What the teacher can do and will do depends on the nature of the child's handicap and the extent of support service provided. It is quite clear that a child who is orthopedically handicapped but is intellectually gifted will be handled differently from one who is physi-

cally fully functioning but is mildly—or severely—retarded intellectually. In this context, the Individualized Education Program makes
good sense because the learning needs of children vary greatly from
one to another. Likewise, what the teacher does or does not do will
depend on how much technical assistance and support service is available. If the classroom has the services of an interpreter-tutor who
can work with the handicapped child for part of the time in a one-
on-one setting and who works with the teacher on a cooperative
basis, it becomes easier for the regular teacher to integrate the handicapped child into the day-to-day life and activities of the classroom.

In the case of a child who is severely disabled, the chances are
good that a teacher trained in special education will prepare the Individualized Education Program. The classroom teacher may only be
responsible for a small part of the implementation of the IEP. On the
other hand, if the teacher has a child in the class who is mildly retarded, that teacher may have full responsibility for the preparation
and implementation of the IEP. Even in cases of mildly handicapped
children, the regular classroom teacher may have available the assistance of a special education teacher in preparing the IEP. In those
cases where the handicapped child is attending both regular and special education classes, ordinarily the IEP goals and objectives will
focus on compensating for the child's handicap, and it is the special
education teacher who attends the IEP meeting.[1] The regular classroom teacher, the special education teacher, and other support personnel must, of course, work in close cooperation with each other to
ensure a coordinated program of instruction for the handicapped
child.

The Individualized Education Program must take into account the
child's present level of attainment or development. In other words,
a learning needs assessment must be made, and the current status
established. Based on that information, the IEP stipulates the long-
range goals that are to be met by the end of the year and the short-
term objectives to be achieved in order to attain the long-range goals.
The short-term objectives should be listed in the sequence in which
they are to be achieved, not unlike a programmed learning document. Although the regular teacher may exercise some initiative in
preparing the IEP, the program planning and development *must* include, on a firsthand basis, the principal or other school representative and the child's parents or guardian. Teacher-prepared IEPs that
are sent to the child's parents or guardian for signature are not acceptable in terms of the mandate of PL94-142.

The actual format of the IEP will vary from district to district, although the substance of what is included will remain pretty much the
same. The sample form provided on pages 131–133 illustrates a standard IEP that includes components required by federal regulations.

---

[1]*Policy Paper on Individualized Education Programs*, U.S. Department of Education,
Office of Special Education, May 23, 1980.

IN TEACHING SLOWER-LEARNING CHILDREN

1. Provide generously for experiences of a concrete firsthand nature. These children learn best by handling, manipulating, sensing, feeling, and doing, and they learn least well by reading, analyzing, generalizing, and finding new solutions to problems.
2. Learning tasks must be specific and simple; learning goals must be definite, clear-cut, and short-ranged. The children must know precisely what to do and how to do it. Use detailed study-guide material.
3. Learning experiences should be presented in one small step at a time with successful completion of each step before advancement to the next.
4. Recognize that lessons should be short in duration because of the brevity of the attention span of many slow learners.
5. Expect them to show less initiative and less ability to plan for themselves than average or gifted children. They are also less able to evaluate their own work, making close supervision and direction by the teacher imperative.
6. Reduce their load of abstract and verbal materials to a level they are able to handle. Work in references, if used at all, must be specific; reading and research must be held to a minimum.
7. Recognize that it will be difficult for them to sense relationships, to make generalizations, or to do inferential thinking. They are more skillful in dealing with *who*, *what*, and *where* questions than they are with *why* type questions.
8. When teaching crucial items such as those of health, safety, laws or conventions of society, or simple elements of social studies skills, plan to provide for much practice and repetition of the material to be learned.
9. Set realistic levels of expectation for them. Plan in terms of their most pressing needs with a view toward their future life as happy and productive members of society. Try to visualize what the child is likely to be doing a score of years in the future.
10. Above all, maintain a patient and encouraging attitude toward them. Help them establish security and status in the classroom. Provide opportunities for a degree of success for them.

IN TEACHING GIFTED CHILDREN

1. Provide a generous amount of challenging reading material that will allow them to read for informational purposes.
2. Plan learning activities that call for problem solving, making logical associations, making logical deductions, and making generalizations.
3. Give them many opportunities for the planning aspects of their own work; allow for a considerable amount of individual initiative, commensurate with their degree of maturity.
4. Provide for individual study and research. This should include use of the library and references, as well as note keeping, outlining, summarizing, and reporting.
5. Expect and encourage much originality in self-expression—in discussions, dramatizations, projects, and activities.
6. Recognize that they have less need for extended firsthand and concrete experiences than do slow-learning or average-learning children, because they are able to work with abstractions more easily, see associations and relationships more quickly, and have quick reaction time.

PIEDMONT PUBLIC SCHOOLS
INDIVIDUALIZED EDUCATION PROGRAM

Standard Form

Student _____

Birthdate _____

C.A. _____

Address _____ (include zip) _____

Lives With _____ Relationship _____ Home Phone _____ Work Phone _____

Home School _____ Grade _____ IEP Conference Date _____ Projected Review Date _____

Teacher _____ Program _____ School _____ Date Enrolled _____ Terminated _____

PLACEMENT OFFICE ONLY:

Date Enrolled _____

Teacher _____

Building _____

Program Assigned _____

I. SUMMARY OF PRESENT LEVELS OF PERFORMANCE
(Include statements of progress in each area from last reporting period)

SCHOLASTIC:

PHYSICAL:

ADJUSTMENT:

II. ANALYSIS OF ASSESSMENT DATA
(Report of significant changes since initial IEP)

ELIGIBILITY CRITERIA: _____

PROGRAM AND/OR PLACEMENT CHANGE:

Team Leader: _____ Date _____

Parent: _____ Date _____

PROGRAM RECOMMENDATION:

_____ Date _____

Psychologist: _____ Date _____

Parent: _____ Date _____

131

III. STUDENT GOALS & OBJECTIVES

Academic Year _____

Special Classroom Teacher _____

Support Services _____
(Specify Service)

Name of Student	B.D.	Grade	Program	Building	Teacher	Date Enrolled	
						Date Started	Date Completed
Goals:							
Initial Objectives:				Evaluation Criteria & Progress Notes (include pre-test, post-test data, and grades)			

_____ _____
Signature of person or persons responsible for reporting   Parent Signature   Date
progress on goals and objectives

Student: _____

IV. RELATED SERVICES

Regular Education Program:	Estimated Time/Week	Anticipated	
		Start	End

Support Services: (C.D.S., P.E., Voc. etc.)

Regular P.E. ☐   Adaptive P.E. ☐

My rights and responsibilities have been explained to me in a manner which I understand.

I have had the opportunity to participate in the development of this Individualized Education Program.

I understand all programs and services listed above and give my permission for my child/ward to participate in these programs/services.

I have been informed that the objectives listed on this form are initial objectives and that the person(s) responsible for implementing the objectives will revise and/or add objectives in keeping with the student's progress toward the stated goals.

Parent Signature: _____

Date: _____

V. I.E.P. Committee Members:

Name	Position

The School District shall provide the parent (or the adult student) a copy of the individualized education program.

133

7. Encourage these pupils to develop self-evaluative skills; these children are generally capable of effectively evaluating their own work.
8. Give them many opportunities for leadership responsibilities. Provide opportunities for gifted children to use their talents in helping slower-learning children on a tutorial basis. In some schools children of the intermediate grades with high intellectual abilities also work with primary-grade children.
9. Remember that gifted children have many of the common needs of all children. Although it is true that they are ordinarily accelerated in other aspects of their development as well, their physical growth, muscular coordination, social development, and emotional stability cannot be equated with their rate of growth in mental development.
10. The complete acceptance by the teacher of the high intellectual abilities of gifted children is essential to planning an effective program for them. The teacher who sees gifted children as a threat becomes defensive and is unable to work with them satisfactorily.

DISCUSSION QUESTIONS AND SUGGESTED ACTIVITIES

1. Do you believe that a teacher's expectations of a pupil relate in any way to the child's achievement? Explain.
2. Develop a floor plan of a room environment that would lend itself well to the individualization of instruction.
3. How can the teacher ensure that the social values of social studies education are being attained in a program that individualizes instruction to a high degree?
4. Prepare a small learning kit or package that could be used by pupils in a grade of your choice.
5. Design a sketch of a classroom learning center for social studies and show what you would include in it.
6. Develop a pupil contract suitable for use in a grade of your choice.
7. What procedures for individualizing instruction might be used in groups that (a) have a high percentage of low readers; (b) have limited language ability; (c) have a high percentage of high-achieving, capable pupils; or (d) present difficult management problems?
8. If you visited an elementary school classroom, what would you look for that would suggest that individualizing of instruction is taking place in social studies?
9. What new knowledge and skills does a regular teacher need to have in order to work effectively with handicapped children who are assigned to his or her classroom?
10. What differences can you identify between the practice of "mainstreaming" and that of placing handicapped children in "least restrictive learning environments"?

SELECTED REFERENCES

Affleck, James Q., Sheila Lowenbraun, and Anita Archer. *Teaching the Mildly Handicapped in the Regular Classroom*, 2nd ed. Columbus, Ohio: Charles E. Merrill Publishing Company, 1980.

Barbe, Walter B. and Michael N. Milone, Jr. "Modality," *Instructor*, 89 (January 1980), pp. 44-47.

Cheyney, Arnold. *Teaching Children of Different Cultures in the Classroom: A Language Approach*, 2nd ed. Columbus, Ohio: Charles E. Merrill Publishing Company, 1976.

Dunn, Rita and Kenneth J. Dunn. "Learning Styles/Teaching Styles: Should They . . . Can They . . . Be Matched?" *Educational Leadership*, 36 (January 1979), pp. 238-244.

Guenther, John and Patricia Hansen. "Social Studies Activity Centers," *The Social Studies*, 68 (March-April 1977), pp. 65-69.

Hennings, Dorothy Grant, George Hennings, and Serafina Fiore Banich. *Today's Elementary Social Studies*. Chicago: Rand McNally College Publishing Company, 1980. Chapters 7 and 8.

Herlihy, John G. and Myra T. Herlihy, eds. *Mainstreaming in the Social Studies*, Bulletin 62. National Council for the Social Studies. Washington, D.C.: The Council, 1980.

Joyce, William W., ed. "Mainstreaming: The Least Restrictive Environment," *Social Education*, 43 (January 1979), pp. 57-68. Elementary Education Supplement: six articles.

Maxim, George W. *Methods of Teaching Social Studies to Elementary School Children*. Columbus, Ohio: Charles E. Merrill Publishing Company, 1978. Chapters 9 and 11.

Ochoa, Anna S. and Susan K. Shuster. *Social Studies in the Mainstreamed Classroom*. Boulder, Colorado: ERIC Clearinghouse for Social Studies/Social Science Education, Social Science Education Consortium, Inc., 1980.

Reynolds, Maynard C., ed. *Futures of Education for Exceptional Students: Emerging Structures*. A publication of the National Support Systems Project, University of Minnesota, Minneapolis, Minnesota, 1978.

Turnbull, Ann P. and Jane B. Schulz. *Mainstreaming Handicapped Students: A Guide for the Classroom Teacher*. Boston: Allyn & Bacon Books, Inc., 1979.

SOURCES of CONTENT

6

The Contributions
of the Social Sciences

The prime sources of subject matter for social studies programs through the years has been history and geography. Great faith has been placed in these subjects as vehicles for achieving the goals of the social studies. Along with these subjects, civics was usually included at the upper-grade or junior high school levels. In recent years, increasing use has been made of concepts and subject matter from a broader range of the social sciences. Interesting and exciting social studies programs are being planned that incorporate concepts and content from economics, anthropology, sociology, political science, and, to a lesser extent, psychology, social psychology, and philosophy. It is not accurate to say that these disciplines have replaced history and geography in the social studies program or that their inclusion has reduced the importance of the more traditional subjects. The attention given the newer disciplines simply indicates that there is a growing awareness that they have an important contribution to make in the quest for a better understanding of humankind, society, and institutions.

Although the importance of the social science disciplines to the elementary social studies curriculum is generally conceded, there is not agreement as to how they are to be built into programs. A number of experimental and developmental projects have tried possible patterns and designs. In some cases, the discipline provides the central organizing focus for the study. Some of the programs in economic education have done this. In others, the approach to topics has been cross-disciplinary, with systematic treatment of important concepts from several of the social sciences. Commonly, programs have retained history and geography as organizing frameworks (or *integrating disciplines*) and have incorporated related concepts from supporting disciplines in such studies. It is not possible to say which of these organizational formats is best, because good programs have been developed using several different plans. The teacher's willingness to incorporate ideas from the various social science disciplines, a knowledge of the possibilities they present for social studies instruction, and an imaginative approach to teaching are probably more important to the conduct of good instruction than is the particular organizational scheme followed.

Some of the methods of inquiry of the social sciences can be adapted and applied in a simple way to social studies instruction in

139

the elementary school, and this can do much to stimulate good teaching and learning. For example, the local community and state provide excellent laboratories for the examination of primary source materials. Pupils can examine firsthand some of the same traces of events used by historians in studying local history. They can visit museums and historical sites and can examine original documents. Instead of simply keeping a boxful of photographs or newspaper clippings of early life in the community, the class might arrange and label them, thereby making a good study collection. Pupils can be taught to be more precise in the statement of questions to which they seek answers. This is not to suggest that all pupils are to become miniature social scientists or that all of the instruction needs to follow this pattern.

GEOGRAPHY AND THE SOCIAL STUDIES

Geography has traditionally occupied and continues to occupy a position of central importance in the social studies curriculum. Events in modern times have underscored the need to study geography from a global perspective at all levels. Social studies units and topics have a place in space, and geography is concerned with the character of those places. The nature of an area and the way it relates to other areas are both of great significance in understanding human occupancy and use of the earth.

The teaching of geography has suffered somewhat because of the persistence of traditional and stereotyped notions about the nature of geography. School geography has been dominated by a preoccupation with describing and naming various features of the physical environment: locating rivers; naming mountains; learning places, products, capes, and bays. Such descriptive teaching allows little if any opportunity to approach geographic concepts in a thoughtful and reflective way.

Geography is a science that is concerned with the study and description of the earth. Traditionally, this has meant physical geography, with studies focusing on the unequal distribution of such phenomena as water, minerals, climate, productive land, vegetation, land forms, and so on. Undoubtedly, the intense interest that people have in the world in which they live and their desire to find out what lies beyond the immediate surroundings gave rise to the development of the science of geography. As early people began to move from one place to another on the earth, they began to notice that one place differed from another, and to make observations of these differences. In time, these observations were systematically recorded and were gradually brought together into the discipline of geography. Geographic knowledge became extremely useful, and indeed essential,

140

for travelers, explorers, military leaders, and those engaged in trade and commerce.

As people found their way into all parts of the world, knowledge of the physical geography of the earth greatly increased. All parts of the world were explored in a gross way and were to some extent described and mapped. Then the emphasis in geography began to shift from simply describing phenomena to explaining the differences that were found from one place to another. In addition, the relationships between the physiographic and biotic elements within those areas were beginning to be explored. The study of the uniqueness of a particular area—the study of the factors that make an area different from any other area of the earth—is embodied in the concept of *areal differentiation*. Also, relationships between areas were explored; that is, the links and bonds, either natural or human-made, that develop between places. Such studies concern themselves with the concept of *spatial interaction*. These two concepts—areal differentiation and spatial interaction—are central to the understanding of the concerns and approaches of modern geography. Although there are other important concepts in geography, these two serve as the backbone of modern programs of geographic education at all levels.

Teaching Suggestions

The primary-grade teacher will have no difficulty finding ways to include geographical elements in social studies units. Much of the early geography teaching centers about the local community. The primary-grade child may experience and observe firsthand in the local community various land and water forms—lakes, creeks, islands, gullies, slopes. The teacher encourages children to explore the various forms of native plant and animal life and observe the characteristic changes of these with changing seasons of the year. With some help from the teacher, the children can build their understanding of ideas such as the following:

1. People adapt themselves to conditions in the environment.
2. Transportation plays an important part in the distribution of food.
3. Nature changes the character of the earth.
4. The same land can be used for many different purposes.
5. Every day we use things that have come from all over the world.

The opportunities for children to explore geographically in and around the school site should not be overlooked. A primary-grade class visits a nearby basement excavation for a new home. The children observe the various layers of soil and the teacher calls their attention to the many roots found in the fertile topsoil. The class is able to obtain samples of the various strata of soil to take back to their classroom for an experiment in seeing how well plants grow in

141

the various layers—an early beginning in the appreciation and understanding of the value of soil conservation. The presence of earth-moving equipment suggests that human beings are not completely at the mercy of natural phenomena but can, within certain limits, do things to modify the environment. Pupils learn that sometimes these modifications are helpful, but other times they are destructive and harmful. The imaginative teacher can plan similar experiences in purposeful exploration in connection with soil, water, water bodies, minerals, rocks, local vegetation, and surface features. Experiences of this type provide an opportunity to learn and apply an important method of study used by geographers: careful observation of phenomena.

Weather and climate present another area of exploration. Children have viewed weather forecasts on television. The frequency of reference to weather in adult conversations indicates the degree to which weather and climatic conditions have an effect on the lives of people. In primary-grade classrooms, children will want to have their own charts on which they can record various weather data observed each day. The teacher reads the daily temperature, or the children report the official daily temperature that they have heard over an early morning radio broadcast. These temperatures can be shown graphically, thereby applying knowledge of numbers and graphs. Over a period of several weeks or months the graph will show the changes occurring in temperatures and seasons of the year. Children can also record data dealing with wind velocities, cloud formations, precipitation, and similar subjects. They can also make their own predictions based on the data they have collected. Sensitivity to weather changes will again call attention to the changes in native plant and animal life as well as to the adaptations people make to changing seasons. Here the teacher can apply another technique of the geographer: recording data and using simple charts.

A number of opportunities for teaching geography may grow out of the reading and language program of the class. In the basic reading series one will find many stories and selections with a geographical setting. The children read about the family that took a weekend trip to the lake or spent a summer in the mountains. They read about the antics of the monkeys in the zoo and wonder about their natural habitat. Brief explanations and discussions of accompanying geographical elements are helpful in gaining a better understanding of the meaning of the story. Primary-grade teachers spend much time reading to children, and many of these stories present opportunities for geography education. These situations, plus the selections the children read in their classroom periodical and the current affairs that children report, present many opportunities not only for language development but also for developing geographical concepts.

The following is an example of a plan used by one teacher to familiarize primary-grade children with geographic concepts and skills using the globe.

PURPOSE: To develop a familiarity with concepts relating to the globe.

READINESS: Give the children free time to manipulate a globe and explore it on their own.

WORK/STUDY ACTIVITIES: The teacher directs the following questions to the children:

What shape is a globe?
Can you find the North Pole? Place your finger on it.
Where is north on a globe?
Where is south on a globe?
Is south the opposite direction of north?
What divides the north from the south?
Have any of you been to the equator?
Is the equator really a line?
How much of the globe is north?
How much of the globe is south?
What is half of a sphere?
Does anyone know what we call the northern half of the globe?
Does anyone know what we call the southern half of the globe?
How can we tell water from land on the globe?
Does anyone know what we call these large pieces of land?
Can you find a continent in the Northern Hemisphere?
Can you find a continent in the Southern Hemisphere?
Are there any continents that are in both hemispheres?

SUMMARY: How is the globe divided?
                Can you name the parts of the globe we talked about?
                Can you point to the Northern Hemisphere?
                Can you point to the Southern Hemisphere?
                Can you point to a continent?

MATERIALS: As many globes as are available in order that each child can easily explore and manipulate the globe.

Children in the middle and upper grades can delve more deeply into the relationships between the earth and the activities of human beings than they could in the primary grades. They learn that people the world over attempt to satisfy their basic needs in ways that are influenced by their environment, their past experiences, and present resources. Even though the methods various people use to meet these needs in specific regions of the world may seem strange to us, they are not unusual for those who inhabit that region. Although children will *not* be taught that geographic conditions determine how people live, they should learn that geography sets certain limits on the choices available to them. (For example, people in the Arctic are

143

probably not going to find it profitable to grow oranges and bananas no matter what their level of technological or cultural development.) In this connection, children learn that historical and cultural items as well as natural ones have significance in the development of geographic relationships. A few examples of some of the key geographical ideas that should be stressed in the middle and upper grades are

1. Places on the earth have a distinctiveness about them that differentiates them from all other places.
2. Physical and human changes in one part of the world affect people's lives in other parts of the world.
3. The relationship between agricultural resources and human life is less direct in highly urbanized societies than it is in other regions.
4. Areas of the earth develop bonds, interconnections, and relations with other areas.
5. The wasteful exploitation and pollution of natural and human resources pose serious problems for the welfare of the earth's rapidly growing population of human beings.

In the study of various regions of the world, the middle-grade child will follow somewhat the same pattern of exploration and problem solving as in the primary grades. When studying a specific region, such factors as these will be included, although not necessarily in this sequence: the surface features of the region; the plant and animal life characteristic of the region; and the relationship of this life to the climatic and weather conditions that affect the occupations and way of life of the people of the area. From this systematic study of communities in various natural regions of the world, the children can discover some relationships between various geographic conditions and the activities of human groups. For example, they might discover that in places where one finds similar physical geographic conditions, people may live quite differently. The reverse could also be true. How people use natural surroundings depends mainly on cultural factors.

The study of particular communities and regions presents difficult instructional problems, no matter what system is used in selecting them. Too often they are treated in a superficial or romantic way. It becomes easy to make unwarranted value judgments about the people studied, to arrive at hasty and inaccurate generalizations, and to develop stereotyped ideas of people. The tendency has been to stress traditional or legendary aspects of a people's culture rather than coming to grips with their way of life in modern times. The need for accurate information and a proper instructional emphasis is essential if valid understandings are to develop.

The natural regions selected for study should be sufficiently different from one another to help the child learn the characteristic adjustments people make under varying conditions. These then may be compared with life in the local community, stressing the similarities

144

that exist between people. Such a study should, of course, include historical and cultural elements as a natural part of geographic study.

Intensive continental studies are usually not well suited for elementary school grades because the natural, cultural, and historical backgrounds of various sections are generally so diverse that it is difficult to select a unifying set of concepts for the study. Consequently, pupils often learn a number of facts regarding natural items but fail to relate these to the people who inhabit the area. It is ordinarily better to select specific communities in representative regions of the world and study those intensively.

At the beginning of the study of a community or a region, it is helpful, however, to make an overview of the continent on which the region is located. This places the area properly in its larger geographical setting. At the beginning of such units, the teacher often will use a globe and a series of wall maps. Beginning with the globe, attention will be focused on the continent on which the study is to be made, and its location in terms of other known places on the earth will be noted. Then a wall map of the continent can be used to point out the particular area to be studied. This can be followed with a brief study of the geographical features of the continent in terms of their relationship to the particular area to be studied in greater detail. Such a spot location of places will make it easier for the pupil to visualize the types of interrelationships and associations that are possible for a given area.

Some elementary schoolteachers cling to the concept of environmental determinism, although geographers rejected it years ago as an explanation of differing ways of living. Geographic conditions should be taught as factors that relate to, or affect, ways of living but do not *cause* them. If geographic conditions caused people to live the way they do, everyone in a given area of the world would live the same way; and, of course, this is not the case. For example, some of the people of the world who inhabit the deserts live in tents, tend sheep, and live nomadic lives; others who live in desert areas have air-conditioned ranch-style homes, work in comfortable office buildings, and drive modern automobiles.

The teaching of the earth's climatic zones also persists even though this concept, too, has been discarded by geographers. Traditionally, children were taught that the earth had climatic belts known as the Frigid, Temperate, and Torrid zones that encircled the earth at certain latitudes. The implication was that these areas are homogeneous with respect to climatic conditions. This conclusion is in error, because there are places in the so-called Torrid Zone that have snow the year around; places in the so-called Temperate Zone that have winter temperatures as low as forty degrees below zero; and places in the Frigid Zone that record fairly mild temperatures even in the winter months. These zonal designations with respect to climate should *not* be taught. The terms *low latitudes*, *middle latitudes*, and *high*

145

latitudes are acceptable in referring to these parts of the world because they do not imply that a specific climatic condition prevails throughout the area so designated. Climate should not be explained entirely in terms of latitude.

In the study of ways of living around the world, usually at the fourth grade, many programs focus on nonindustrialized societies because these people relate so directly to their surroundings in meeting their basic needs of food, clothing, and shelter. They make their homes and clothing from materials close at hand, and these necessities are usually entirely functional. All food is grown, gathered, or hunted. Where there is trading or other contact with the outside world, ways of living begin to change. Much of value can come from studies of this type, but the teacher needs to be careful not to develop the idea that just because these people meet their basic needs in simple ways, their social organization is easy to understand. Often the customs, mores, and taboos of these cultures are exceedingly complex. When studies of pre-literate or pre-industrial societies are undertaken, the units should be used to demonstrate specific points: people can live under a variety of geographical conditions; these people have less need for the great variety of resources needed by industrial societies; certain human qualities are apparent in all people no matter how they live; people do not need great material wealth in order to be happy; these people spend a disproportionate amount of time seeking basic needs; ways of living change when people meet others from another culture; and so on.

In the fourth grade, one also finds the study of home states to be fairly common. Many of the states are sufficiently diverse in geography to allow parallels to be drawn with similar places around the world. If the state has plains, for example, pupils might find out where else in the world one finds plains and how the people there make use of them. Or the state might have mountains, or deserts, or good harbors—any of these can be used to teach geographical concepts to children on a broad basis.

The same principles hold true in the fifth-grade social studies curriculum, which in many schools deals with communities or sections of the United States, its history, and the movement of people from one section to another within it. In the consideration of historical developments, life in early America, or contemporary life in various communities of the United States, the teacher should relate geographical factors to the study of such units. What did the geography of the region have to do with the way people lived and how they made their living? Why did large cities grow where they did? Why did the people moving west follow certain routes? How were people able to make use of the resources they found? All these questions relate to geography, and geographical understanding should be used to help explain them.

In the upper grades, many social studies units provide the opportunity to relate human activities to the environment. Children should learn how such social functions as making a living, producing goods, building homes, making clothing, transporting goods, and communicating ideas relate to the specific region in which people live. They should also develop skill in the use of the tools of geography—charts, graphs, source books, and, most particularly, maps and globes.

In the middle and upper grades, some attention should be given to the historical dimension of geography. For example, in studying the location of cities, teachers frequently have pupils explain why the particular place is a good location for a city. What is often overlooked in such an exercise is that the choice was made a hundred or two hundred or even more years ago. *At that time* in terms of the technology of the period, the site may have been a good one, but in terms of present-day technology it may be a bad site. If the choice of a place for a city were made today, perhaps it would be located somewhere else. Ghost towns are good examples of poor site selection for permanent settlement. The same applies to many other features of the environment that bear the imprint of human presence. Roads today were formerly cow paths and horse trails or old logging roads. Industrial centers grew up in places that were easily accessible to employees who walked to work or who rode trolleys. Downtown shopping centers were established before automobile parking became a problem. Instructive and interesting studies can be made of areas as they were in early days: land division and use, the pattern of transportation, the location of processing and manufacturing facilities, the location and distribution of markets, and interactions with surrounding areas can be noted. The study then shifts to an examination and analysis of these factors in the same area as they are today, the pupils thereby gain an understanding and appreciation of the problems related to area growth and change.

In this connection, too, geographic thinking can be stimulated through the consideration of hypothetical propositions. For example, a fifth-grade class might consider the following proposition: Suppose instead of being located in northern Minnesota, the large iron deposits of the Mesabi had been discovered in southern Missouri. What effect might this have had on the location of northern cities? Would the major transportation systems and routes of the area be the same as they are today? Would major industrial and manufacturing centers be located where they are today? Teachers can easily devise problems of this type from time to time by selecting a situation and shifting a critical variable. Pupils cannot arrive at final answers to such problems, but they can speculate on possible alternatives and can demonstrate their ability to apply their geographic knowledge. Hypothetical propositions, if well selected, provide good ways for a teacher to evaluate children's understanding of important concepts and their ability to transfer such knowledge to other situations.

One teacher used the following exercise to alert children to the origins of place names in the local area, which led the class to the development of the geographic concept of successive occupance.

PURPOSE: To explore the origin of names within a specific geographical area.

READINESS: Brainstorm a list of names of places with which you are familiar within a geographical area. After brainstorming, compile an additional list from maps that have been distributed (example: a map of the home state or local county). Perhaps a total of fifty to sixty names would be a good stopping point.

ACTIVITIES: Categorize the names as to their origin: Indian names, names of explorers, famous people, early settlers, ethnic names, and so forth.

Have the children decide on the fairest way of distributing the names so that each has two or three place names to research.

Each child will then research the names using resource books, interviews, letters to various city or community information sources to determine the origin of the name. This is done over an extended period of time.

SUMMARY: As each child obtains the information, display it on a bulletin board attaching it with yarn to the particular geographical location on a map. Relate this information to the history and settlement pattern of the area.

MATERIALS: Maps of the area under study.

HISTORY AND THE SOCIAL STUDIES

Many lay persons as well as educators believe that history can and should contribute directly to attaining the broad goal of citizenship education. For this reason most states have legislative requirements calling for the teaching of state and national history. A knowledge of history supported by actual experiences in the practice of responsible citizenship in the school and classroom unquestionably contributes to a strengthening of loyalties and helps children identify with their historical background. Persons develop love of country, loyalty, and fidelity through a knowledge, appreciation, and understanding of the struggles of the people who contributed to the building of this great and powerful nation. History teaching is valuable in this respect if it provides opportunities for the child to identify with the past. The historical experiences of the nation then become part of the heritage of individual children and, thus, a part of the common culture. This was amply demonstrated by the interest generated in historical and

148

heritage studies resulting from the celebration of the nation's Bicentennial in 1976.

Knowledge of history does not lend itself to the practical solution of everyday problems *in the same way* as does a knowledge of spelling words, or skills in reading or mathematics. Because little direct relationship between a knowledge of history and daily problems of living exists, it cannot and should not be thought of as an entirely practical subject. In this sense, history resembles literature, art, and music in that its contribution may lie along cultural lines rather than along strictly practical ones. Although children will not apply their knowledge of history directly to the solution of the many complex problems of the 20th century, it will give them an insight, appreciation, and understanding of these problems.

Teaching Suggestions

The teaching of history in modern elementary programs occurs within the various social studies units of the grades, and history contributes substantially to such units. The emphasis in modern programs is on understanding the past, the people who lived during those times, their problems and ways of living, and their struggles to meet basic needs. History taught in this way helps the child develop a better understanding and appreciation of human growth through the years—not only along political lines but in all ways—that contribute to a richer and more abundant life. This would include a study of the growth of the arts, sciences, literature, humanitarian movements, and other cultural aspects of human development.

The following represent *samples* of major generalizations from the field of history that have been used as organizing ideas in developing programs in historical study:

1. The history of a country has a definite bearing on the culture, traditions, beliefs, attitudes, and ways of living of its people.
2. People are influences by values, ideals, and inherited institutions as well as by their environment.
3. Several civilizations have risen and fallen in the history of human societies; many have contributed to existing civilizations.
4. Human societies have undergone and are undergoing continual, although perhaps gradual, changes in response to various forces, but not all change is progress.
5. Guidelines for understanding thought and action in contemporary affairs can be derived from the historical backgrounds of society.

A good social studies program in the elementary school will help the child build psychological bridges or links with the past through a series of planned experiences. The following are a few examples of activities that may be helpful for this purpose.

149

Opportunity to Examine Objects of Historical Significance

Children are intensely interested in objects of historical significance, particularly if they can examine them closely and handle them. Items from the past that will be helpful in teaching are such things as: Indian arrowheads, artifacts from past wars, a facsimile of a slave contract, a family Bible, deeds, photographs, church membership rolls, school records, a hymnal, and branding irons. Children may bring items of this type to school to share with their classmates. Such objects may have some monetary value and must be handled accordingly. If a particular item is highly valued, it is best for the adult owner to bring it to the school to show the children and tell them of its significance.

In addition to historical realia that can be brought to the classroom or to those that may be in a school museum, the teacher should look into the permanent museum resources of the community. Most larger communities maintain exhibits of historical materials significant to the local community and state. School groups are always welcome to make visits to local museums and are frequently taken on guided tours through the exhibits. Some museums change their displays from time to time and will on request furnish schools with information concerning their current exhibits. These resources

This sixth grade girl is not sure she is enjoying the first hand lesson in how hair was curled in earlier times! A local museum provides opportunities for direct experiences of this type for schoolchildren. How was the curling iron heated?

present valuable opportunities for teaching history and need to be used extensively.

The best use of the museum can usually be made by pupils after they have had an opportunity to develop an understanding of the material on display. This means that visits will be made after the pupils have been able to explore ideas and concepts in the classroom through reading, study, and discussion rather than at the beginning of a unit. They will then be ready for the clarification of ideas: they can ask intelligent questions and can enrich their understanding through the museum visit. In taking pupils to a museum, teachers will want to ready the class beforehand by identifying a few relevant questions concerning the items to be observed.

Many museums in the country have assembled artifacts, pictures, and other items of interest into kits that are available to schools on a rental basis. Study kits ordinarily have a teacher's guide providing background information for the teacher as well as providing practical suggestions concerning the use of the material.

Opportunity to Talk with Older People of the Community

Children are fascinated when old-timers talk of their exciting experiences in the early community. They are surprised and electrified by the thought that the person now speaking to them served with General Eisenhower or shook President Kennedy's hand. These experiences make real people out of historical figures and remove them from the realm of myth and unreality. Interviewing persons who have had firsthand experience with an event under study is a technique often used by historians.

Almost every community has one or more persons who has devoted a substantial amount of time to the study of local history as a hobby. These individuals are excellent resources for the classroom teacher, not only in their personally speaking to the pupils but in directing the teacher's attention to other resources that might otherwise be overlooked. To catch some of the enthusiasm and interest such persons ordinarily have for history is, in itself, a valuable experience for both the teacher and the pupils.

Oral History

The structured interviews or informal conversations with persons of historical significance in the local community can be preserved as oral history by using cassette tape recorders. This procedure has the added instructional value of involving pupils themselves on a firsthand basis in gathering historical data. The taped interviews should be structured to the extent that pupils have identified the questions to be asked and the sequence in which they are to be presented. Pupils should, however, be encouraged to include follow-up questions that emerge as the interview progresses. Oftentimes the interaction between the pupil interviewer and the subject becomes stilted because the pupil asks only the questions that are prepared in advance.

151

It helps if pupils simulate the interview, or a portion of it, in advance with a classmate serving as the subject of the interview. The cassette tape recorder should be used for the simulation, too, just as it will be used in the real interview. A good-quality taped interview will result only if the interviewer has good interaction skills, and if the substantive aspects of the subject matter and the technical elements of the recording are well planned and implemented.

If good classroom preparation precedes the interview, pupils may obtain taped interviews of a quality that can become a part of a central collection of materials dealing with local history. It is necessary to obtain a signed release from the person being interviewed if the material is to be used beyond the work of the class. Where it is possible to do so, pupils may also want to secure a photograph of the person being interviewed.

Use of Historical Films and Recordings

A number of films and recordings dealing with historical incidents and personalities can help place children in the setting of the historical period under study. These may be biographical sketches of persons or an authentically portrayed reproduction of a historical incident. Through these mediums children can at least for the moment identify so strongly with the portrayal that they share the anxieties, fears, joys, and disappointments of the historical figures. The popularity of this type of program on television and in commercial movies attests to its appeal to children.

Reading Materials

There is a plentiful supply of well-written, exciting books of a historical nature that have great value in helping children identify with the past. Children do this when they become "lost in a book." In the vivid accounts of the adventures of early explorers, the child relives the perils, dangers, and excitement of Lewis and Clark, the disappointments and trials of Abe Lincoln, the hazards of a trip across the western plains, or the rugged winters of Wisconsin.

Using Interesting Study Projects

In addition to the learning activities planned specifically to help the child build psychological bridges with the past, the teaching of history in the elementary school can be enlivened and made more meaningful through the use of a variety of other activities. The following are examples of only a few that have been used successfully by elementary schoolteachers:

1. *Collect and exhibit* old photographs that show the history of the community.
2. *Collect and try* pioneer recipes, learn folk dances, investigate local cultural contributions of various nationality groups.

These pupils are participating in candle dipping, a process of ancient origin. Teachers often use this activity to help children gain a sense of appreciation for the hardships of life in earlier times. Suggest other activities that could be used for this purpose when studying local, state, and national history.

3. *Write items* of local history for the school paper or for the local newspaper.
4. *Write biographical sketches* of early settlers in the community.
5. *Investigate the history* of some important old buildings in the community.
6. *Trace the history* of some local industry such as mining, manufacturing, or lumbering.
7. *Make models* or sketches of oxcarts, prairie schooners, canoes, spinning wheels, or other pioneer equipment.
8. *Paint a mural* of some aspect of the history of the local community or state.
9. *Write and present* a pageant telling the story of some aspect of local, state, or national history.
10. *Collect songs* of various periods of history and present a costumed recital of them.
11. *Make a model* of the town as it looked 50, 75, or 100 years ago, or a diorama of life in the town at an earlier time.
12. *Make a topographical or relief map* of the local area indicating points of historical significance.
13. *Use historical settings* for creative dramatics activities.
14. *Make pictorial time lines* tracing periods of national, state, or local history.

153

15. *Prepare bulletin boards* and other exhibits having a historical theme.
16. *Write, plan, and prepare* short plays or presentations in connection with holiday observances.
17. *Organize a junior historians club* in the classroom and establish contact with the local and state historical societies.

Holiday Observances

Some of the most satisfying and long-remembered experiences children have in the elementary school are those associated with the observance of holidays. Many schools and states require observance of holidays such as Presidents' Day, Thanksgiving Day, Veterans' Day, Martin Luther King Day, and other days of import to the local community and to the state. Although school programs related to the observance of such historical holidays are often guided more by fancy than by historical fact, these occasions, nonetheless, present excellent opportunities to teach effectively the associated historical material.

The chief contribution that holiday observances can make to the education of young children is to acquaint them with their rich cultural heritage and help them grow in their appreciation of it. With this in mind, the teacher can plan a short unit related to the holiday, keeping the content simple but truthful. Commonly, such short units have as their culminating activity a dramatization that is shared with another class.

If the teacher does not plan to devote more than a class period or two to such an observance, the reading of an appropriate story or poem, followed by discussion, can be a profitable experience. After the reading, the children can participate in a suitable follow-up activity such as drawing, painting, singing a related song, writing an original poem or story, or listening to a recording, or they can use the story for creative dramatics. This is also an appropriate time to view a film dealing with some aspect of history related to the holiday or to listen to a recorded dramatization of a historical event. In this same connection the teacher may discuss with the class the significance of a classroom picture or a symbol such as the flag, the Declaration of Independence, the Constitution, or the national anthem. The amount of time spent on activities of this type ought always to be weighed against their value as educational experiences.

Helping Children Understand Time Concepts

The teaching of historical material to elementary-age pupils must take into account the problems they encounter in dealing with time concepts. The young child in the primary grades deals almost entirely in the here-and-now. Birthdays seem a long way off; Christmas seems never to come; mother and father are "old" people. Young children are interested in what will happen this afternoon, tomorrow, or today after recess. Anyone who has traveled with young children knows how endless the time seems to them and knows how frequently they ask, "Aren't we there yet? How many more towns?"

The understanding of time in the historical sense represents a fairly mature level of dealing with time and, therefore, should not be expected of young children. The development of time concepts should begin with time situations that are within their realm of experience. Children should be given help in learning to read clock time and in understanding references to the parts of the day, days of the week, months, seasons, and the year. Even though primary-grade children make statements about things that happened "a hundred years ago," they have little comprehension of the real meaning of the expression and simply use it as a vague reference to something that happened in what seems to them a long time ago.

The placing of related events in chronological order requires considerable maturity and, except for the events within the child's own experience, should not be expected of children below fifth or sixth grade. The use of time lines in the upper grades may be helpful in teaching the extent of time separating one historical event from another. They must, of course, be accurately drawn and are more effective if events are represented pictorially. Research on this problem seems to indicate that below the sixth grade the use of time lines is questionable.

ECONOMICS AND THE SOCIAL STUDIES

Of the newer social sciences that are gaining a place in the social studies program, none has received more attention or been promoted with more enthusiasm than has economics. In one form or another, economic education has been a part of the American school curriculum for many years. The Joint Council on Economic Education, representing business, labor, education, agriculture, and other groups, organized in 1948, has along with its affiliated local and state councils actively promoted economic education in the schools.

Economics is the study of the production, distribution, exchange, and consumption of goods and services that people need or want. In a modern industrialized society such as ours, wants and needs are great because individuals have an expectation of a high standard of living. Moreover, the processes involved in the production, distribution, exchange, and consumption form an interrelated web of relationships. So directly are individuals enmeshed in it that almost everything they do is, in one way or another, related to our economic system. Economic education concerns itself with helping pupils achieve an understanding of some of the basic relationships between our economic system and our way of life, thereby enabling them to make informed decisions on economic matters.

155

These samples represent major generalizations from economics that have been used as organizing ideas in developing programs in economic education:

1. The wants of people are unlimited, whereas resources needed to fulfill wants are scarce; hence, societies and individuals have to make choices as to which needs are to be met and which are to be sacrificed.
2. The interdependence of peoples of the world makes exchange and trade a necessity in the modern world.
3. Economic systems are usually mixed with both public and private ownership and with decisions made both by the government and by individual members of society.
4. Increased specialization in production has led to interdependence among individuals, communities, states, and nations.
5. In the complex, modern industrialized society of today, government plays an important role in the economic life of society.

Teaching Suggestions

The elementary school program of instruction should be built around basic economic concepts (such as production, distribution, exchange, and consumption) that are related to one or more generalizations of the type listed previously. Each of these fundamental concepts can be developed with pupils in many of the unit studies. There may be times, however, when particular units are selected because they have special usefulness in developing specific economic concepts. Units on The Market in the primary grades are of this type and ordinarily focus on the distribution of needed goods.

Learning resources and teaching materials for economic education in elementary schools are available in increasing quantities. Perhaps the best source of such learning resources is the Joint Council on Economic Education, 2 West 46th Street, New York City 10036. From this source, the teacher can secure sample units, scope and sequence charts, background information, and other teaching materials, as well as information concerning other sources of aids for teaching economic concepts.

Learning activities such as the following can be used in developing economic concepts:

1. Examine ways that people depend on each other in their families, neighborhoods, and communities. Relate this to the need for many different kinds of jobs.
2. Compare work roles of today with those in colonial times to discover differences between cottage-industry procedures with assembly-line production.
3. Study different types of advertising to learn how producers create consumer needs and wants.

4. Compare wages paid to workers in terms of such things as the (a) level of education required for the job; (b) extent to which the job requires highly developed skills; (c) length of the preparation or training program for the job; (d) amount of risk to the worker.
5. Role-play negotiations between buyers and sellers; employers and employees in a salary dispute; a consumer with a complaint about a product and a retailer; a customer who has been overcharged and the repairman who did the work.
6. Use newspapers to compare prices of items among various retailers. Relate this to factors that affect pricing policies.
7. Study the concept of seasonal employment as it relates to employment patterns in different parts of the country.
8. Study government regulation of business operations in terms of consumer protection, quality control, and ethical business practices.
9. Familiarize children with local businesses through the use of field trips and resource persons.
10. Study personal and family budgeting procedures to illustrate the relationship between income and expenditures, the difference between wants and needs, and the necessity of choice making.

The following sequence illustrates how a primary-grade teacher developed the concept *division of labor* with a class.

OBJECTIVE:	Pupils will be able to give an example of division of labor.
READINESS:	Have children discuss jobs they know about in their family or neighborhood by responding to these questions:
	Do *you* have a job at home? What do you do?
	What is the difference between your job and the jobs of grown-ups?
	Explain that during the next few days they are going to learn about different kinds of jobs in the community.

WORK/STUDY ACTIVITIES: Have the children make a chart with the following headings:

	Name of job	*Reasons for the job*
1.	_____	_____
2.	_____	_____
3.	_____	_____

Instruct the children to take the chart home with them and complete it with the help of their parents, naming three different jobs in the community.

157

On the following day have the children compare and discuss their lists with each other.

Compile a list of as many different jobs as possible on the chalkboard. Children should pick one from their individual lists until everyone has had a turn to name one. Keep going as long as *different* jobs are named.

Have children discuss the need for a variety of jobs by responding to these questions:

Why is it that we have so many different jobs in our community?

Why couldn't each family do all these jobs itself?

Why do you suppose people in a community divide the work the way they do?

Do you mean that people who have these jobs have special skills? What do you mean?

Do you think people can do their jobs better when each person has a special job? Why do you think so?

Tell the pupils that when people divide work so that each one does something special, we call that *division of labor.* Write this term on the chalkboard. Discuss this term by having pupils respond to these questions:

Does anyone know another word for *labor?* (Pupils suggest *work* as a synonym for labor. This is discussed and examples are provided.)

Can anyone tell us in his or her own words what division of labor means? (Pupils respond that "division of labor means dividing the work.") This is discussed and examples are provided.

CONCLUSION: Have the pupils tell in their own words how they see the division of labor in these places:

in their school	at the shopping center
in their families	in a hospital
in the supermarket	at the airport
at the post office	anywhere else they may have visited recently

POLITICAL SCIENCE AND THE SOCIAL STUDIES*

The problem of precisely defining the scope, concerns, and limits of political science is a difficult and technical one, and most writers in this field have their own definition of it. For purposes of the elementary school social studies curriculum, political science can be regarded as a discipline concerned with the study of government, political processes, and political decision making. Some of this is handled through content in courses that are nominally history. In the upper grades, many schools have had courses called civics comprised of instruction in the role, function, and organization of government with

*Political science concepts and content are closely related to law-related education discussed in the next chapter, and it is reasonable to assume that the two would be combined in the social studies curriculum of the elementary school.

some attention to political processes, political institutions, and political decision-making as these apply to citizenship behavior.

Three ideas are basic to the understanding of the organization of human societies. One is that all societies have developed ways of establishing and maintaining social order; the second is that the central order-maintaining instrument has great power over the lives of individuals subjected to it; and the third is that all such systems demand and expect a loyalty to them when they are threatened by hostile opposing forces. It is apparent that if individuals are to function in a society, they must conduct themselves in politically appropriate ways. Not to do so might result in disastrous consequences. Therefore, societies provide ways of inducting the young into the political life of the society. Through this process, children internalize a set of values, beliefs, and attitudes that are consistent with the political system of the society. They learn how the system functions and eventually they contribute to its perpetuation. This process of learning has come to be called *political socialization.*

All of this is relevant to the elementary schoolteacher of social studies. Recent research suggests that the values and attitudes undergirding political socialization are formed fairly early in life. Pupils are able to add to their fund of information and knowledge, to be sure, but basic political orientation is well established during the early years. When children are in the elementary and junior high schools, they are still relatively flexible in their political outlook, making these years extremely important from the standpoint of their political socialization.

As is the case in all the other disciplines contributing to the social studies curriculum, certain organizing ideas from political science are used to provide a focus for studies. The following represent samples of major generalizations from political science that have been used as organizing ideas in developing units:

1. Every known society has some kind of authority structure that can be called its government; such a government is granted coercive power.
2. A stable government facilitates the social and economic development of a nation.
3. All societies have made policies or laws about how groups of people should live together.
4. The decisions, policies, and laws that have been made for a given society reflect and are based on the values, beliefs, and traditions of that society.
5. Throughout history human societies have experimented with many different systems of government.

Teaching Suggestions

The school program needs to begin early in helping children develop a political orientation. They need school experiences that fa-

The class in this photograph is visiting the chambers of the state legislature. Why is it important that each generation of schoolchildren have some firsthand contact with various governmental bodies at the local, state, and national levels?

miliarize them with the techniques of democratic procedures and that help develop a sense of appreciation for the liberties enjoyed by citizens of this nation. Such appreciations and skills must be built in part on a foundation of knowledge. Accompanying the development of these understandings, children should be given practice in using their knowledge and skills in the regular work of the class and the school.

Perhaps the best way to teach concepts drawn from political science at the early levels is to select those that can become a part of the immediate life of the child. For example, primary-grade children can learn that when people live together they must establish and observe rules. When people have rules, they know what they can and what they cannot do. Rules are made so that everyone is treated fairly. Children can understand this because they have rules in their classroom, in their school, and in their homes. They can learn that grownups have rules, too. These are written down and are called laws. When people break the rules, or laws, they are usually punished in some way. If some people keep on breaking the law or do things that are very harmful to other people, they are not allowed to live with other people in the community. In this way, children learn not only that laws limit what one can do but also that laws have a protective function. As a result of instruction and firsthand experiences in group life, children's concepts of rules and laws, as needed for

160

orderly living, develop. Naturally, such concepts are given increasingly greater depth as the pupils progress through the grades. For example, later in the grades, they will learn that rules and laws are not exactly alike; laws are more binding than are rules.

The program for building civic competence begins with the introduction of the most elementary concepts relating to people living and working together under a system of order than preserves individual freedom. Great stress is placed on applying learnings as they are presented. Theoretical and complex explanations of the structure of government are inappropriate at this level. The main goals are to get children to handle themselves in responsible ways, to see the need for order in living, to govern their actions with consideration for the rights of others, and to realize that the whole realm of human activity is based on a system of rules and laws. Although children at this level are too immature to comprehend the meaning of freedom as an abstract concept, they can, nevertheless, understand it in terms of activities in which they can choose their own pupil leaders or help to establish their classroom rules.

As pupils advance to the middle grades, more can be done in direct teaching of the ways our system of government functions. At this level, pupils also have greater opportunity to participate in school activities that promote civic learnings. For example, they can take a more active part in the school council if there is one, they can serve as members of the safety patrol or as playground monitors, and they can assume greater responsibilities for affairs within their own classroom.

The exact concepts and learnings to be included in each of the three middle grades will depend on the content of the school curriculum. In the fourth grade, units on the home state are filled with good possibilities for civic learnings. Pupils can study the early beginnings of their state and learn how its government developed. The teacher will need to be careful not to make the concepts relating to state government too difficult for children of this age. Even the matter of differentiating between a city, a state, and a county, for example, may be quite difficult for some fourth-graders. Should the curriculum call for a study of communities around the world, a part of the study should stress that all of them have some type of government. Pupils will learn that governments are not all like ours, and the teacher will have to guard against having children make unwarranted value judgments about other governments. The essential learning here is that all peoples have some type of government, and although we would not choose their systems for ourselves, their governments may serve the people of those particular countries very well. There may be other cases, of course, where the teacher will want to call attention to unfair actions of governments.

Grade five units dealing with the development of the United States emphasize ways of living during the periods of exploration, colonization, and the westward movement. However, this does not mean that

161

early beginnings in representative government should be ignored. Youngsters at this level can achieve substantial understanding of some of the foundations of the government of this country. They are particularly interested in and ready to learn of the lives of some of the great champions of American freedom. Pupils can learn the differences in the way Spain, France, Portugal, and England ruled their colonies in the New World and relate these colonial attitudes to the kinds of governments that developed in the colonies ruled by these countries. They can learn how local representative government developed in the English colonies and can grasp simple concepts relating to the development of our own national government. It is easy to make such studies too technical and difficult for fifth-graders; ideas will have to be dealt with at a level suitable to the pupils.

The sixth-grade program affords opportunities for pupils to learn something of the governments of other nations, because, at this level, units often deal with countries in various parts of the world. Some schools include a study of early civilizations on the Mediterranean, and this affords an opportunity to show the origins of the democratic concept of government and law and how this idea found its way into our own system of government. If countries of Western Europe are studied, children can learn of the growth of freedom and that modern-day monarchies are based on democratic principles of government. They can also learn that in many nations of the world, individual citizens have little or nothing to say about the way they are governed. Units on Africa are popular in this grade, which makes it possible to show the problems of the governments of new nations.

A unit on the United Nations may be included in the sixth grade, in which case the need for lawful international relations can be developed. This will provide an opportunity for pupils to learn how and why national governments join together for the fulfillment of mutual self-interests. The concept of alliances and their purpose can be studied as it applies to the United States.

The program of the seventh grade depends on the sixth-seventh grade sequence followed in the school. If nations of the Western Hemisphere are studied in the sixth grade, the Eastern Hemisphere nations are usually studied in the seventh grade; or the order can be reversed. Some schools also include home-state studies in the seventh grade. Whatever pattern is followed, there will be many opportunities to include learnings relating to government in connection either with other nations or with the home state.

In most schools, grade eight deals with the development of the United States, and there is ordinarily a heavy emphasis on the growth of the government of this nation. Attention is directed to the early Colonial governments, events that led to the American Revolution, and the formation of the new government. Pupils study the significance of such documents as the Declaration of Independence, the Articles of Confederation, and the Constitution. They learn of our political system and how it functions. They learn how the government of the United States grew in power and how it relates to the private lives of citizens. When pupils complete the eight grades, they should have a functional, citizen's knowledge of government and civic responsibility. They also should have had a great many experiences that will have given them the opportunity to learn, practice, and use democratic citizenship skills. This does not mean that they need not or cannot learn more; it means simply that they have completed the basic, introductory work in civic education that serves as the common foundation for all citizens of the United States.

The following example illustrates how a teacher might create a sensitivity to the need for responsible participation in political decision-making.

TOPIC: Citizen Participation in Government.

PURPOSE: To develop awareness of alternative ways to act on a community problem.

INTEREST BUILDING: "What if I were to tell you that there was going to be a new street in our neighborhood that was going to link 60th Street and the shopping center and that it was going to run straight through Tomkin Park?" Display a map showing the area and the proposed street corridor.

Discuss the feelings of the group concerning this issue. You might list all of the activities that occur in the corridor and put checks next to those that would be disrupted.

"Suppose you did not want this to happen. What could YOU do? The highway department is scheduled to make a final decision in a few weeks and the adults in your neighborhood seem to think that nothing can be done to prevent approval of the project."

"I am going to give you a list of some alternative actions that could be taken. You will be divided into groups of five. In your groups, decide on four actions that seem to be *responsible* and *useful*. Then we will get back into our large group to discuss your decisions. Place your decisions on a chart such as this":

Action	Likely Consequences?	How Responsible?	How Useful?
1.			
2.			
3.			
4.			

The children might also create a list of alternatives that might contain such things as:

163

Arrange to speak with someone from the area Planning Commission.

Hold a meeting of interested children and teachers from your school.

Speak before the PTA or PTSA, the local Garden Club, the Community Club, and other civic groups.

Write an article for your school newspaper and for your community newspaper.

Survey the neighborhood to look for other possible routes, or find out if the new street is really necessary.

Provide time for the groups to do their work, then reassemble. Discuss each alternative in accordance with information asked for on the chart. Try for consensus on the four options that best meet the requirements of being *responsible* and *useful*.

CONCLUSION: Have pupils identify a local problem in which citizen action was involved. Have pupils analyze and evaluate the effectiveness of citizen participation in terms of their earlier discussion.

SOCIOLOGY AND THE SOCIAL STUDIES

Sociology is a broad social science that deals with the study of the structure of society, its groups, institutions, and culture. Sociological studies often focus on the diverse societal and cultural phenomena that influence the behavior of individuals and groups. Sociology is especially concerned with social organization and the way people organize themselves into groups, subgroups, social classes, and institutions. It is difficult to draw a sharp line between the content of sociology and some of the other social sciences because their areas of concern overlap.

Social psychology and sociology concern themselves with somewhat the same social phenomena. Whereas sociology focuses on groups, social psychology studies the individual in a social situation. Social psychology is particularly concerned with the effects of group life on the behavior of individuals. Studies in social psychology deal with the problems of the individual's role in groups, the development of the self-concept, the effects of group pressure on individual behavior, attitudes, and how they are formed, leadership, followership, and the effects of social-class structure.

The following are representative samples of major generalizations from sociology that have been used as organizing ideas in developing social studies units with a sociological emphasis:

1. The family is the basic social unit in most cultures and is the source of some of the most fundamental and necessary learnings in a culture.
2. Social classes have always existed in every society, although the bases of class distinction and the degree of rigidity of the class structure have varied.
3. Every society develops a system of roles, norms, values, and sanctions to guide the behavior of individuals and groups within the society.
4. All societies develop systems of social control; conflicts often arise between individual liberty and social control in societies where both values are sought.
5. The social environment in which a person is reared and lives has a profound effect on the personal growth and development of that individual.

Teaching Suggestions

A considerable amount of content of the elementary school social studies is drawn from sociology. This is particularly true in the primary grades. One of the units studied in first grade is "The Family." Children learn about the structure of this basic group in our society, some of its functions, and the roles of various members. This is usually followed in the primary grades by units dealing with the neighborhood, community workers, community living, and community institutions. As children study the diversification of work that is done in a modern community, they begin to see how various groups are formed, and learn of the purposes of these groups. Later, in the higher grades, pupils will learn that the interests of such community groups are often in conflict and that this sometimes results in disorganization and community problems.

Studies of various cultures should focus on basic social processes rather than on the quaint ways used by the group to achieve them; that is, all groups have systems of communication, worship, education, and government. Much of value can be learned by showing what factors tend to disrupt conventional ways of living and cause people to change to other ways. Pupils in the middle and upper grades can also learn the consequences that befall cultures that do not make necessary changes in their way of living as external conditions change.

In units on the growth of the United States in grades five and eight, as well as in home-state units in the fourth grade, pupils will want to study the cultural, religious, and racial backgrounds of the people who live there. Such a study will show that the United States has benefited from the contributions of many other peoples in the world. Often it is possible for pupils to see concrete evidences of contributions of other cultures in the life about them in things such as the names of towns, cities, bodies of water, festivals, customs, language, and famous men and women in our history. A knowledge of,

165

and appreciation for, the contributions of other cultures to our own can be a strong force in combating harmful aspects of ethnocentrism. Such studies provide a setting in which to deal realistically with pluralism and with the multiethnic quality of the United States.

Certainly a problem that will be receiving increasing attention in the social studies is that of population growth. In its simplest form, the study of population might call for the examination of the location of settlements and population centers. Which areas are densely populated? Which are more sparsely settled and why? In the upper grades, pupils can study more intensively some of the problems that develop in areas of high population density. They can trace the movements of peoples and discover why they move when and where they do. They can study population trends, birth and death rates in countries, and examine problems faced by countries with rapidly increasing numbers of people.

ANTHROPOLOGY AND THE SOCIAL STUDIES

Anthropology, with its several divisions, is often thought of as a unifying social science, because it is by definition the total study of human beings, their culture, and their growth toward civilization. Anthropology is concerned with the development of language, social institutions, religion, arts and crafts, physical and mental traits, and similarities and differences of cultures. Much of the research that has been done on the characteristics of various racial groups has been done by anthropologists. Anthropological concepts become a part of the social studies in the culture studies that are made of human societies.

Anthropological studies are often comparative. Such comparative, cross-cultural studies show the wide range of capabilities of human beings: modern medical practice and the primitive medicine man; affluence and poverty; humanitarian behavior and cruelty and war; urban living and rural life; life in extremely cold areas and life in hot, desert regions. People are, therefore, contradictory creatures, highly adaptive in their behavior, capable of remarkable achievements, rational yet often acting in irrational ways. They can, within limits, control and shape their environment and build a culture. They rely on their ability to think, imagine, and innovate to solve problems of living. This characteristic results in great diversity among the people of the world in how they live, what they believe, and how they conduct their affairs. Nonetheless, people are all part of the human family; all are a part of what is called humankind and all have many common physical and social needs.

A considerable amount of interest has developed in the exciting possibilities for social studies programs with an anthropological ori-

The skillful hands of the adult demonstrates for this cross-age group of children in an alternative classroom the ages-old process of spinning wool into yarn. Experiences of this type can help build a sense of appreciation for the skills and ingenuity of those who lived in bygone days. What processes do persons engage in today that might be demonstrated to school-children a couple hundred years from now as representing "skills and ingenuity of those who lived in bygone days"?

entation. This may be, in part, a result of the increased importance of the non-Western world in international affairs and the traditional interest of the anthropologists in non-Western cultures. The increased interest in anthropology may also stem from the concern of the discipline with concepts that are so closely related to the shaping of the human personality, human institutions, and the evolution of human societies.

The following are representative generalizations from anthropology that have been used as organizing ideas in developing social studies units:

1. Every society has formed its own system of beliefs, knowledge, values, traditions, and skills that can be called its culture.
2. Culture is socially learned and serves as a potential guide for human behavior in any given society.

167

3. Although people everywhere are confronted with the same psychological and physiological needs, the manner in which they meet these needs differs according to their culture.
4. The art, music, architecture, food, clothing, sports, and customs of a people help to produce a national identity.
5. Nearly all human beings, regardless of their racial or ethnic background, are capable of participating in and contributing to any culture.

Teaching Suggestions

Anthropological studies will deal with the concept of culture from many different perspectives—cultural determinism, cultural relativity, cultural diffusion, cultural borrowing, cultural change. Other concepts included in anthropological studies are environment, languages, tools, adaptation, technology, human variation, values, authority, institutions, socialization, and of course, many others. These concepts cut across several of the social science disciplines. Thus, social studies units often contain a substantial amount of information that could be defined as anthropological even though it may not be made explicit in the curriculum. The point is that there is already much in the social studies curriculum of most schools that is anthropological in content. Indeed, the unified concept of social studies has a closer kinship to anthropology, in terms of its attempt to deal with the totality of social phenomena, than it does to any of the other social sciences.

Pupil activities such as the following have been used by elementary schoolteachers in studies having an anthropological emphasis:

1. Trace the development and use of certain tools; associate ways of living with the use of tools.
2. Follow the development of language and communication systems from early signs and symbols to modern information dissemination devices.
3. Discover ways that inventions have changed civilizations.
4. Serve as participant observers in groups of which they are a part, such as their families.
5. Prepare data-retrieval charts to compare the use of resources, tools, technology, or other variables by different groups.
6. Use role playing, simulations, and creative dramatics for cross-cultural comparisons of human behavior.
7. Use music and art to gain insight into the culture of a people.
8. In the upper grades participate in a simulated archaeological dig.
9. Provide experiences in the exchange of goods and services, as, for example, the simulation game involving medium of exchange in Chapter 12.
10. Study artifacts from the local area that provide traces of the early history of the community.

The following sequence illustrates how one teacher used a concept from anthropology in a social studies unit entitled "Changing Ways of Living."

PURPOSE:	To learn how contact with another culture changes ways of living.
READINESS:	Begin the presentation by discussing with pupils changes in ways of living with which they are familiar. This should lead to the idea that the ways of living of people all over the world are changing. Display a photograph of the tundra region showing a sled being drawn by a snowmobile with sled dogs and a tent in the background. Ask pupils whether they think the photograph is one that was taken a long time ago or in recent years and why they think as they do. This should lead to a discussion of the presence of the snowmobile, which means that the group has had contact with the industrial world.
ACTIVITY:	Divide the class into groups of three, and using the resources available have pupils make an inquiry into the specific changes that have taken place in Eskimo life as a result of contact with the outside world and the impact of those changes on traditional Eskimo life. Their findings should be recorded on a chart as follows:

Change	Result
Motorboats	
Snowmobiles	
Guns and steel traps	
Canvas tents	
Sewing machines	
Schools	
Others (specify)	

Provide sufficient time for the groups to do their research, then reassemble as a whole group. Summarize the findings of all groups on a master chart on the chalkboard. Discuss the findings along these lines:

How have these changes been helpful to Eskimo life?
How have these changes been harmful to Eskimo life?
Is it important to keep Eskimo traditions and skills alive?
How might this be done?

Lead the discussion toward the more general problem of what happens when people of one culture have contact with another culture. This deals with the concept of cultural borrowing, although that term need not be introduced to the pupils at this time.

169

CONCLUSION: As a follow-up have pupils, again in groups of three, find other examples of cultural borrowing in back issues of *National Geographic* magazines you have provided. Have them explain how their examples illustrate cultural borrowing.

DISCUSSION QUESTIONS AND SUGGESTED ACTIVITIES

1. Develop inquiry-oriented learning experiences for pupils in a grade of your choice for one or more of the disciplines discussed in this chapter.
2. What are some ways that geographical concepts are important in the study of history? Provide other examples that illustrate the interconnections among the social sciences.
3. Suggest five community resources that might be used in teaching social science-related concepts to children in a grade of your choice.
4. What specific out-of-school experiences of children enhance their ability to understand social science concepts?
5. Select one of the disciplines discussed in this chapter and find out what particular methods of inquiry are used by scholars in that discipline. Explain how—or if—any of these might be adapted for use with elementary school pupils.
6. Examine a social studies textbook and its accompanying teacher's manual. Which of the social sciences are included? Are any not included? Does the text or the manual explain how the content of the book relates to the social sciences?
7. Visit your curriculum library on campus and examine two or three curriculum guides to see how the social sciences are incorporated in the program.
8. What holidays are observed in the schools of your state? Develop a calendar of such days for the school year.
9. How can the study of the various disciplines discussed in this chapter help pupils learn social roles such as *family member, consumer, friend, worker, member of social groups, citizen,* and *self identity?*
10. School librarians frequently organize exhibits around selected themes during the year. For example, "Black History Week" in February provides an opportunity for librarians to draw attention to their Black studies material. Visit an elementary school library. Ask the librarian about other special weeks or events during the year. How might these be tied to the social studies program?

SELECTED REFERENCES

Alleman-Brooks, Janet, Ambrose A. Clegg, Jr., and Alberta P. Sebolt. "Making the Past Come Alive," *The Social Studies*, 68 (January–February 1977), pp. 3–6.

Allen, Rodney F. and John R. Meyer. "Beyond Collecting Information: Oral History as Social Education," *The History and Social Science Teacher*, 15 (Winter 1980), pp. 101–108.

Banks, James A. with Ambrose A. Clegg, Jr. *Teaching Strategies for the Social Studies: Inquiry, Valuing, and Decision-Making*, 2nd ed. Reading, Massachusetts: Addison-Wesley Publishing Co., 1977. Part 2.

Branson, Margaret Stimmann, guest ed. "Teaching American History," *Social Education*, 44 (October 1980), pp. 450–485. (Special issue on the teaching of American history includes six articles and list of sources and resources.)

Fox, Karen F. A. "What Children Bring to School: The Beginnings of Economic Education," *Social Education*, 42 (October 1978), pp. 478–481.

Hennings, Dorothy Grant, George Hennings, and Serafina Fiore Banich. *Today's Elementary Social Studies*. Chicago: Rand McNally College Publishing Company, 1980. Chapters 11, 12, and 13.

Leon, Warren. "Preparing a Primary Source Package on Your Community's History," *Social Education*, 44 (November–December 1980), pp. 612–618.

Lowderbaugh, Thomas E. "Museums, Language, and the Hearing-Impaired Child," *Social Education*, 45 (January 1981), pp. 60–62.

Machart, Norman C. "Doing Oral History in the Elementary Grades," *Social Education*, 43 (October 1979), pp. 479–480.

Mazuzan, George T. and Gerald Twomey. "Oral History in the Classroom," *The Social Studies*, 68 (January–February 1977), pp. 14–19.

Muessig, Raymond H. and Vincent R. Rogers, eds. *Social Science Seminar Series*, 2nd ed. Columbus, Ohio: Charles E. Merrill Publishing Company, 1979. Six volumes.

Rossi, Tom. "Sell 100 Shares When It Reaches $20\frac{1}{8}$," *Instructor*, 90 (March 1981), pp. 71 and 74.

Rushdoony, Haig A. "California's Population Geography: Lessons for a Fourth Grade Class," *Journal of Geography*, 77 (November 1978), pp. 221–224.

7

Social Concerns as Emerging Priorities for Social Studies Education

Social issues and comtemporary challenges that confront society do not always fit neatly within the subject matter boundaries of a social science discipline. Indeed, the implications of many of the problems of modern social life are so far-reaching that they must be studied from an interdisciplinary perspective that goes quite beyond any or all of the social sciences. Moreover, these problems and issues cannot be studied by the learner only once and then filed away. If they are to be understood, the child must return to them time and time again at various grades, each time at an increased level of complexity. Often schools handle these topics as recurring themes that are recycled at higher levels of sophistication throughout the curriculums of the elementary and secondary schools. This chapter deals with six such vital topics that are thought by many to be emerging priorities for society and, therefore, for social studies education.

ENERGY AND ENVIRONMENTAL EDUCATION

One of the essential characteristics that distinguishes a modern nation such as the United States from a less well developed nation is its use of and dependence on various forms of energy. Modern nations have taken burdens off the backs of human beings and animals and have substituted inanimate sources of power and energy. The dependence on various forms of such energy—and in huge and escalating amounts—is absolute in modernized nations. Their economic systems cannot survive without it. They could not sustain their present standards of living if their energy sources were curtailed. The United States consumes more energy on a per capita basis simply to provide food for its people than developing nations such as the Peoples Republic of China use for the entire operation of the country. Perhaps no topic is related more directly to the day-to-day lives of citizens than is energy.

173

Energy is, of course, related to the environment. The relationship occurs at all stages of the energy production–delivery–consumption sequence. Extracting energy sources such as coal, gas, and oil from the earth either scars or pollutes the environment. Processing the raw materials of energy into usable forms and delivering the finished products also does violence to the environment. Similarly, the consumption of energy in most instances has some environmental impact. Thus, one of the major profound social issues of our time is that of providing for the vast energy needs of our modern industrial society while at the same time preserving an environment that can sustain human and other forms of life at an acceptable level of quality.

When European settlers first came to this country, the incredible vastness and abundance of resources they found produced no concern in their minds for the environment. There was fresh water aplenty. Forests and trees were in such abundance that they were perceived as obstacles to land use. There was no shortage of places to dispose of solid wastes. There were no internal-combustion engines or other devices creating large quantities of harmful hydrocarbons to pollute the air. The forests and streams were well stocked with wildlife and fish. What happened in the 300 years that followed provides us with a shocking case study of unbelievable exploitation and waste and an almost total lack of concern for the consequences of this behavior. All this is now too familiar history.

Serious efforts to reverse this trend got underway about two decades ago. National and state leadership, combined with publicity in the popular press and, most importantly, concerned citizen groups, raised the consciousness of the general public to the violence being perpetrated on the ecosystem. More than that, these forces were successful in securing state, national, and local legislation that mandated a halt to environmental abuse. Scientific data relating to the use of certain energy-producing fuels raised the frightening possibility that the planet could experience something in the way of an "eco-catastrophe" in the foreseeable future. The most significant danger signals seemed to be those associated with (1) the use of pesticides, (2) the disposition of solid wastes, (3) air pollution, (4) water pollution, (5) radiation and radioactive substances, and (6) overpopulation.

The present concern for energy use and the related problems of environmental contamination are extensions of earlier efforts in the general area of conservation. The concept of conservation—meaning prudent use—has a reasonably long history in this country. Even during the colonial period some of the thoughtful men of the time (among them Washington and Jefferson) were concerned with conservation in the broad sense. During the middle of the 19th century, conservation efforts were institutionalized, largely as a result of rapidly diminishing forest resources. The U.S. Department of Agriculture established a Division of Forestry in 1880. Federal legislation during the latter half of the 19th century and extending into this century encouraged conservation and conservation education. The amount of federal, state, and local legislation dealing with environmental control has grown at a phenomenal rate in recent years.

It is clear that the turning point in the battle against pollution has now been reached and that people—in this country at least—will henceforth not be allowed to contaminate their surroundings with the same abandon as they have been able to do in the past. Almost everywhere in this nation local and state laws, following the lead of the federal authorities, are becoming much more strict in their control of human behavior that further contributes to environmental problems. More is being done to encourage citizens to be sensitive to the needless use and waste of energy. Similarly, educational programs are being implemented to help citizens use their surroundings more wisely. Recognition of the need for major remedial efforts to alleviate environmental pollution is growing.

Energy and environmental studies are, of course, not the sole province of the social studies. The subject is such a comprehensive one that it can be studied from many points of view. It can be approached from the standpoint of science education, for, clearly, much of our polluted environment is a direct consequence of science and technology. Likewise, the subject is appropriate for health education, because research has established relationships between air pollution and respiratory ailments such as asthma, emphysema, lung cancer, and bronchitis. Certainly energy and environmental studies have geographic, esthetic, sociological, economic, and even political dimensions. Thus, the broad topic is highly appropriate for social studies programs because of its implications for human societies and human life. It is an ideal subject for interdisciplinary studies.

A program of energy and environmental studies should concern itself with three types of broad goals:

1. It should provide pupils with an opportunity to develop a basic understanding of the dimensions of problem's surrounding energy and the environment, the causes and consequences of ecological disaster, the remedial measures now underway, the need for additional corrective legislation and action, *and* similar inputs of information that bear on these important topics.
2. It should help pupils develop an attitude of responsible concern for energy use and the quality of the environment. It should leave them with the feeling that they have a personal investment in their natural surroundings—that energy and environment truly are everybody's business.
3. It should provide pupils with the opportunity to do something themselves about improving the environment. That is, if goals 1 and 2 are concerned with knowledge, thinking, and valuing, this goal constitutes the action dimension of the program.

Studies of energy and of the environment as broadly defined here should be included in the social studies curriculum in at least two ways. First, every unit studied should include attention to energy and related environmental problems throughout the entire curriculum when the topic under study lends itself to such an emphasis. This will include most topics, as can be seen by examining the typical unit titles on pages 13–16. Second, every grade should include one unit of study each year devoted entirely to the systematic treatment of energy and the environment. This program should be planned on a K–12 basis in order to develop important learnings cumulatively as children progress through the grades.

Key Ideas in Energy and Environmental Education

The program of instruction in energy and environmental education should focus on a limited number of basic ideas. These key ideas can be defined along a continuum of complexity and be included in the curriculum at several points. Such a basic idea as the need for food by all living creatures can be dealt with in a simple way in the primary grades in the context of the units on family living, the local community, changing seasons, or meeting basic needs. In the upper elementary school grades, this idea can be expanded and made more complex by getting into such dimensions of it as food chains and webs of life. The planned curriculum should provide ideas, identify emphases, suggest activities, and list learning resources but at the same time should allow for and encourage inspired teaching and learning in this field.

What gives environmental studies vitality and freshness is a spontaneity and originality that are not often found when teaching conventional unit topics. Children can easily relate to energy and environment because these topics are so much a part of their day-to-day lives. Much of what they hear discussed by the adults around them, what they see on television, and what they hear and read in the news has to do with subject matter related to energy and the environment. Teachers can capitalize on this readiness in planning interesting and engaging studies on these topics.

The following key ideas are being suggested to provide a focus for studies dealing with energy and the environment. They are not the only ones that could be used; indeed, they are probably not even the best ones for all parts of the country. They are, rather, a *sample* of ideas that can be, and have been, used as central organizing ideas for energy and environmental studies:

Environment

1. People are now facing critical environmental problems of their own doing.
2. The most imminent problem facing people of the world is food shortage.

3. The problem of food shortage is presently differentially distributed around the world but could ultimately affect all people.
4. Some rehabilitation of the environment and greater restraint of its use are needed in order to maintain an acceptable quality of life.
5. Most of what human beings do has a detrimental effect on natural balances because it interferes with natural communities.
6. The earth is a self-contained, self-sustaining life-support system, consisting of an infinite number of ecosystems.
7. All living organisms fit into a complex environmental interrelationship known as a *food chain*.
8. The food supply for all living organisms depends ultimately on sunlight, soil, air, and water; consequently, anything that destroys these essential resources disturbs the quality of life.
9. All living organisms in some way affect and are affected by their environment.
10. Living things must have minimum space requirements for optimum development.
11. The quality of human life depends ultimately on the natural environment.
12. Increase in human population, if continued at the present rate, will, in the long run, have disastrous consequences for human societies.
13. Waste disposal potentially is at least as severe a problem as is the fulfillment of basic food needs.
14. The effects of the presence of people on the environment has esthetic as well as survival dimensions.

Energy

1. All life depends on energy, the most basic being energy supplied by the sun.
2. Food provides energy for the bodies of human beings.
3. Energy is the ability to do work.
4. The amount of energy is constant; it cannot be created or destroyed, it simply changes form.
5. Energy can be changed from one form to another: mechanical to electrical, electrical to heat, chemical to electrical, and so on.
6. Through the years human beings have discovered new sources of energy.
7. Most of the serious environmental problems that we face are the result of economic growth that has a high dependence on energy consumption.
8. The standard of living of a society is related to productivity; productivity is related to energy use.
9. Energy resources and their use are related to the level of cultural and technological development; industrial societies place heavy demands on the earth's resources.

177

10. Economic development is highly dependent on industrialization, which in turn demands a high level of energy consumption.
11. The introduction and use of new energy sources often result in significant social changes.
12. Energy resources are unevenly distributed around the world; thus, as more nations become developed, interdependence among them is imperative if energy is to be shared.

These ideas are suggested as providing a focus for planning instruction. The specific subject matter should and probably will, in most cases, be selected from topics relating to the local region. Quite naturally, there will be a considerable overlap because many problems are common throughout the country. But case studies and examples should be drawn from the local area.

What follows is a series of specific types of energy-related environmental problems around which studies have been planned, along with a few examples of activities that teachers have used successfully with elementary school pupils.

POPULATION

Pupil Activities to Build Awareness of Rapid Growth

1. Using a *World Almanac* or a copy of the U.S. Census, compare the population of the twenty leading American cities in 1940, 1950, 1960, 1970, and 1980. Are they still ranked in their original order? Which one has increased the most? Why?
2. Make a chart comparing the present-day population of a selected area with its population 20 years ago, 100 years ago, 200 years ago.
3. Make a chart comparing the present birth and death rates of a particular area with the birth and death rates of 1900.
4. Use the telephone directories of 1940, 1950, 1960, 1970, and 1980, to discover growth in such things as (a) schools, (b) hotels and motels, and (c) service stations.

Pupil Activities to Discover Population Distribution

1. Using a map and reference books, compare the populations of various parts of the United States. Why do people live where they do? What areas have the fewest people? Could people be moved to those areas? Why or why not?
2. Construct a map showing areas of heavy population in the city, state, nation, or world. Identify sparsely populated areas. Have pupils give reasons for both conditions.
3. Make a chart of the most rapidly growing areas of population in the state, nation, or world. Discuss the reason for the rapid increase in these areas.

Pupil Activities to Understand the Meaning of Rapid Growth

1. Have pupils use a checkerboard or other similar squares and kernels of corn and try doubling the number of kernels in each square, starting with one. How many squares can be used before there is no longer room to double again? Discuss how this relates to population growth and its implications.

2. Encourage pupils to suggest problems that would be caused by an increase of twice as many persons in their environment.
3. Find pictures of the local area 10, 15, and 20 or more years ago. Have pupils discover how it has changed.

LAND AND WATER USE

Pupil Activities to Build Awareness of Need for Concern

1. Creative dramatics: A public meeting is held to protest closing of a lake to fishing. A biologist explains why it was closed. Have pupils discover what he or she should say. Conduct the drama and include the discussion that followed the biologist's presentation.
2. Compare status reports of your state from the 1850s with those of the present day on some animal, fish, or bird. Identify the reasons for the change.
3. Collect pictures from newspapers and magazines showing misuse of land. Have pupils suggest remedial measures for improved use or what might have been done by foresighted planners to have prevented the misuse from occurring.
4. Obtain data on acres of land under cultivation in 1940, 1950, 1960, 1970, and 1980, in the local area. Have pupils find out why changes occurred.
5. Have pupils list ways that productive farmland is used for other purposes, for example, for urban sprawl, for freeway construction, as land flooded or submerged behind dams. Have them also consider other problems that might have resulted if urban growth had been stopped and no freeways built.

TRANSPORTATION

Pupil Activities to Understand Problems of Congestion

1. Construct a chart to compare the amount of space on a highway required to transport 40 persons in 40 cars as compared with that required to transport 40 persons in a bus. Have them also suggest differences in residential patterns and concentrations of workplaces that would result if everyone were required to ride a bus to work.
2. On a local map, identify points of congestion and hours of highest congestion. Study traffic flows and suggest alternative routes.
3. Prepare a map of the local area showing existing transportation routes. Prepare another map showing an improved arrangement.
4. Show by illustration how air, water, and noise pollution are related to transportation.
5. Carry out a roadside improvement project. This could be a cleanup campaign or the planting of trees, shrubs, or flowers.

NOISE POLLUTION

Pupil Activities to Build Awareness of the Problem

1. Make a tape of various sources of noise pollution. Use this to build awareness of sounds in the environment.
2. Demonstrate instruments that measure the level of sound. Measure the level of sound in and around school at various times of the day.

179

3. Demonstrate familiar sounds of noise pollution such as that of jet planes, stereo rock music, motors, machines, horns, and construction.
4. Take a field trip into the local area to build an awareness of sound. Identify points of especially high noise pollution.
5. Make a map of the local area and label the places with most noises.
6. Prepare guidelines to reduce noise at home and at school. Develop a program of action to reduce noise. Suggest costs of these measures. Where would money come from? What would have to be sacrificed?

AIR POLLUTION

Pupil Activities to Understand Dimensions of the Problem

1. Construct a map of the local region showing places of highest pollution. Explain why these areas have a high level of pollution.
2. Have pupils discover the major sources of air pollution. Present these on charts.
3. Have the class attend a meeting of the local Air Pollution Control Board. Discuss issues considered by the board.
4. Show by illustration why air pollution cannot be only a local problem.
5. Relate air pollutants to problems of health.
6. Discover effects of air pollution on vegetation.

WATER POLLUTION

Pupil Activities to Understand the Relationship of Polluted Waters to Recreation

1. Have pupils discover major sources of water pollution in the local area. Prepare a chart showing those sources. Discuss. Present the chart to local government officials.
2. Make a map of a specified area through which a large river flows. Find out if and/or to what extent the river becomes polluted as it flows.
3. On a map of the United States, identify water bodies that once were contaminated but that have been rehabilitated.
4. Select a water body in the local area that is not available for recreation because of contamination. Plan a strategy to have it rehabilitated. Present the plan to local officials. Begin a movement to mobilize public opinion in support of such an action.

ENERGY USE

Pupil Activities to Build Awareness of Energy Dependence

1. Through discussion, establish the relationship between increasing wants and needs and increased energy consumption. Have pupils find pictures from magazines to illustrate points.
2. Develop a class project to encourage energy conservation in their homes (turning off lights, turning down thermostats, shutting off TV and appliances not in use, and so on).
3. Prepare a bulletin board display of energy-related news stories. Through discussion, establish the importance of energy to the everyday lives of everyone.
4. Have pupils make a survey of their homes to identify energy uses that

180

would not have been in homes 50 years ago, 100 years ago. Discuss in terms of new demands on energy resources.

5. Secure data on sources of energy on which we depend and construct maps, globes, and other visuals based on the data.

6. Have pupils identify values that emphasize increased energy use and values that emphasize energy conservation.

7. Relate energy use to the production of goods and services and to standard of living.

8. Have pupils identify recreational activities that contribute to increased energy consumption and those that do not. Pupils can prepare displays to illustrate points.

9. Familiarize pupils with state and federal agencies that are concerned with energy matters.

10. Have pupils determine the relationship between energy cost and energy use. For example, what impact have higher gasoline prices had on gasoline consumption?

The activities just listed are provided simply as examples of things that pupils can do. They are not meaningful unless they are placed within the context of a larger study. Just to do the activity would hardly be sound teaching and would probably not lead to good learning.

Not all schools in the country have instructional resource centers that provide the teacher with the tools needed for teaching. But in the case of energy and environmental education, every school does have an instructional resource center immediately at hand. All that is required is an imaginative teacher who will open the door of the classroom and step outside. What better instructional center is there for energy and environmental education than the local natural surroundings? Happily, it makes no difference if the school is located in the most congested section of our largest cities or in a remote rural area. Wherever one is, there is an environment that can profitably be studied, and we are all surrounded by energy resources.

Activities for Conservation Education

Some schools may choose to focus on conservation education rather than on the broader topics of energy and environment. Although it is not possible to suggest a great number of learning activities and resources for soil, water, wildlife, mineral, and forest conservation education because of space limitations, the teacher may find the following suggestions helpful. They are intended to serve as *samples* of activities that have been used with success with elementary school-age children.

Use the many good films now available on the topic of conservation. They are thoughtfully prepared, use modern photographic techniques and color to present forcefully the problem of waste and the need for better conservation practices.

181

These young people are participating in the stripping of fish eggs during the class visit to a fish hatchery in connection with their study of the environment. What opportunities can you identify in studies of this kind for the integration of science and social studies?

Take field trips to local conservation or ranger stations, fish hatcheries, farms, and local parks.

Invite speakers to class such as the county agent, a ranger, an agriculture teacher from the local high school, or a member of an outdoor or recreation club.

Relate soil fertility in various ways to plant food elements and community prosperity.

Develop and exchange correspondence with children from different parts of the country, asking for firsthand information of their local conservation problems and what is being done to correct them.

Illustrate in various ways the time needed to recover resources and the impossibility of recovering some resources lost through waste.

Familiarize the pupil with the interest and action of government (local, county, state, and national) in conservation.

Integrate conservation education of such groups as Boy Scouts and Girl Scouts, 4-H club, Future Farmers of America, Camp Fire Girls, and other youth groups with the school program.

Place instructional emphasis on new developments in conservation through the application of scientific knowledge—new uses of resources, more productive farmland, new flood-control techniques, new energy sources.

182

Conduct experiments dealing with conservation:
1. Collect runoff water and determine what it carries.
2. Test a sample of soil for organic matter.
3. Discover how and why grass protects soil.
4. Demonstrate the effect of rapidly falling water on soil.
5. Test the productivity of various types of soil.

Contact various agencies that have an interest in, or dedication to, the cause of conservation for suggestions, teaching materials, or help. Such a list can be obtained from your local county agent or the Department of Natural Resources of your home state.

Conservation education requires a multipronged approach if effective attitudes of conservation are to be developed. The inclusion of occasional units on conservation in the elementary school social studies program are, in themselves, an inadequate response to the need for conservation education. It requires the combined efforts of communities, parents, and schools. It also requires a sensitivity to the relationship of such attitudes as thrift, frugality, economy, and temperateness to conservation.

SOCIAL STUDIES AND THE WORLD OF WORK

Elementary school social studies has for many years concerned itself with aspects of the world of work. The treatment was perhaps not as systematically focused nor handled in as sophisticated a way as it is today, but the emphasis on the world of work was nevertheless there. Units on family life, neighborhood relationships, workers in the community, transportation and communication, food, clothing and shelter, and ways of living in societies past and present are familiar to elementary school social studies. Even though many changes have been made in the social studies program in recent years, these topics are still in the curriculum of most schools. These units and others like them stress work roles, jobs, the importance of work to the community and to the individual, interdependence, and simplified producer and consumer economics. In this context it is obvious that the social studies program is a natural vehicle to teach important ideas and attitudes relating to the world of work.

In the early 1970s, influential persons in this country argued persuasively that preparation for work, including the attitudes and skills needed to perform work, should be the primary emphasis of the school curriculum.[1] No less a figure than the U.S. Commissioner of Education challenged school leadership of America to attend to what

[1] Larry J. Bailey and Ronald W. Stadt, *Career Education: New Approaches to Human Development*, Bloomington, Ill.: McKnight Publishing Company, 1973.

he called "career education" of its children and youth.[2] By this he meant that the school experience should equip all children and youth with saleable skills that would be useful to them in relating to the world of work. The term *career education* was and is used to describe the schools' effort to help children and youth relate to the world of work. Federal funds were made available to schools and colleges to encourage and promote career education. In the 1980s career education as an educational movement lacks the high priority it had a decade earlier, but concern for preparing individuals for the world of work remains a central concern of schools.

In career education, as is the case with energy and environmental education, safety, law-related education, and other such topics, a systematic integrated approach is probably more effective than special units spaced throughout the grades. This, of course, does not preclude the possibility of having special units with a world of work focus, but simply to suggest that such an approach is not in itself adequate. Teaching is strengthened when career education concepts are built into many of the existing units of the social studies program. Most who have been involved in curriculum work in this field suggest that awareness building should be a major goal of a program relating to the world of work in the elementary school. The major components of such a program are these:

Information About the World of Work

Persons are often uninformed about choices available to them when they decide on a vocation. They simply select from those few occupations they have learned about on a firsthand basis from a close relative or from a friend. This explains why some occupations seem to "run in families." Children should *not* be encouraged to make occupational choices when they are in the elementary school. But they can begin to build a background of knowledge about a broad spectrum of occupations, which will one day help them make an intelligent career choice.

Opportunity to Explore Work Values

Children need to see the connection between values that are stressed in school, such as responsibility, dependability, punctuality, cooperation, trustworthiness, and others, and the world of work. They need to develop a sense of appreciation for a job that is well done. They need to learn what it means to take pride in one's work.

Personal Choice Making

Part of the awareness building of career education should include the opportunity to make decisions and to exercise choices. De-

[2]Sidney P. Marland, Jr., "Educating for the Real World," *Business Education Forum*, 26 (November 1971), pp. 3-5.

cisions surrounding career choices will one day be an extension of decision-making skills the child has exercised throughout life. One can hardly expect wise career choices from one who has had a life history of thoughtless conformity, wholly lacking in decision-making experiences.

Society and the World of Work

Children need to learn about the relationship of the individual to society *through* the world of work. What one does for a living does not simply have to be a job that has no purpose other than as a way of earning enough money to pay bills and stay alive. Work contributes to the life and health of the larger society. Society's need to have jobs performed and performed well can be learned by the youngest children. All of us depend on others to help us meet our basic needs. Social studies units that deal with so-called "community helpers" provide opportunities for learning outcomes of this type. Work is so important to society that individuals are often identified by others in accordance with what they do for a living, "he is a cabinetmaker," "she is an airlines attendant," "he is an accountant in town," "his wife is a kindergarten teacher in a local school," and so on.

Many of the outcomes sought in career education are affective, dealing with attitudes, appreciations, and feelings. This means that pupils will need a broad exposure to the world of work and opportunities to respond to it in a variety of ways. Such experiences have feeling as well as knowledge dimensions. For example, children may want to express their own feelings about certain occupations, and the strength of those feelings should be explored. Children should be encouraged to find out the attitudes of their parents toward the jobs they hold. Why do they like them or dislike them?

Some attention should also be given to basic economic concepts such as producer, consumer, goods, services, division of labor, and interdependence. Children must understand the importance of work both to the individual and to society. Instruction should stress society's need for a wide range of talents and abilities in order that the many jobs that need doing will get done. Society has a need for a constant flow of competent persons in order to operate the complex systems that go into making up our way of life. The study of basic economic concepts can help the child develop a sense of appreciation of our absolute dependence on others for the things we need in ordinary everyday living.

Career education clearly must be sensitive to sex-role and ethnic-role stereotyping in the world of work. Traditionally, women have been stereotyped along the lines of domestic roles, and a certain limited number of occupational roles—elementary school teaching, nursing, secretarial services, food services, and so on. School programs have often reinforced these stereotypes, with the result that women have a much more restricted set of occupational choices than do men.

185

Boys and girls need to learn that the traditional ideas about what is "woman's work" and what is "man's work" no longer apply, and that people now have greater opportunities to do the things *they* want to do to lead self-fulfilling, productive lives. Much the same can be said in connection with ethnic-role stereotyping. Although a great deal has been done in recent years to eliminate stereotyping in learning resources, the teacher still must be careful not to associate certain occupations with specific national, ethnic, or racial groups.

Key Concepts in Career Education

The staff of a career education project based at Eastern Illinois University[3] made an extensive search of the literature and existing K-6 career education materials. This search identified some 1,500 career education concepts. Further analysis indicated that these concepts could be clustered into eight categories that the Project defined as "Dimensions": (1) Attitudes and Appreciations, (2) Coping Behavior, (3) Career Information, (4) Decision-Making, (5) Educational Awareness, (6) Economic Awareness, (7) Life-style, (8) Self-development. Additional sorting surfaced generic concepts that were associated with these Dimensions. Other important but less encompassing ideas were identified as "Subconcepts."

The seven Dimensions and Major Concepts (stated as generalizations) of the Eastern Illinois University Project are shown in chart form on pages 186–187. The number of subconcepts is too large to be included here. The Dimensions and Concepts were then spread along a continuum of complexity ranging from kindergarten through grade six and serve as the organizing framework for the curriculum. Appropriate subject matter and learning activities were developed for each grade. Altogether the Project developed some 224 activities that integrate career development concepts in mathematics, science, language arts, and social studies programs of the elementary school.

CAREER DEVELOPMENT MAJOR CONCEPTS[4]

Attitudes and Appreciations

Society is dependent upon the productive work of individuals.

Career Information

Basic career information will aid in making career-related decisions.

---

[3] Conducted by The Center for Educational Studies, School of Education, Eastern Illinois University, Charleston, Illinois, under Part I of Public Law 90-576—*Curriculum Development in Vocational and Technical Education*, Dr. Marla Peterson, Director. This project was known as the "Enrichment of Teacher and Counselor Competencies in Career Education: K-6."

[4] Ibid., p. 67. A decision was made not to include Economic Awareness.

Coping Behaviors

Certain identifiable attitudes, values, and behaviors enable one to obtain, hold, and advance in a career.

Individuals can learn to perform adequately in a variety of occupations and occupational environments.

Decision-Making

Life involves a series of choices leading to career commitments.

Basic components of the decision-making process can be applied to the establishing of personal goals and the making of career-related decisions.

Educational Awareness

Educational skills and experiences are related to the achievement of career goals.

Life-style

Work affects an individual's way of life, in that a person is a social being, an economic being, a family being, a leisure being, and a moral being.

Self-development

An understanding and acceptance of self is important.

Social, economic, educational, and cultural forces influence self-development.

Individuals differ in their interests, aptitudes, values, and achievements.

Activities for Career Education

Conduct interviews to find out how adults in the community earn money. Have the pupils compile a list of categories for their questionnaire such as these:

> People Who Produce Things
> People Who Fix Things
> People Who Create
> People Who Work with Ideas

Analyze these data in terms of different subpopulations in the questionnaire compilation, such as women, minorities, and so forth.

Brainstorm a list of reasons why people might have selected particular occupations. This list should include such things as "It provides me with a chance to be my own boss" or "I earn a good salary." Have this list refined and duplicated, and then use it in a survey with working adults in your community. Have the adults choose three reasons from the list and ask them to rank them in order of most important to least important.

187

Administer an interest inventory on possible career opportunities. Then invite adults from the community to come to talk to your class in the areas in which the most interest was expressed.

Have pupils identify four or five careers that interest them (upper grades). Have them arrange to visit at least one of the work settings so they can see what the career is actually like. Create a checklist with such topics as Working Conditions and Job Requirements to use as a guideline for the children's investigations.

Brainstorm a list of occupations—say 25 to 50. In groups have the children organize the data into four categories using any system they wish to devise. Have each group explain its system. Discuss the standard career area classifications.

To sensitize pupils to sex-role stereotyping, *have them generate lists of occupations* that are associated with males, those associated with females, and those that are neutral. Discuss these in terms of equality of job opportunity and whether or not a person's sex has anything to do with performance of the jobs listed in the male and female categories.

Have pupils analyze television commercials and newspaper and magazine advertisements to detect evidence of sex-role and racial stereotyping in certain occupations.

Use "classified ad" sections of local newspapers to discover the types of jobs that are most available. Relate this to a study of changing needs of the work world over a period of time, e.g., what jobs are available now that were not available 10, 20, 50, or 100 years ago?

Study the relationship between the number of producers, consumers, and the growing demand for increased social services. Relate this to taxing policies and the increasing need for persons employed by various levels of government, i.e., local, state, and federal.

LAW-RELATED EDUCATION

The escalating rate of crime, the negative attitudes of young people and adults toward the legal system, and the evidence of widespread ignorance of the justice system among citizens are a few of the reasons why there is a growing interest in, and concern for, what has come to be called "law-related education." Law-related education seeks to help pupils develop an understanding of the legal and justice system and to provide pupils with a functional knowledge of the operation of legal institutions. It stresses law as an essential component of social life, not as a set of abstract and theoretical concepts relating to the organization and structure of the legal system and government. Support for law-related education has come not only from educators and educational groups but from prominent jurists, the legal profession through the American Bar Association and local bar associations, political leaders, parents, and virtually every segment of responsible leadership in society.

This narrative may remind the reader of boring lessons on law and government endured in a ninth-grade civics class. If so, the reader should have a sense of appreciation of the urgency for doing a more effective job of law-related education with the present generation of schoolchildren. Traditional approaches to teaching about the legal and justice systems were tied to courses in civics, history, and government. Often the learners would find little in these courses that would provide them with any practical sense of how the legal system actually operates. Learners might study the functions of the three branches of government, memorize the Preamble to the Constitution and the Bill of Rights, define a few legal terms, and know the difference between petty larceny and grand larceny, and yet be unable to relate such learning to their day-to-day living. School programs dealing with the law are often criticized because substantive content is either inappropriate or lacking altogether and because teaching methods are such that they engender no pupil interest in the subject. Recent thrusts in the law-related education field have attempted to correct both of these deficiencies.

The object of the school program of law-related education is not to make lawyers out of pupils. Nonetheless, a sophisticated knowledge of the legal system and the skills associated with legal education and the practice of law are not beyond the grasp of ordinary citizens. These skills and this knowledge can no longer be reserved for those who have had legal training, namely lawyers. When we live in a time in which aspects of the law touch our lives on a daily basis from our birth to our death, we cannot remain ignorant of its pervasive influence and uphold our responsibilities as free citizens. Accordingly, a program of law-related education should concern itself with broad goals such as the following:

1. Develop an understanding of concepts that are basic to the legal system, such as liberty, justice, fairness, toleration, power, honesty, property, equality, and responsibility.
2. Develop an understanding and appreciation of the Constitutional basis of the American legal system.
3. Develop a functional knowledge of how the institutions of the legal and justice systems operate.
4. Develop an understanding of and respect for the need for a system of law and justice as prerequisite for orderly and harmonious living.

A vast number of national, regional, and local projects have dealt with law-related education in recent years. Perhaps the best known are those projects conducted by the following groups:

National Street Law Institute
605 G Street, N.W.
Washington, D.C. 20001

Law in a Free Society Project
5115 Douglas Fir Drive, Suite 1
Calabassas, California 91302

Constitutional Rights Foundation
1510 Cotner Avenue
Los Angeles, California 90025

Special Committee on Youth for Citizenship
American Bar Association
1155 East 60th Street
Chicago, Illinois 60637

Key Concepts in Law-Related Education

There is no agreement on the exact list of concepts to be included in a law-related program but the overlap of concepts identified by various projects is considerable. The Law in a Free Society Project develops its program around eight basic concepts: Authority, Justice, Privacy, Responsibility, Participation, Diversity, Property, Freedom. These are typical and are included in most programs. Such concepts as equality, power, honesty, fairness, and others could reasonably be subsumed in the eight listed by the Law in a Free Society Project. Instructional resources, pupil materials, teacher training materials, study guides, and other related instructional materials that develop these concepts are available through the projects and through commercial publishers.

Activities for Law-Related Education

Invite a local police officer to talk to the class about law enforcement problems in the community.

Bring in news clippings describing acts of vandalism.

Discuss rights versus responsibilities along lines familiar to the pupils such as "Can we go to the movies and talk out loud even if we disturb others?"

Have the pupils research the latest legislation on drugs (upper grades). Find out if the legal penalties for drug abuse are the same for adults as for juveniles.

Take a field trip to the juvenile court admissions office in the county (upper grades). Talk with the screening officer at the court. Take a tour of the detention center.

Have pupils find out how a jury is selected. Invite someone who has recently served on a jury to speak to the class about the responsibilities and duties of jurors.

Relate rules and laws to personal safety. For primary grades this could include moving to and from school, bicycle safety, and safety in the neighborhood. For older children this could be extended to laws relating to trespass, vehicle use, drug and alcohol use, assault, and other activities that are at the edge of experience of preadolescents.

Have pupils find examples of advertisements from magazines, newspapers, radio, and television that they think may be deceptive. Relate this to consumer protection laws. Find out about agencies that deal with consumer protection.

Make use of whatever services are provided the school by local law enforcement agencies and the local bar association.

With the help of a local attorney, *have the pupils discuss the accuracy* of a law-related television program (upper grades).

MULTIETHNIC EDUCATION AND ETHNIC HERITAGE STUDIES

In recent years a process of reconceptualizing society has been underway, shifting the emphasis from the traditional melting pot ideology to one of pluralism. Many implications may be found in this shift for all of education and most especially for the social studies. There can be little doubt that sensitivity to ethnic diversity grew out of racial conflicts of the 1960s. Race and racism remain serious problems for this society, and although many believe that ethnic heritage studies will help combat some of the evils that flow from racism and racist practices, multiethnic education and ethnic heritage studies serve broader purposes. Ethnic heritage studies are intended to acquaint young people with the multiethnic composition of this society to help them become more fully aware of who they are as individuals and as a nation. Viewed societally, multiethnic education and ethnic heritage studies should be directed toward the ultimate goal of improving the quality of human relations in this country.

The society of the United States is multisocial class, multiracial, and multiethnic. Consequently, considerable confusion over terminology and meanings occurs when discussing issues relating to the pluralistic character of this society. Social class groups have to do with grouping individuals on the basis of income, occupation, lifestyles, and in the case of upper classes, family background. These are status groups and represent a hierarchical arrangement from high to low on some basis of preference. Racial groups result from genetically transmitted physical characteristics that are innate and immutable. They are often visibly different from other groups on the basis of physical qualities. Ethnic groups, on the other hand, are formed on

191

the basis of common cultural variables such as language, customs, religion, nationality, traditions, and history that give some groups a sense of "peoplehood." It should be clear that socioeconomic level or social class membership has nothing whatever to do with one's ethnic identity. All ethnic groups have individuals who are wealthy and those who are poor; all have individuals in upper social classes and those in lower social classes.

Race and ethnicity are often confused because in some cases they overlap. For example, the Japanese have physical characteristics that set them apart as an Asian racial group. At the same time, the Japanese people have a language, tradition, common heritage, and history that give them an ethnic identity. A blond European baby who, at the moment of birth, was adopted and raised by a Japanese family would as an adult be ethnically Japanese in spite of his physical (racial) characteristics that he inherited from his European ancestors. Perhaps it would be difficult for such an individual to be fully assimilated by the Japanese society because of clearly differing physical characteristics. This is because social attributes tend to be associated negatively with physical qualities when the individual is a member of a visible minority group in a society. This is an obvious illustration of *racism*, which is the practice of attaching nonphysical characteristics to physical qualities of human beings. It should also be obvious that this practice has been and continues to be quite common in the United States. *Race and racism are problems not because of the reality of physical differences between human beings but because there are social values attached to those differences.*

This country is exceptional among the nations of the world because it is composed of representatives or their descendants of almost all of the world's many cultures. In terms of ethnic heritage, we are among the most diverse people on earth. But Americans vary greatly in the extent to which they retain their ethnic identity. Many have no knowledge or even interest in their forebears. Others lack a clear ethnic identity because of intermarriage, name changes, and migrations. Others may be nominally members of an identified ethnic group but do little more than attend a once-a-year picnic of such groups as "Sons of Norway." Still others are more active in retaining their ethnicity by maintaining a fluency in the language of their ancestors, observing traditional holidays associated with their ethnic group, continuing traditional church affiliations, and so on. A small group remains totally immersed in its ethnic culture, as for example the Navajo people. Thus, the level of enthusiasm for ethnic heritage studies can vary greatly from one individual to another and attempts to impose interest in such studies is not likely to be productive or even desirable.

The major purposes of multiethnic education and ethnic heritage studies ought to be along the lines of the following:

1. to present truthful accounts of the multiethnic composition of this society.

2. to develop a sense of pride in the multiethnic heritage of this nation.
3. to develop a respect for the contributions of all groups to the life and culture of this nation.
4. to develop harmonious social relations resulting from the use of acceptable methods of resolving social conflicts.
5. to develop a reasoned pride in one's own ethnic heritage.
6. to understand that much of the strength of this nation derives from the diversity of its ethnic heritages and cultural origins.

Multiethnic education and ethnic heritage studies should be firmly rooted in the local community but should not be limited to the study of ethnic groups of the local area. In order to present social reality as accurately as possible, a broad spectrum of ethnic groups should be represented in the program. Much of the content of ethnic studies is affectively toned, and thus it can be expected that providing knowledge alone is not likely to be very powerful in achieving the goals of ethnic education. Activities need to be planned that will engender positive feelings toward others.

Ethnic studies can be interesting and enriching and can do much to build social cohesiveness by helping all children gain a better understanding of the diverse people we really are. There is much of which we, as a nation, can be proud that comes as a direct consequence of our multiethnic backgrounds. However, there is a clear danger that ethnic studies may contribute to social disunity and the development of ethnocentric attitudes. If ethnic studies are allowed to become rallying grounds for the advocacy of political and social goals of specific ethnic groups, if groups become polarized over issues that are ethnically based, or if these studies become politicized, they can do little to enhance human relations. It must be emphasized that there are all-embracing common societal values that all groups share regardless of their cultural or ethnic identity. The concept of "one Nation under God, indivisible, with liberty and justice for all" must be made a reality if the nation is to escape internal conflict and strife of untold proportions.[5]

Instructional resources for teaching multiethnic education and ethnic heritage studies are available in generous amounts from many suppliers. The Council on Interracial Books for Children (1841 Broadway, New York City 10023) produces many materials useful to teachers, as does the National Council for the Social Studies (3615 Wisconsin Avenue, N.W., Washington, D.C. 20016), and the Anti-Defamation League of B'nai B'rith (345 East 46th Street, New York City 10017). The Social Science Education Consortium (855 Broadway, Boulder, Colorado 80302) has assembled materials sold as "Packet K" that includes a handbook for school librarians; a materials

[5]For a detailed statement of curriculum guidelines for ethnic heritage studies, see the National Council for the Social Studies position statement, *Curriculum Guidelines for Multiethnic Education.* Washington, D.C.: National Council for the Social Studies, 1976.

analysis instrument; and an annotated bibliography of over 1100 films, publications, human resources, publishers, and ethnic organizations. Another annotated list of multiethnic resources for children is available from Multicultural Resources, Box 2945, Stanford, California 94305.

Activities for Multiethnic Education and Ethnic Heritage Studies

Research contemporary groups that have been organized because of particular ethnic identities. Discover their purpose and identify their leaders, if possible.

Make a scrapbook of outstanding individuals in an ethnic group. Include their accomplishments and what they have contributed to the whole society, to their ethnic group, and to the individual.

Read a fiction book in which the main character is a member of an ethnic group. Have a discussion about the main character with another person who has read the book or with the teacher. How was the life of the main character affected by his or her ethnic background?

Create puppets and act out a folk tale or legend from a particular ethnic culture.

Write a newspaper article advocating the position of an ethnic group in a conflict situation, such as an Indian tribe in its land or fishing disputes.

Have pupils find out about their own ethnic origins. Show on a world map where their ancestors came from. Discuss this in terms of the areas of the world represented in the class. Study settlement patterns in the United States of various immigrant groups. (Note: Activities such as this one or studies of family genealogy ought always to be optional. Some parents and pupils do not wish to divulge personal family information, and their wishes must be respected.)

Learn folk songs and folk dances of various ethnic groups.

Prepare a bulletin board or other displays that show the contributions of various ethnic groups to American life and culture. Have children bring newspaper clippings and photographs of various ethnic groups in the news.

Use the local telephone directory to find names that can be identified with a particular ethnic group, e.g., French, Irish, German, Chinese, Slavic, Scandinavian. Try to detect a pattern in terms of the dominance of any group. Check, also, the yellow pages to find out which ethnic restaurants are found locally. If possible, compare data found in the local telephone directory with that found in a directory of a city in some other part of the country.

Invite representatives of various ethnic groups in the community to your class. Ask them about their cultural roots. Have them discuss their language and customs. Inquire about their connections, if any, with the homeland of their forebears.

Encourage children to view television programs or listen to radio broadcasts of ethnic groups in the local area.

Visit museums that display exhibits, artifacts, and collections of ethnic groups of the community and state.

Have pupils learn about holidays and festivals of ethnic groups in the community.

Have pupils conduct a survey of the school or the local area to find out the number of different languages spoken and identify each.

Survey the community to find places of business or service groups (food stores, funeral homes, specialty shops, churches) that cater to particular ethnic groups.

STUDIES IN SEX EQUITY

In August, 1920, the Nineteenth Amendment to the Constitution became the law of the land, and thereby women were given the right to vote, a right enjoyed by most free men since the founding of the Republic. The discrimination against women, however, did not end with the Nineteenth Amendment. The evidence is clear that women have not achieved full status with men in the business and professional worlds, in education, in political affairs, or in any field that has been traditionally dominated by men. For a variety of reasons, the traditional roles of men and women in society have undergone great changes in the second half of the 20th century, resulting at long last in the emancipation of women. The independence of women, which without question is one of the most significant social developments of our time, has many implications for social studies education in the elementary school.

Many believe that school programs have actually contributed to discrimination against women because they have reinforced conventional sex roles that emphasized male superiority. Where this can be studied with a degree of objectivity, as, for example, in analyzing school textbooks, the evidence is overwhelming that males have had a clear advantage. They have been consistently represented in positions of greater prestige, and as being more courageous, more clever, more witty, and more skillful than women. Women have tended to be represented in subservient positions and most generally in social-service roles or in roles that require serving men, as, for example, secretarial service and nursing. Thus, discrimination against women became institutionalized in that both boys *and* girls came to believe in the superiority of the male.

Discrimination on the basis of sex is explicitly forbidden by sev-

195

eral pieces of federal legislation, the best known being Titles VI and VII of the Civil Rights Act of 1964, and Title IX of the Education Amendments of 1972. Title IX deals with discrimination in education, and the intent of the law is made clear by its opening statement:

No person in the United States shall on the basis of sex be excluded from participation in, be denied the benefits of, or be subjected to discrimination under any education program or activity receiving Federal financial assistance...

Because nearly all schools receive federal financial assistance in some form, the law is for all practical purposes universal. In addition to these federal laws, many state laws and constitutions prohibit discrimination.

There is much greater awareness of sex-role stereotyping now than there was even a decade ago, and many of the practices that contribute to this attitude are being eliminated. The contributions of women to the life, culture, and development of this nation are becoming more visible in the curriculum and in learning resources. Women are seen in prestigious occupations as being coequal with men. Men and women are shown sharing responsibilities associated with maintaining a household, caring for children, and providing family income. Other forms of invidious distinctions between men and women are being eradicated from the printed and visual material used by children in school.

These changes obviously represent great gains for women in broadening the potential for their self-fulfillment. What is often overlooked is that it does the same for men. Both sexes will have greater opportunity for choice if neither male nor female roles are stereotyped. This applies not only to career choices but to leisure-time activities, hobbies, reading interests, school activities, sports, and, indeed, all other aspects of life except those specifically limited by biological differences between the sexes.

Major Goals of Sex Equity Education

A major overall goal of the socialization of American children is that of engendering values and attitudes based on principles of equality among human beings. Many groups and institutions in the community contribute toward the achievement of this goal, including, of course, the family, religious institutions, and the school. Regrettably, children may not always receive consistent direction from all of the socializing influences. Nonetheless, sexism and sex-role stereotyping are forms of discrimination against others because they are the result of arbitrary judgments based on the sex of the individual. Social studies programs have a responsibility to combat the formation of such values and attitudes because they are contrary to the goals and purposes of the school curriculum and are repugnant to the ideals and laws of the nation. Instruction in sex equity should be directed toward the attainment of objectives along such lines as these:

196

1. To develop a sensitivity in children to the stereotyping of males and females along the lines of occupations, home life, lifestyles, community life, recreation, and other life choices.
2. To learn about the contributions of both men and women to American life and culture, especially in areas that have traditionally been closed to one or the other of the sexes.
3. To have pupils become aware of the nature and impact of sex bias in all walks of life and having them become familiar with some of the more obvious examples of sex bias and inequities based on sex.
4. To stress the importance of providing both sexes with the right of *choice* in directing the affairs of their lives and in considering career options.
5. To gain an understanding of sex roles in terms of physiological and biological differences between males and females on the one hand, and in terms of gender distinctions influenced by cultural beliefs on the other.

Activities for Sex Equity Education

Compare and contrast roles of men, women, boys, and girls in an earlier historical period, such as in Colonial times, with those same roles today. Similarly, compare and contrast those roles in other cultures with those in the United States. Discuss reasons for such differences. Have pupils provide reasons why roles change.

Have pupils list as many different behaviors associated with males and females that are based on customs and traditions (e.g., ladies first, women wear dresses and men do not, etc.). Have pupils speculate on how these customs may have originated. Discuss items on the list in terms of changes that may be taking place in them.

Have pupils generate a list of different tasks members of the family do at home. Have pupils identify the person best able to do each task. Discuss whether or not the task could be performed by other members of the family.

Ask pupils to bring to school pictures from magazines or newspapers of men and women engaging in various occupations. Post these on the bulletin board in terms of those almost always performed by men and those almost always performed by women, and those performed by either. Discuss reasons why some occupations attract men, others women, and others are attractive to both men and women.

In a brainstorming session have children name as many important people in American history—living or dead—as they can think of in a 10-minute period. Write names on the chalkboard. Then have pupils group the individuals on some self-determined criteria (occupation, ethnic or racial minority, living or dead, men or women, etc.). Have pupils note discrepancy between the number of men and the number of women. Have pupils speculate on why this is so. Conduct an inquiry to test their hypotheses.

Have pupils read children's biographies of prominent women who have championed the cause of sex equity.

Invite men and women who have made non-traditional career choices (e.g., male nurses, female airlines pilot) to speak to the class about their experiences in pursuing their career goals.

GLOBAL EDUCATION

It is unlikely that any single event in human history had as profound an effect in providing a feeling of worldmindedness and world identity than did the moon landings by the American astronauts. Throughout the world, human beings watched or listened, hoped or prayed for the safe return of the men, and contemplated the concept of the one-ness of the world community. The event truly did mark "one giant leap for mankind" as was so aptly put by Neal Armstrong.

Barring some global catastrophe, it is likely that worldmindedness will continue to grow among the people of this planet. This has many implications for social studies instruction. Today international relations are dominating the attention of our nation. It could hardly be otherwise given the realities of the modern world. Consequently, social studies programs are being planned to equip the young citizen to deal thoughtfully and intelligently with problems of international import.

We live in a world fraught with danger, which is likely to increase as modern instruments of destruction become available to more and more nations. Even a minor power—armed with modern weapons, constitutes a threat to the entire world. To ignore the real danger that exists or to minimize it could result in disastrous consequences for the entire human race. But if nations can spare themselves from destruction during this delicate time of the present, perhaps more sensible approaches to human relations will eventually prevail. Perhaps through educational programs directed toward the understanding of others and toward a search for world peace, a more satisfactory method of resolving international disputes can be found than the oldest and least effective method, war.

A global perspective that engenders worldmindedness, therefore, is essential if humankind is to survive. Such programs cannot be allowed to become based on sentimentalism and naïve optimism. The harsh realities of the world are ever present and must be faced. Teachers will want to help pupils develop feelings of goodwill, mutual trust, and understanding of others, but at the same time, it must be understood that these feelings cannot be one-sided in their application. No

Pupils learn about life in other cultures in many ways besides formal studies. Here we see a group from Japan visiting an American classroom. What other experiences can you name that help pupils develop a global perspective on human affairs?

matter how strongly men and women of goodwill of *any* nation long for peace, it cannot be a realizable goal so long as huge sections of the world's people are taught to hate and distrust others. As has been said many times, we deal with the world the way it is, not as we wish it to be.

The policy of the United States as a government and the personal philosophy of most Americans is one that supports peaceful and harmonious relationships among people of all countries. This policy has been announced publicly in a variety of ways countless numbers of times. The behavior of Americans as a nation as well as individually has given testimony to support our policy. This is not to say that the actions of our government or of individual Americans in dealing with people of other countries has in all cases been faultless. It is precisely because there have been instances of poor judgment in our relationships with others that our policies and intentions can be misconstrued or distorted. Moreover, because the United States is a rich and powerful nation, in a position of world leadership, the actions of its government and individual citizens come under constant and extraordinarily careful scrutiny by the rest of the world. A diplomatic blunder by a

199

small obscure nation might go almost unnoticed in the stream of world events; the same actions by the United States or one of its citizens could precipitate an international crisis. Heavy responsibilities are thrust on those who find themselves in leadership positions, and the standard of expectation for performance is correspondingly high. Global education in American schools is crucial, therefore, when viewed in this context. American schoolchildren must be alerted to these realities, for it is they who will be representing the United States to the rest of the world in the years to come and who will be the decision-makers of the future.

When education for a global perspective is regarded as one of the broad goals of education, it becomes apparent that the addition of a new subject to the curriculum is not necessary. Rather, it should represent an *extension and broader interpretation of what is already taught in most schools*. Teaching for worldmindedness can occur through experiences the child has in music, art, science, literature, reading—in fact, in almost any of the various curricular areas.

In order to broaden instruction as described in the previous paragraph, teachers will need to be imaginative in exploring and discovering new avenues to a world view. For example, when children in the primary grades are studying homes and home life, that is the time to begin developing the understanding that people all over the world need homes and that they build them in a variety of ways. Or, when the food market is studied, time might be spent on an examination of food markets around the world. Units on transportation and communication can, likewise, be expanded to familiarize the child with these functions on a broader basis than the local community. Almost any topic has within it such possibilities for teaching global relationships.

If a school accepts global education as one of its primary purposes, it will concern itself with ideas such as these:

1. the interdependence of peoples.
2. the need for peaceful relations among nations.
3. basic similarities and differences in peoples because of geographic, cultural, and historical considerations, to include an elementary understanding of the ways of living in the modern world.
4. the philosophy and practice of respect for the dignity of the individual irrespective of race or other factors over which he or she has no control.
5. the need to develop a sensitivity to and respect for the cultures of other people.

Experiences to Help Build A Global Perspective

Use Experiences from the Everyday Lives of Pupils to Initiate Such Projects

These experiences might include the return of a parent from an overseas assignment, the presence of a foreign visitor, a curio from another country, a story or television program about children in other lands, or a news item familiar to the children. Successful activities of this type usually begin in class discussions under the guidance of an alert teacher who can identify experiences of children that lend themselves to such a study.

Be Sure Information About Other Peoples
Is Accurate and Authentic

Misguided teaching resulting in erroneous concepts of other peoples, the development of stereotypes, or overemphasis on those aspects of the lives of others that are drastically different from our own leads to distorted ideas about other cultures and should be avoided. In order to get up-to-date information about the society being studied, the teacher might consult the local library or local travel bureaus, write to the appropriate embassy in Washington, D.C., or the nearest consulate, or request information about the country through the United Nations. Other good sources of information are persons who were or are citizens of a foreign country—exchange students, recent immigrants to the United States, or foreign nationals visiting here.

Keep Instruction and Experiences for Primary-Grade
Children Simple, Child-Oriented

Difficult concepts relating to international understanding, geography, and intercultural relations should be avoided in teaching young children. One of the major purposes of these studies at the primary-grade level is to develop the concept of friendliness and neighborliness among the people of the world. Experiences planned should be simple ones, dealing with ideas and things that are consistent with the experience and maturity of the young child. Specifically, this means experiences concerning the way children in other lands live, play, dress, and eat. The primary-grade child can understand that everyone needs a home, a family, and friends, must go to school, and feels sad, happy, or angry at times.

Make Direct Contact with the Life of
the Group Studied

One of the best learning experiences for young children in making a study of people in other lands is to have direct contact with a person from the country, especially a child their own age, who can answer questions about the clothes they wear, their schools, games, celebrations, homes, foods, stories, and similar ways of living. Other types of contacts include material things that have come from other countries. These are especially interesting to children if the items are similar to something they use in their own lives each day. A doll, an article of clothing, a musical record, a book, and a toy are examples of items that help children understand that there are differences in the ways of doing things but that children everywhere do many of

201

the same things. With help from the teacher and their parents, even primary-grade children can carry on correspondence with children abroad, which invariably leads to the exchange of photographs and other objects. Teachers who wish to have their classes or individual pupils correspond with children in other lands may obtain information and addresses from the following sources:

International Friendship League
40 Mount Vernon Street
Beacon Hill
Boston, Massachusetts 02108

Student Letter Exchange
Waseca, Minnesota 56093

Use Story and Literature Resources Related to Other Lands

The amount of fictional reading material dealing with children's lives in other lands has been increasing substantially in recent years. Typically, these little books are illustrated vividly, and primary-grade children get as much from the pictures as from the story as the teacher reads it to them. As children advance to the second and third grades, some of them can read the stories themselves.

In addition to the principles discussed in connection with the primary-grade program, the following suggestions apply to the middle and upper grades.

Explore More Deeply Some of the Reasons for the Differences in Ways of Living

People everywhere are products of their backgrounds—historical, geographical, sociological, psychological, and religious factors help explain how and why people live the way they do. Children in the middle and upper grades can begin to sense these relationships. They can learn, for example, how the presence of natural barriers such as mountains has tended to isolate people and that these barriers usually stabilize borders between nations; they can see the cultural impact of missionaries, explorers, and colonists; they learn that modes of dress or types of homes people select are related to climatic conditions of the region; they can understand why island people turn to the sea for their livelihood and why desert people move toward water and food. In studying other cultures, pupils need experiences that will help them perceive the world through the eyes of the people of that culture, insofar as that is possible. They need to imagine how the world would look to them if they were a member of the culture studied. When children begin to see even partially how others view themselves and the world, they come to understand some of the reasons for differences in ways of living, and the differences tend not to seem unusual to them. Rather, they come to the conclusion that people the world over are resourceful, logical, and show considerable ingenuity in dealing with environmental factors and forces.

Teach About the United Nations and Its Specialized Agencies

Whether schools should teach about the United Nations has been a controversial issue in some communities in the United States. Because under our educational system such issues are resolved at the local level, teachers will need to decide how much emphasis should be placed on studies of the United Nations. As a nation, we support the United Nations and are members of it. It has its headquarters within the boundaries of our country. Our national policy is to trust that it will be influential in averting wars and in settling international disputes equitably and peacefully.

Activities for Global Education

Have pupils compile an international cookbook, a game book, a book of holidays, or a book of national sports.

Invite foreign-born local residents to the classroom to display traditional national costumes or skills.

Set aside one bulletin board for current events in other countries around the world. Associate such news stories with their map and globe location.

Have pupils write to embassies, consulates, airlines, or travel bureaus for material on the countries being studied.

Develop simulated situations and instructional games to teach about other countries. This can be combined with role playing for additional insights. Topics such as city life, education, agricultural problems, and government would be appropriate for this activity.

Teach folk songs, national anthems, poems, dances, and games of other countries.

Study the origin, growth, and *change* of languages. Examine the derivation of specific words.

Develop dramatic activities based on legends, myths, or stories of other peoples around the world.

Study contributions to American culture that have been made by immigrants.

Have pupils prepare a travel brochure on a country, continent, or region; role-play the part of a tourist representative from that country telling about a fifteen-day tour of the country.

Enter into correspondence with a class in another country.

Have children organize an International Club as a means of sponsoring all-school activities with an international emphasis.

203

Develop a tape exchange with children of another country. See page 202 for address of contact.

Exchange artwork with a school in a foreign country or with children from a sister city if one exists.

Contact a local agency for foreign student placement and arrange to have a foreign student spend a day with your class.

DISCUSSION QUESTIONS AND SUGGESTED ACTIVITIES

1. Develop inquiry-oriented learning experiences for pupils in a grade of your choice based on one or more of the topics discussed in this chapter.
2. Visit the curriculum library on your campus and examine some of the newer materials related to the topics included in this chapter.
3. How are *racism* and *ethnocentrism* alike and how are they different? What danger does each present in terms of desirable human relations?
4. How do you define *ethnicity*? Are all ethnic groups also minority groups?
5. What resource persons in the local community might be of help in teaching the topics included in this chapter?
6. Select one of the key concepts listed on pages 176–178, and show by a short example how it could be taught meaningfully to children in each grade of the elementary school.
7. What benefits are there to the larger society of career education programs in school? Or, is it only the individual learner who benefits?
8. Locate a photograph relating to an environmental problem. Prepare six interpretation and analysis questions (see page 77, Chapter 3) based on the photograph.
9. The inclusion of energy and environmental education, career education, law-related education, and multiethnic education in the social studies curriculum is being challenged by a parent at a public meeting. If you were asked to respond to such a concern, what points would you make?
10. Explain how topics discussed in this chapter relate to the goals for social studies education listed on pages 6–8.
11. Some parents, for religious or other reasons, object to the teaching of sex equity. How do you define your boundaries of responsibility in dealing with this topic while at the same time respecting the right of parents to believe as they do?
12. Provide specific examples of how social studies topics in a grade in which you have a special interest can be studied from a global perspective.

SELECTED REFERENCES

Abramowitz, Norman, Andrew J. Leighton, and Stephen Viederman. "Global and International Perspectives," Chapter 5, *Improving the Human Condition: A Curricular Response to Critical Realities*, 1978 Yearbook. Association for Supervision and Curriculum Development. Washington, D.C.: The Association, 1978, pp. 129-162.

Banks, James A. *Teaching Strategies for Ethnic Studies*, 2nd ed. Boston: Allyn & Bacon, Inc., 1979.

Cogan, John J. "Implementing Global Education in the Elementary School: A Case Study," *Social Education*, 42 (October 1978), pp. 503-505.

Gillespie, Judith A., guest ed. "Teaching About the Energy Crisis," *Social Education*, 44 (April 1980), pp. 259-291. (Several authors contribute articles to a special section on energy and environment in this issue.)

Gilliom, M. Eugene and Richard C. Remy. "Needed: A New Approach to Global Education," *Social Education*, 42 (October 1978), pp. 499-502.

Grambs, Jean Dresden, ed. *Teaching About Women in the Social Studies: Concepts, Methods, and Materials*, Bulletin 48. National Council for the Social Studies. Washington, D.C.: The Council, 1976.

Grant, Carl, ed. *Multicultural Education: Commitments, Issues, and Applications*. Washington, D.C.: Association for Supervision and Curriculum Development, 1977.

Gratz, Pauline. "Environment and the Quality of Life," Chapter 3, *Improving the Human Condition: A Curricular Response to Critical Realities*, 1978 Yearbook. Association for Supervision and Curriculum Development. Washington, D.C.: The Association, 1978, pp. 68-93.

Greenberg, Selma. *Right from the Start: A Guide to Nonsexist Child Rearing*. Boston: Houghton Mifflin Company, 1978.

King, Edith W. *Teaching Ethnic Awareness: Methods and Materials for the Elementary School*. Santa Monica, California: Goodyear Publishing Company, Inc., 1980.

Loyd, Bonnie and Arlene Rengert, coordinators. "Women in Geographic Curricula," *Journal of Geography*, 77 (September–October 1978). (Special issue on women in geography.)

Lucas, Christopher J., ed. "The New Vocationalism: Career Education," Chapter 4, *Challenge and Choice in Contemporary Education*. New York: Macmillan Publishing Company, Inc., 1976.

National Council for the Social Studies. "Law-Focused Education," *Social Education*, 41 (March 1977), pp. 168-193. (Four authors contribute to a special section on law-focused education. A list of curriculum materials and resources is included along with the names and addresses of many suppliers.)

National Council for the Social Studies, Task Force on Ethnic Studies Curriculum Guidelines. *Curriculum Guidelines for Multiethnic Education*. Washington, D.C.: The Council, 1976.

Pasternak, Michael G. *Helping Kids Learn Multi-Cultural Concepts*. Champaign, Illinois: Research Press Co., 1979.

Puglisi, Dick J. and Alan J. Hoffman. "Cultural Identity and Academic Success in a Multicultural Society: A Culturally Different Approach," *Social Education*, 42 (October 1978), pp. 495-498.

Reilly, Mary Ellen. "Eliminating Sexism: A Challenge to Educators," *Social Education*, 43 (April 1979), pp. 312-316.

Remy, Richard C., James A. Nathan, James M. Becker, and Judith V. Torney. *International Learning and International Education in a Global Age*. Washington, D.C.: National Council for the Social Studies, 1975.

Tonkin, Humphrey and Jane Edwards. "A World of Interconnections," *Phi Delta Kappan*, 62 (June 1981), pp. 695-698.

Wheeler, Ronald. "Law-Related Education," *Social Education*, 44 (May 1980), pp. 381–397. (Special Elementary Education Supplement on law-related education, including a list of children's literature with strong law-related content.)

Wood, Dean and Robert Remnant. *The People We Are: Canada's Multicultural Society*. Agincourt, Ontario: Gage Publishing Limited, 1981.

Wood, Jayne Millar, guest ed. "Science and Technology for a Global Society," *Social Education*, 43 (October 1979), pp. 420–455. (Several authors contribute articles to this special section on science and technology for a global society. Many lists of classroom materials and their sources are provided.)

8

CURRENT Affairs
in the Social Studies

"But they can't *do* that! It's against the Constitution!"

"What Constitution?"

"The *United States* Constitution!"

"What does the United States Constitution have to do with it?"

"I don't know; but it just doesn't seem right. If a person has some land with some trees on it, he shouldn't have to get permission from the Ecology Department to cut them. They're *his*."

This lively exchange took place between a boy and a girl in a fifth grade class as a result of a story in the local newspaper under the headline:

COURT STOPS FURTHER TREE REMOVAL

Orders Environmental Impact Statement

The teacher brought this article to class because it dealt with an issue of local interest that had been in the news for several weeks and because it illustrated so well the conflict between individual rights and community values, something the class had been dealing with in social studies. The example also illustrates how the use of current affairs can add vitality and meaning to what might otherwise seem to be abstract and remote concepts. Although these pupils may not have the facts of the case straight, it is obvious that they have strong feelings about the issue. This discussion has motivated them to get additional information, and their teacher can help them and their classmates get the facts they need.

The point of view to be developed in this chapter is that the program of current affairs is a matter of importance in the school program and, as such, requires careful planning and teaching. Pupils cannot be subjected to several years of boring experiences with current affairs in school and leave convinced that they have any responsibility to keep themselves informed on the affairs of the world. Pupils cannot have news sharing while the teacher takes roll, collects lunch money, completes plans for another lesson, or does other things about the room that draws full attention from the news reports. The teacher could not successfully teach mathematics, reading, or spelling in this way, and there is no reason to believe that current affairs can

207

be taught with any degree of success in this way either. Poor teaching of current affairs is worse than none at all, for such depressing experiences subvert any natural curiosity the child might have had about current happenings.

If the nation expects its adults to have an abiding interest in news and current developments and have a desire to keep informed, the groundwork for these attitudes, interests, and skills must be laid in the elementary school. The first major purpose of current affairs teaching at the elementary school level is, therefore, *to promote interest in current affairs and news developments.*

Intelligent consideration of current affairs requires the use of a variety of skills and abilities: (1) to read news materials; (2) to discriminate between important and less-significant news items; (3) to take a position on issues based on a knowledge and a critical evaluation of the facts of both sides; and (4) to predict likely consequences in terms of present developments. *Promoting the growth of these skills and abilities represents the second major purpose of current affairs instruction at the elementary school level.* These skills evolve over several years through the study of current affairs under the direction and guidance of capable teachers and do not appear full blown when the child enters high school or achieves voting age. It is unrealistic to hope for an adult population that can exercise critical judgment concerning current problems and issues unless individuals have at their command the fundamental skills and abilities such action demands.

The third major purpose of current affairs teaching is *to help the child relate school learning to life outside school.* The constant reference to current affairs is good insurance against the separation of school activities from the nonacademic life of the child. Good teachers recognize that printed material begins to become obsolete shortly after it is written, and there is always a gap between the information contained in books and changing developments in the world. A generous use of current affairs materials helps to close this gap. Some encyclopedia publishers recognize the need for timely information and issue annual supplements that include changes that have occurred during the preceding year. Because textbooks and supplementary books usually are not revised each year, it is necessary to depend on such sources as newspapers and magazines for the latest information on some topics. The practice of selecting topics for social studies units from the immediate surroundings and life of the child also underscores the need to use current materials.

THE PROGRAM OF CURRENT AFFAIRS INSTRUCTION

The three most common methods of including current affairs in the elementary school program are (1) teaching current affairs in addition to social studies, (2) using current affairs to supplement or rein-force the regular social studies program, and (3) using current affairs as the basis for social studies units. A discussion of each of these methods follows.

Teaching Current Affairs in Addition to Social Studies

Mrs. Hansen, who teaches fourth grade, plans to spend a few min-utes each morning during the sharing period for the discussion of im-portant news stories. She encourages children to bring news clippings from daily newspapers or from weekly magazines for the class bulle-tin board. Children are encouraged to bring news stories related to classroom work, and Mrs. Hansen helps interpret these stories for the children by her comments and leading questions, such as

"How do you suppose the new highway will help our town?"
"What are the explorers looking for on these expeditions?"
"Why do you suppose the animals died when they were brought here?"
"Can you show the class on the map the exact location of the new airport?"

Mrs. Hansen uses a classroom periodical and plans to spend a half-hour on it with the children each week. This consists of reading the material, or portions of it, with a discussion following. She varies the procedure from week to week and uses the suggestions provided in the teacher's edition that accompanies the classroom periodical.

This method has the advantage of providing a regularly scheduled time for news each day. Such periods can be useful in building pupil interest in current affairs and in teaching skills of interpreting news stories. It has the clear disadvantage of isolating current affairs from the remainder of the school program, most especially from the social studies. If current affairs teaching is handled as is done by Mrs. Han-sen in the example, time should be taken to relate news content to topics and units in social studies. This can be done by (1) interpret-ing news stories within the context of topics that have been studied or are under study; (2) extending the meaning of concepts developed in social studies; (3) applying social studies skills, such as map, graph, or chart reading to the news stories; or (4) comparing and contrasting events in the news with events encountered in social studies units.

Using Current Affairs to Supplement or Reinforce the Regular Social Studies Program

Mr. Ray schedules his social studies period immediately following morning opening activities for his fifth-grade class. As a part of the beginning activities, he provides time for the reporting of news arti-cles and encourages children to report news items related to social studies. He and his class maintain a news bulletin board as well as a small table on which are placed news articles, magazines, current maps, or similar materials of a timely nature related to the social studies unit. He uses current affairs materials in this way to augment other instructional resources and as a means of reminding his class of the need for up-to-date information.

Mr. Ray often suggests parallels to his pupils between events that happened long ago and events that are occurring today, thereby illustrating recurrent problems in the conduct of human affairs. For example, in the study of the struggle for freedom and independence in America, he used examples from present-day affairs to show that some peoples of the world are still struggling for the right to govern themselves. When the class studied early explorers, Mr. Ray related this study to present-day exploration. In the unit on the Westward Movement, he called the attention of the class to current population movements and trends in the United States.

The difference between this method and the one used by Mrs. Hansen is that the connection between current affairs and social studies is much more deliberate in Mr. Ray's approach. He is concerned mainly with those news stories that can be related to his social studies program. He builds an awareness in his pupils of the relationship between what is currently happening in the world and what they are studying in social studies. He is using the affairs of the world as reported in the news media as a current data source for social studies. This method has the advantage of keeping the information base for social studies up-to-date. It has the disadvantage of restricting the range of news stories that are appropriate. Therefore, if this approach is used, the teacher should provide some opportunity for the pupils to examine news items that are significant and timely, yet may not be directly related to the social studies unit under study at the time.

Using Current Affairs As the Basis for Social Studies Units

Miss Bell likes to develop social studies units with her sixth-grade class around topics that are currently in the news. She does this between the regular units she is required to teach during the year. During her years of experience as a teacher, she has found that units of this type must be carefully selected because it is not always possible to find a sufficient amount of instructional material suitable for children that deals with topics in the news. Units that she has taught with success in this way in the past have dealt with alliances, such as NATO; meeting our needs for oil; migration of the world's people as a result of news of newcomers to the United States; 20th-century explorers; progress in science, medicine, and industry; and elections. When Miss Bell selects the unit topics carefully, she finds it possible to include much of the subject matter ordinarily included in her social studies curriculum under other unit titles. She believes that the use of current news happenings as a starting point for units does much to stimulate interest and discussion among her pupils.

This method has the advantage of being highly motivating to pupils because it deals with subject matter that is of immediate interest. It also bridges school learning with life outside of school. It has the disadvantage of being difficult to plan because news events may not relate directly to the social studies curriculum. Also, news stories may not provide a continuing or sustaining source of information on topics, and, therefore, other data sources would need to be available. This method works best for short, minitype units as described in the example, rather than as a structure for the entire social studies program.

TEACHING CURRENT AFFAIRS SUCCESSFULLY

Any of the three current affairs programs described here can be used successfully. In good programs there will be time during the school day devoted to the study and discussion of current affairs that may be entirely unrelated to topics under study in the social studies units or unrelated to any other curricular area for that matter. At the same time, in guiding unit work, the teacher will not ignore current affairs relating to the topic being studied but will, in fact, seek with enthusiasm the current affairs materials that will add strength to the unit. From time to time, too, the teacher and children can plan an entire social studies unit from current news developments. Units dealing with the topics of energy, environment, safety, intercultural relations, law and justice, housing, food, elections, discoveries in science, and items of local news may, and frequently do, grow out of current affairs. When the social studies program includes these three methods, the teacher and class will use any or all of the procedures described in the following sections.

Daily Discussion of News

Children enjoy discussing the news and should be given the opportunity to do so within the school program. It is a fairly common procedure for classes to have a morning meeting or sharing period at the beginning of each school day, during which time the children can report news items. Children in the primary grades frequently report only news that affects them directly: Daddy took an airplane trip, the family has a new baby, the pet cat had kittens, or other similar items of "news." As children mature, they move away from news items that are of concern only to them personally to news of more general interest.

In reporting, discussing, and considering daily news occurrences, elementary schoolchildren frequently report the sensational headline news that may or may not be particularly significant. Without guidance, children are likely to report murders or robberies or hold postmortems on the previous night's television programs. The teacher should help children evaluate the importance of news stories and teach them to discriminate between significant news and the sensational.

In general, the practice of reporting news should be encouraged by the teacher rather than required. Some teachers require children to bring a news clipping on specified days. This usually means a hurried breakfast for the child while Mother peruses the morning or evening paper hoping to find a suitable item that she can explain to the child before the child leaves for school. A better procedure for the teacher is to build the children's interest in news to the extent that they voluntarily bring news clippings that they believe are important enough to bring to school. Similarly, in the reporting of news items, on some days there will be many items and much discussion; other days there may be none. The teacher must bear in mind that the purpose of this procedure is to *develop the children's interest* in current affairs and that this is usually not done by requiring children to spend specified amounts of time on news whether the content justifies the time or not.

As children approach the middle and upper grades, they will not only report news events but will begin to include issues on which there are conflicting points of view. This should be encouraged, and eventually the emphasis can be placed almost entirely on problems and issues rather than on simple events. The movement from the consideration of simple events to simple issues to complex issues is a gradual one for the child.

When controversial issues are considered by the class, the teacher will find a number of special problems presenting themselves. Some teachers are so fearful of precipitating community ill will and pressure that they avoid consideration of any problems that are even mildly controversial. This is unfortunate and unfair to the child who needs to develop skill in handling problems of this type because the real world is filled with controversy and conflict. The National Council for the Social Studies takes a strong position on this issue in its statement on academic freedom.

It is the prime responsibility of the schools to help students assume the responsibilities of democratic citizenship. To do this, education must impart the skills needed for intelligent study and orderly resolution of the problems inherent in a democratic society. Students need to study issues upon which there is disagreement and to practice analyzing problems, gathering and organizing facts, discriminating between facts and opinions, discussing differing viewpoints, and drawing tentative conclusions. It is the clear obligation of schools to promote full and free contemplation of controversial issues and to foster appreciation of the role of controversy as an instrument of progress in a democracy.[1]

Good sense and mature judgment would dictate that the teacher avoid issues that may cause severe and intense feeling among parents

---

[1]National Council for the Social Studies, "Academic Freedom and the Social Studies Teacher," (a policy statement of the National Council for the Social Studies), *Social Education*, 35 (April 1971), p. 378.

and that can cause the wrath of the community to descend on the school. Problems of this type are usually not well suited for study by the elementary schoolchild anyway. The best problems for discussion are those that are mildly controversial but that deal with material that is significant and within the realm of experience of the child. This does not mean that issues must be limited to local problems. Many adults would be surprised at the extent of knowledge that elementary schoolchildren have on problems of national or international import and the intelligent manner in which they are able to discuss them.

In teaching controversial issues, the teacher has a special responsibility to help children develop habits of critical judgment and open-mindedness, to evaluate sources of information, and to appraise the soundness of facts. Young children are impressionable, and the habit of insisting on getting multiple sides of a question before taking a stand can be taught to youngsters by the teacher's example. There has been some discussion of the necessity of keeping the teacher's stand on issues unknown to the pupils. This is not possible or entirely desirable. To be sure, the teacher does not begin the discussion of an issue by stating his or her own bias to the class. It is the teacher's responsibility to see that all sides of the issue being discussed are presented fairly and impartially and that the reasons underlying points of view are thoroughly aired. If the class requests the teacher's own views on an issue, it is clearly the teacher's right to express them and to state the reasons for the position taken. The professional obligation remains, however, not to attempt to impose a personal point of view on the children on issues that are unsettled and on which there may be honest differences of opinion among well-informed persons. In such cases, the teacher should encourage children to discuss the matter with other adults whom they respect whose views may be different. The child thus learns that there may be honest differences of opinion among intelligent, well-educated persons who consider problems in good faith. The children will respect the teacher who is willing to take a stand on issues, who gives reasons for the position taken, and who accepts and honors the differences in points of view of others.

HOMEOWNERS PROTEST AIRCRAFT NOISE

More than two hundred irate homeowners jammed the chambers of the Metropolitan Airport Commission last evening to protest noise from jets at the International Airport. Property owners are demanding that the Commission secure funds to purchase homes immediately adjacent to the airport. They insist that the noise has reached a level that is intolerable and that it is endangering the health of residents.

"When a plane flies over our home, all conversation must stop," claimed one resident. Similar complaints were made by other homeowners. "It is

213

impossible for us to conduct instruction when planes fly overhead," said Brian Sorokin, a teacher at Stevens School, located near the airport.

Marvin Sherwin, attorney for the homeowners, said his group would resort to legal action if appropriate measures are not taken immediately by the Airport Commission. He could foresee no satisfactory solution to the problem short of clearing the area of homes. "These families bought their homes without knowing that an international airport was to be placed next door to them," he said. "They cannot sell their homes and they cannot live with the present noise level. The Commission must deal with this problem," he added.

Members of the Airport Commission refused comment except to say that the problem is a serious one and that funds were not presently available for the mass evacuation being proposed by the residents. Robert Randall, Chairman of the Commission, said he did not know whether federal monies are available for such removals, but that "all possibilities would be explored."

This news story is a good example of the types of controversial issues that can be found in nearly all communities, large or small. Here are a few other examples:

Whether or not to

- allow an area to be rezoned for a shopping center.
- permit freeway construction through a residential or farming area.
- close an elementary school.
- build an athletic stadium.
- allow a golf course to be built.
- pass a dog leash ordinance.
- allow animals to be used for medical research.
- allow certain forms of gambling.
- restrict trash burning.
- construct a new hospital.

These issues present good opportunities for teaching pupils how to deal with controversy. A teacher might proceed as follows:

1. Have the pupils identify the facts of the case. In examining the airport news story, some of the facts are:
   a. Jet aircraft produce objectionable noise.
   b. A sizable number of homeowners are disturbed over the noise level.
   c. The homeowners are insisting that the Airport Commission do something about the problem.
   d. The homeowners have engaged an attorney to represent them.
   e. The noise problem reduces the possibility of sale of the homes in the affected area.
   f. Money for the purchase of the homes by the Airport Commission is not now available.

214

g. Modern urban areas must have conveniently located jet plane air service.

In identifying facts, it is important not to confuse them with opinions or with issues. For example, one would need further documentation that the noise "is endangering the health of residents" as is claimed in the story. Also, it is *not* a fact that the only solution to the problem is the purchase of the homes by the Commission.

2. Have pupils identify the *issues* in the case. In looking for issues, one is seeking to find out why there is a problem. Usually this involves conflicts of values. In the airport case, for example, the following are some of the issues:
   a. Is it possible to locate metropolitan airports completely away from residential areas?
   b. Have the dollar values of these homes been reduced because of the airport location?
   c. Should the homes of those residents who moved into the area *after* the airport was in operation be purchased?
   d. How can the residents insist on the Commission's purchasing their homes when there is no money available?
   e. Who should bear the cost of the purchase of the homes? The local taxpayers? Travelers who use the airport? The airline companies whose planes make the noise? The federal government?
   f. Does a public facility that results in a nuisance to nearby residents require that the homeowners be paid for damages?
   g. How severe must the nuisance be before a claim can be justified?

3. Have pupils identify alternative solutions to the problem and list the consequences of each alternative. In this type of analysis it is not necessary to come to consensus as to the best solution. In the airport case, these alternatives might be proposed:

Proposals	Consequences
a. Reduce jet noise by reducing landing and takeoff speeds.	a. May not be safe; would not solve the problem completely.
b. Develop less noisy jet engines.	b. Would take too long to develop quieter engines. May not be possible to develop such engines.
c. Relocate the airport.	c. Would be very costly. Would simply move the problem somewhere else.
d. Purchase homes and relocate only those residents	d. Does not solve the problem for the remaining residents.

who owned their property before the airport location was established.

e. Purchase all homes in the affected area.

f. Do nothing.

It is unfair and probably not legal.

e. Would require huge sums of money not now available. Would establish a precedent for other cases of a public facility creating a nuisance.

f. Commission would be subject to legal action and would eventually have to do what the court directs rather than making the decision themselves. Would generate additional public ill will.

Cases such as this lend themselves well to role-playing and simulation. For example, some pupils could play the parts of the Commission members, the homeowners, the attorney, the teacher, and others. The data could be secured by the pupils from the point of view of the role they are playing. If a local issue is the focus of the study, pupils can get data from the community by interviewing individuals, researching background information on the problem, and through local news stories. If the airport case were used, the teacher would need to provide data for the various roles. For example, each player or group of players would receive information prepared by the teacher such as:

Homeowner. You have owned your home ten years. The airport planning began three years after you made the purchase. You and your wife have three children, ages eight, six, and two. You are worried that your children's hearing will be damaged by the noise. You have had your home for sale for a year. Three buyers looked at it, but decided not to buy when they found out about the jet noise problem.

Similar instructions would need to be prepared for all other players in the simulation. Directions for developing simulation games along with an example are provided on pages 335-340.

Situations such as this also can be used to have pupils speculate about the future. For example, how might we deal with the problem of jet aircraft noise (or any of several other issues) in a futuristic setting? Here the pupils do not need to be constrained by what is practicable and feasible—or even possible. They simply let their creative minds imagine what might possibly become alternatives at some future time.

Use of a News Bulletin Board

The teacher should prepare to display interesting news pictures and stories to which the child can turn for information concerning current affairs. Because items on the news bulletin board are changed frequently, it should be in a place in the room where children pass regularly. A point near the doorway is a good location because pupils can stop to examine it for a moment or two on their way in and out of the classroom.

It is good procedure to discuss the significance of the news articles in class before they are posted on the bulletin board. The display should contain items of national and international import as well as items of local interest, sports stories, developments in science, people in the news, perhaps even oddities and jokes for variety and spice. It is helpful to have various sections of the bulletin board specifically designated for such groupings as local news, science in the news, news of our country, and global happenings. This serves as a means of organizing the display in a meaningful way.

Use of a News Map

In the middle and upper grades, the news map can be used to teach current affairs. A world map is displayed in the center of a bulletin board allowing sufficient space around the map for the posting of current news clippings or pictures. Colored string can be used to connect the news story with the location of the spot where the event occurred. This has the value of combining the study of current affairs with map-reading skills. Children should have a major responsibility for keeping the news map up-to-date and for handling the mechanics of its preparation. It is also possible to subscribe to a commerically prepared news map published weekly during the school year.[2]

Use of a Classroom Newspaper

Many teachers consider the classroom newspaper or periodical an indispensable tool in the teaching of current affairs. These materials have a number of definite strengths as well as some limitations that are frequently overlooked. The limitations of classroom current affairs periodicals lie not so much in their makeup but in the manner in which they are used. The papers themselves are generally well prepared. Companies producing these materials have editorial advisory staffs composed of nationally recognized educators in the field of elementary education, and their editorial staffs consist of carefully selected and highly qualified personnel. Three of the better-known sources of classroom periodicals are:

[2]World News of the Week, 100 Subscription Processing Center, South Milwaukee, Wisconsin 53172.

The Civic Education Service, Inc.
1733 K Street
Washington, D.C. 20006
(*Junior Review*, grades 6 through 9)

Scholastic Book Services
Division of Scholastic Magazines
906 Sylvan Avenue
Englewood Cliffs, New Jersey 07632
(*Let's Find Out*, kindergarten)
(*News Pilot*, grade 1)
(*News Ranger*, grade 2)
(*News Trails*, grade 3)
(*News Explorer*, grade 4)
(*News Citizen*, grade 5)
(*Newstime*, grade 6)
(*Junior Scholastic*, grades 6–8)

Xerox Education Publications
Education Center, P.O. Box 16629
Columbus, Ohio 43216
(*My Weekly Reader*, kindergarten through grade 6)
(*Current Events*, grades 7 and 8)

The chief strengths of the classroom newspaper are (1) its careful attention to reading difficulty, (2) its selection of current materials that are significant yet within the comprehension of the pupil, (3) its unbiased presentation, and (4) the common background of information it presents to the class. These advantages cannot be obtained through the use of any other single source. They are designed and published for use by pupils in a classroom, and, therefore, their writing style, readability, and illustrations are suitable to children.

Classroom periodicals also have some limitations of which the teacher should be aware. Even though the readability is carefully controlled, there is no published material that will meet the reading needs of every pupil in class. Some children will find the material too difficult; others will find it too simple. In a sense, the classroom periodical is the "textbook" for current affairs, and its use should be governed by the same pedagogical principles that apply to the use of textbooks generally.

There is a tendency for teachers to formalize the teaching of current affairs through the use of such a classroom periodical. One period a week is set aside for "current events" consisting of the reading of the paper followed by what is called "discussion" but amounts to the presentation of some questions by the teacher to be answered by the pupils. Overemphasis on the formal use of classroom periodicals crowds out the consideration of current affairs from the remainder of the curriculum.

A third limitation of classroom periodicals is that they select items of general interest either nationally or internationally and cannot deal adequately with local news. The teacher will find it necessary to turn to local sources for such news items. This is another reminder to the teacher not to depend entirely on the classroom periodical to carry the entire current affairs program.

The service bulletins that accompany classroom periodicals often suggests ways to make good use of the papers. A procedure similar to this should be followed:

The teacher prepares and preplans—
Read the periodical and accompanying teachers' edition.
Keep up-to-date on current affairs by regularly reading an adult newspaper and news magazine and by listening to radio and television newscasts.
Build your own background on topics included in the classroom periodical.
Plan how to use the periodical and vary the procedure from week to week.

The teacher prepares the classroom—
Post related pictures, maps, and diagrams on the bulletin board.
Have additional references available.
Place new words and terms on the chalkboard.

The teacher prepares the pupils—
Present the periodical to the class by calling attention to a picture, a map, or a particular story.
Discuss reasons why certain topics are in the news.
Develop meanings of new words and terms.
Use maps and the globe to orient pupils.
Develop purposes for reading.
Differentiate requirements to provide for individual differences.
Use the bulletin board, pictures, or other visual aids to motivate the class and to develop concepts.
Plan any special activities relating to the news stories, such as reports, dramatic presentations, and panels.

The pupils read the periodical—
Vary the reading assignments according to reading ability.
Have specific purposes for the reading.
Be available to assist with difficult vocabulary.
Direct the study of slower reading pupils.
Have additional references on topics for more advanced pupils.

The teacher and pupils conduct discussion and follow-up—
Discuss the periodical in terms of the purposes established.
Relate news stories to other classroom work.
Have pupils present any special activities that were planned.
Make generous use of maps and the globe.
Synthesize and summarize ideas and conclusions reached.
Plan further research or other creative follow-up activities.

Use of Daily Newspapers

Some teachers in the middle and upper grades find a daily newspaper helpful in promoting the goals of current affairs instruction. In units dealing with aspects of communication, the newspaper is an important learning resource. Pupils will profit from classroom instruction on the use of the newspaper that focuses on items such as these:

1. the organization of newspapers, purposes of various sections, where to look for certain kinds of information.
2. the nature of news stories, why some appear on the front page and others elsewhere.
3. the purpose and use of headlines.
4. newspaper illustrations: wire photos, maps, charts, graphs, cartoons.
5. the editorial page and its function.
6. detecting bias in news stories.
7. how to read a newspaper.

From time to time the teacher can devise practice exercises such as the following one to help pupils develop their skills in using a daily newspaper.

WHERE WOULD YOU FIND IT?

Features in Today's P-I

Bridge	B-2	Horoscope	B-2
Business	B-3–6	Landers	D-6
Classified	C-7–15	Lifestyle	D-1–6
Comics	D-7	Marine	B-6
Crosswords	B-2	Obituaries	B-10
Dr. Coleman	B-2	Sports	C-1–6
Editorial	A-14, 15	Television	B-9
Films/Arts	B-6–B-8	Travel	D-8, 9
Graham	B-2	Word Sleuth	B-2

In what section of the newspaper would you look if you wanted to know

the results of a major league baseball game?

what movies were showing at local theaters?

if your mother's "For Sale" ad was carried in the newspaper?

something about a person who had died?

the newspaper's position (or opinion) on some current issue?

OR

In what section of the newspaper might you find expressions such as these?

"the series of double plays along with the bases-loaded homer in the ninth . . ."

"nominated for five Oscars . . ."

"For Sale. Three-year-old duplex . . ."

"Dear Ann . . ."

"some influence from Gemini . . ."

"She died in a local hospital after a long illness."

"The market was sharply up today. . . ."

NEWS MEDIA LINGO

Persons who report the news often use expressions that are peculiar to their profession. Here are a few common ones. Can you tell what they mean?

"A usually reliable source . . ."

"The information was leaked to newsmen . . ."

"The story was scooped by the *Post* . . ."

"The Senator tried to extricate his foot from his mouth . . ."

"In a news release from the White House . . ."

"There is a touch of irony in the President's statement . . ."

"This is a live broadcast . . ."

"Both Moscow and Peking said last night . . ."

"In its lead story this morning . . ."

"The story was first carried by syndicated columnist . . ."

SHOULD YOU BELIEVE EVERYTHING YOU READ IN THE NEWSPAPER . . .?

PURPOSE: To learn to detect bias in news accounts.

READINESS: Secure two accounts of the same news story, such as those included in the following example. Make copies and distribute one of each to members of the class.

OPPOSITION TO GUN CONTROL REMAINS STRONG

Legislation pending in Congress would ban possession of the kind of handgun used in the attempted assassination of President Reagan in Washington, D.C., in March, 1981. But opposition remains strong, especially in the House.

The present law banning imports of manufactured cheap handguns was passed in 1968 after the killings of Senator Robert F. Kennedy and Rev. Dr. Martin Luther King, civil rights leader. The law permits importing parts that can be assembled and sold in the United States.

A much tougher bill was approved by the Senate in 1972 after

LITTLE HOPE SEEN FOR GUN CONTROL LEGISLATION

Long overdue legislation pending in the foot-dragging Congress would ban possession of the kind of vicious handgun used in the nearly successful assassination attempt on President Reagan in Washington, D.C., in March 1981. But the carefully coordinated opposition to tough gun controls remains strong, especially in the politically sensitive House.

The present mild law banning imports of manufactured cheap handguns was reluctantly passed in 1968 after the ruthless murders of the popular and respected Senator Robert F. Kennedy and Rev. Dr.

221

the shooting of Governor George C. Wallace, but the House never acted on it. Senate sources said that members have shown a willingness to pass tough gun control laws but are waiting for some sign that the House is ready to do so, too.

Meanwhile, the lobbyists opposing gun control continue their efforts to stop such legislation. They remain consistent in their view that there is not necessarily a correlation between gun control and the actions of fanatics.

Martin Luther King, Nobel prize-winning civil rights leader. The so-called "gun control" law permits importing parts that can be easily assembled and freely sold to fanatics in the crime-ridden United States.

A much tougher bill was approved by the Senate in 1972 after the brutal shooting of Governor George C. Wallace, but, as usual, the conservative House never acted on it. Senate sources said that enlightened members have shown a willingness to pass much-needed tough gun-control laws but are waiting patiently for some hopeful sign that the House is ready to do so, too, however, belatedly.

Meanwhile, the lobbyists opposing reasonable gun controls continue their clandestine efforts to sabotage such legislation. They remain consistent in their warped view that there is no correlation between gun control and the actions of fanatics.

ACTIVITIES: Have the pupils underline the *facts* in each story.

Using a chart, analyze the stories separately according to FACTS AND NONFACTS. Compare the facts in each account to determine if there are any discrepancies.

Analyze the two accounts sentence by sentence by having pupils identify all nouns and the words that describe them (adjectives). List these on the chalkboard or a chart as follows: (Last sentence, first paragraph.)

Account No. 1		Account No. 2	
Nouns	Adjectives	Nouns	Adjectives
opposition	strong	opposition	carefully coordinated, strong
		gun controls	tough
House		House	politically sensitive

CONCLUSION: Have pupils search newspapers and listen to news programs on television and radio on their own and bring to class examples of stories that contain elements of bias in the way they were reported.

Discuss with the pupils the conditions under which it is appropriate for news media to express opinions on issues. (editorials)

Use of a Variety of Activities

A number of learning activities can be used profitably to study current affairs:

Conducting round-table discussions—dividing the class into five or six discussion groups, each to discuss a question related to some item in the news. Each group would be responsible to present to the entire class a short four- or five-sentence summary of its major ideas.

Having panel discussions—selecting five children to prepare a 20-minute presentation to the class on some topic currently in the news. These five children would be given a few days or a week to prepare the presentation and would be the class "experts" on the topic discussed. After the presentation, the remainder of the class could ask questions, clarify points, or add to what the panel has said.

Making charts, maps, graphs—showing increases in school population, steps in an event that led to a crisis, decline or increase in employment, the number of highway accidents over a holiday weekend, the route of a recent air flight of importance, and so on.

Constructing posters, murals—to emphasize safe living, progress in preventive medicine, changes in air travel, progress into space, and other topics.

Keeping scrapbooks of news stories or pictures—clipping and keeping the headlines from the evening paper for several weeks. This helps children to distinguish between news stories that are of continuing interest and those that are transitory in nature. Collections of news clippings can be a valuable resource if the topic selected is one that is likely to be in the news for a period of several weeks or months. Careful selection of articles in the scrapbook will allow the class to follow the development of the news story on a continuing basis.

Drawing cartoons to illustrate news—can be used effectively with older children. Care must be taken to avoid having children draw cartoons that might be offensive to individuals or groups. Cartoons dealing with a community fund drive, a sports story, safety or health habits, conservation practices, good citizenship, and other topics can be used.

Giving reports—is a widely used technique for handling current affairs by having individuals report news items to the class.

Conducting television news programs—can be used from time to time to dramatize news stories. Children can take turns as reporters; variety can be obtained by using a tape recorder and playing the recorded "broadcast" for the class.

Dramatizing news events—when they lend themselves to dramatization. Not all do, but items dealing with festivals, meetings, conferences, and negotiations can be used.

Viewing telecasts of special events—reporting inaugurations, visits of foreign dignitaries, dedications, and other newsworthy programs can be used for in-school viewing in the elementary school. Children can also be encouraged to view news programs out of school and report on these to their classmates.

This chapter concludes with a created news story that is a typical example of the type of controversial issue that can be useful in teaching social studies concepts and skills. As you read this story, based on an actual incident in the Puget Sound area, think of (1) the issues it presents, and (2) what possibilities it holds as a teaching vehicle in the middle and upper grades. At the conclusion of the story, a few teaching suggestions are provided.

WHALE CAPTURE CREATES WAIL

Six killer whales are being held inside the Aqua Life, Inc., nets at Cook Inlet while Bill Holberg decides which ones, if any, will be kept for aquarium exhibits. Hundreds of people watched the capture from boats and shore yesterday afternoon.

The huge mammals swam slowly round and round inside two purse seine nets today, surfacing to "blow" for only moments. They stayed under for five minutes at a time. A large bull whale and a small calf that escaped the capture were nowhere to be found.

Governor Reconsidering

Meanwhile, a political storm was gathering over the capture operation. The governor today interrupted his skiing vacation long enough to say that he was "reconsidering" the state's position on making the inlet a sanctuary for killer whales. The state's senior senator in Washington said that a declaration of support for the governor for a whale sanctuary would clear the way for protection of the sea animals. Earlier efforts to get support from state officials for the idea were unsuccessful. The senator also said, "Apparently this man [Holberg] had a valid permit. But there aren't going to be any more. This is the end!"

Depth Charges Used

An assistant to the State Game and Fisheries Director, Jack Binns, watched the capture from about fifty feet away. Binns said Aqua Life, Inc., boats used "sonar, radar, and 'depth' charges" to drive the whales into smaller and smaller coves and finally into the nets. He said he watched three men in power boats racing across the water atop the whale school, "dropping 'depth charges' as fast as they could light them. I've never seen anything so disgusting in all my life," he said today. "This ought to be stopped right now."

A federal enforcement officer who supervised yesterday's operation said, "there is nothing in the permit that prohibits the use of such explosives."

Use of Charges Denied

Many citizens complained about the capture operation. An automobile dealer from South Harbor said he saw an airplane dropping "tomato can"-size cannisters that apparently exploded as the plane herded the whales. Bill Moss, veterinarian for Aqua Life, Inc., said no such charges were used. He said the whale chasers used "firecracker"-type explosives thrown from boats to herd the whales. Holberg himself was aboard the Aqua Life, Inc., boat, *KANDU*, and was unavailable for comment.

Court Action Threatened

Environmentalists and others bitterly opposed the capture of the whales. Fred Russell, president of the state's largest environmental protection group, PROTEX, demanded that the whales be released. He said his group was prepared to take the matter to court if necessary to prevent Aqua Life, Inc., from keeping the creatures. "This is an outrage," he said, "and we are not going to sit by and let it happen."

Russell cited a Canadian biologist who found that only about sixty-five killer whales remain in the Straits of Georgia and Juan de Fuca and in Puget Sound. Earlier data had placed the number of whales at about three hundred.

Overlapping Jurisdiction

The power to create a whale sanctuary rests with the federal government, but federal law says the governor of a state that contains the sanctuary may veto its creation. This overlapping of jurisdiction sometimes creates confusion or results in no action being taken.

Until today, federal officials thought the governor opposed creation of a killer whale sanctuary in this area. The governor's staff said that no record could be found of the governor's ever having opposed such a proposal.

The senior senator renewed his call for a sanctuary, something he has advocated since 1974. There is no reason to believe that the governor will oppose the creation of the killer whale sanctuary.

How can a news story of this type be used for social studies instruction? Here are a few suggestions:

1. Use the strategy discussed on pages 214–216 in making an analysis of this situation—that is, (a) have the pupils identify the *facts* of the case; (b) have pupils identify the *issues* in the case; and (c) have pupils identify *alternative solutions* to the problem and list the consequences of each alternative.
2. Use this story as a springboard for an in-depth study of endangered species. More than five hundred kinds of animals are listed as rare or in danger of extinction, including blue whales, Indian and Siberian tigers, Asiatic lions, snow leopards, eagles, condors, grizzly bears, alligators, and whooping cranes. Pupils should get into the values question of whether or not an animal has to be "useful" in order to be protected.
3. Have pupils study the roles of federal, state, local, and volunteer groups in decision making regarding issues of the type presented in this story. This should get them into local and state regulations concerning the conservation of natural resources and environmental contamination. It should also confront the matter of what individual citizens or groups of citizens can do when they see something happening that they believe to be unconscionable, even if legal.
4. This story provides an excellent setting for the study of the issue

225

of capture of wild animals for use in circuses and zoos. Should zoos be allowed at all? Do animals benefit from zoos?

5. This story can provide the basis for the study of the web of life food chains—that is, how changes in the population of one animal change the number of another animal on which it feeds. This can be coupled with a study of wildlife management, hunting and fishing regulations, and the concept of *open season.*

6. Study the lives of individuals who have dedicated themselves to the preservation of wildlife and other natural resources: John Muir, Jack Miner, Gifford Pinchot, and local environmentalists.

7. Develop this news story into a role-playing activity in which the issues are highlighted and satisfactory resolutions played out.

8. Have pupils in committees develop "position statements" to represent the point of view of the various principals in this controversy: the whale hunter, the governor, the president of the environmentalist group, an irate citizen, the director of Aqua Life, Inc., who would receive the captured whales, and so on.

9. Use the story to build interest in developing a social-action project dealing with ecology or conservation. A second-grade teacher in Wisconsin reports the following activities that were developed in such a project:

   a. The children helped others become aware of the problems faced by endangered wildlife by sharing their research findings with their family, friends, schoolmates, clergymen, and neighbors.

   b. They wrote letters to state and federal officials to urge their support of legislation designed to protect wildlife.

   c. They presented programs that dealt with the potential threats to wildlife by land developers, trappers, poachers, snowmobilers, hunters, pesticide programs, campers, and so on.

   d. They compiled a list of guidelines and distributed them to each pupil in the school, explaining ways individuals can help. These are some of the guidelines:

      (1) Refuse to shoot birds and other wild creatures "just for the fun of it."

      (2) Refuse to participate in cruel and senseless "chases" of wild animals on snowmobiles, in cars, on bikes, on foot, or in boats or planes.

      (3) Refuse to destroy animal homes.

      (4) Refuse to disturb baby birds and animal babies in their nests.[3]

These suggestions provide interesting extensions of a news story. Of course, no one class would engage in all of them; indeed, it is unlikely that more than one would be used. Perhaps the teacher could create others even more suitable than those provided here. The point

[3] Marsha Gravitz, "You and Me in the Classroom," *Instructor*, 82 (8), April 1973, 43.

of this list is simply to illustrate the wide range of possibilities that inhere in well-selected current news stories. They provide the excitement of controversy, they are relevant to the current stream of human events, they deal with public policy issues, and they lend themselves exceedingly well to social action projects.

DISCUSSION QUESTIONS AND SUGGESTED ACTIVITIES

1. How can map and globe reading be related to the study of current affairs? What possibilities do you see for relating social science concepts to current affairs and vice versa?
2. What would be the strengths and weaknesses of a social studies program built entirely around current affairs?
3. Examine copies of a children's periodical such as those published by Scholastic Book Services. What can a teacher do to ensure imaginative use of such material?
4. Develop appropriate exercises of the types on pages 220–222 based on a newspaper story.
5. In what ways can current affairs topics be used for inquiry and valuing experiences for pupils?
6. Select a news story and explain how it could be used as a springboard for a role playing or simulation exercise.
7. Find a local news item that would be appropriate for teaching the skills needed to deal with controversial issues.
8. In dealing with controversial topics, what issues relating to the teacher's academic freedom are involved?

SELECTED REFERENCES

Degler, Lois Sauer. "Using the Newspaper to Develop Reading Comprehension," *Journal of Reading*, 21 (January 1978), pp. 339–342.

Donohue, Judith Higgins. "Beyond Journalism: The Newspaper as Universal Teaching Tool," *Media and Methods*, 16 (April 1980), pp. 57–58+.

Fairleigh, Roberta Anne. "Extra! Extra! The Newspaper Center," *Teacher*, 94 (February 1977), pp. 50–52.

Gregory, George P. "Using the Newspaper in the Mainstreamed Classroom," *Social Education*, 43 (February 1979), pp. 140–143.

Junior Scholastic, Teacher's Edition. 902 Sylvan Avenue, Englewood Cliffs, New Jersey 17632. Published biweekly during the school year.

Kroen, William C. Jr. "Here and Now," *Teacher*, 96 (January 1979), pp. 82–84+.

Potter, Rosemary Lee. "Newspaper-TV Connection: A Way to Teach Skills," *Teacher*, 95 (December 1977), pp. 36–38.

Turkel, Abby S. "News Center," *Teacher*, 93 (March 1976), pp. 28–30.

See also: Newspaper in the Classroom (NIE) program sponsored by the American Newspaper Publishers Association (ANPA) Foundation. For information about the NIE program and the several materials available through it, contact your local newspaper, or write to the ANPA Foundation, Box 17407, Dulles International Airport, Washington, D.C. 20041, or call 706-620-9500. The NIE program provides many teaching and learning resources; two that are especially recommended are (1) *The Newspaper as an Effective Teaching Tool* and (2) *Biography: Newspaper in Education Publications*, 3rd ed.

Processes and Skills

9

READING TO LEARN
Social Studies

Reading continues to be the most important and essential skill for learning in the curriculum of the elementary school. Children who are retarded in reading are likely to have difficulty with most of their other schoolwork. Some things can be learned visually or through careful listening, but these experiences cannot completely substitute for reading. In spite of the introduction of new materials and media that reduce the reading requirement for some pupils, school programs still depend heavily on reading as a means of learning.

Most elementary schools provide time during the school day when a major effort is made to teach basic reading skills. In this developmental reading program, children acquire a basic reading vocabulary, and learn to use various word recognition techniques along with other skills and abilities that characterize the fluent, independent reader. But a strong basic reading program will not be able to meet all the reading needs of children because each area of the school curriculum requires reading tasks that are somewhat unique to that special area. Helping children develop the specific reading skills and the abilities associated with each area of the curriculum must, therefore, go hand in hand with other instruction in the special-subject area. This point of view is widely supported by authorities in the field of reading.

The special reading skills and abilities needed to handle social studies material intelligently may be identified by examining textbooks and supplementary references written for children. The following are typical of those found in most programs:

In social studies the capable reader

- uses chapter and section headings as aids to reading.
- uses context clues to gain meaning.
- recognizes author bias.
- adjusts speed of reading to purpose.
- interprets what is read.
- detects cause-and-effect relationships.
- understands essential terms and vocabulary.
- gains information from maps, pictures, and illustrations.
- uses various parts of a book as aids to reading.
- is able to skim to locate facts.
- distinguishes between fact and opinion.

231

- compares one account with another.
- recognizes topic sentences.
- interprets quantitative data accurately.
- obtains the literal meaning of the material read.
- relates what is read to reality.
- uses reference aids and references to find information.
- is able to locate a book in the library.

Reading in the social studies is an intellectual process and therefore requires the reader to think while engaging in it. Thus, problems in reading social studies in the middle and upper grades are often a reflection of a pupil's inability to conceptualize and to handle the ideas being presented through the symbolic system of print. Drill and practice on sounding out words is not likely to be of much help in dealing with this type of reading requirement.

This is not to say that the reading task cannot be simplified by careful attention to vocabulary and structural elements. The essential point is that explanations of specialized subjects and topics in print require the use of the terms, words, and concepts that are peculiar to those subjects and topics. The reader will not understand the passage unless the meanings of the terms, words, and concepts used are understood. It is inevitable that pupils with limited conceptual ability will have difficulty reading social studies material.

LEARNING ABOUT THE READING LEVELS OF PUPILS

Elementary teachers in self-contained classrooms provide basic reading instruction to pupils, and, therefore, should be well acquainted with their reading levels. Unfortunately, however, teachers who may be sensitive to pupil differences in reading ability while conducting reading instruction may ignore those differences when it comes to social studies. Or, they conduct social studies instruction as if those variations in reading ability did not exist. Most elementary teachers have had good training in the teaching of reading, and although they are not expected to do intensive diagnostic analyses of the reading problems of pupils, they should be able to make informal assessments of pupil performance in reading. We are assuming here, therefore, that through daily contact with pupils in the basal reading program, through standardized test data, and through observation, the teacher already has some understanding of the ability of individual pupils to apply word-attack skills and to comprehend what is read.

In social studies the teacher should regard diagnostic and instructional procedures as two essential components of the same process. Suppose, for example, the teacher wanted to teach a relatively simple skill such as learning to skim to locate facts. As an initial step, the teacher ought to prepare a diagnostic exercise that will indicate how well pupils are able to perform this skill. For example, an exercise such as the following might be devised:

SKIMMING TO LOCATE FACTS

Directions:

1. Open your book to the correct page.
2. Find the answer as quickly as you can.
3. Write your answer in the space.
4. You will have exactly twenty minutes to do the exercise.

(1) Page 117. What does "VP" mean?_____

(2) Page 121. The goods and services a worker can get in exchange for his money wages are called_____

(3) Page 149. The number of farm workers in 1870 was _____

(4) Page 152. The per cent of women doctors in the Soviet Union is _____

(5) Page 192. The cause of the crisis was _____

(6) Page 209. The number of miles of inland waterways in the United States is _____

(7) Page 209. The cheapest transportation in the United States is by _____

(8) Page 230. Places in cities that have no business buildings are called_____

(9) Page 241. Towns and villages outside large cities are called_____

(10) Page 246. The date San Francisco opened its Bay Area Rapid Transit System—BART—was _____

If a child cannot do this sample exercise, it may be that he or she cannot read well enough to know what the questions ask him or her to do. In that case the reading instruction must begin with attention to more fundamental skills and abilities relating to decoding and comprehension. However, if the child can read the questions but does not know how to locate the answers quickly through skimming, this skill can be taught and practiced. This sequence—diagnosis, instruction, and follow-up practice—can be applied to any of the social studies skills listed on pages 231-232.

A few other sample exercises are these:

I. Using Context Clues to Gain Meaning

Select the words that belong in the blank spaces in this paragraph from the list of words that follows the paragraph.

The work of the TVA was started by building _____ . A _____ is a wall or bank built across a river to stop its flow. The _____ hold back the water so the rivers do not overflow their banks and cause floods. Lakes, or _____ , are formed behind the _____ . Water from the _____ is allowed to flow into the streams when the rivers are low. This makes them _____ at all times. Power plants were built at the foot of some _____ . These plants _____ , or make, electricity. The electricity generated in the plants supplies _____ and _____ to factories, towns, and farms for a 200-mile area.

reservoirs   navigable   power
generate   dams   light
dam

II. Recognizing Topic Sentences

Open your book to page 57. This page contains four paragraphs. Read each paragraph and find the sentence that best tells what the paragraph is all about. In the spaces here, write the beginning two words of the sentences you select.

Paragraph 1. _____   _____

Paragraph 2. _____   _____

Paragraph 3. _____   _____

Paragraph 4. _____   _____

III. Understanding Terms and Vocabulary.

Acronyms (AK' - row - nimz) are words that are formed from the first letter of each word in the full name of something. For example, NOW is an acronym for *N*ational *O*rganization for *W*omen. Acronyms are abbreviated expressions.

Use your text to find the full title of the following acronyms:

1. NATO _____

2. AMVETS _____

3. UNICEF _____

4. NASA _____

5. SALT _____

6. AMTRAK _____

7. BART _____

USING STUDY AIDS AND STUDY SKILLS TO IMPROVE READING

In contrast with reading a library book simply for enjoyment, much of the reading in social studies involves a search for information. Social studies materials, almost without exception, provide many aids to the pupil in doing reading of this type. The teacher cannot assume, however, that pupils will make use of such aids unless they are taught to do so. The skills associated with the use of study aids must be taught, reviewed, and retaught each year throughout the elementary school grades.

Using Various Parts of a Book

The parts of a book should be taught as aids in getting information. For example, if a fifth-grade pupil, Sara, in her study of famous women in American history, wanted to know the name of the Indian woman who assisted Lewis and Clark, how would she find it? She might find a reference to the Lewis and Clark Expedition in the Table of Contents, but that would be less likely than finding it in the Index. She looks in the Index and finds

leather industry, 91–92
Lee, Robert E., 192–195, 197, 307
Lewis, Meriwether, 251, 348, 371
Lewis and Clark Expedition, 251, 371–373
Lewiston, Ida., 348
Lexington, Ky., 214, 217[1]

She turns to page 251 but does not find the information. She then turns to pages 371–373. On page 372 she reads, "During the winter they met a Shoshoni woman whom they asked to be their guide. The Indian's name was Sacajawea, or 'Bird Woman'."[2]

Thus, in a matter of moments, Sara is able to find precisely the information she seeks. Contrast this with the girl sitting next to her who needs the same information, but lacking an efficient way of finding it, goes through the book, page by page, looking for a picture or a clue that will reveal the name of that famous Indian woman. She may never find what she is looking for.

Rather than teaching parts of a book in an expository mode, exercises should be used that require pupils to apply these skills. Often such exercises are included in the book itself. The following is an example:

In the right-hand column are listed the parts of your book. In the left-hand column are listed some thing you might want to find out. For each item in the left-hand column, tell what part of the book you would turn to *first* in order to get the information.

You want to know	Parts of your book
the number of chapters in the book	title page
the meaning of *treaty*	copyright page
how to say the word *bauxite*	preface
when the book was published	table of contents
the population of various states	list of maps
the date the Dutch bought Manhattan Island	list of illustrations
what a sod house looks like	glossary
the route of the first railroad to the west coast	pronunciation key
whether the book tells anything about Canada	appendix
	index

[1]King, Allen Y., Ida Dennis, and Florence Potter, *The United States and the Other Americas*. New York: Macmillan Publishing Company, Inc., 1980, p. 531.
[2]*Ibid.*, p. 372.

Other more complex variations of this exercise are possible. For example, the right-hand column can be omitted and the pupil can be asked to find and supply the information. Or the pupil can be asked to indicate the specific page on which the information appears. Once learned, many of these skills can be transferred to other situations. If the pupils can use an alphabetical arrangement, as in the case of an index, they should also be able to use the dictionary, the encyclopedia, and the card catalog. Also, if they develop the habit of knowing exactly what information they seek before beginning the search, information gathering will be more efficient.

Naturally, the complexity of activities of this type should be appropriate to the age and maturity of the pupils. The examples provided were drawn from the middle grades. But even in the first grade, children learn that books have titles and that pages are numbered. They also learn that sections of their books and/or stories have titles. In the second and third grades they can begin to make use of the Table of Contents to find a particular story. In the third and fourth grades they can learn simple variations of alphabetical arrangements that assist them in using an index.

Using the Organization of a Book

Units, chapters, section heads, and subheads; ends of section, chapter, or unit study aids; maps, charts, or picture captions; introductory questions—all of these make sense to the mature reader who uses them as valuable aids in understanding the organization of a book. But left unguided, a child is not likely to make good use of them as aids to reading. Even teachers may not be familiar with the way a particular book is organized. Chart 5 illustrates some organizational components that are commonly found in social studies texts.

Recognizing Topic Sentences

If pupils learn to recognize the main idea developed in a paragraph, they can organize the ideas developed by the author in some order of importance. They learn to separate the topic being discussed from the elaborative and supporting detail. Before they can deal with topic sentences, however, they have to understand that a paragraph is a group of sentences all of which deal with the same topic or idea. They learn that the *topic sentence* is the critical one in the paragraph because it tells the reader what the paragraph is about. A little practice will help pupils understand the singleness of purpose of paragraphs. Exercises such as the one on page 234 can be used.

Read these selections and decide which is easier to understand.[3]

A

As they drove on, he told them stories he'd heard about the old days on the Chathams, about the ships and the men who hunted the whales and seals, about the Morioris and how they had been almost killed out by the Maoris who came out here over a hundred years ago. "There's lots of people here with Maori blood," he said. "But there's not many with Moriori blood." The road curved round the lake, through hills, paddocks and beside smaller lakes. Ducks and swans were on all the lakes. They bumped across some paddocks and came to the airstrip. There were a lot of Land-rovers and the yellow truck beside two sheds. They heard the plane before they could see it. It came low over the trees and bumped along on the grass of the airstrip. People got off, and others got on. Bags of mail and parcels of goods were carried off through the big doors, and others were put on. The fisherman was carried on.

B

As they drove on, he told them stories he'd heard about the old days on the Chathams, about the ships and men who hunted the whales and seals, about the Morioris and how they had been almost killed out by the Maoris who came out here over a hundred years ago. "There's lots of people here with Maori blood." he said. "But there's not many with Moriori blood."

The road curved round the lake, through hills, paddocks and beside smaller lakes. Ducks and swans were on all the lakes. They bumped across some paddocks and came to the airstrip. There were a lot of Landrovers and the yellow truck beside two sheds.

They heard the plane before they could see it. It came low over the trees and bumped along on the grass of the airstrip. People got off, and others got on. Bags of mail and parcels of goods were carried off through the big doors, and others were put on. The fisherman was carried on.

1. Why is one selection easier to read than the other?
2. Why did the author group the sentences the way he did in selection B?
3. Is there something about the grouping of sentences that makes them a paragraph?
4. Which sentence in each paragraph in selection B tells what the paragraph is about?

An exercise of this type should be followed by practice in identifying topic sentences in paragraphs selected from the pupils' text. They should learn (1) that the topic sentence tells what the paragraph is about, (2) that other sentences in the paragraph elaborate on the topic, and (3) that the topic sentence is usually, but not always, the first sentence in a paragraph.

[3] From *The Chatham Islands* by Jack Lasenby. (A Bulletin for Schools) Wellington, New Zealand: Department of Education, undated, p. 32.

UNIT 3—Life Ways Around The World ←

CHAPTER SEVEN — THE EARTH AS THE HOME OF MANY PEOPLE ←

How Do People Use The Earth?

Where Do People Live On the Earth?

How Are People Alike In What They Need? ←

How Are People Different In The Way They Live?

Soon the days become shorter. Often one can see birds flying south. Nearly every night the temperature drops below freezing. The *growing season* is over even though there may still be many warm days. The growing season is that time between the last killing frost in the spring and the first killing frost in the fall.

Finding the Main Ideas ←

Go back to the section called "How Do People Use The Earth?" on page 212. Which of the following is the main idea of that section?

a. All people must have certain things from the earth in order to live.

b. People who live in cities need the earth less than people who live on farms.

Understanding Key Words and Terms ←

Producer   Exchange   Culture

Use these words to complete the paragraph below

In every_____ people _____ goods and services. How people_____ etc. . . .

Using What You Have Learned ←

On page 143 there are listed several fire hazards . . .

Getting the Facts ←

Skim the section "How Do People Use The Earth?" on page 212 and tell which of the following statements are true. . .

Thinking About What You Have Read . . . ←

Why do you suppose . . .

CHART 5.

Using Picture Captions

Publishers invest huge sums of money to provide instructive illustrations for social studies textbooks. Unfortunately, the full value of these exercises as aids to reading are not realized unless pupils are taught how to make good use of them. Illustrations are not simply decorative afterthoughts included to make the book more appealing. They are, or should be, an integral part of the message system of the text.

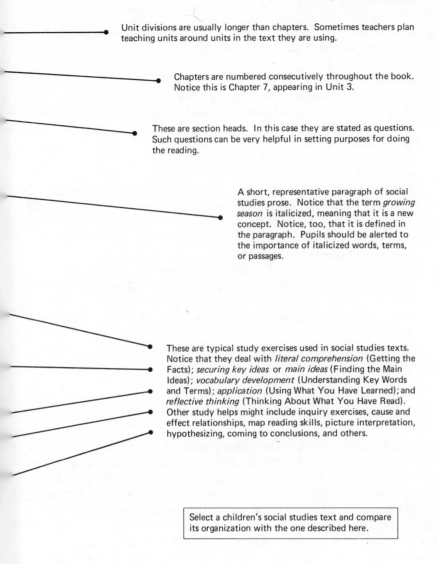

Unit divisions are usually longer than chapters. Sometimes teachers plan teaching units around units in the text they are using.

Chapters are numbered consecutively throughout the book. Notice this is Chapter 7, appearing in Unit 3.

These are section heads. In this case they are stated as questions. Such questions can be very helpful in setting purposes for doing the reading.

A short, representative paragraph of social studies prose. Notice that the term *growing season* is italicized, meaning that it is a new concept. Notice, too, that it is defined in the paragraph. Pupils should be alerted to the importance of italicized words, terms, or passages.

These are typical study exercises used in social studies texts. Notice that they deal with *literal comprehension* (Getting the Facts); *securing key ideas* or *main ideas* (Finding the Main Ideas); *vocabulary development* (Understanding Key Words and Terms); *application* (Using What You Have Learned); and *reflective thinking* (Thinking About What You Have Read). Other study helps might include inquiry exercises, cause and effect relationships, map reading skills, picture interpretation, hypothesizing, coming to conclusions, and others.

Select a children's social studies text and compare its organization with the one described here.

CHART 5 (*Continued*)

Pictures and illustrations elaborate concepts presented in the narrative but usually do not repeat exactly what is said in the text. Neither do picture captions simply tell what would be obvious to the reader only by looking at the picture. Thus, captions should call attention to some element or relationship in the picture or illustration that might be missed by the casual viewer. Often this is done by using a question or series of questions. In this way pictures and illustrations can provide the reader with a wealth of information. In teach-

239

ing children how to use pictures and illustrations, questions such as these may be appropriate:

1. Exactly what is being shown in the picture?
2. What relationships are illustrated by the picture?
3. When was this picture taken? (recently, years ago, time of day, and so on)
4. How does the picture illustrate something we discussed in class?
5. What influences (causes or effects) can be detected in the picture?
6. What does the picture tell about the life-styles of the people?
7. How does the picture illustrate something valued by people?
8. How does the picture show conflicts between traditional and modern ways of doing things?
9. What does the picture show that illustrates the roles of men, women, and children in that society?
10. What characteristics of the culture are shown in the picture?
11. What can you say about the geography of the area shown by the picture?
12. What conversation might be going on between the persons in the picture?

BUILDING SOCIAL STUDIES VOCABULARY

The vocabulary load of social studies reading material is one of the major causes of poor comprehension and faulty reading in social studies. Even with the more careful attention that contemporary authors give to word difficulties, the social studies vocabulary remains a stumbling block for many children. Although a degree of simplification is possible, it is true that there are limits beyond which the use of a specialized vocabulary cannot be avoided. If one is speaking or writing about social studies concepts, appropriate vocabulary must be used. This is not altogether undesirable if the teacher accepts vocabulary development as one of the goals of the total social studies program. The same situation exists in other areas of the curriculum; the child must learn the language associated with mathematics, science, art, music—all of which have their own peculiar words, terms, or phrases. The following chart shows some of the types of words and terms that are peculiar to social studies.

WORDS AND TERMS NEEDING SPECIAL ATTENTION IN SOCIAL STUDIES

Technical terms—Words, terms, and expressions peculiar to social studies and usually not encountered when reading selections from other fields of knowledge. *Examples:* veto, meridian, frontier, latitude, longitude, legislature, polls, franchise, temperate, plateau, hemisphere, mountainous, wasteland, balance of power, capitalism, democracy, nationalism, civilization, century, ancient, decade.

Figurative terms—Expressions that are metaphorical; having a different connotation from the literal meaning usually associated with the word. *Examples:* political platform, cold war, closed shop, iron curtain, log rolling, pork barrel, open door, hat in the ring.

Words with multiple meanings—Words that have identical spelling but whose meaning is derived from context. *Examples:* cabinet, belt, bill, chamber, mouth, bank, revolution, fork, court, assembly, range.

Terms peculiar to a locality—Expressions peculiar to a specific part of the country that are not commonly used elsewhere. *Examples:* truck, meeting, borough, gandy, draw, coulee, right, prairie, section, run, butte, arroyo.

Words easily confused with other words—Words that are closely similar in general configuration. *Examples:* peasant for pheasant, alien for allies, principal for principle, longitude for latitude, executive for execution, conversation for conservation.

Acronyms—Words that are abbreviated expressions. *Examples:* NATO, NASA, OPEC, SALT, NOW, UNICEF.

Quantitative terms—Words and terms signifying amounts of time, space, or objects. *Examples:* shortly after, century, fortnight, several years later, score, one hundred fifty tons.

The teacher should anticipate word difficulties *before* pupils are asked to read a social studies selection. Two types of word problems must be expected. One is the inability to recognize the word in print; the other is not knowing the meaning of the word once it is recognized. Therefore, new words and terms should be presented and developed in the context of a phrase or a sentence rather than in isolation.

Vocabulary development should be conducted in relatively short, highly motivated settings. Having pupils look up a long list of terms in the dictionary prior to reading a selection is not productive. A better arrangement is to write the key terms in a phrase or sentence on the chalkboard and discuss their meanings. Better still, the sentence in the text in which the word or term appears can be selected for directed study.

Maintaining a sensitivity to, and interest in, new words and terms is essential. Pupils should be encouraged to use the specialized social studies vocabulary in their discussions. From time to time the teacher may want to involve them in word games such as "Twenty Questions." Devising riddles, providing synonyms or antonyms, making or completing crossword puzzles, or constructing variants of words are helpful in maintaining an awareness to new terms. Also, bulletin board displays and other classroom exhibits can feature new words encountered in social studies.

Teaching how known words can be used to construct new words can be of help in recognizing new words and understanding their meanings. Among the simplest variations are compound words or

241

the addition of prefixes or suffixes. Some examples are these: construct, construct*ed*, construct*ing*, construct*ion*; consume, consum*er*, consum*ed*, consum*ing*; loyal, *dis*loyal, loyal*ist*; front, front*ier*, frontiers*man*.

One of the most useful skills in reading social studies materials is the use of context clues. A reader, for example, should have no problem gaining meaning from the following passage even though many of the words are missing.

> At exactly 4:05 P.M. the _____ landed at the _____. Hundreds of _____ were waiting in the _____. It was the first time many of them had seen our nation's leader. When the _____ came down the _____, he _____. The crowd _____. He made a short _____. The crowd _____ again. In a few _____ he was on his way again, this time in a _____. As the _____ went straight up, the _____ could see the _____ through the window of the _____.

Gaining meaning through context is especially appropriate to social studies because it ensures that the reading is done thoughtfully. This contrasts with defining words and terms in isolation, in which case the wrong meaning might be selected. Many social studies terms and words have multiple meanings. For example:

- He established the first *bank* in the region.
- The river overflowed its left *bank*.
- "You can *bank* on that," he said.
- Directly ahead was a big *bank* of snow.
- As he looked west, he could see a large *bank* of clouds.
- Just before crashing, the plane seemed to *bank* to the left.
- The assembly line consisted of a long *bank* of machines.

When terms that have multiple meanings are encountered in a passage, only the meanings being used in the passage should be developed at that time and they should be developed in context.

Glossaries do not provide the meanings of words and terms in context and, therefore, have some limitations in providing the meanings of new terms. For instance, a pupil may read the following sentence:

Several well-known people from this city were killed in the crash of a charter flight.

Looking in the glossary of a text for the meaning of the word *charter*, the pupil finds

242   char'ter: a paper giving a person or company special rights

It happens that the definition of *charter* given is only one of about five that correctly defines that word.

After anticipated word difficulties have been attended to and the purposes for doing the reading have been established, pupils will usually read selections silently the first time through (middle grades). The teacher should be available to assist those who encounter problems with words. Children should be encouraged to figure out the meaning of words for themselves, but if a child cannot do so in a couple or three tries, the teacher should explain the term, pronounce it, and have the child proceed with the reading. Reading of the entire selection should not be held up because of a problem with a few unfamiliar words or terms.

It is often helpful to keep a special social studies vocabulary list posted in the classroom. Lists can be developed by individual children, too, and made into a social studies picture dictionary. If a word is likely to be used frequently in writing, such a word might be added to an individualized spelling list. However, many social studies words are not often used by children in their writing and, therefore, do not make good selections for spelling lists. They are more likely to be a part of children's reading vocabulary than their writing vocabulary.

Most social studies texts provide extensive study aids to assist with vocabulary development, including any or all of the following:

1. Contextual definition of words and terms.
   Examples: Thousands of persons in this city earn their living by *processing* food. Processing means preparing food for marketing.

   In recent years people have become concerned about *pollution.* Pollution comes about when something harmful is placed into the water or air.

2. Use of boldface type and/or italics.
   Examples: The things from which products are made are called **raw materials**. Three *raw materials*—iron ore, coal, and limestone—are found in the Midwest.

3. End of unit, chapter, or section exercises.
   Examples: Matching exercises.
   Selecting terms for incomplete sentences.
   Finding definitions of key terms in the text.

4. Glossaries.
   Examples: **Pig iron:** melted iron that hardens into bars
   Pilgrim: a person who travels to holy places to worship
   Plantation: a large farm that specializes in one crop
   Polar regions: areas in the high latitudes

5. Pronunciation guide.
   Examples: **tropics** (trop′ iks)
   volcano (vol-ka′ no)

243

IMPROVING READING COMPREHENSION

Reading with comprehension means that the reader is able to extract from the selection the essential facts and understandings, visualize details, and sense the relatedness of the facts. It is a process of obtaining an understanding of the meaning the author was attempting to convey. Comprehension depends on a number of factors, some of which reside within the reader and others that deal with the selection to be read. Because of the complexity of the psychological processes involved in comprehension, as well as the limitations of printed symbols to convey meaning, it is doubtful that the reader is ever able to obtain the precise shade of meaning intended by the author. Teachers can help children read social studies materials with greater understanding, however, if proper attention is given to the factors known to affect reading comprehension.

It is obvious that the child who brings the most to a reading situation will receive the most in return. What the child brings that will enhance reading social studies materials are intellectual ability and experience background. Although there is not much a teacher can do about the intellectual capacities of pupils, there is a great deal that can be done to broaden their life experiences. Extensive use of field trips, films, pictures, stories, exhibits, displays, and real objects will materially assist the child in comprehending the ideas encountered in reading.

Comprehension is sometimes, but not always, related to the speed of reading. The poor reader may read at a snail's pace and also comprehend very little. The good reader, on the other hand, may read rapidly and have an adequate understanding of the ideas presented. Under ordinary conditions, the difficulty of the material *as it appears to the reader* will determine the rate of speed at which it should be read. Children should be taught that rate of reading should vary in accordance with the degree of comprehension required.

Some topics in social studies are more easily understood than others, and therefore, reading comprehension is more of a problem in dealing with some topics than it is with others. A narrative account of early plantation life in the South is straightforward and relatively easy to understand. Most children can read selections of this type rapidly and keep their comprehension high. On the other hand the child may encounter a passage that explains the topic "Why Seasons Change." This is an exceedingly complex idea and will require the most careful reading the child can muster if it is to be understood.

Reading comprehension in social studies consists of at least four components: (1) getting the literal meaning or a general understanding of what is being communicated; (2) understanding and remembering facts and details that support key ideas; (3) recognizing and remembering the sequence of ideas or events presented; and (4) following directions. Sometimes interpretation is regarded as a component of comprehension, but in this treatment, we deal with interpretation in a separate section. What follows are suggested procedures that can be used to build better comprehension.

Preview for the General Idea

Because comprehension involves getting meaning, it helps if the reader has a general idea as to what the material is all about before starting to read it. Such an overview will usually be directed by the teacher, but pupils should develop the habit of previewing material themselves. Let us say that a class is about to read *part* of a new unit entitled "The World of Carmelita and José." The teacher speaks to the class:

Teacher: Boys and girls, for the next few days we will be reading from our social studies books. I would like to introduce you to two children we will visit in this unit whose names are Carmelita and José. Please open your books to page 86. (The children take time to find the page.) Notice that the large print says "The World of Carmelita and José." Just looking at this page, what do you think this unit is about?

Frieda: Mexico.

Teacher: Why did you say Mexico, Frieda?

Frieda: Because Carmelita and José are Mexican names. Besides, it shows their pictures and they are dressed in Mexican clothes. . . . We learned that when we studied the community in Texas. . . .

David: That doesn't mean they are from Mexico. They could be from several other countries in South America and have names like that. They would dress like that, too.

Teacher: Those are both good ideas. Perhaps if we page through this unit, we can discover the country it talks about. Turn to the map on page 88. . . .

It is established that the unit is, indeed, Mexico, and the teacher continues. . . .

Teacher: As you look at these pages, what do you suppose you will be reading about in the world of Carmelita and José?

Eric: Well, it looks like . . . uh . . . it tells like . . . you know . . . what they do every day . . . in school . . . at home, you know. . . .

Lisa: It shows how they do many of the same things we do.

Teacher: What do you mean?

Lisa: Well, we have homes and families, we go to school, we go shopping, and things like that, and they do, too.

The discussion concludes after the teacher is satisfied that the pupils are oriented to the material to be read. Previews should do the following:

1. Help the reader get the general idea of what the selection is all about.

2. Help the reader understand how the material is organized and understand the nature of the narrative.
3. Help the reader see how the subject matter to be read relates to prior studies or experiences.
4. Help the reader understand how illustrations relate to the subject matter to be read.

Anticipate and Attend to Potential Word Difficulties

As has been indicated earlier, word difficulties and word meanings should be attended to before the reading is attempted. Often this can be done during the time the material is being previewed. In the example cited in the foregoing section, for instance, the teacher might have called the attention of the class to such words as *serape*, *fiesta*, *tortilla*, and *hacienda*. Specific suggestions for vocabulary development are provided on pages 241-243.

Establish Clear Purposes for Doing the Reading

Reading for a purpose is critical to comprehension. Many pupils pore over their social studies texts for endless hours without really knowing what they are looking for or why they are doing the reading. Clearly, it is the teacher's responsibility to make sure that the reading pupils do is purposeful. In a directed study situation, these purposes may be given orally by the teacher:

Find the sentence near the top of page 115 that begins, "Each time this happens. . . ." Put your finger on that sentence. (The teacher sees that all pupils have the correct place.) Now read the next three paragraphs to find out three different ways of controlling air pollution.

If the reading is to be done independently, that is, not directed by the teacher, as in the example given, the purposes of the reading can be written on the chalkboard:

As you read the section "Dangers to Health" on pages 143-146, find the answers to these questions:

1. Why are scientists worried about air pollution?
2. Why has the government stopped the sale of some products?
3. What does the author mean on page 145 when he says, "Time is running out"?

The book itself may provide aids for setting purposes for reading. For example, the teacher says:

For several days we have been learning about life in and around Big City. Today we will be doing some reading about how people get to work in Big City. On page 25 of your book there is a section that begins with the question "How

Do People in Big City Get to Work?" Open your book to page 25. Can you find that question? Fine. As you read this part, find out as many ways as you can how people get to work in Big City. When you are finished reading, we will talk about the ways you found. See if each of you can find all the ways the author tells about.

The teacher should vary the purposes from time to time in order that pupils can get practice on a variety of skills. Purposes can relate directly to the four basic components of comprehension; namely, getting the literal meaning, getting facts and details, sensing a sequence of events or ideas, and following directions.

Use Study and Organization Aids Provided in the Book

The use of study and organization aids was discussed earlier in this chapter (see pages 234-239). Attention is called to these aids again here because their use can be enormously helpful to a pupil in comprehending what is read. It should be stressed that time must be taken to explain the organization of material and to instruct pupils in the use of the various aids presented. In learning about the organization of the material, children are also learning skills that are associated with organizing their own ideas to gain a better understanding.

Teach Pupils to Vary Their Rate of Reading

As a regular part of social studies instruction, the teacher should devise reading situations that will require children to vary their rate of reading for a particular purpose. This may be in the form of questions, some calling for rapid reading or skimming, others for more detailed careful reading and rereading. Commonly, the answers to names of places, persons, situations, dates, and similar factual data can be obtained through skimming, whereas answers to reflective questions will require slower, more careful reading.

Relate What Is Read to Pupils' Life Experiences

This procedure not only helps comprehension but is motivating as well. It tends to give the material an added dimension of meaningfulness. Here are a few examples:

The pupils read about:	*The pupils relate this to:*
1. fire hazards	1. danger spots in their homes
2. discoverers, explorers, pioneers	2. present-day mountain climbers, adventurers, astronauts
3. ecology	3. local environmental contamination
4. occupations and careers	4. their own career interests and ambitions

247

5. the law and justice systems

5. their own involvement with the law (in the civil, not criminal area)

6. the interdependence of nations

6. the energy crisis, foreign-made products they use

Check Comprehension Regularly and Keep Individual Records

When one wants to improve, it helps to record progress. In working toward improved reading comprehension, the teacher should follow a systematic cycle of instruction, practice, evaluation, and feedback to the learner. Social studies education is or should be more than reading. But beginning at about the third grade and continuing through the middle and upper grades, indeed, through high school, reading (especially reading *comprehension*) is critical to success in social studies. Comprehension suffers when the teacher assumes that the pupil has the skills developed well enough to meet the reading requirements of the social studies.

Short teacher-made tests similar to several of the examples provided in this chapter can be used to assess pupil comprehension. It is recommended that time limits be set for such evaluations and that these be kept constant from one test to the next. Providing the children with information about the improvement they have made in reading over a period of time is likely to encourage greater effort on their part to improve their reading comprehension.

LEARNING TO INTERPRET IDEAS

Reading comprehension in the strictest sense involves getting the facts as they are presented by the author. Social studies materials often require that the reader interpret the ideas. This involves making inferences, sensing relationships, noting cause-and-effect occurrences, detecting the emotional bias of the author, reading critically, evaluating the material, and being able to anticipate or predict likely outcomes. It requires the reader to go beyond the literal presentation of the facts and to sense the significance of them. This process is referred to as "reading between and beyond the lines." Consider the following example that might be a passage from a selection read by fifth-graders:

All day long the wagon train moved slowly westward. The travelers were tired and weary from the long, dusty journey. The wagonmaster looked at his watch. It was four o'clock, but the sun was still high in the sky. Directly ahead was the river that had to be crossed. On the other side was high ground. Near the river bank was a fine grove of trees. The wagonmaster wondered if he should have the tired travelers cross the river yet today or camp on this side of the river and cross over the first thing in the morning. He decided to make the crossing that evening.

Now answer these questions: (1) In what season of the year were the people traveling? (2) Why do you suppose the wagonmaster decided in favor of crossing that evening? Notice that the material does not give the answers to either of the questions, yet the answers can be inferred from the information given. Many passages in social studies books lend themselves to questions of this type.

Being able to interpret ideas and grasp their significance is a complex, thinking, creative process. Obviously, children in the elementary school are not going to master such skills, but they can be helped to make a good beginning toward that end. This can be done by having them draw conclusions and state generalizations, by making comparisons, by suggesting relationships, by helping them sense the need for suspended judgment, and by other similar experiences. Research in children's thinking supports the view that reasoning and problem-solving abilities begin at about age three and develop continually with increasing age and experience. Stimulating experiences in critical thinking and problem-solving during the formative years of early childhood can do much to foster the growth of such skills. The following example shows how two different kinds of questions can be based on the same piece of prose, each requiring different reading skills and different intellectual processes.

INDIAN "OLD FIELDS"

The Indians, we have seen, lived in villages. After eight or ten years in one place, an Indian village area became very dirty and had many rats, mice, and insects in it. The Indians knew, from long experience, that these conditions led to disease. Also they knew that, after a few years, their fields did not grow as large crops as did new fields. Therefore, every eight or ten years the people would find a new area, perhaps three or four miles away. There they would build a new village. They had to clear away the forest to build the new village and to start new fields around their new homes. The clearings and fields left behind became "old fields."

The records of all the colonies, from Canada to the Gulf of Mexico, mention large numbers of old fields. The early settlers called them "fair meadows," "broad grassy plains," "fine savannas," or "grassy glades." But there were few *natural* grassy places in this forest-covered land. All these names for open places referred to the same thing: Indian old fields.

By using Indian old fields, the settlers saved themselves the long, hard labor of cutting away the forest to start farming. Everywhere the old fields were a great help in getting settlements started.

The reason that there were so many old fields lies in an unhappy experience in Indian history. We believe that an epidemic swept through the Indian population in the 1500's. The disease was probably smallpox or some other disease to which the Indians had never before been exposed. They probably caught the disease from European fishermen who had gone ashore somewhere along the Atlantic Coast. Then it spread from one Indian group to another. The epidemic killed many—or even most—of the Indians from the Gulf of Mexico to Canada. As a result, there were many deserted clearings—old fields—where villages had once stood.[4]

[4]Prunty, Merle and Bertha Davis, *This Favored Land*, 2nd ed., New York: Macmillan Publishing Company, Inc., 1974, pp. 26–27.

Questions requiring comprehension of literal meaning	Questions requiring interpretation of ideas
1. How often did the Indians move from place to place?	1. If the Indians did not find the fields productive, how did it happen that the white settlers did?
2. Why did the Indians move so often?	2. How large would you say the Indian farms were?
3. How far away did the Indians build the new village from the old one?	3. What can you tell about the kinds of homes the Indians had?
4. What did the early settlers call these Indian old fields?	4. Why would the Indians' old fields not be as productive as the new ones?
5. Why did the settlers use the Indian old fields?	5. What time of the year would the Indians have cleared their fields?
6. What disease caused the epidemic among the Indians in the 1500's?	6. What evidence would lead scientists to think that an epidemic swept through the Indian settlements?
7. How did the Indians get the disease?	7. Why couldn't these open areas have been caused by fires started by lightning?
8. What did the disease have to do with the Indian old fields?	8. Do you think that the smallpox disease might have been more deadly among the Indians than among the European whites? Why or why not?

In comparing these two sets of questions, it is obvious that one set can be answered directly from the text and that the other cannot. In the latter case the readers must go beyond the information provided by the author; they have to bring prior knowledge to bear on the questions. They have to be able to speculate, to wonder, and to imagine. Moreover, there are probably no absolutely correct answers to these questions. In the case of the first set of questions, right answers can be established if one uses the authority of the narrative in determining correctness. Clearly, questions such as those in the right-hand column are best suited for discussion in class and should not be given as homework assignments.

LOCATING AND USING REFERENCE MATERIALS

Pupils should make use of a wide variety of reference material in studying social studies topics. The value of such references depends not only on their availability but also on the ability of the children to make optimum use of them. The teacher's responsibility in this respect is, therefore, twofold: teaching children (1) which references to use for various purposes and (2) how to use the reference efficiently once it is found. These are continuing responsibilities of the social studies program and cannot be completely taught in any one grade or any one year. A beginning will be made in the primary grades, but the child will continue to extend and refine the ability to use references throughout high school, college, and in later life. Instruction usually will begin as soon as the child develops a degree of independence in reading.

The reference materials used in the social studies may be grouped meaningfully as follows:

Books
Textbooks
Supplementary reading books
Picture books
Biographies
Historical fiction

Special References
Encyclopedias
Maps and globes
Atlases
Dictionaries
World Almanac
Charts and graphs
Yearbooks
Legislative Manuals
Who's Who in America
Junior Book of Authors
Statesman's Yearbook

Reference Aids
Card catalog
The Reader's Guide
Bibliographies

Miscellaneous Materials
Advertisements
Magazines and periodicals
Recipes
City and telephone directories
Labels
Guidebooks and tour books
Letters and diaries
Travel folders
Postcards
Newspapers and news clippings
Comic books
Pictures
Schedules and timetables
Pamphlets and booklets (such as those from the information services of foreign countries, Superintendent of Documents, conservation departments, historical societies, art galleries)
Weather reports
Manufacturers' guarantees and warranties
Money, checks, coupons for premiums, receipts
Reviews, government documents

Much of the instruction given on the use of references will have to be specific to the particular resource used. For example, one uses the *World Almanac* differently and to obtain different information than one does the atlas or a tour book. Moreover, the references may be used at varying levels of sophistication. The library may be used by primary-grade children under teacher guidance to check out books, to look at magazines, or to have stories read to them, whereas upper-grade children should be able to use the library independently, making use of the card catalog and locating books themselves. The use of the various references should be taught as the need for them arises in the social studies.

The following suggestions will be helpful.

LEARNING TO USE REFERENCES

In the Primary Grades

1. Acquaint the children with the school library and provide pleasurable experiences for them with this facility by having them look through books, check out books, look at magazines, and have stories read to them. Enlist the help of the librarian if there is one.
2. Provide learning centers that are well stocked with easy reading and picture books related to the topic under study.
3. Make frequent use of references in the regular work of the classroom. This may mean comparing a seashell that a child has brought with the picture of one in the book of shells; finding out whether we eat the roots, stems, or leaves of broccoli; finding out about the different kinds of boats and their uses; and hundreds of other questions that children wonder about during the course of the unit. It is helpful to have an encyclopedia handy for this purpose. Not all children will be able to use it, but its presence and use by the teacher provides an excellent means of developing positive attitudes toward reference materials.
4. Identify the children who are progressing rapidly in reading and teach and encourage them to use references such as the encyclopedia, magazines, pamphlets, and other material from which they can profit but that may be too complex for the rest of the class.
5. Give children experiences in helping to locate materials—finding appropriate pictures, stories, or sections of books that relate to the social studies topic.
6. Develop prerequisite competencies for the efficient use of a dictionary: alphabetical ordering, use of guide words, antonyms, synonyms, multiple meanings of words. Primary-grade children could make a class picture-dictionary of social studies words and terms they encounter.

In the Middle and Upper Grades

1. Make certain that children know how to use the various parts of a book. (See pages 234–239).
2. Take time out to teach children how to use the library, card catalog, the *Reader's Guide*, and other aids for the purpose of locating information.
3. Teach the various skills needed to use each of the special references: encyclopedia, *World Almanac*, atlas. Provide for practice as well as application in purposeful settings.
4. Plan social studies activities that require the use of a wide variety of references.
5. Have children browse through the library and other sources to locate material that is appropriate for the unit under study.
6. Teach children how to identify key words in using reference material. Children may know how to use the references but not know what to look for with regard to the information they are seeking.
7. Teach children how to use titles of books as guides to their content, and select books that are appropriate for the purpose.

Skills needed to use references can be practiced and learned on an individual basis by pupils by using Task Cards, as is illustrated in the following example:

SIDE ONE

Find Out for Yourself

(If you cannot do any one of these, look for a clue on SIDE TWO of this card.)

1. Find the article on "Safety" in the *World Book*.
2. Into how many sections is the article divided? _____
3. Skim through the article to find these two facts:
   a. Where do most accidents happen? _____
   b. What do the letters *UL* on electrical wiring and appliances stand for? ___
   _____
4. Suppose you heard that someone had been killed in an accident in his or her home but you did not know what kind of an accident it was. You would be right most of the time if you guessed that the accident was a _____
   _____ or a _____ or _____
5. Suppose you questioned the accuracy of this article. What is there about the article that might renew your confidence in its authority? _____
   _____

SIDE TWO

CLUES

1. Select volume S–Sn. Look for the article according to the alphabet.
2. See the "Outline" at the end of the article.
3. a. Look under the section "Safety/Home."
   b. Look under "Safety with Electricity."
4. What does the article say about the major causes of accidental deaths in the home?
   _____
   _____
   _____
5. What group critically reviewed the article?
   _____
   _____
   _____
   _____

An example of teacher-prepared task cards.

If teachers regard the teaching of reading as something that is done in three small groups during the reading period and ignore the reading needs of children during the remainder of the school day, they may expect children to have many disappointing experiences reading social studies material. The feeling that children learn to read in the basic reading program and read to learn in the social studies, for example, is not an entirely correct concept of reading growth and development. Actually, these two processes occur simultaneously; children improve their reading ability *as they read to learn*. Children can extend and improve their reading skills and abilities quite apart from the basic reading program as they use reading for a variety of purposes.

USING WRITING SKILLS IN SOCIAL STUDIES

The learning activities associated with social studies present many opportunities to teach all of the communication skills, not only reading. Children read for information and often share that newly gained knowledge through oral reports and in class discussions. In such interactions, pupils use speech and speaking skills, and, correspondingly, others are listening to what is being communicated. Or, children may prepare written notes or reports on what they have read or heard. We see, therefore, that there is a constant and close relationship between and among the several language arts—reading, speaking, listening, writing—as skills that are essential to learning social studies. The reverse is also true; social studies presents excellent functional settings in which to teach such skills.

The elementary school curriculum often becomes badly fragmented with bits and pieces of subjects and skills without being tied into some type of integrated organized framework. Moreover, subjects and skills such as writing, reading, spelling, and listening often become make-believe exercises when they are taught in isolation, outside of a subject matter context. How much more meaningful these skills become for a learner when they are taught in purposeful settings. The child is then reading to find out something of importance to the subject under study. Or, the child is writing something that will be shared with others as a contribution to knowledge about a topic. With greater attention to the inclusion of important communication skills in the units planned for social studies, the teaching of social studies *and* the language arts would be improved. We have discussed this subject as related to one component of the language arts, namely reading; now let us direct our attention to writing skills.

Whereas reading has to do with the use of coded symbols to intake ideas and feelings, writing reverses the process. Nonetheless, there is a reciprocal relationship between the two skills. One always reads what has already been written. One writes something with the expectation that either the writer or someone else will read what has been written. In addition to the skills associated with the mechanics of writing, such as capitalization, spelling, punctuation, and handwriting, the following writing skills can and should be taught within the context of social studies:

254

- note taking
- letter writing
- organizing and outlining
- preparing written reports
- record keeping
- summarizing ideas in writing
- preparing notices, announcements, advertisements
- expanding written vocabulary
- completing routine forms, e.g., checks, deposit slips, applications, order blanks, library slips
- writing creative material, e.g., poems, stories, plays

Writing skill is developed when the individual engages in a considerable amount of writing and is provided instructive and supportive feedback on what is written. In short, writing requires practice with the intent to improve. Therefore, if the only writing children do in the social studies consists of filling in single words or short phrases in workbooks or worksheets, one cannot expect much growth in any of the important writing skills identified in the foregoing paragraph. Accordingly, the teacher must involve pupils in social studies related writing assignments as a regular part of the work of the class. Such writing tasks need to be appropriate to the developmental level of the children.

Simply providing the *opportunity* for children to write is not in itself enough to develop writing habits and skills. Pupils also need instruction and they need to be motivated. Writing is often drudgery because the individual does not know how to go about doing it and/or has no inclination to want to do it. Consequently, school writing assignments frequently stifle writing abilities rather than encourage them. Teachers who have taught writing successfully create an environment or climate that places high value on writing and makes it seem an exciting adventure for young learners. A few techniques that have been used successfully by teachers follow.

Techniques That Make Writing Easier

1. List and post difficult, technical words that pupils might find useful in their writing.
2. Use imaginative springboards to encourage creative writing. For example, (1) write a story about a pioneer girl, a pony, and a snowstorm; (2) keep a one-month diary of a newly arrived immigrant child; (3) describe how you ordered breakfast in a restaurant in a country where no one knew how to speak your language; (4) write what happened to you when you were lost in a large city.
3. Have pupils list main ideas about a topic. Have them order the ideas sequentially. Then have them write three more sentences about each main idea.
4. Remind pupils of forms and skills already learned (indenting para-

255

graphs, using exclamation marks, using quotation marks for conversations, etc.).

5. Provide opportunities for children to share their written work with others and display it on the bulletin board.
6. Demonstrate writing skills through the use of group activity.
7. Use word games to develop more elaborate vocabulary—rhyming words, synonyms, antonyms, "happy" words, "sad" words, night sounds, city noises, etc.
8. Develop and encourage pupils to use self-evaluating checklists.

Writing Activities for Social Studies

The best writing activities for social studies are those that pupils do within the context of what they are studying. Writing assignments take on a sense of importance and purpose when they are needed as a part of the process of achieving other objectives. A letter written to obtain information, for example, is likely to be more meaningful to a pupil than is a make believe letter written to a fictitious person. Thus, insofar as possible, writing activities in social studies should be functionally related to the classwork.

The activities on the following list have been used by elementary teachers who have successfully related the teaching of writing skills to social studies:

1. Write endings to reaction stories or situations in which the outcome is in doubt.
2. Prepare a classroom newsletter or newspaper.
3. Prepare an original script for dramatization.
4. Maintain a class or personal diary ("Today I learned how to jump rope," "Today I lost a tooth," "Today we had a visitor from China.")
5. Prepare outlines or notes for an oral report.
6. Prepare captions for pictures, illustrations, exhibits, cartoons.
7. Write explanations of events, of exhibits, or after a field trip.
8. Make holiday greeting cards and write appropriate messages.
9. Write letters requesting information and/or material, inviting visitors to the classroom, thank-you letters, get-well messages to classmates and teachers.
10. Create "news" stories about historical events; create descriptive headlines for historical events.
11. Keep minutes of meetings.
12. Write directions for doing something, such as making soap, reading a chart, operating a machine.
13. Take notes from several different sources for use in a discussion.
14. Take notes while listening to a speaker.
15. Organize material and prepare a written report for others to read.
16. Make lists of things studied, e.g., rice, cocoa, oranges.
17. List questions during study period.

18. Label items on maps.
19. Write answers to questions.
20. Summarize ideas into topic sentences to be developed into paragraphs.
21. Prepare short annotations of trade books used in social studies.
22. Write a script for a tape-recorded program.
23. Write a short history of the school and the community.
24. List words that describe particularly well some event or period.
25. Write a poem to express feelings about a topic or period studied.
26. Write entries in a diary that might have been kept by an explorer or a pioneer.
27. Prepare maps of various types and write accompanying explanations.
28. Write book reviews.
29. Write a short story based on subject matter studied in social studies.
30. Write a letter home as it might have been written by a member of the Lewis and Clark Expedition.

DISCUSSION QUESTIONS AND SUGGESTED ACTIVITIES

1. If social studies textbooks are written for the average reader, why is it that all good social studies textbooks tend to be difficult for the average reader?
2. Select a children's social studies text and examine it to find examples of the reading skills listed on pages 231–232.
3. Select a children's textbook and provide sample exercises based on the points made in the section entitled "Using Study Aids and Study Skills to Improve Reading."
4. Using the text you selected in your answer to question 3, find examples of the social studies words and terms listed on page 241.
5. Select a passage from a children's social studies textbook and develop comprehension questions as is done on pages 77–78 and 250. Develop an equal number of interpretive-type questions.
6. What reference books do you believe are the most useful to children? Why do you think so?
7. Pick a social studies topic for a grade of your choice. Make a list of poems, stories, biographies, and other reading sources that develop a strong mental set or mood appropriate to the topic. Read selected passages to your classmates.
8. Choose one of the references listed on page 251. What prerequisite skills must the child have in order to use that reference effectively and efficiently?
9. Prepare a lesson plan for social studies that incorporates the teaching of a related writing skill.

257

SELECTED REFERENCES

Chapin, June R. and Richard E. Gross. *Teaching Social Studies Skills*. Boston: Little, Brown and Company, 1973. Chapter 2.

Criscuolo, Nicholas P. "More Miracle Motivators for Reluctant Readers," *Instructor*, 89 (March 1980), pp. 72–74.

Hurst, Joe B. "Images in Children's Picture Books," *Social Education*, 45 (February 1981), pp. 138–143.

Kapel, Marilyn. "Can Your Students Read the Assigned Materials?" *The Social Studies*, 69 (January–February 1978), pp. 14–20.

Lamberg, Walter J. and Charles E. Lamb. *Reading Instruction in the Content Areas*. Chicago: Rand McNally College Publishing Company, 1980. Chapter 12.

Lunstrum, John P. "Reading in the Social Studies," Chapter 4, *Developing Decision-Making Skills*, 47th Yearbook, National Council for the Social Studies. Dana G. Kurfman, ed. Washington, D.C.: The Council, 1977, pp. 109–139.

Lunstrom, John P. "Reading in the Social Studies: A Preliminary Study of Recent Research," *Social Education*, 40 (January 1976), pp. 10–18.

Mahony, Joseph E. "Improving Reading Skills in Social Studies," *How to Do It Series*, 2, No. 1. National Council for the Social Studies. Washington, D.C.: The Council, 1977.

Robinson, H. Alan. *Teaching Reading and Study Strategies—The Content Areas*. Boston: Allyn & Bacon Books, Inc. 1975, Chapter 7.

Schneider, Donald O. and Mary Jo McGee Brown. "Helping Students Study and Comprehend Their Social Studies Textbooks," *Social Education*, 44 (February 1980), pp. 105–112.

Thomas, Ellen Lamar and H. Alan Robinson. *Improving Reading in Every Class*. Boston: Allyn & Bacon Books, Inc., 1976.

Tovey, Duane and Thomas D. Weible. "Extending Social Studies Understandings Through Language Activities," *Social Education*, 45 (May 1981), pp. 367–369.

West, Gail B. *Teaching Reading Skills in Content Areas: A Practical Guide to the Construction of Student Exercises*, 2nd ed. Oviedo, Florida: Sandpiper Press, Inc., 1978.

10

Space and Time Dimensions
of Social Studies:
Maps, Globes, and Graphics

Suppose someone came into a roomful of people and announced, "There has been a disastrous earthquake!" What would be said by the others present? Most likely the next things to be said would be,

"Where did it happen?"
"When did it happen?"

Only after these questions were answered would there be an interest in whether anyone was injured and the extent of the damage. Events hold little meaning for us unless we know the *place* and the *time* of their occurrence. Consequently, in social studies we find ourselves constantly making references to *where* something happened and *when* it happened. Such references to time and place may be specific, such as Lexington, Massachusetts, April 18, 1775; or they may be general, such as "a long time ago, in the area where three continents meet." These definite and indefinite references to time and space also involve *quantitative* concepts:

Space	Time
A great distance	Soon thereafter
Forty miles	A long journey
1,500 acres	Three decades
Largest continent	Four centuries earlier
55,000 square miles	A fortnight later
23½° north latitude	A four-hour interval

Both definite and indefinite references to time and space can be bothersome for children. For example, if children read that Columbus's ship, the *Santa Maria*, was 98 feet long, such a reference to distance probably will mean something different to every child in the class. It might be conceptualized as a distance ranging from one not greater than the length of the classroom to one of several city blocks. When there is such confusion over a relatively simple and definite

259

reference to distance, one can only speculate on the misunderstandings that must abound when we use such references as the following:

A township was to be a square, six miles long on each side. Each township was to be divided into thirty-six sections. A section, therefore, was one mile square and had 640 acres in it.

The research that has been conducted on time, space, and quantitative concepts in social studies confirms that children often misunderstand them. The tendency is to overestimate the ability of children to handle such concepts. As a result, maps often are used that are more complex than they should be in view of the maturity of the children using them. Also children may make and use time lines that they really do not comprehend. Because children so easily verbalize quantitative concepts such as decade, century, thousands, hundreds, several miles, many years, and 10 per cent, the assumption is that they are understood. Research on this subject indicates that such assumptions are often in error.

When the abstractness of these concepts is reduced, they are made meaningful to children. We try, therefore, to provide children with a concrete reference to space and time, preferably one that is a part of their experiences. This is why current news events provide such a good vehicle for teaching some concepts and skills. The children read about current happenings in the classroom periodical or hear and see them reported on radio and television news. Thus, finding places on a map is a natural extension of everyday experiences.

The social studies curriculum operates within a matrix that might be represented very simply as follows:

Experiences that could be charted at point A would be the least abstract and would usually be found in the early grades. Experiences at point B would be most difficult to make concrete for children because they are remote not only in space but also in time. Because many children today have firsthand experiences that acquaint them with places beyond their immediate environment, it is not as necessary to confine the social studies program to the local area as it once was. There can be more movement from the near at hand to the far-away even at early grade levels. This is more difficult to do with the time dimension, however. The reality of events of the past needs to be tied to the present, again calling attention to the importance of using current news events.

There are many instructional aids that can help one deal with these complex concepts, provided one has the skills to use them. For example, globes and maps are indispensable tools for working with space and spatial relationships. Time lines and charts can make time and chronology meaningful. Graphs and tables can make some types of quantitative relationships easier to comprehend. It is imperative, therefore, that the social studies program teach children how to use these tools.

MAP AND GLOBE SKILLS ESSENTIAL TO THE SOCIAL STUDIES CURRICULUM

Maps and globes are vehicles for representing space symbolically. The essential features of all maps and globes are a gridwork, color, scale, symbols, and a legend that explains the symbol system used. The ability to read and interpret maps and globes, like conventional reading, is a summarizing skill in that it represents a composite of several subskills. These subskills can be inferred by making an analysis of the behavior of someone reading a map who is skillful at it. Fortunately, this will not be necessary because it has been done by specialists several times and always with somewhat the same results. One list that has been widely used by school districts throughout the nation in developing their map and globe skill sequence appears in two yearbooks of the National Council for the Social Studies:

1. Ability to orient the map and to note directions.
2. Ability to recognize the scale of a map and to compute distances.
3. Ability to locate places on maps and globes by means of grid systems.
4. Ability to express relative locations.
5. Ability to read map symbols.
6. Ability to compare maps and to make inferences.[1]

Directional Orientation

In order to deal with directional relationships on maps and globes, the child must first understand them in reality. The easiest directions to use are those that express relative location, such as close to, near, over here, and over there. These can be learned in the primary grades. The cardinal directions are also learned in the primary grades by hav-

---

[1]This list was developed by Professor Clyde F. Kohn for the 1953 NCSS yearbook. It is cited and elaborated on by Dean Lorrin Kennamer, "Developing a Sense of Place and Space," in *Skill Development in Social Studies*, 33rd Yearbook. Washington, D.C.: National Council for the Social Studies, 1963. pp. 157 ff. The chart in the appendix of that yearbook provides a list of related subskills along with a suggested curriculum sequence.

ing them pointed out and by referring to places that are known to children as being north of, east of, south of, and so on. Placing direction labels on the various walls of the classroom helps remind children of cardinal directions. They can associate east and west with the rising and setting of the sun. They can learn how a compass is used to find direction. While on field trips, children should be given practice in noting directions, observing especially the directions of streets and roads. Gradually, pupils learn the purpose of the poles, the meridians of longitude, and the parallels of latitude in orienting a map and noting directions. When maps with unfamiliar projections are introduced, pupils should be taught how to establish correct directional relationships on them.

Using Map Scales

In making a map the cartographer tries to reproduce as accurately as possible that portion of the earth being represented. Because globes are models of the earth, they can represent the earth more correctly than can maps. No map can altogether faithfully represent the earth simply because the earth is round and maps are flat. The flattening process inevitably results in some distortion.

Scaling is the process of reducing everything in the same amount. In working with children in the primary grades, scaling should be done in the relative sense. Some things are larger or smaller than other things and the maps should show their *relative size* as accurately as possible. For example, a 50-foot high tree in the schoolyard should be about five times larger than the 10-foot-tall playground set. On conventional maps, three types of scales are used:

1. The graphic scale

   ```
   |____|____|____|____|____|____|
   0   100  200  300  400  500  600
   ```

2. The inches-to-miles scale

   ```
   |_____|_____|_____|
   0         300        600        900
   ```

3. The representative fraction   1:250,000.

Of these, the graphic scale is the easiest to use and can be taught at about fourth grade. The inches-to-miles scale is more complex, but it can also be taught in the middle grades. The representative fraction is usually considered beyond the scope of the elementary school program.

As pupils become more global in their experiences, they will encounter map scales in metric measures. Using metric measurement, the distance on a graphic scale would be recorded in kilometers. Likewise, rather than inches-to-miles, the scale would show the relationship as centimeters-to-kilometers. The following graphic scale illustrates the same distance expressed in miles and in kilometers:

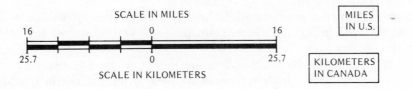

Locating Places

The ability to locate places on maps and globes comes with a familiarity with these devices cultivated over a period of several years. Children first learn to locate places that are known to them on simple maps and layouts that they make in the classroom. In the early grades, too, children can learn the names and shapes of some of the major geographic features, such as continents, oceans, the equator, and the poles. The commercially prepared maps and globes designed for the lower grades are quite plain, having only a few features shown. Gradually, children increase their repertoire of known places they

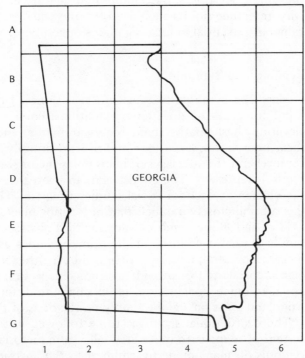

FIGURE 6. Middle-grade pupils can learn to use a grid in locating places by using road maps that have coordinates of the type shown on this map. Test your own memory of place locations by responding to these questions:

1. What major city is located at C2?
2. What major city lies near the intersection of the squares D1, D2, E1 and E2?
3. Describe the location of Savannah by using the coordinates provided on this map.

Check your answers by consulting a map of Georgia that shows cities.

can find on the map and globe because of frequent references to the location of important cities, countries, rivers, mountains, and other physical features.

In the middle grades, children are taught to use coordinates to locate places. Local highway maps are well suited for use in teaching this skill because they deal with an area familiar to the children. One set of lines of the gridwork—perhaps the north-south lines—is identified with letters; the other set of lines is numbered as is done in Figure 6. The teacher can have the children (this is usually done in fourth grade) find several places located on or very near to a north-south line, say D. Then several places can be found on an east-west line, say 7. If the teacher is clever enough to pick two coordinates that intersect on a major point of interest, the children will discover that some city or other important feature is located at the point where D and 7 intersect. Figure 6 is an example of an exercise of this kind. This experience provides readiness for the use of meridians of longitude and parallels of latitude in locating places on wall maps and the globe. At this stage, children are mature enough to understand why reference points such as poles, the equator, and the prime meridian are essential in locating places on a sphere.

Reading Map Symbols

Maps use symbols to represent real things: Dots of varying sizes stand for cities of different populations; color is used to represent elevation; hash marks stand for escarpments; and lines are used to show boundaries, coastlines, and rivers. Naturally, the reader will not comprehend the messages of maps unless he or she knows what these symbols represent. The child begins to learn their meanings early in the elementary school social studies program. The development of this subskill closely parallels that of locating places on maps.

Map and globe symbols vary in their abstractness. Indeed, some simple maps for children in the primary grades use symbols that are pictorial or semipictorial. These symbols either look like the object being represented or provide a strong clue as to its identity. It would not take much imagination, for example, to differentiate water areas from land areas on a globe simply on the basis of their color.

The instructional sequence to be followed in teaching the symbol system of maps is to move gradually from pictorial and semipictorial symbols on maps made by children to the abstract symbols used on conventional wall maps, globes, and maps that are included in the textbooks of the middle and upper grades. It is essential that children learn to consult the map legend or key in order to confirm which symbols are being used. In most cases children in the middle and upper grades will be dealing with maps that use conventional map symbols, but special-purpose maps such as those showing vegetation, rainfall, population density, and so on, often use symbols that are unique to the particular map.

FIGURE 7. Pupils can be introduced to the concept of symbols through pictorial representations that they encounter in real life, such as the ones shown here.

It is always a good idea to make generous use of photographs of the areas shown on a map in order to help the children associate the map symbol with what the place actually looks like. Similarly, when children go on field trips, they should be encouraged to observe carefully the appearance of landscapes and other features that are shown on maps. In time they will be able to visualize the reality that the abstract map symbols represent.

Understanding Relative Location

Understanding relative location is an interpretive skill that requires information beyond that provided by the map itself. It has to do with thinking about how places relate to each other in terms of political, cultural, religious, commercial, or historical perspectives. It has nothing to do with how close or how far away places may be in the absolute sense. For example, the non-Asian people, and even many Asians, of the British Crown Colony of Hong Kong feel closer to Great Britain (10,000 miles away) than they do to the People's Republic of China (less than twenty miles away) because of political, economic, and cultural ties.

Relative location may also be thought of in terms of the amount

265

of time required to get to a place using the kind of transportation available. This is commonly expressed nowadays in ordinary conversation and small talk as people say, "It takes me 30 minutes to get to work," or "I'm about two hours from Washington." Distances that now take two hours to traverse would have taken two days a hundred years ago and two weeks or even more at the time of the founding of the Republic. Increasingly, we reckon distances in terms of time. Consequently, places may be thought of as being remote or near in terms of how difficult it is to get to them. Air crash survivors stranded in the High Sierras in the dead of winter, no more than 50 miles from Fresno, California, might be as far away from civilization in the relative sense as they would be if they were in Antarctica.

Comparing Maps and Making Inferences

Comparing maps and making inferences is also an inferential skill because to some extent the reader has to project what he or she already knows on the map data. In this process the map reader discovers relationships among the sets of data presented by different maps. In the middle elementary grades, teachers often have children compare vegetation maps with rainfall maps. They also have them compare maps showing the location of important resources, such as iron and coal, with maps showing the location of industrial centers, population densities, and so on. It is quite common to find special-purpose maps of the same region in the children's textbooks, making comparisons easy. These provide excellent settings for inquiry exer-

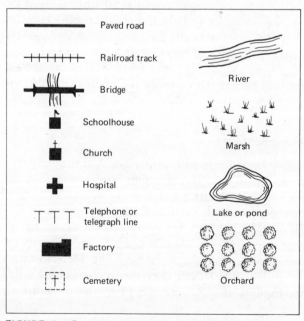

FIGURE 8.   Examples of standard symbols used on maps.

cises, as the children can study the data presented on two or more maps, make predictions or hypotheses about these data, and then go on to the next step of verifying or rejecting their speculations.

Children in the late middle and upper elementary grades should study maps based on different projections and compare the shapes and sizes of known areas with those same areas as shown on the globe. This will familiarize them with the concept of distortion, which, in greater or lesser amounts, is present in all flat maps. Pupils should learn why distortion occurs and what cartographers have done to minimize its effect.

INSTRUCTIONAL EXPERIENCES WITH THE GLOBE

Every elementary school classroom should have and use a globe. In grades one, two, and three a simplified twelve-inch globe is generally recommended because small children find this size easier to handle than the larger 16-inch one. For primary grades, the globe selected should have a minimum amount of information on it. It should not use more than three colors to represent land elevation or more than two colors to represent water depth. Only the largest cities, rivers, and water bodies should be shown. In the middle and upper grades, a 16-inch globe is recommended because of its easy scale of one inch to 500 miles. Moreover, its larger size allows more detail to be shown without the globe's becoming a confused collection of facts. Globes for middle- and upper-grade children will ordinarily use seven colors to represent land elevations and three colors to represent water depths.

The chief value of the globe in grades one, two, and three is to familiarize the children with the basic roundness of the earth and to begin to build an awareness of global relationships. The primary-grade child does not necessarily need formal lessons on the use of the globe. If the globe is in the classroom, it will provoke curiosity and a desire to know more about it and how to use it. Parents speak of places in the news, and the children wonder where those places are. They hear of earth satellites and wonder about their orbits. Perhaps a pupil has just joined the class; her family has recently moved to this country from another part of the world, and she wants to show the class the location of her former home. The teacher will use situations such as these, and hundreds more like them, to acquaint the young child with the globe.

The teacher should help children discover other things about the globe—differences between water and land areas and that these are represented by different colors; the line that separates the water and the land is called the sea coast. Children may be shown pictures to help them visualize different kinds of coastlines. In a like manner,

267

the teacher extends their understanding of other concepts—oceans, cities, rivers, mountains. Children learn that most of the brown areas that represent land are on the half of the earth that has the North Pole and that it is here that the majority of the people of the world live.

In addition to the incidental references made to the globe, the teacher should make frequent use of the globe when teaching social studies and other subjects. For instance, in a reading lesson, pupils might find where their book friends "live." Thus, the globe can be used in a great variety of ways to lay a good foundation for more formal aspects of the teaching of these skills later on.

The following are examples of the *types* of learnings and experiences that can be planned with the globe for pupils in the lower grades:

1. Stress with pupils that the globe is a very small model of the earth. Good models look exactly like the real thing but are smaller. The globe is a good model of the earth.
2. Show the children how land areas and water bodies are represented on the globe. Have children find land areas and water bodies. Names of these need not be taught at this level, but children might already know the large water bodies such as the Pacific and Atlantic oceans. Similarly, they might be familiar with North and South America, Africa or the Antarctic, and these can be pointed out. Explain that all water bodies and land areas have names.
3. Have children discover that there is considerably more water than land shown on the globe. Ask children to find the half of the globe that has most of the land. Explain that this is the half on which we live and is the part of the earth where most of the world's people make their homes.
4. Show children the location of the North Pole. Explain that most of the land of the world is on the same half of the world as the North Pole. We call this the northern half.
5. Show children the location of the South Pole. Explain that most of the water areas of the world are on the same half of the world as the South Pole. We call this the southern half.
6. Explain that our earth is a planet.
7. Show children how they can find their country, their continent, their state, and possibly their city on the globe.
8. Use the globe to find places that are familiar to the children—places they have visited on vacations, places in the news, homes of book friends and visitors from other countries, or places in the world from which some circus or zoo animals are brought.
9. Encourage children to handle the globe and to find places on it themselves.
10. Answer questions the children ask concerning the globe in simple, nontechnical language.

As the child moves into the middle and upper grades, instruction in the use of the globe should take two forms. First, the teacher should take time from regularly scheduled unit activities to teach skills needed in reading and interpreting the globe. Second, in unit work and other classroom activities there should be frequent reference to the globe and maps. Both of these aspects of instruction are important, and one should supplement the other. To hope that children will become skillful in the use of a globe or maps simply by making incidental references to them when the occasion presents itself is wishful thinking. At the same time, formal lessons in the use of these devices without application of the newly acquired skills in purposeful situations is equally ineffective. The best arrangement is to provide for systematic instruction in the use of map- and globe-reading skills as a part of unit activities, reinforcing this with direct teaching of these skills as the need arises.

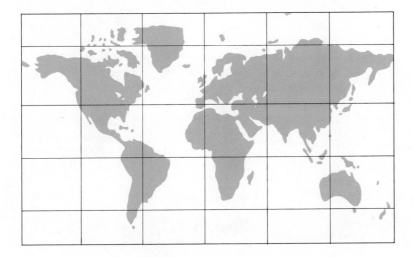

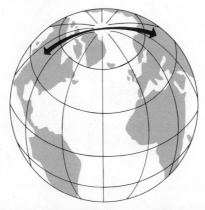

FIGURE 9. Notice how differently the map and globe portray global relationships. In the Space Age we need to think of the world more as it is shown by the globe than the map.

269

Maps may be used to find distances between points only under certain conditions, but the globe represents distances accurately and true to scale at all points on the surface of the earth. It is a simple procedure for the pupil to place a flexible ruler on the globe and measure directly the distance between two points in question, then refer to the scale and determine the actual distance between the two places. The air routes of the world use great circles because these are the shortest distances from place to place on the earth's surface. If nothing but flat maps are used, it is difficult to understand the concept of great circle routes, and, therefore, of airplane routes. The

FIGURE 10. A land area such as North America may take a variety of shapes on maps, depending on the projection that is used. A classroom globe shows shapes and areas more accurately than maps and should be used in conjunction with the study of wall maps.

globe can help clarify this for the youngster. In this connection, the slated globe (sometimes called the project globe) is useful because it is possible to write on the surface of it with a piece of chalk.

Globes are helpful, too, in establishing concepts of direction. It is not difficult for the child to think of north as being in the direction of the North Pole when using a globe. On the other hand, this may be confusing if only a flat map is used. Furthermore, the relative direction of various parts of the earth can be better understood through the use of a globe. Many Americans are surprised, for example, when they learn that Great Britain lies in a more northerly latitude than do any of the forty-eight midcontinent states of our country; that Boston has nearly the same latitude as Rome; that our most westerly state is not Hawaii but Alaska; that our most southerly state is not Florida but Hawaii; that Moscow and Glasgow have approximately the same latitude, both being farther south than any city of Norway or Finland. These facts are not important except to demonstrate that one perceives the earth differently on a globe than on a flat map.

A definite advantage that globes have over maps is that they show size and shapes of areas exactly as they appear on the earth's surface, whereas maps cannot. The classical examples of distortions in the size and shapes of land areas are Greenland on the Mercator projection and Australia on the polar projection. On the Mercator projection, Greenland appears as a very large area—larger than South America. On a polar projection, Australia appears to have a greater east–west distance and a shorter north–south distance than is actually the case. Notice the different shapes North America takes on various maps as illustrated in Figure 10. A globe will show all of these map shapes and sizes to be inaccurately represented. Therefore, a globe should be used with maps to prevent wrong conceptions.

INSTRUCTIONAL EXPERIENCES WITH MAPS

A number of complex skills are involved in map reading and interpretation; therefore, early experiences with maps should be kept simple. This can best be done through the use of diagrams and maps that the teacher and the pupils make of their immediate vicinity. These experiences may take the form of a layout on the classroom floor using blocks and other objects for houses, streets, trees, and public buildings. The layout can be done on a sand table, or the map can be drawn on a large piece of wrapping paper on the classroom floor. When the floor material will permit, masking tape can be placed on the floor itself to represent boundaries, streets, or roads.

Opportunities to teach and apply these skills often arise in the everyday life of the classroom. For instance, children in one class

271

learned about map direction when a new pupil joined the group. Soon after the child arrived, the teacher used a map to show the class the location of the child's previous home. They determined the direction the child's family traveled to reach their new home. The teacher then used a map of the local area and had the children discover the direction they travel in going from their homes to school each day.

A fundamental skill in map reading is to learn that a symbol represents a real and actual thing. The symbol may be arbitrarily chosen and bear no resemblance to the object represented, or it may be one that would suggest to the reader what is intended. A school might be represented by a small circle or by a small square with a flag placed on top. It is easier to associate the flag and square with a school than to associate the circle with it. The flag and square are, therefore, less abstract. With young children, it is better to use pictorial or semipictorial symbols of this sort than to use completely abstract ones. In

This pupil is making a practical application of map skills by pinpointing the places visited on the previous day by presidential hopefuls. Suggest other uses that can be made of map skills in the regular work of the classroom.

teaching map-reading skills to children it must be remembered that both reading and interpretive skills are involved, and the interpretive skills depend heavily on maturity and background knowledge. Primary-grade children will do less with interpretive skills than they will with reading skills.

The idea of objects representing other objects, people, or things is not new to the children; they have substituted symbols for the actual things many times in the imaginative play of childhood. The teacher can begin by explaining that they are going to draw a map of the schoolroom, schoolyard, or some segment of the immediate vicinity. It is best if this can be done on the classroom floor, so the layout can be oriented exactly as it appears in relationship to the classroom; this sidesteps the matter of orientation to directions at this early stage. Trees, doors, playground equipment, parking areas, and other objects appear in relation to other objects, and only the major ones should be included. The purpose of this experience is simply to show that it is possible to represent space symbolically and that symbols stand for real things. Their map should have a title and a key to tell what the symbols stand for. This is the first experience in the development of skill in comprehending the significance of symbols, and it will be continued and extended as long as maps are used.

As the children become ready for more abstract symbols, such symbols will be introduced, taught, and used, as will more conventional map symbols. As a part of this instruction in the middle and upper grades, it is important to make generous use of pictures and other visual aids that will help children visualize the area represented. It is helpful, too, to take children to some high point of vantage in the community where they can look down on an area and see what it actually looks like from above. In most localities it is possible to purchase inexpensive aerial photographs of the local community, and these can be used in studying map symbols and in making maps of the local area. Some map companies have prepared wall charts designed to help children visualize things represented by map symbols; these are excellent devices for teaching this skill to middle- and upper-grade children. The teacher also should take advantage of the many fine photographs in social studies textbooks to acquaint the pupils with the appearance of various areas, landscapes, surface features, land and water forms, and people-made things that are represented symbolically on maps.

For reasons of simplicity, orientation to direction may be avoided in the children's first attempts at making diagrams or maps. But the need to orient a map properly for direction will become apparent to them if their classroom map is rotated. Being able to note and read directions is a prerequisite to serious map study and this skill should be introduced fairly early, perhaps in the second grade. Children learn the cardinal directions by having the directions pointed out to them. They learn which wall of the room is north, south, east, and west because the teacher may have placed labels on the walls. They learn that if one knows the direction of north, the other directions can be determined; for if one faces north, the direction of south will be to one's back, east to the right, and west to the left. To extend their ability to orient themselves, children should be taken outdoors and the directions pointed out to them. If this is done at noon on a sunny day, the children's shadows will point in an approximate northerly direction. After the children have this basic orientation to direction, subsequent mapwork should include reference to direction and should become increasingly more complex as the pupils mature.

Finding directions on conventional wall maps can be facilitated with the aid of a globe and perhaps should not be taught much below the fourth grade. When this concept is introduced, it should be done through reference to north–south and east–west grid lines. Pupils are taught that north is in the direction of the North Pole and that south is in the direction of the South Pole. The poles can be easily found by following the meridians of longitude. The east–west directions can be found by following the parallels of latitude. Generalizations such as "north is at the top of the map" and "south is at the bottom of the map" should not be taught because they are not correct and because they may be confusing when one uses a variety of different map projections. Similarly, references to north as "up" and south as "down" should not be taught in connection with either maps or globes. When we speak of the earth, the term *down* means toward the center of the earth and *up* means away from the center of the earth, and both terms should be taught only in that way. The matter of associating up with north introduces many instructional problems as children learn more of the geography of the earth. For example, if north is up, how can so many of the world's rivers flow north? The children will invariably ask why we say "way down South" or "the Land Down Under"; these can be explained as being colorful expressions and figures of speech similar to "way out West" or "out at sea" that have crept into our language but have nothing at all to do with direction itself. (See Figure 11.)

There is merit in taking time to have children point out and discuss directions on the map. In the middle and upper grades the teacher should duplicate maps on various grids and have the children place directional data on them. When this is done the need to use east–west and north–south lines should be emphasized. This will give the children experiences noting directions on various map grids as well as keeping the teacher up-to-date on the progress that the children are making in the development of this skill.

Children can be made to understand the need for map scales by indicating to them that maps must be small enough to bring into the classroom or carry around. We cannot make maps as big as the area we wish to show because that would make the map so large it could not be used. It must, therefore, be made smaller, and everything on the map must be made smaller in the same amount. Just as a photograph of the family shows everyone smaller in the same amount, so must the map; otherwise, it would not give a true picture. Children

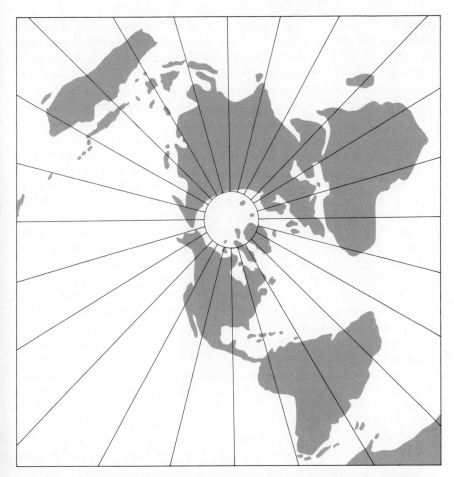

FIGURE 11.   This map illustrates why generalizations such as "north is at the top of the map" are incorrect. East–west lines or parallels of latitude have been omitted in order to draw attention to north–south directions. What questions might you pose to pupils studying this map?

should learn that maps are precise and accurate instruments. In primary grades, the scaling is not done in the mathematical sense, but the reductions are made in a relative way. In middle grades, when children have had sufficient background in mathematics, they can deal with graphic reductions more precisely. They learn that wall maps have the scale printed on them and are taught how to read the various ways in which scale can be indicated. The experiences children have using map scales provide a good time for the teacher to call their attention to distances between various places. Children can be helped to visualize these distances through an appreciation of the amount of time needed to traverse the distances in question by air travel. These times may be obtained from commercial airlines.

When the children have learned the meaning of map symbols, are skillful in orienting themselves to direction on a map, and can recognize and use map scales, they are well on their way toward an understanding of the language of maps. This does not mean, however, that

275

they find them especially useful or that they regard them as a valuable source of information. The development of skills that deal largely with map language must be accompanied by associated interpretive skills. Proficiency in the interpretive aspects of map use will vary considerably among the children. One who is skillful in map use has developed the ability to visualize what an area actually looks like when it is seen on the map. Looking at the map color, one in a sense "sees" the rugged mountains of our West, the waving grain fields of western Montana, the rich farmlands of the Midwest, and the rolling countryside of Virginia. Because the child cannot visualize places not actually seen except in an imaginative way, the generous use of additional visual material along with maps is suggested. Good-quality pictures are especially important, and the class should see several pictures of an area in order to avoid fixing a single impression of the area in their minds. Filmstrips and slides can be used for the same purpose, and motion pictures and television are also excellent aids. As was previously noted, in the early stages of map reading, an excellent procedure is to have an aerial photograph of the local area as well as a conventional map. When these are placed side by side, the child can see how the area actually looks and how it is represented on a map. Stories and other narrative accounts also are helpful in assisting the child to visualize areas represented on maps.

Activities such as the following can be used to relate the abstractions of maps to the reality they represent:

1. Observing local landscapes and geographic features, preferably from a high point of vantage.
2. Using pictorial and semipictorial symbols, especially at the lower grade levels.
3. Using three-dimensional models of the areas mapped; using blocks and models to represent buildings.
4. Making maps of the local area with which pupils are familiar.
5. Making generous use of pictures, films, and filmstrips of the areas shown on maps.
6. Relating aerial photographs (angle shots rather than perpendicular ones) to maps of the same area.
7. Comparing areas shown on the wall map with the same area shown in a picture.
8. Developing descriptive words (adjectives) that apply to a particular area shown on a map.
9. Making use of current events that relate to the area shown on a map.
10. Visiting places shown on the map, such as the airport, harbor, park, and downtown area.

Map- and globe-reading skills are learned through direct teaching and by application in situations where the skill is normally used. In many instances these processes can be combined. Let us say, for example, that pupils in a fifth-grade class read that "Permafrost is a condition found only in high latitudes." The teacher can use this encounter with *high latitudes* to teach map-reading in connection with that concept. That is, class time can be taken to teach the meaning of *high*, *low*, and *middle latitudes* on maps and globes, and the teaching would occur in what we refer to as a functional setting. Teachers are encouraged to teach as many map and globe skills as possible in this way, rather than to isolate the skills from their relevant subject matter. After direct teaching there must be a generous application and use of the skills if proficiency is to be developed and maintained.

Because these skills are *developmental*, one cannot expect to teach them once and assume that they have been learned. Most skills are introduced early in the grades and then are retaught, reviewed, or expanded later on. We expect that children will show increased proficiency and maturity in their use of these skills each year that they are in school. Such development comes through continued teaching and use, not automatically through the natural process of maturation.

MAKING A TRIP MAP

The teacher showed children color photographs of several states and discussed the many interesting things that can be seen and done in the various states. Pupils shared some of their own travel experiences. The teacher provided pupils with road maps of several different states and asked them to find places that might be of interest to someone visiting those states. These places of interest were discussed briefly. Pupils were then asked to think about and select a state they would enjoy visiting. Choices were to be made by the next day.

The following day the pupils made their selections of states they wanted to "visit." Using a road map of that state provided by the teacher and using references available in and outside the classroom, pupils were to plan a route of travel through the state of their choice, making at least five stops at places that would be interesting to a visitor. These places were to be marked with a large dot. A short narrative description was to be written to accompany the map telling about the travel route, state or national parks, natural areas of interest, historical landmarks, or other items of interest. If the children preferred, they could prepare a verbal rather than a written narrative by using the cassette recorder in the classroom.

The children responded to the teacher's encouragement to be creative in describing their imaginary trips, and several prepared travel brochures and recorded travelogs. The children began a classroom exhibit of their trip maps and narratives, and in a week the room resembled a travel agency office. This generated a considerable amount of discussion and sharing of ideas and, of course, numerous opportunities to learn about maps. Also, through this activity the children acquired a great deal of information about their country, applied important skills (reading, research, writing, discussion, speaking), and developed an appreciation for the diversity and variety of their own country.

The use of color has caused confusion for children trying to visualize elevations. Children seem to believe that all areas represented by one color are precisely the same elevation, not recognizing that there

277

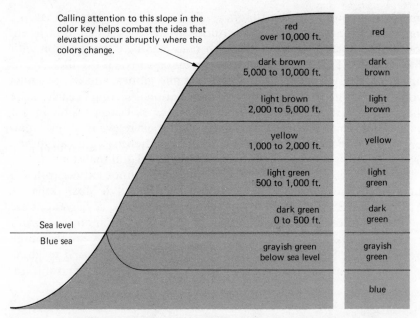

Calling attention to this slope in the color key helps combat the idea that elevations occur abruptly where the colors change.

red over 10,000 ft.	red
dark brown 5,000 to 10,000 ft.	dark brown
light brown 2,000 to 5,000 ft.	light brown
yellow 1,000 to 2,000 ft.	yellow
light green 500 to 1,000 ft.	light green
dark green 0 to 500 ft.	dark green
grayish green below sea level	grayish green
	blue

Sea level

Blue sea

FIGURE 12. This diagram shows two methods of illustrating keys to colors used to express elevations on classroom maps. Some teachers find it helpful to construct a three-dimensional paper-mâché model of the key shown on the left.

are variations in elevations that occur within the limits of the interval used by the color representation. (See Figure 12.) Moreover, children develop the mistaken idea that elevations occur abruptly where colors change. Conventional color symbols give no impression of gradual elevations or depressions and create the illusion that changes are abrupt. The use of a relief map is helpful in showing that changes in elevation occur gradually. Comparing colors of a wall map with elevations on a relief map helps children gain a better understanding of map color as used to represent elevations. It is important to remember, however, that relief maps use two scales—one for vertical distances and another for horizontal distances. If the horizontal scale were used for vertical distances, the elevations would be imperceptible on a relief map of the size usually found in elementary classrooms. Some maps combine shaded relief with altitude colors; this adds a third-dimensional effect to the mountains and valleys. Oblique shading and blending of color from one elevation to the other gives a graduated effect to land elevations that more accurately portray the surface of the earth. Children must also be taught that color may be used to designate political divisions such as states, nations, and territories and that the color chosen is an arbitrary one having nothing to do with the way the area actually looks. Pictures of state boundaries, for example, will illustrate that if it were not for the boundary marker, one would not be able to tell where one state ends and the other begins.

278   Landform maps are often used in middle- and upper-grade social

studies textbooks. The usual land forms shown are plains, plateaus, hills, and mountains; each is represented by a different color. Difficulty in using these maps arises when the pupil mistakenly thinks of the colors as representing elevations in absolute amounts. For example, there are high mountains and low mountains, yet on a landform map they appear in the same color. Some high plateaus are actually higher in absolute elevation than some low mountains. Some hills may be lower in elevation than plateaus and plains. Pupils need to learn that landform maps only show where the plains, plateaus, hills, and mountains are located, not how high they are above sea level.

Through years of experience with maps, the children will develop skill in the location of places and become familiar with the shape and size of better-known areas on the map. Places should be located precisely on maps. In pointing to Chicago on the map of the United States, for example, children should locate it exactly—not by sweeping a hand across the general location of Chicago, thereby including parts of Iowa, Illinois, Wisconsin, Michigan, and Indiana. But the location exercises must go beyond simply pointing to places and objects that appear on the map. What information can be obtained from the map that might account for the large settlement of people in the Chicago area? What features tend to encourage or discourage settlers? Such factors as natural transportation routes, waterways, waterfalls, mouths of rivers, coastlines, temperature, gaps in mountains, and outlets for products of the surrounding areas will become apparent as being important in population density and settlement. Why do certain areas of the Red River Valley in Minnesota and

The globe in this photograph shows elevations in raised relief. Maps are also available that illustrate the earth's surface in relief. Why must a different scale be used to represent vertical distances from the one used to represent horizontal distances?

North Dakota experience frequent spring flood problems? The facts that the Red River is north-flowing and its headwaters thaw while the sections farther north are still frozen help explain this recurring problem. What is the relationship of the grazing lands of the West to the farmlands of Iowa to the meat-processing plants of South St. Paul, Chicago, and Kansas City? Map study, along with some knowledge of the geography of these areas, will help answer questions of this type. Children gain insights into geographical relationships by having a helpful teacher who can assist them in seeing possibilities for interpreting and making inferences from facts gained through map study.

The types of information that can be read directly or inferred from map study can be classified as follows:

Land- and water forms—continents, oceans, bays, peninsulas, islands, straits.

Relief features—plains, mountains, rivers, deserts, plateaus, swamps, valleys.

Direction and distance—cardinal directions, distance in miles or kilometers and relative distance, scale.

Social data—population density, size of communities, location of major cities, relationship of social data to other factors.

Economic information—industrial and agricultural production, soil fertility, trade factors, location of industries.

Political information—political divisions, boundaries, capitals, territorial possessions, types of government, political parties.

Scientific information—location of discoveries, ocean currents, location of mineral and ore deposits, geological formations, air movements.

Human factors—cities, canals, railroads, highways, coaxial cables, telephone lines, bridges, dams.

What follows is a list of map and globe activities that will provide the teacher with a few examples of the kinds of pupil activities that can be used to stimulate interest and at the same time teach important concepts and skills relating to map and globe reading.

1. After an on-the-spot observation of the school grounds or the immediate vicinity, construct a three-dimensional floor map of the area.
2. Locate the place where stories about children in other lands take place or where news events are occurring.
3. Find pictures in magazines that illustrate various landforms: plains, plateaus, hills, and mountains.
4. Make maps of the same area, such as the local county, using different scales for each map.
5. Trace great circle air routes on maps and on globes and compare the two.

6. Compare the shapes of known areas on different map projections.
7. Develop a classroom exhibit of maps found in current newspapers and periodicals and compare them with conventional maps and globes.
8. Develop an illustrated glossary of concepts and terms associated with map reading.
9. Secure an outdated political map of the world (1940–1950 vintage) and have the class compare it with a current political map of the world.
10. Illustrate *mis*conceptions about maps such as "north is at the top of the map" or "the climate is temperate in the Temperate Zone."

Teaching map and globe skills does require some amount of special resources and equipment. Every classroom should have a globe along with wall maps appropriate to the curriculum content of the grade. Outline maps are needed in the middle and upper grades. It helps to have available a three-dimensional relief map of the United States and of the home state. Additional equipment might include charts showing conventional map symbols, slated maps and globe, and special-purpose maps showing vegetation, historical development, and natural resources. When children engage in map making, they will need to have available essential construction materials: boxes, blocks, butcher paper, black tape, tracing paper, colored pencils, pens or crayons, paints and brushes, papier-maché, plaster, salt and flour, or other modeling material.

Regular social studies unit work and the current events program provide natural settings for teaching map and globe skills. Children can use maps to record their data or observations as they study unit topics. They can analyze the relationships they detect in maps. They can use maps as a means of communicating ideas and findings to their classmates. It has been said that maps are the constant companions of geographers, and the same might be said about children as they engage in the social studies.

Children develop skill in map- and globe-reading in settings where teachers know which variations of the skills are to be taught at each level and where there is some method of accountability for such teaching. Regrettably, this does not occur as often as it should, and, as a result, the systematic teaching of these important skills becomes vulnerable to neglect. If we depend only on incidental references to maps and globes as a way of having children learn these skills, it will only be a fortunate accident if children become proficient in their use.

As a first step in developing a program of instruction in maps and globes, therefore, the teacher must determine which variations of the essential skills will be taught during the year. Naturally, it is helpful if the school district provides this information in a curriculum document. If such a document is not provided, the teacher should develop his or her own list of skills to be taught, looking for guidance to such sources as the textbook teacher's guide, the appendix of the thirty-third yearbook of the NCSS,[2] curriculum documents from other districts, or college methods books in social studies. The summary on pages 282–284 is an example of material that could be used for this purpose.

A SUMMARY OF MAP AND GLOBE SKILLS

Elementary school pupils should develop map and globe skills associated with the following concepts and generalizations.

1. Primary grades.
   - A map is a drawing or other representation of all or part of the earth.
   - On maps and globes, symbols are used to stand for real things.
   - The earth is a huge sphere.
   - A globe is a small model of the earth and is the most accurate representation of the earth.
   - Half of the earth is called a hemisphere.
   - The earth can be divided into several hemispheres. The most common ones are the Eastern, Western, Northern, and Southern Hemispheres; land hemisphere and water hemisphere; and day hemisphere and night hemisphere.
   - Any part of the globe can be shown on a map.
   - Large bodies of land are called continents.
   - Large bodies of water are called oceans.
   - Terms such as *left*, *right*, *near*, *far*, *above*, *below*, *up*, and *down* can be useful in expressing relative location.
   - A legend or key on a map tells the meaning of colors and symbols used on the map.
   - Directions on a map are determined by the poles; to go north means to go in the direction of the North Pole, to go south means to go in the direction of the South Pole.
   - North may be shown any place on a map; north is *not* always at the top of a map.
   - The North Pole is the point farthest north on the earth; the South Pole is the point farthest south.
   - The scale on a map or globe makes it possible to determine distances between places.
   - Maps are drawn to different scales; scale ensures that all objects are made smaller in the same amount.

[2]*Ibid.*, pp. 313ff.

- Maps and globes use legends, or keys, that tell the meaning of the symbols used on the map.
- The cardinal directions are north, south, east, and west; intermediate directions are northeast, northwest, southeast, and southwest.
- All places on the earth can be located on maps and globes. Different maps provide different information about the earth.

2. Intermediate and upper grades.
   - The larger the scale used, the larger each feature appears on the map.
   - The same symbol may mean different things from one map to another; the legend tells what the symbols stand for.
   - The elevation of land is measured from sea level; some maps provide information about elevation.
   - Physical maps can be used to determine land elevations, slopes of land, and directions of rivers.
   - Parallels of latitude can be used to establish east–west direction and are also used to measure distances in degrees north and south of the equator.
   - All places on the same east–west line (parallel of latitude) are directly east or west of one another and are the same distance north or south of the equator.
   - All places north of the equator are in north latitudes; all places south of the equator are in south latitudes.
   - The Tropic of Cancer and the Tropic of Capicorn are lines of latitude lying north and south of the equator. The part of the earth between them is known as the tropics.
   - The Arctic and Antarctic Circles are imaginary lines that define the polar regions.
   - The low latitudes lie on either side of the equator; the high latitudes surround the poles; and the middle latitudes lie between the low and high latitudes.
   - Parallels of latitude, parallel to the equator, get shorter as they progress from the equator to the poles.
   - Knowing the latitude of a place makes it possible to locate its north–south position on the earth.
   - Meridians of longitude can be used to determine north–south direction and are also used to measure distances in degrees east and west of the prime meridian.
   - The zero or *prime* meridian passes through Greenwich, a suburb of London.
   - Meridians of longitude are imaginary north–south lines that converge on both poles.
   - Meridians of longitude are *great circles* because they divide the earth into two hemispheres.
   - The shortest distance between any two places on the earth follows a great circle.
   - West longitude is measured to the west of the prime meridian

283

from zero to 180°; east longitude is measured to the east of the prime meridian from zero to 180°.

- All places on the same north–south line (meridian of longitude) are directly north or south of each other and are the same distance in degrees east or west of the prime meridian.
- The latitude and longitude of any place determine its exact location on a globe or map.
- Longitude is used in determining the time of day at places around the world. The earth rotates through 15° of longitude every hour; the earth is divided into 24 time zones.
- Globes give such information as distance, direction, relative and exact location, and sizes and shapes of areas more accurately than flat maps can.
- Maps and globes often use abbreviations to identify places and things.
- An imaginary line through the center of the earth, running from pole to pole, is called the earth's axis; the earth rotates on its axis from west to east.
- Night and day are the result of the rotation of the earth.
- Maps and globes provide data about the nature of areas by using color contour, visual relief, and contour lines.
- All flat maps contain some distortion because they represent a round object on a flat surface.
- Different map projections provide different perspectives on the sizes and shapes of areas shown.

DEVELOPING A SENSE OF TIME AND CHRONOLOGY

There is much in the modern urban, industrialized world to remind one of the importance of time. Airlines, trains, and buses operate on time schedules, as do places of business, factories, churches, public institutions, sports events, and television programs, to name just a few. Benjamin Franklin said, "Remember that time is money," this being one of several such proverbs that equate time with economic gain. When we speak of persons making "wise use" of their time, we usually mean that they are busy at something perceived to be "productive." Because time is such an important commodity in the lives of most of us, we have little tolerance for time wasters and loafers.

In spite of the substantial amount of research that has been conducted on the ability of human beings to deal with time concepts and chronology, much about this phenomenon remains shrouded in mystery. There can be no question that one's perception of time grows out of cultural conditioning. There are few cultures in which people are as compulsive about punctuality as are Americans. To some extent, one's time orientation relates to one's social-class membership, but research suggests that human beings vary greatly in their ability to understand time concepts. Circumstances also condition one's perception of time so that in some cases we say that "time flies," whereas in other settings time seems to drag on endlessly.

Children, of course, learn much about time relationships through ordinary living outside of school. Undoubtedly most children would learn how to tell time, would learn the days of the week and months of the year, and would become familiar with terms ordinarily used in referring to units of time, such as noon, midnight, afternoon, and morning, even if these were not taught in school. The school program can ensure that these skills are correctly and are adequately learned, however, and can provide children the opportunity to practice using them. A few lessons with a simulated clock, supported by practical application in noting when things happen in the schedule of activities during the day, will be adequate to teach most children how to deal with clock time. It is rare to find a mentally competent grown person who cannot tell the time of day. In any case the increased use of digital clocks should eliminate entirely any problems in reading clock time.

The main thrust of the school program should be, therefore, on those aspects of time and chronology that are not likely to be learned outside of school. This includes (1) the more technical language of time and chronology, such as century, decade, fortnight, fiscal year, calendar year, generation, score, millennium, A.M., P.M., B.C., and A.D.; (2) placing events in chronological order; (3) developing an understanding of the time spans that separate historical events. References to *indefinite* units of time—such as many years ago, soon thereafter, several years had passed, and in a few years—need special attention because they are apt to mean almost any amount of time to young children. Definite references to time can more easily be made meaningful by associating them with units of time that are known to the children: their own ages, the length of time they have been in school, when their parents or grandparents were children of their ages, and so on. The teaching or these relationships can and should take place within the context of social studies units, especially those that focus on history, and in connection with current news stories.

Time lines are often used to show how related events are arranged in chronological order and to show the relative amount of time that separates them. Though widely used, experts are not in agreement as to the value of time lines in clarifying time and chronology for young children. Children can develop the concept of representing time on a continuum by first charting events that they experience on a firsthand basis. This helps them arrange the events in the correct sequence. They can make time lines that show things that happened to them yesterday, today, or are being planned for tomorrow. The amount of time included on the line can gradually be expanded to cover several months and then years. Time lines are more interesting to children if events are shown pictorially, rather than simply as dots and dates. With middle- and upper-grade children, frequent use can be made of time lines in connection with historical studies of their home state and their nation. Such time lines need not stop with the present date but may be projected into the future, thus illustrating that time is continuous and that the present stands between the past and the future.

TEACHING CHILDREN THE USE OF GRAPHS AND CHARTS

Because of the widespread use of graphs and charts in social studies materials and in printed material outside of school, it is imperative that children develop the skills needed to read and interpret them. Just leafing through a daily newspaper or a weekly news magazine reminds one of how commonly these graphics are used and how powerfully their messages are conveyed. Citizens today are "digest" oriented. They do not have the time or the inclination to wade through a mountain of narrative that explains social events or conditions. They want to see these ideas in summary form and in stark relief. Besides, the complexity of social data, much of which is in statistical form, lends itself well to a graphic format.

Graphs

Graphs are used to illustrate relationships among quantities. These relationships may be spread over a period of time, thus showing trends. The most commonly used graphs are some variation of the *bar graph*, the *pie* or *circle graph*, and the *line graph*. Any of these graphs may include pictorial representations, thereby making them more interesting to young children and making the content less abstract. For instance, with primary-grade pupils, stick figures can be used to represent children in a bar graph showing the number of pupils absent from class each day. It is easy to visualize the relationships of the parts to the whole in a circle graph, but to construct one accurately requires the ability to compute percentages, usually not possible in the elementary school grades. Modern elementary school textbooks make liberal use of graphs in presenting data, but pupils need to be instructed in how to read and interpret them. Because graphs can be designed to present distorted pictures of data, children in the middle and upper grades should be taught how bias is introduced in a graph.

Children can learn much about graphs and how to read them by constructing their own graphs. Such pupil-made graphs can be used in making oral or written reports and for bulletin board displays. In making graphs accuracy in the presentation should be emphasized rather than artistic perfection.

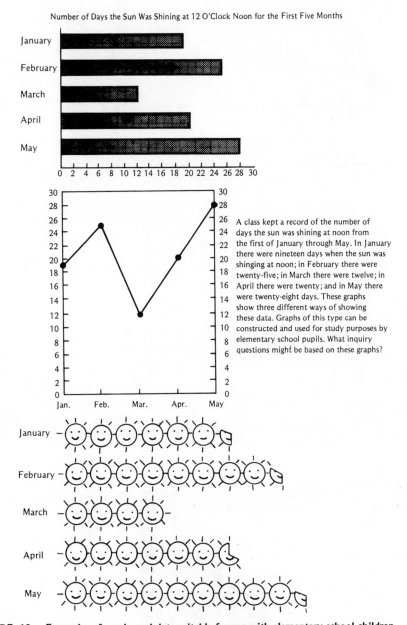

Number of Days the Sun Was Shining at 12 O'Clock Noon for the First Five Months

A class kept a record of the number of days the sun was shining at noon from the first of January through May. In January there were nineteen days when the sun was shinging at noon; in February there were twenty-five; in March there were twelve; in April there were twenty; and in May there were twenty-eight days. These graphs show three different ways of showing these data. Graphs of this type can be constructed and used for study purposes by elementary school pupils. What inquiry questions might be based on these graphs?

FIGURE 13. Examples of graphs and data suitable for use with elementary school children.

Formal Charts

Like graphs, charts are widely used to present ideas in a vivid and forceful way. Formal charts are often designated as follows:

1. Narrative chart: Tells a story; shows events in sequence. (Example: how plywood is made, stages of

287

FIGURE 14.   The drawing illustrates how the popular "pie" graph is sometimes used to create an incorrect impression. Because the sketch is shown in perspective, the sizes of the sections are distorted. Thus, sections that seem to be farthest from the viewer appear smaller than those in the foreground, although arithmetically they represent equal amounts.

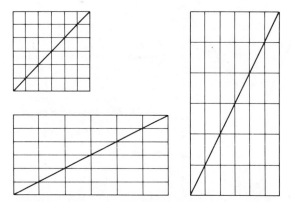

FIGURE 15.   It is important for children to learn that graphs can create false impressions. In these line graphs, the same data were used on three different grids, resulting in varying steepness in the slopes of the lines. Consequently, although the facts are the same, the rate of change appears markedly different.

FIGURE 16.   How much larger were profits in 1981 than in 1979? The chances are that you have said "about twice as large." This graph illustrates how wrong impressions are conveyed when pictorial graphs are improperly constructed. Careful examination of this graph will show that the 1981 profits are not even twice those of 1978. The basic error in this graph is that it does not show the first $500,000 of profit. A more accurate perception of the growth in profits can be made if the correct position of the base line is established. Can you locate the place where the base line should be?

the development of civilization, how to use the telephone, or the construction of homes)

2. Tabulation chart: Lists data in table form to facilitate making comparisons. (Example: data placed in tabular form to show infant mortality rates, illiteracy rates, or per capita income among nations of the world)

3. Pedigree chart: Shows events stemming from a common origin. (Example: a family tree, the development of a political party, or the history of language)

4. Classification chart: Groups data into various categories. (Example: the various types of restaurants, types of personal services available, or different modes of transportation)

5. Organization chart: Shows the structure of an organization. (Example: the three branches of government, the structure of a corporation, or the organization of a city government or a school district)

6. Flow chart: Shows a process involving change at certain points. (Example: how raw materials are transformed into finished products, the break of bulk in shipping as at a harbor facility, or how scrap iron is converted into a usable raw material)

The frequent use of formal charts in children's books provides a good basis for inquiry learning. In the process children not only learn how to read and interpret the chart, but broaden their substantive knowledge and build their understanding of associated concepts.

Informal Charts

Informal charts are charts that are developed and constructed by the teacher or by the children. They are commonly placed on wrapping paper, oak tagboard, newsprint, "butcher" paper, chart paper, or the chalkboard. They may contain diagrams, sketches, pictures, or other illustrative material or simply may be written accounts of experiences or activities related to the unit under study.

When charts are constructed for use with primary-grade children, it is essential that the mechanics and makeup of the charts conform exactly to the patterns that are taught in the basic language arts program. For example, the style of lettering used should be exactly the same as that used by the children in manuscript writing; capital letters and punctuation marks should be used only where they are used in ordinary writing; and the reading vocabulary should follow as closely as possible the vocabulary being developed in the basic reading program. Careful attention should be given to the format to facilitate ease of reading: uniform margins; well-spaced letters, words, and lines; natural phrases of appropriate length; and sharp, clear lettering. Phrases should not be broken at the end of a line such as:

Cross the street at
the crosswalk.

But rather:

Cross the street
at the crosswalk.

Middle- and upper-grade children can be encouraged to make and use charts in connection with their reports, committee work, and displays. As was true with graphs, the children need be less concerned with the artistic perfection of the chart than with the manner in which it conveys ideas. Simplicity, vividness, concreteness, and accuracy of the idea presented are more important considerations than artistic finish.

Data-Retrieval Charts

The *data-retrieval chart* was developed by the late Hilda Taba and her associates in connection with curriculum development work in social studies. It consists of a set of questions related to the inquiry and an indication of the groups or situations from which data is to be

CHART 6.   Data Retrieval Chart

Our Next-Door Neighbors		
Analytical Concepts	Canada	Mexico
Geographical features 　Size 　Climate 　Physical features 　Natural resources		
History 　Native people 　Foreign influences 　Relations with U.S. 　Type of government today		
Economic development 　Main occupations 　Average per capita income 　Exports		
Population 　Ethnic groups 　Density 　Major cities 　Levels of education 　Religious groups 　Languages		

secured. It provides a convenient way for pupils to record data they gather in the process of study. It also has the advantage of displaying the data in a form that can be used or "retrieved" for study and analysis at a later time. The data retrieval chart is useful in making comparisons and contrasts because comparable data can be secured from two or more samples.

TEACHING CHILDREN THE USE OF CARTOONS

Almost everyone enjoys the humor of good cartoons. In cartoons we see a part of our own experience reflected because they deal with situations commonly known to all of us. They exaggerate, the sub-

FIGURE 17.[3] This cartoon illustrates how much the reader must bring to such visuals if they are to have meaning. Rather than using word symbols in a caption, the cartoonist has relied totally on the illustration itself to communicate the message. What message does this cartoon convey to readers?

[3]Artwork by Christine E. Meyers, Graphic Artist, *The Seattle Times.*

jects are presented in caricature, and they are designed to show all the vices or virtues associated with a particular character in our culture. They give us a chance to laugh at ourselves and thereby add spice and variety to living.

When dealing with social or political matters, however, cartoons may be anything but funny—especially to the person or group represented in them. The same techniques of symbolism, the use of familiar situations, exaggerations, satire, and caricature are used to present forcefully a single point of view. The cartoon does not allow the reader or the person portrayed in it an opportunity for rebuttal. Recognition of the fact that only one point of view is represented in cartoons is important in their interpretation. Older children need to be taught the general makeup of cartoons that deal with social and political problems and need the experience of critically evaluating them. It is well for the children to present an opposite point of view from the one presented in the cartoon.

The symbolism used in cartoons causes much confusion in the minds of some children. When the characters are portrayed as animals, the children tend to associate those animals with various national groups. Cartoons use stereotypes of people that add little to the type of international understanding we are attempting to foster and encourage in the social studies program. Figurative terms such as *iron curtain* are represented as walls of iron, leading the child to believe that such a wall exists in a literal sense. Cartoons usually demand a high level of understanding of the issues involved if they are to tell their story accurately; thus, the child needs to be instructed and helped in developing the skill of interpreting cartoons. (See Figure 17.)

DISCUSSION QUESTIONS AND SUGGESTED ACTIVITIES

1. Select a topic for a grade of your choice and plan specific map- and globe-reading activities that could be incorporated in a study of it.
2. Prepare a series of posters showing map symbols and accompany each symbol with a photograph of the object being represented.
3. Make a list of words or phrases related to the understanding of maps and globes that are misleading (for example, up, down). For each entry suggest an alternate word or phrase that would be more accurate.
4. What misunderstandings might develop when characters in charts and cartoons appear in caricature? What might be done to prevent such misunderstandings from occurring?
5. Develop an inquiry-oriented learning experience based on a map, chart, or cartoon. Arrange to teach it to your peers.

6. How might a data-retrieval chart constructed by the pupils be useful to them in unit study? Suggest a specific topic and variables that could be used in constructing such a chart.
7. Select a map-reading skill and show by examples of learning activities how it is sequenced through the elementary grades on a simple to complex continuum.
8. Select a social studies textbook and examine it in terms of its treatment of the skills discussed in this chapter.
9. If you are teaching or if you have access to a class, try these three activities with the pupils:
   a. Have pupils find indefinite references to time and space in their social studies texts or in a newspaper (expressions such as "many years ago," "shortly after," "several ships," "few resources"). Discuss the meaning of these terms with the pupils. How accurate are their understanding of these terms? Report your findings to your classmates.
   b. Have the class discuss situations in which they think "time flies" and others in which they think time "moves at a snail's pace." Encourage them to identify reasons for this difference. Are the situations the same for all pupils?
   c. Have the class think of as many popular expressions or proverbs as they can that have to do with time. Conduct this activity for a period of days and as expressions or proverbs are suggested, place them on the bulletin board. Have children make drawings to illustrate them. Discuss this in terms of the importance of time in our lives.

SELECTED REFERENCES

Anderson, Charlotte C. and Barbara J. Winston. "Acquiring Information by Asking Questions, Using Maps and Graphs, and Making Direct Observations," Chapter 3, *Developing Decision-Making Skills*, 47th Yearbook. National Council for the Social Studies, Dana G. Kurfman, ed. Washington, D.C.: The Council, 1977, pp. 71–106.

Davis, Arnold R. "Reading Maps: A Much-Needed Skill," *The Social Studies*, 65 (February 1974), pp. 67–71. (The author annotates 39 journal articles dealing with teaching map reading.)

Harris, Ruby M. *The Rand McNally Handbook of Map and Globe Usage*, 4th ed. Chicago: Rand McNally & Company, 1967.

Nixon, William D. and Richart E. McCormack. "LANDSAT: A Tool for Your Classroom," *Social Education*, 41 (November–December 1977), pp. 606–622.

Sunal, Cynthia S. and Dennis W. Sunal. "Mapping the Child's World," *Social Education*, 42 (May 1978), pp. 381–383.

Whiteford, Gary T. "Space and Place: Recognizing the Ties that Bind," *The History and Social Science Teacher*, 15 (Spring 1980), pp. 173–176.

11
Skills for
Group Interaction

Social studies education provides a natural setting in which to teach, promote, and practice social and group-work skills. The learning activities that characterize soundly-based social studies programs require pupils to plan and work together, to strive toward common goals, and to share materials, tools, and resources. Although it is true that the total elementary school curriculum assists in the growth of social behavior, the social studies program should contribute to its attainment in a special way.

The term *group* must be understood to mean something more than a collection of individuals. Groups develop a solidarity—a unit or cohesiveness—resulting from working and thinking together. A fourth-grade class at the beginning of a school year is an aggregate of individual children assigned to a particular room because of their similar chronological ages. This class of individuals may develop into a *group* as the year progresses and the children develop feelings of belonging to it, identifying with it, developing an *esprit de corps*, and growing in their concern for the welfare and success of the class. It will be a *group* to the extent that the actions of individuals are influenced by other members and the extent to which the behavior of individual members affects the group.

SETTING A DESIRABLE ATMOSPHERE FOR HUMAN RELATIONS

Why is it that some teachers are able to build a classroom atmosphere that is emotionally supportive, one in which children feel comfortable and secure, and other teachers have difficulty doing so? Doubtless, part of the reason can be attributed to personality variables. Some teachers have a greater tolerance for flexibility and ambiguity than do others. Quite apart from these variations in personalities of teachers, however, it is possible to identify teacher behaviors that contribute to or detract from setting a desirable atmosphere for human relations in the classroom.

We are not unmindful of the fact that groups of children also vary considerably and that the task of developing a wholesome classroom climate is more challenging with some groups than it is with others. Children who have developed hostile and aggressive life-styles outside of school bring those dispositions and behaviors to school with them. Groups that have been together for a few years may have formed in-groups, cliques, and bad feelings toward each other that persist from year to year. In some cases, children are so lacking in any sense of self-discipline and common courtesy that even the most skillful teacher would have a difficult time trying to develop some sense of group feeling based on unity and cooperation. Where such conditions prevail, effective teaching cannot take place unless and until basic problems of classroom management are resolved. We do not deal with such chronic problems of pupil behavior because they are beyond the scope of this text.

An emotionally supportive atmosphere is one that is characterized by trust and by evidence that individuals care about each other. When a child volunteers, "Robin's group had more to do than the rest of us. They should have more time to finish," the observer senses

This photograph captures the warmth of feeling between these two young children. Working together, sharing ideas and things, engaging in play activities in a secure, caring environment— all of these opportunities foster growth in human relations skills. What other social studies objectives are being attended to when pupils of various ethnic backgrounds are placed in the same classroom?

that he or she is in a caring environment. Or, when a minor classroom accident results in damage to material or broken equipment, and the teacher treats the incident as an accident, one concludes that the teacher values human beings more than things. Teachers who develop comfortable classroom environments for children are concerned with a broad range of educational outcomes, including those that relate to the emotional and social growth of children, rather than attending only to subject matter and skills goals.

Perhaps the most significant characteristic of a desirable classroom climate is the lack of hostility between pupils and the teacher and among the children within the group. The level of hostility and aggressive behavior in a classroom is related to what the teacher says and does. Teacher behavior can best be illustrated by such contrasts as the following:

Practices and Procedures That Tend to Increase Hostility in a Classroom

1. *Negative statements by the teacher*—Here are a few examples of ridicule, sarcasm, criticism, negative, and tension-producing statements made by a teacher. Such statements to children invariably lead to hostility, emotional disturbance, selfishness, fear, and criticism of others:

"I wish you would start acting like fourth-graders instead of kindergarteners."

"Someone is whispering again, and I guess you all know who it is."

"Most fifth-grade classes could understand this, but I am not sure about you."

"Sit up straight. Don't you have a backbone?"

"Why don't you listen when I give directions? None of you seems to know how to listen."

2. *Excessively competitive situations*—Fair competition in classrooms is highly desirable. It can stimulate good work, motivate children to do their best, and help children learn the graces

Practices and Procedures That Tend to Decrease Hostility in a Classroom

1. *Positive statements by the teacher*—Friendly, constructive statements by the teacher tend to reduce tension and hostility in the classroom. Here are a few examples:

"We will all want to listen carefully in order not to miss anything Sue is going to tell us."

"All of us did our work so well yesterday during our work period. Do you suppose we can do as well today?"

"It is really fun for all of us when you bring such interesting things for sharing."

"It's nice to have Bill and Sue back with us again. The boys and girls were hoping you would come back today."

2. *Successful cooperative enterprises*—The successful achievement of cooperative activities, involving all members of the class, tends to reduce hostility within the group because it demands the

297

associated with winning and losing. It becomes undesirable when it is of the "dog-eat-dog" variety where each child is pitted against every other child whether the competitive situation is fair or unfair.

3. *Disregard for individual differences*—Classrooms where some children are made to feel "this place is not for me" contribute much toward breeding hostility in children. Such rooms are characterized by one level of acceptable performance applied to all, uniform assignments, one system of reward, great emphasis on verbal intellectual performance.

4. *Rigid schedule and pressure*—A rigid time schedule and constant pressure associated with "hurry up," "finish your work," "you will be late," or stopping lessons exactly on time whether completed or not create insecurity in children that leads to hostility. A class that is always "one jump behind the teacher" is likely to be one where children blame others for their failure to finish, invent excuses for themselves, and seek scapegoats.

5. *Highly directive teaching practices*—Teachers who must make every decision themselves, give all the assignments, allow for very little participation on the part of children in the life of the classroom are encouraging feelings of hostility. Such practices usually mean that teachers refer to the pupils as "my children," or in addressing the pupils, say

combined efforts of everyone in the successful attainment of a common goal. Children depend on one another in such situations and, therefore, feel a need for one another.

3. *Recognition of and adaptations made in accordance with individual differences*—In such classrooms, children are challenged at a level commensurate with their abilities. Boys and girls feel that they "count for something" in the classroom and that they belong to it.

4. *Relaxed, comfortable pace*—Good teachers working with young children maintain a flexible schedule and will not place undue pressures on pupils. They will have a plan and a schedule, yet will not be compulsive in adhering to it. They will deviate from their plan and schedule now and then in the interest of the needs of the boys and girls they teach. Good teachers recognize that feelings of insecurity are related to hostility and will do everything they can to develop feelings of security in the classroom.

5. *Pupil involvement in planning and managing the class*—Giving pupils some opportunity to plan and manage the affairs of the classroom does much to develop feelings of "we-ness," of identification with the group. Children under such circumstances are less inclined to want to think of ways to disrupt Miss So-and-so's orderly room but will

"I want you to...," or more subtly, "Miss So-and-so wasn't very proud of her class this morning."

6. *Lack of closeness between teacher and pupils*—Some teachers feel they must "keep children in their place," meaning they must remain socially distant from them. This leads to a cold objective relationship between the children and teacher, causing the children to feel that the teacher lacks affection and warmth for them. This "holier-than-thou" attitude on the part of the teacher is likely to engender feelings of hostility in some children.

7. *Lack of satisfying emotional experiences*—Some classrooms sorely lack experiences of an affective nature. Everything is deadly serious business—work, work, work. Even the music, art, storytime, or dramatic activities are made to seem like work. Little time is spent on teaching children to enjoy one another, feel the inner joy that comes from a good poem or music selection, or express their feelings in some art medium.

work hard to make "our" room a good place to work.

6. *Warm and friendly relationship between teacher and pupils*—One of the basic needs of children is that of love and affection. They need it in their homes, in their playgroups, and in their schools. The feeling that children will not respect the teacher who is friendly with them is in error. They are likely to respect the teacher more who they feel is a "human being" capable of cordial and warm personal relationships with others. This is a professional relationship, however, not one of oversentimentalism.

7. *Many opportunities for pleasurable emotional experiences*—Teachers can reduce tensions that build up in children during the course of classroom life by providing opportunities for the release of these tensions through various emotional experiences. Children have the opportunity to express their feelings orally, in writing, or through art forms. They talk together and enjoy one another's company. They prepare skits, do creative dramatics, and role-play situations to help get the feelings of others. All of these activities tend to reduce feelings of hostility.

ORGANIZING SUBGROUPS FOR SOCIAL STUDIES INSTRUCTION

Committee work or small-group enterprises are effective instructional procedures in the social studies and have many values for children. It is in the small group that the children get experience with and develop skill in group processes. These experiences should begin in a limited way even as early as the kindergarten. In block play, for example, the teacher can let some children choose the things they wish to build with blocks. Some will want to build an airport, some a house, others a post office, others a supermarket, and so on. The teacher can let each of these children choose two other children to help build the project. The children proceed with the building and, when it is completed, tell the class or their teacher a story about their building. Early experiences in such block play will consist mainly of parallel play—three children may be building an airport but each is working independently of the other two. As the year progresses, there will be more evidence of cooperative endeavor. Children become more conscious of what others in their group are doing and will plan their own contribution in terms of the other children and the group goal.

A good way to familiarize primary-grade children with small-group work is to have committees responsible for various housekeeping duties in the classroom. Jenny's committee has the responsibility of keeping the library table neat, Paul's committee is in charge of the game shelf, Peter's committee is responsible for the care of the aquarium, and Kathy's committee keeps the coat corner orderly. Membership on these committees can be changed from time to time to include all the children in the class. Such experiences will help prepare

These two girls are gathering wood to construct a survival shelter. They are involved in the school district's outdoor education program, which provides many opportunities for learning in all areas of the curriculum. Identify a few objectives important to the social studies that could be achieved through an outdoor education program.

children for the committee work that is done as a part of the instructional program. Small-group enterprises in the primary grades need careful supervision and direction. The goals or purposes of the group should be well defined, concrete, and easily understood. Materials needed for the group to do its work must be immediately at hand. Rules and responsibilities of working on committees should be discussed, explained, and posted conspicuously in the room. Group-work skills develop slowly and gradually and require practice as do any other skills. The skills of group work can be learned only by working in groups.

In the middle and upper grades, small group work becomes an increasingly greater part of the social studies instructional program. Committees are used to prepare reports; discuss topics; plan activities; do construction, art, or dramatics activities; write plays; gather resources; interview resource persons; and so on. Through instruction and experience, children will learn responsibilities of committee chairpersons and committee members and will learn that the success of the group depends on the initiative and cooperation of individuals within the group.

When teaching is planned on a unit basis, there will be many occasions when the class will be divided into small work groups. These subgroups will be organized in accordance with the ages of the pupils and the nature of the task to be performed. Such subgroups are *task-oriented*; they are formed to do things that need doing. Task groups tend to be relatively flexible and short-lived. A committee may be assigned the task of finding out why pioneers moved westward. When the committee has obtained its information and has reported to the larger group, it can be dissolved and its members can either join other groups or work on individual activities.

Teachers who have experimented with small-group instruction commonly feel that group work breaks down either because some children within the groups do most of the work or because the children waste time and accomplish very little. This is characteristic of immature groups and is an indication that the children need more guidance in small-group activities. Actually, a group has two types of tasks that it must carry out in any cooperative endeavor. First, it is important that members of the group have the appropriate skills necessary to carry through the assigned task to completion. It would be unwise, for example, to send a group of fifth-graders to the library to find information about population growth and food distribution if none of the children knew how to use the library for this purpose. Similarly, pupils who do not have well-developed reading skills should not be placed on group projects that demand a considerable amount of reading and research activity. The nature of the task assigned to a committee should be consistent with the ability of the individual members who comprise the group. Because the finished product presumably represents the combined efforts of all members, each must be able to contribute in some measure to its successful completion.

301

The second type of task faced by a group involves the use of skills needed in order to function as a group: organizing, selecting a leader, designating responsibilities, deciding on controls, and various ways of working together. If, for example, the group sent to the library to find materials was unable to organize itself, plan how it would go about its work, assign specific responsibilities, decide who was the leader, and how it would report its findings, its efforts would not be that of a group but rather would be that of individuals working independently. It would be trying to move in several different directions at one time, making progress as a *group* impossible.

In organizing subgroups within a class, the teacher may find the following suggestions helpful:

1. Defer small-group work until the management of the class has been firmly established and until the work habits, capabilities, and special needs of individual children are known.
2. Begin group work slowly. Select responsible key children for the first group and keep the group small—perhaps not more than five children.
3. Assign a task that is simple, well defined, and one that the group is certain to accomplish successfully.
4. Have the remainder of the class engage in individual assignments while giving guidance and direction to the smaller group. Either designate a leader for the small group or have the children choose a leader. Explain the nature of their assigned task and begin to discuss some of their special responsibilities when working in a small group.
5. Have resource materials available for the pupils. Later on, as they become accustomed to working in groups, they will be able to secure needed materials themselves.
6. Meet with the small group every day for a few minutes before they begin work and again at the end of their work period to make sure things are moving along as planned. If possible, have them make a progress report to the other, larger group during the summary and evaluation that should come at the close of each social studies period.
7. Give them specific help and suggestions in how to organize their work and how to report what they are doing.
8. Have their report to the class be short, concise, and interesting. Have members of the group explain to the class how they did their work as a group. Begin calling attention to some of the responsibilities of persons working in small groups.
9. Follow the same procedure with another group of children as soon as possible. Gradually include other children, selecting some who have had previous experience in group work and some who have not. Observe carefully the children who need close supervision and those who are responsible and work well in groups.

10. After all the children have had an opportunity to work in a small group under close supervision, more than one group can work at one time. Eventually, the entire class may be able to work in small groups simultaneously. When this is attempted, it should be preceded by a review of the standards of group work, goals should be clearly defined beforehand, and a careful evaluation should follow.

These principles are apparent in the following example of a teacher's getting a small group started on a task.

> The children in Mr. Shigaki's class have been involved in a career awareness study and are going to have resource persons visit their classroom. The children have indicated careers they would like to have included. Mr. Shigaki has asked four children to meet him in the rear of the classroom and is now speaking to them.
>
> "Because the four of you are particularly interested in learning about computer science careers, I am asking that you take responsibility for introducing Miss Timms tomorrow. You will have to select some one person to actually do the introducing. The others can help by suggesting things that should be said about her in the introduction. Also, all of you should help develop some questions to ask her after her presentation. Remember one of our goals is to find out what kind of training and skills computer scientists need and what opportunities there are in that field. Is there anything else you think you will need to prepare in order to be the host group tomorrow?" (Pause)
>
> One member of the group asked if they were to thank the visitor for coming.
>
> "Yes. Good point! I'm glad you thought of that, Mark. You will need to select someone to thank Miss Timms. Anything else?" (Pause; no further suggestions are offered.)
>
> "I guess you are ready to begin your work then," says Mr. Shigaki. "Lisa, would you act as the group leader and report to me when your group is finished planning?"
>
> Mr. Shigaki then left the group to its task and supervised the remainder of the class who had been working on individual assignments.

MANAGING SMALL-GROUP INSTRUCTION

Careful attention to each of the following suggestions will facilitate the effectiveness of small-group endeavors.

Help Children Learn Group-Process Skills

This text has repeatedly stressed the need to place pupils in group-work settings if they are to learn group-work skills. However, if pupils are only given the *opportunity* to work in groups without receiving instruction in how a group is supposed to go about its business, they

303

may likewise not learn to function effectively in small groups. Simply dividing the class into groups and assigning each a task is not likely to help children grow in group-work skills.

Before attempting a small-group endeavor, the teacher should discuss with the class some of the responsibilities of the persons who are a part of a group. It is helpful if the children and the teacher can summarize these and place them on charts that are posted in the room. These standards can be used as evaluative criteria after the children have had an opportunity to work in small groups. Such standards would vary some depending on the age of the children; but, in general, they might include any or all of the following:

Group Members

1. Help the leader carry out plans.
2. Do your share of the work.
3. Work without disturbing other group members.
4. Ask other members for their ideas.
5. Select only the ideas that help the group do its best work.
6. Cheerfully take the jobs the group wants you to do.
7. Make other members of the group feel welcome.
8. Be courteous; respect the ideas of others.
9. Support the group's decisions.

Group Leaders

1. Help make everyone become a part of the group.
2. Let everyone have a turn at the "good" jobs.
3. Get ideas from all members of the group.
4. Let the group decide which ideas are best.
5. Keep the group moving to get its job finished in the best way it can.
6. Keep from being "bossy"; be a leader, not a dictator.
7. Help your group know what its job is.

Some teachers find role playing to be a valuable technique in teaching the skills needed in small-group work. By selecting four to five children to serve as group members, the teacher can demonstrate to the class what it means to "help everyone become a part of the group" or any of the standards that have been discussed. When the role playing is completed, the remainder of the class can analyze the situation to determine why the group was functioning well or poorly. It is helpful to have children observe certain specific elements in the situation to be presented. For example, they might try to answer such questions as these:

1. What did individual members do to help the group do its job? What did members do that did not help the group?
2. What did the leader do to help the group get its job done?
3. How did the group find out exactly what it was to do?

4. Did the group use good resources in solving its problems?
5. Did the group seem to be working together as a team? Why or why not?
6. How could the group be helped to do its job better?

Following the role playing, the class can discuss the situation in terms of the specific points being observed. It may then be helpful to re-play all or a portion of the situation to help children appreciate the forces at work in group situations. With young children it may be de-sirable to have an older group demonstrate such things as a domineer-ing leader, an uncooperative group member, a member who wants only the choice tasks, the noncontributor, the irresponsible leader, the member who must always have his or her own way, the member who talks too much, and so on. In teaching group-work skills the teacher will want to do more than talk about what should or should not be done. Children really need an opportunity to see and experi-ence "how it works" as well as an opportunity to experiment and try their hand at doing productive group work. Role playing can do much to sensitize them to the various subtleties and forces that come into play in small-group situations.

Cooperative group work skills can take many forms. Here, with assistance from their parents, pupils are working together on a school improvement project. Do you believe that group work skills learned in a setting such as the one in the photograph transfer to in-class activi-ties? Do you think that group work skills learned in the intellectual setting of the classroom transfer to situations outside of the classroom?

Keep the Size of the Group Small

The size of a subgroup within a classroom has considerable effect on its productivity. If groups are too large, there will be a duplication of responsibilities, less opportunity for individuals to carry their share of the group effort, a tendency for some members to fade out of the group activity, and problems of management will become more severe. On the other hand, if groups are too small, the collective talent of the group is restricted, demands on individuals may be excessive, and the work product may represent little more than the effort of one or two individuals. In general, however, groups should be kept small, possibly not more than three to five children and rarely more than six.

Keep in Mind the Status of Members Within the Class

Within the classroom there develops a prestige or status system that reflects itself in pupil interaction. This status system involves every member of the group, including the teacher. Under favorable classroom conditions the teacher is considered a high-status member, usually at the top of the status scale. The pupils distribute themselves on a continuum of status ranging from the children who are generally well accepted and highly thought of by most members to those who are almost universally rejected by the majority of the class.

Some insight into the status of various members of the class may be obtained informally by observing the children in and out of the classroom. These observations can be made in any situation where the children exercise a free choice of the partners they wish to play or work with. The teacher may observe, too, whether the preference is a mutual one or whether the child doing the selecting is simply attempting to identify with a high-status classmate. It is also possible to obtain information relative to the social structure of the class through the use of sociometric devices. More specifically, sociometric data may be used to

1. identify leaders within the class.
2. determine the social status or social position of any child with respect to other children.
3. spot in-groups, cliques, or rival factions within the class.
4. locate children who are rejected by others.
5. obtain information that will be helpful in arranging the classroom seating pattern, forming committees, work groups, play groups.

The teacher will want to give careful consideration to status in setting up work groups. Children should be placed with others with whom they can work, but the selection should not be left entirely to the children. When this happens, high-status children are selected first, leaving the low-status children that no group wants. Even allowing children to choose the group with whom they wish to work is not entirely satisfactory. Possibly a combination of children's choices and teacher placement is the best course of action, because the teacher knows the capabilities of each child and can make a sound judgment about how and with whom each is likely to work best and make the greatest growth. Some teachers find the assignment of low-status children to group activities with high-status children has the effect of helping the low-status children obtain greater acceptance and prestige. A grouping of children that almost duplicates the "in-groups" and "out-groups" of a class rarely works well because it does not make for good human relations within the classroom.

Reward Group Work Appropriately

Part of the reason that group work is at times ineffective is the feeling on the part of the children that this type of work is not rewarded to the same extent that more formal aspects of the classroom work are. This stems from the teacher's attitude toward the value of group activites. If the rewards (recognition, praise, value statements, reports to parents, grades) go only to those who do well in paper-and-pencil activities, the pupils rightly conclude that group activities do not count much in the entire scheme of things. Group work will be enhanced if the teacher regards it as an important part of the instructional program and rewards appropriately the children who have done commendable work in group endeavors.

TEACHING AND USING DISCUSSION TECHNIQUES

One of the most widely used and most valuable techniques in social studies teaching is *discussion*. Its value lies chiefly in the fact that it represents a type of intellectual teamwork, resting on the principle that the pooled knowledge, ideas, and feelings of several persons have greater merit than those of a single individual.

Because the strength of discussion is obtained from the information and viewpoint of many members of the group, it is necessary that it be based on broad participation. It is a thinking-together process that breaks down if one member or group dominates it. It is the responsibility of the teacher to encourage the more reluctant children to participate. Although there cannot be a single answer to the question of what to do with the child who dominates the discussion, skillful teachers usually take care of the matter with a statement such as "Jackie, you have given us so many good ideas today, and I know you have many more good suggestions, but we want to find out what some of the others think would be a good way to. . . ."

In good class discussions, children should talk freely and voluntarily. There should be no set pattern of soliciting contributions, nor should letter grades be given on individual discussion contributions. It will take a while to develop effective discussions because the skills needed develop gradually. If the leadership and atmosphere are conducive to discussion, the children will make progress in developing skill in this important problem-solving procedure.

The physical arrangement of the classroom may either contribute to or inhibit discussion. For example, it is difficult to interact with someone when one is not facing the person with whom one is speaking. When classroom seating is arranged so that all pupils face the teacher, the pattern of interaction will be *through* the teacher, that is, "pupil A-teacher-pupil B-teacher-pupil C-teacher." A preferred discussion pattern is to have pupils interacting directly with each other; this can be encouraged by having them face one another. This also can be achieved by arranging the seating in a semicircle fashion for at least some of the discussion sessions. Through careful and patient teaching, a teacher can bring pupils to a point where they interact courteously with one another—without always agreeing with each other—and do so without raising their hands to speak. Such maturity in discussion procedure, however, requires a considerable amount of good teaching, practice, and time.

If discussions are to have some purpose beyond ordinary social conversation, the participants must have certain skills and attitudes, both of which can be learned. These skills should be taught to pupils directly. Skills and attitudes may be stated as standards or guides that characterize harmonious, productive discussion. For example, one participating in a discussion should:

1. Listen attentively when others are speaking.
2. Remain objective and not become emotional.
3. Be open-minded, respect and accept the contributions of others, but think independently.
4. Assume responsibility for contributing ideas.
5. Prepare adequately for the discussion and be able to support ideas with factual evidence.
6. Speak loudly and clearly enough for all to hear.
7. Not be offended when one's ideas or suggestions are not accepted by the group.
8. Not dominate the discussion; contributions should be stated concisely and briefly.
9. Ask for clarification of ideas that are not understood; ask for evidence to substantiate statements.
10. Recognize the problem of semantics in arriving at group decisions or in discussing a controversial issue.
11. Assume responsibility for moving the group toward its goal; help keep the group from becoming sidetracked from the central issue.

12. Have confidence in the ability of the group to come to a satisfactory decision and support the decision of the group once it has been made.

Standards such as the ones listed here are not appropriately stated for use with children, but the ideas can be discussed and understood by them when stated more simply. It is generally more effective if children themselves contribute to the setting of standards. For example, children will state ideas, such as the preceding ones, in the following manner:

1. Stick to the topic.
2. Be considerate of others' viewpoints and feelings.
3. Use facts to back up statements.
4. Ask questions when you don't understand.
5. Listen carefully while others are speaking.
6. Let everyone have a turn.

It is usually better to use positive rather than negative statements in developing standards. It is more helpful, for example, to say, "Speak clearly and loudly enough for all to hear," than to say, "Don't mumble." Positive statements help the child know what *to do*, whereas negative statements tell what *not to do* but suggest no alternative.

Suggestions for Improving Classroom Discussions

Use a Variety of Springboards to Stimulate Pupil Interest

Social studies content is loaded with issues that are emotionally toned and can serve as the basis for productive discussions. Additionally, the teacher can use issues raised in stories and books read by the children, news stories, sporting events, and pupil conflicts in school. Good topics for discussion are those with which pupils can identify. In relating themselves to the problem, pupils are able to gain some insight into their own behavior and at the same time maintain a measure of detachment.

Keep Discussion Groups Small for Greater Participation

If pupil involvement is wanted, discussion groups should be limited in size, and preferably not larger than five or six children. Of course, there are other values in discussion besides the ability to say something. Pupils also learn by listening to others discuss a topic. Therefore, a discussion that includes the entire class can be defended, but the teacher will have to expect some nonparticipation by children who are shy or who, for one reason or another, do not wish to talk in the large-group setting. Those same children might contribute their ideas in smaller groups.

309

Use Questions That Require an Elaborative Response

Discussion questions must be open-ended, suggestive of more than one point of view. They should require the respondent to provide an explanation. If questions can be answered by responding "yes" or "no" or with a single word or phrase, there is little to discuss. Questions that call for the reproduction of facts are not good for discussion, either, as for example:

1. By what three routes did people travel to the gold fields of California?
2. What are the Pacific states? Which is the largest? Which is the smallest?
3. Who was John Sutter?
4. Who were the Forty-Niners?
5. Who was the founder of the California missions?

As these questions are stated, there is nothing to discuss. However, the subject matter of these questions might be used for discussion if the questions were framed differently, as for example:

1. If you had been a gold seeker in 1849, what route would you have taken to the gold fields of California, and why would you have gone that way?
2. Washington, Oregon, and California face the Pacific Ocean. On the east coast of the United States, *fourteen* states occupy the same north-south distance as these three western states. What problems do you suppose are brought about by the size of a state?
3. How might the history of California and the United States have been different if John Sutter had found gold near Los Angeles instead of where he did?
4. How has the San Francisco Bay area changed since the days of the Forty-Niners?
5. What is there about California today that relates directly to the system of missions started by Father Junipero Serra and the Franciscan Fathers?

The two types of questions presented serve different purposes. For a quick check of literal reading comprehension, the first set might be appropriate, but would not make good discussion questions.

Point Out Inconsistencies and Confusions
in the Pupils' Thinking

Imagine a class discussing the merits of a law prohibiting smoking in public places such as meeting rooms, auditoriums, elevators, and restaurants. The discussion might proceed as follows:

Pupil: I think there ought to be such a law because a person has a right not to have to breathe someone else's smoke.

Teacher: Is that a right?

Pupil: Well, if some people have the right to smoke, others should have the right not to smoke.

Teacher: Isn't that the way it is now?

Pupil: Yes . . . but not really . . . when they have to be in the same room or in an elevator, the people who do not smoke do not have any choice, but the people who do smoke do have a choice.

Teacher: Then you are talking about choices rather than rights?

Pupil: Yes, I think so. With smoking in the room, the people who do not smoke and *have* to be there have no choice.

This is an interesting example because it illustrates how the teacher moved the discussion toward a clarification of the main point the pupil was making.

Keep the Discussion Focused on the Topic

It is difficult for discussants of any age to stay with the topic, but this is especially so with young children. Almost anything said reminds them of a personal experience that they want to share but which may be irrelevant to the topic being discussed. When the discussion strays away from the main theme, the teacher must refocus the group's thinking with a comment such as, "But let's get back to our main question. . . ." or, "I wonder if we could look at this problem from another angle. . . ."

Maintain a Low Profile in Leading Discussions

If the object of discussion is to encourage pupil talk, the teacher talk should be limited to whatever is needed to keep the discussion moving. Give pupils time to think about what they want to say. Allow extended periods of silence. Use nonverbal clues generously, such as a nod, an encouraging glance, or some other gesture along with verbal encouragement. Confine your own remarks to probing or clarifying comments or questions and to the acknowledging of contributions. Avoid having discussions become teacher lectures.

Discussion can be used to encourage children to speculate, to imagine, and to think of alternatives, as in the following example.

Miss Fowler's second-graders have been making discoveries about changes in their community. To stimulate discussion, Miss Fowler asked, "If you were a second-grader in the year 2050, and lived where you do now, what might you see on your way to school? Don't raise your hand for the next minute; I just want you to think."

After a minute, the children were bursting with ideas. Miss Fowler was careful to accept all ideas and to try to hear a comment from every child. When a couple of the ideas were silly, she very adeptly brought the discussion back to the main focus by asking these children to clarify what they meant. Miss Fowler was aware of the children who were too shy to volunteer and called on them, also. She encouraged all children to give evidence for their suggestions.

Many of the same principles and procedures used in group discussions involving the entire class also apply to other forms of discussion procedure. The advantage of smaller groups lies chiefly in allowing for greater participation by individual members. The teacher may find each of the following forms of discussion procedure helpful in social studies instruction.

Round-Table Discussions

A *round-table discussion* usually involves a small number of persons, perhaps no fewer than three and no more than eight. It requires someone to serve as a moderator to introduce the members of the discussion group, present the problem to be discussed, and keep the discussion moving. The leader's role is one of guiding the group rather than one of dominating it. A permissive atmosphere needs to prevail and the presentations are conversational rather than oratorical.

Round-table discussions can be used in the middle and upper grades by having a group of children discuss a problem before the remainder of the class or by dividing the class into several small discussion groups that function without an audience. It is perhaps best to use this procedure with one group at a time, either with or without an audience, until the children have learned how to participate in discussions of this type. It will be necessary for the teacher to introduce the procedure to the class and to explain and demonstrate its purposes and the way it works. Such points as the following need to be emphasized:

1. *Responsibilities of the moderator:* To be informed on the problem to be discussed, introduce the problem, keep the discussion moving, avoid having the group become sidetracked, ask members to explain more fully what they mean, avoid having members argue and quibble over irrelevancies, summarize and state conclusions.
2. *Responsibilities of members of the discussion group:* To be well informed on the problem to be discussed, especially some phase of the problem, speak informally while avoiding arguing and quibbling, stay with the problem under discussion, have sources of information available, back up statements with facts, help the group summarize its conclusions.
3. *Responsibilities of the audience:* To listen attentively, withhold questions until presentation is completed, ask for clarification of ideas, ask for evidence on questionable statements, confine remarks to the problem under discussion, extend customary audience courtesies to members of the round table.

Round-table discussions may be used for any of the following purposes:

1. to discuss plans for a major class activity.
2. to evaluate the results of a class activity, the merits of a film, school assembly on citizenship, the decision of a student council.
3. to make specific plans, such as the best way to present the work of the class to the parents.
4. to get facts related to a topic.
5. to discuss current affairs.
6. to present differing views on a community problem or a school problem.
7. to make decisions and recommendations to the class (the student council wants to know how the grade feels about a new play schedule. A committee of five children discusses this problem and presents its findings and recommendations to the class).

Panel Discussions

A *panel discussion* is similar to a round-table discussion in many respects, but there are also some important differences. The responsibilities of the moderator are approximately the same as they are for the moderator of the round table, as are those of the participants. The procedure is more formal than that of the round table. It usually begins with a short statement or presentation by each discussant before the panel is opened for free discussion by members. Panels are usually more audience-oriented than round tables, and frequently some provision is made for audience questions or participation at the end of the panel's presentation. A greater responsibility is placed on participants to prepare themselves well for their particular part on the panel, for each panelist is considered to be more or less an "expert."

One teacher made use of a panel discussion format in the following way.

The topic for the panel to discuss was a community problem involving the conversion of a military base into a community resource. Various special-interest groups were competing for the use of the newly acquired property. In class the teacher asked children to volunteer to represent one of the following special-interest groups:

1. city planner
2. golf enthusiast
3. representative of the local community club
4. condominium builder
5. representative of a local Indian tribe
6. moderator

The children were provided planning time in which to prepare a three- to five-minute statement explaining their point of view regarding the future of this property. Time was allowed for questions to clarify points made in the presentations or to raise other issues.

313

Buzz Groups for Brainstorming

The following is an example of a "buzz" group in operation.

> The members of Mrs. Kryzinski's class were asked to view a television special dealing with energy. The next morning they were anxious to discuss the program and even more anxious to do something about the energy problem.
>
> "What can we do, Mrs. K, to help other kids in our school know about some ways to save energy?" a pupil asked.
>
> "Why don't you decide," Mrs. Kryzinski responded. "You are already arranged in small groups so why don't you take the next ten minutes and come up with some ideas? Be prepared to give us two or three good ideas that would be possible for us to carry out in our school."
>
> After allowing ten to fifteen minutes, the children's attention was refocused and each group presented some ideas. There was no attempt to evaluate suggestions at that time.
>
> All of the suggestions were listed on the board and discussed. The class then voted on the list to determine which three they would implement.

We have here a brief description of a *buzz-group* or "brainstorming" technique. It is an informal consideration of ideas or problems where the chief purpose is to solicit the suggestions, feelings, ideas, or consensus of the members participating. It is slightly more structured than informal conversation and usually has some purpose other than a purely social one. The group may or may not have a designated leader and may or may not be expected to come to some conclusion.

Talking things over in a buzz session can be helpful in clarifying ideas, getting a wide sampling of opinion and feeling, obtaining suggestions and ideas, and getting pupils to participate who might be reluctant or fearful in a more structured discussion situation. Likewise, it has some limitations. Buzz sessions can easily get out of hand and become noisy and boisterous where nothing is accomplished except the creation of confusion. There is need, therefore, for the teacher to have firm control of the class before such a procedure is attempted and to establish standards that are clearly understood beforehand.

MAKING USE OF PUPIL REPORTS

Pupil reports to the class are commonly used in social studies teaching to share information obtained through individual research and study. They serve the purpose of bringing to the group the knowledge and understanding obtained by individuals as well as of giving the child the experience of organizing, planning, and presenting the report. This suggests a mutual value that accrues to the group as well as to the individual making the report. It also implies a responsibility that each must share if the procedure is to have value.

314

There is nothing quite so deadly or lacking in instructional value as the elementary schoolchild giving a "report" that has been copied from an encyclopedia. The speaker stumbles over every other word—meanings are not understood and pronunciation is incorrect. The report lacks continuity and is hard to follow. The listeners become bored and/or disruptive. Under such a set of circumstances no one likes to give reports or listen to them. They are a waste of time.

The primary responsibility for good pupil reports rests squarely with the teacher. How to give reports and how to prepare them should be explained. Through discussion, the teacher and the class can establish standards that will be used in the preparation of reports and the evaluation of them after the reports are given. Examples of such standards are:

Responsibilities of the Speaker

1. Speak in a clear voice.
2. Be well prepared.
3. Speak in your own words.
4. Use charts and pictures to make the report more interesting.
5. Ask for questions at the end of the report.
6. Stick to the topic.

Responsibilities of the Audience

1. Listen carefully.
2. Be courteous; do not interrupt the speaker.
3. Ask questions only at the end of the report.

Children can help each other improve the quality of their reports by holding brief evaluative discussions following the presentation. A good practice to follow is to ask for positive statements first—points at which the report was especially well done. Then, the children might offer suggestions concerning the way the report might have been improved. The teacher must set the stage for sincere evaluation with the attitude of helping one another, rather than only pointing out things that were wrong with the report. Care must be exercised so as not to make the evaluations destructively critical of a child's work.

It is the responsibility of the teacher to take an active part in assisting the child with the preparation of the report. This includes helping select a suitable topic, suggesting references, helping with its organization, and suggesting visual devices to use. The teacher should find a few minutes of time a day or two in advance of the presentation to sit down with the youngster and review what is to be included in the report. Once prepared, the child should be left alone while the report is being given unless help is specifically requested. It is unfair to the child and to the listening group to have the teacher continually interrupting and asking questions. The standards and responsibilities of good listeners apply to the teacher as well as to the children. Of course, when the report is completed the teacher can ask questions, call attention to points that need further clarification, or add pertinent information to the report. Positive comments and concrete suggestions as to how the child might improve future reports should also be offered.

Only a relatively few pupil reports should be scheduled on the same day. It is impossible for children to sustain any degree of interest if they must listen to a dozen or fifteen reports consecutively. A better procedure is to have two or three reports given at a time and to spread the reporting over a period of several days.

A perennial problem with pupil reports is the tendency for them to be "bookish." Some teachers encourage verbalism by being too rewarding, too complimentary of reports that are well presented but are not given in the child's own words. The dependence of the child on the language of the reference material is probably an indication that the topic is not understood. In order to combat the problem of verbalism in pupil reports, the teacher should

1. Not fully accept bookish presentations that are meaningless to the child and are simply repetitions of what has been read. This usually can be handled by a comment such as "Jackie, I know you spent a lot of time and work preparing your report, but we would have found it much more valuable and interesting if you had told it to us in your own words."
2. Encourage children to make and use visual material in their reports—pictures, charts, diagrams, maps, graphs, the chalkboard.
3. Ask pupils to give concrete examples of what they are describing in words they use in everyday conversation.
4. Encourage children to use more than one source for their information.
5. Be more lavish in praising those who avoid bookish presentations.

Oral and written reports are among the most common ways pupils share ideas in social studies. In many classrooms these activities are overused and, in some cases, misused. It is important for children to share ideas with each other, however, and if some variation is made in the traditional reporting format, these experiences can be both interesting and informative. Here is an example.

> To culminate a unit in which the class studied North American Indians, the children were asked to create an illustrated documentary on a tribe of their choosing.
>
> Ms. Pang brought in art materials for the children to use in creating their visuals and several cassette tape recorders. The children planned a narration and tape recorded it. Then they made illustrations to accompany their narrations and presented their completed "documentaries" to their classmates.

The following are suggested as still other alternatives to the traditional oral and written reports.

316

1. Dramatizing an incident, sequence, or situation relating to the topic and incorporating essential data to be communicated in the dramatization.
2. Using pupils' own drawn illustrations, charts, and graphs as the basis for a presentation or using illustrations found in newspapers, magazines, or other sources.
3. Pretending to be a tour guide taking the class through the area studied.
4. Using the overhead projector for visual aids in a presentation.
5. Role playing the part of a newscaster making an on-the-spot report.
6. Interviewing a classmate who is role playing the part of someone who is an expert on the topic under study.
7. Collecting pictures, arranging them in sequence, and using them as the basis for a report.
8. Writing a diary or letter that might have been written by someone in an earlier period.
9. Using artifacts or realia as the basis for a report.
10. Preparing and explaining a bulletin board display or diorama.
11. Preparing a narration for a filmstrip.
12. Doing an original narration for a motion-picture film with sound turned off.
13. Writing news stories that might have been appropriate to a particular period or preparing and publishing a single issue of a newspaper that might have appeared in some historical period.
14. Tape recording a presentation for playback to the class.

DISCUSSION QUESTIONS AND SUGGESTED ACTIVITIES

1. Under what circumstances might a teacher *not* want to clarify in great detail the goals of a small group?
2. How might a teacher build readiness for small-group activities with a class that has always worked on a whole-class basis?
3. Develop a role-playing exercise designed to teach group-work skills.
4. Select a topic that is appropriate for a grade of your choice and develop questions that could be used to stimulate a discussion.
5. The chapter suggests the "use of a variety of springboards to stimulate pupil interest in discussion." Provide examples of such "springboards" in addition to those included in the chapter.
6. Prepare an informal chart that might be used with children to illustrate points to keep in mind when preparing and making oral reports. Illustrate your chart in a way that you think would appeal to children.

7. In visiting a classroom, what specific things would you look for that would provide an indication of the quality of interaction taking place there?
8. Examine the chart on pages 297–299 and add examples from your own experience that tend to increase or decrease the level of hostility in a classroom.
9. Suggest topics or questions that could best be discussed in a *dyad* configuration (a group of two), a *triad* (a group of three), and by a group of five pupils. What reasons do you have for selecting certain topics or questions for a particular group size?

SELECTED REFERENCES

Chapin, June R. and Richard E. Gross. *Teaching Social Studies Skills*. Boston: Little, Brown and Company, 1973. Chapter 3.

Ellis, Arthur K. *Teaching and Learning Elementary Social Studies*, Second Edition. Boston: Allyn & Bacon Books, Inc., 1981. Chapter 15.

Johnson, David W. and Roger T. Johnson. *Learning Together and Alone*. Englewood Cliffs, N.J.: Prentice-Hall, Inc., 1975.

Nelson, Murry R. and H. Wells Singleton. "Small Group Decision Making for Social Action," Chapter 5. *Developing Decision-Making Skills*, 47th Yearbook. National Council for the Social Studies. Dana G. Kurfman, ed. Washington, D.C.: The Council, 1977. pp. 141–174.

Orlich, Donald C. and others. *Teaching Strategies: A Guide to Better Instruction*. Lexington, Mass.: D.C. Heath & Company, 1980. Chapter 7.

12

Pupil Involvement Through Activities, Expressive Experiences, and Social Action

It is a common assumption that when pupils are involved in creative activities, less in the way of "real" learning takes place. Traditional attitudes toward learning suggest that it must be accompanied by a hard-nosed discipline that is joyless. The feeling is widespread that if children enjoy what they are doing in school, it is prima facie evidence that the program does not amount to very much. The following narrative describes a parent's attitude on just this point:

At first we were quite concerned when we found out that Lori was to be placed in Mr. Allison's room the next year. His room had such a relaxed atmosphere about it, and he was very popular with the kids. We just assumed, I guess, that a teacher who was so well liked by all the children could not be very effective in maintaining a disciplined environment for learning. I must say this assumption was wholly unfounded.

Mr. Allison was clearly the most creative, imaginative, and overall the most effective teacher Lori had during the seven years she attended that school. He always had the most unusual things going on in that room that would so hook the kids that they spent hours of unsupervised study on what they were doing. Schoolwork seemed to be a sheer delight, strange as that may seem. They analyzed advertising techniques in a unit on consumerism; they simulated law and justice procedures; they studied the effects of immigrant groups on American life and culture; there were art, poetry, music, and dramatic activities galore. Once they constructed a whole set of authentic models of Indian villages representing various tribes that inhabited this part of North America in pre-Columbian times. This involved the children in an incredible amount of research and information gathering in order to do the constructions. There were always games, puzzles, inquiries—tremendous interest grabbers. It was the only time I can recall that children had literally to be told to go home after school. If not, they would stay until dinnertime.

Mr. Allison convinced my husband and me that disciplined learning did not have to give the appearance of rigidity and drudgery. He seemed to embrace the philosophy that a teacher should obtain "maximum learning with minimum effort." But the "minimum effort" only seemed that way because of the tremendous motivating power of the creative activities he used. Actually, I have not seen children work any harder nor be more productive in their efforts than their year with Mr. Allison.[1]

How does a teacher develop this type of stimulating program for girls and boys in social studies? In part, this comes from an imaginative teacher who is able to capitalize on the natural interests and curiosities of children. The teacher encourages them to raise questions and to suggest ways of working. These, then, are converted into interesting study activities. In this chapter we will discuss ways that creative and expressive activities can be used to enhance teaching and learning social studies.

The chief values of construction and processing, art, music, drama, and simulation games in social studies are (1) the contribution they make toward enhancing learning through the extension and expansion of meanings and understandings, (2) the extent to which they assist in promoting process learnings, and (3) the way they motivate pupil interest in the topics being studied. Teachers must have definite goals and purposes to be achieved through the use of the activity before it is selected. With this in mind, the teacher might use such activities for any or all of the following purposes:

1. to stimulate pupil interest.
2. to stimulate various aspects of thinking.
3. to give direction and purpose to learning.
4. to encourage initiative, exploration, and research.
5. to aid in applying factual information obtained through research to concrete situations.
6. to provide a setting in which to use socialization skills.
7. to clarify complex procedures.
8. to aid in developing an understanding of concepts and generalizations.
9. to relate various aspects of the school program to one another.
10. to provide opportunities for thinking, planning, sharing, doing, and evaluating.
11. to provide an outlet for creative abilities.
12. to provide an opportunity for recognition for the nonverbal, nonacademic child.

CONSTRUCTION AND PROCESSING ACTIVITIES

Most children love to make things. They build villages and castles in their sandboxes; they make windmills with their Tinkertoys; they build boats to float in a nearby pond; they construct birdhouses,

320   [1] An actual case from Minneapolis, Minnesota, reported to this writer.

model airplanes and cars, and handicraft objects. With a hammer, a saw, a few nails, and some scraps of lumber, the young child is off to an afternoon of fun in the family workroom, "making things." These natural sensory-motor play and creative-building activities are valuable for children in and of themselves. They give countless opportunities for thinking and planning as well as for creative expression, use of tools, physical activity, and the development of coordination. Children need many experiences of this type. In social studies, however, these values are only incidental to the chief purpose, which is to extend and enrich meaning of some aspect of the topic being studied. The excellence of the final product is, likewise, not a major concern. What is important is the learning that has occurred as a result of the construction activity. This being true, authenticity, genuineness, and truthfulness in the representations are important considerations in conducting construction activities.

Construction activities often have been misused largely because the teacher has lost sight of their basic purpose. In some cases these activities amount to little more than keeping the children busy at something, without much thought being given to the social studies outcomes the construction is allegedly fostering. If constructions are inaccurate, contrary to truth and reality, they may be detrimental to learning because they reinforce incorrect concepts.

It is possible to use construction activities to motivate children's work and to establish more clearly children's purposes for doing things. For example, the teacher of a primary grade conducting a study of the dairy farm might suggest that the class construct a model farm in the classroom. Naturally, the children will want to make their model as authentic as possible; therefore, a considerable amount of research will be necessary as they proceed with the building of the farm. In fact, they cannot even begin unless they know what it is they want to do. This gives them a genuine need for information. The children's purpose in this case may be to learn about the dairy farm to be able to build a classroom model of it. The teacher's purpose, however, is to have children form accurate concepts and understandings of a dairy farm; the construction activity is being used as a vehicle to achieve that goal. Under this arrangement, both pupil goals and teacher goals will have been achieved.

In selecting a construction activity for social studies, the teacher should make certain that

1. It is useful in achieving a definite purpose related to social studies.
2. It clarifies, enriches, or extends the meaning of some important concept.
3. It requires the child to do careful thinking and planning.
4. It is an accurate and truthful representation.
5. It is within the capabilities of the children.
6. The time and effort expended can be justified by the learnings that occur.

321

7. It is reasonable in terms of space and expense.
8. The needed materials are available.

There is no limit to the items that children can make in projects related to the social studies. The following have been used successfully by many teachers:

Model furniture
Books
Musical instruments
Simple trucks, airplanes, boats
Puppets and marionettes
Paper bag dolls
"Television" set with paper-roll programs
Looms for weaving
Animal cages
Animals of art materials
Maps (pictorial, product, relief, floor)
Candles
Soap
Baskets, trays, bowls
Preparation of foods (making cookies, jelly, butter, ice cream)
Ships, harbor, cargo
Retail food market and equipment
Scenery and properties for stage, dioramas, panoramas
Holiday decorations
Jewelry
Pottery, vases, dishes, cups
Covered wagons, churns, butter paddles, wooden spoons, and other
    pioneer gear
Post office
Bakery
Fire station
Dairy farm and building
Oxcarts
Circus accessories
Playhouses
Model villages
Purses, hot pads, table mats, small rugs
Birdhouses and feeding stations
Seed boxes, planters
Tie-dyeing
Production of visual material needed in the unit, such as pictorial
    graphs, charts, posters, displays, bulletin boards
Block printing

In order to proceed with the construction, the following suggestions may be helpful:

Discuss the Purposes of the Activity with the Children

The practice of having children make stores, build boats and covered wagons, or do Indian crafts without knowing why they are performing these activities is open to serious question. Children may not have any idea of the real purpose or significance of the construction. It is suggested, therefore, that at the beginning of such an activity, the reasons for planning it should be discussed and understood by all. The purposes for the construction should be reviewed from time to time during the activity.

Plan the Method of Procedure with the Children

The initial planning will take a considerable amount of time if every detail is to be taken into account. Such extensive planning is not necessary or entirely desirable, for it tends to make children impatient. Decisions must be made, however, as to the basic materials needed, the major responsibilities and who will assume them, the committees needed and who will be on them, where the construction will take place, where needed information may be obtained, and a general overall plan. After the construction project is underway there will be time each day to do additional specific planning. It is best to plan in a general way and get started, leaving the working out of details for a later time.

Plan Methods of Work with the Children

Construction activities involve working in groups, using tools, perhaps hammering and sawing or other noisy activities, and somewhat more disorder than is usually found in regular classroom work. This means that unless some rules and standards concerning the methods of work are set down, there is likely to be much noise, commotion, and general confusion. Therefore, it is recommended that the teacher and the pupils discuss and decide what the rules of work are to be. These might include

1. How to get and return materials.
2. Use of tools and equipment, including safe handling.
3. Things to remember during the work period: talking in a conversational voice, good use of materials to avoid waste, sharing tools and materials with others, consideration for others, doing one's share of work, asking for help when needed, and giving everyone a chance to present ideas.
4. Procedures for cleanup time. It is well to establish a "listen" signal to get the attention of the class. It can be playing a chord on the piano, turning off the lights, or ringing a small bell. When the listen signal is given, children should learn to stop whatever they are doing, cease talking, and listen to whatever announcement is to be made. In this way, the teacher can stop the work of the class at any time to call their attention to some detail or get them

323

started at cleanup. Cleanup is one procedure that can be done in a routine way. When the signal is given, all work stops and the children listen for directions, restore the room to its prior condition, and assemble at the circle or go to their desks.

Arrange Plenty of Time Each Day for Planning,
Working, Cleaning-up, and Evaluation

Before work on the construction activity is begun each day, time should be spent in making specific plans. This is to ensure that everyone will have an important job to do and that pupils will know their responsibilities. It also is a time when the teacher can go over some of the points the class talked about during its previous day's evaluation. "You remember yesterday we had some problem about which group was to use the tools. Which group has the tools today?" Or, "Yesterday our voices became a little loud at times. Perhaps we can be more careful about that today."

During the work period the teacher will want to move from group to group observing, assisting, suggesting new approaches, helping groups in difficulty, clarifying ideas, helping children find materials, and supervising and guiding the work of the class. Children will be identified who need help in getting started, those who are not working well together, those who seem not to be doing anything, or others who may be having difficulty. The teacher will keep an eye on the time and stop the work of the class in time to ensure a thorough cleanup.

An important part of each period is the group evaluation that occurs after the work and cleanup. During these times, the teacher will want the class to evaluate the progress it is making on the construction as well as the manner in which the children are doing their work.

"Were we able to make progress on our store today?"
"How do you think we might change the color to make it look more real?"
"Does anyone have any ideas how Steven's group could show more action in their mural?"
"Did anyone see signs of safe handling of tools today?"
"I wonder if the mountains aren't too high on Julie's group's map? Did you check that against the picture in your book?"

The precise points discussed in such an evaluation, of course, will depend on the class and its work. In any case, some attention should be given to (1) progress on the construction, (2) methods of working together, and (3) problems that need attention the next day.

Make Use of the Construction in Some Way,
Relating It to the Unit Under Study

When constructed objects are completed, they should be put to good use. In the primary grades such a project may serve well for dramatic play activities. A market in the classroom, for example, gives

324

the children an opportunity to play customer, grocer, butcher, check-out person, or other personnel associated with a market. They read labels and prices, rearrange the material on the shelves, keep the store clean, and so on. In the middle and upper grades, objects made can be examined, discussed, and displayed. A mural can be used for study purposes. A child can explain the way some object is constructed, its main features, how it was used, its history, why it is no longer used, and similar information. Perhaps the best constructions are the ones that can be used in some worthwhile way by the entire group in learning more about an important aspect of unit study. Constructions are of value only insofar as they relate to the work of the class; when they have served this purpose, they should be removed.

EXAMPLES OF CONSTRUCTION ACTIVITIES

Primary Grades

After a study of both the urban and rural communities, the class was divided in half. One group was assigned the project of constructing a rural community; the other an urban community.

Miss Stillwater planned with each group separately, starting with the development of a list of services and facilities needed in each community. Each child was responsible for constructing at least one part of the community.

For several days before construction was to begin, the children brought in cartons, shoe boxes, and other "building materials" that were to become their communities.

Using paint, construction paper, shellac, and team effort, the cartons were transformed into urban and rural communities and were placed on butcher paper streets on the floor around the classroom.

Intermediate Grades

Mr. Russo's class had been studying the state's history and he believed that there was a need for the children to better understand the role that geographical differences had played in the state's development. He thought that the construction of relief maps might be a good method for the children to achieve this understanding.

Because such a construction was too large a project for individual children, he asked them to organize themselves in groups of two or three with whomever they could work best.

Mr. Russo provided the children with a papier-maché recipe and the necessary construction materials. He encouraged them to be innovative in adding things to their maps that would highlight the significance of relief features.

After he was satisfied that the children understood what they were to do, he had the groups begin planning their maps. He provided a regularly scheduled work period each day and supervised and assisted the groups as needed. The completed relief maps were displayed and discussed in terms of the role of geographic features in the development of the state.

Closely related to construction activities are those that help the child understand the various steps or stages in the production of some material item. They deal with the *process* of changing raw materials into finished, usable items and, hence, involve *processing of*

325

materials. These activities help the pupil understand and appreciate the complexities of producing some of the basic material items that most persons use in everyday living. They are commonly used to impress on the pupils the hardships, labor, skill, and ingenuity required of pioneers and early people in a time when it was necessary for them to produce basic materials for themselves. The most common processes used for this purpose are making butter, candles, paper, sugar, salt, bricks, natural dyes, jelly, ink, books, ice cream, and soap and weaving and dyeing cloth.

There are some instructional problems, however, in processing materials. For example, to demonstrate the hardships experienced by pioneers in making candles by dipping, the teacher should not use an electric hot plate as a source of heat nor an aluminum container for the wax! In most classrooms it is, in fact, impossible to duplicate conditions under which candles were made in the 17th century. Almost any raw material the class uses in its processing will in all likelihood *already* be semiprocessed. The child may, therefore, leave such an experience with a lack of appreciation of the complexities involved in the process—a misfire of the precise learning the teacher had hoped to put across.

Some processes require extremely careful supervision by the teacher because of physical danger to the children. Candlemaking means heating tallow, wax, or paraffin that can ignite if allowed to become too hot and cause severe burns if dropped accidentally on one's person. Soap making calls for the use of lye, always potentially dangerous. These points are mentioned not to discourage the use of construction and processing but to alert the beginner to the real need for careful supervision while such activity is taking place.

MUSIC ACTIVITIES

Music activities make an important contribution to social studies instruction. Through the universal language of music, the child may extend communication to other peoples, races, and cultures, both past and present. Various songs and music forms are associated with periods in our national history, and many songs relate directly to heroes or great historical events. Musical expression is an emotional experience, piercing through everyday inhibitions and extending into the inner reaches of one's personality. Music inspires patriotism, love of country, loyalty, and fidelity. It is for this reason that marching bands are used in holiday parades and between halves at football games. Nation-states have used music effectively in building a feeling of national solidarity. Music has a profound effect on individuals as well as on groups.

Music educators have worked diligently to break the shackles of the "music period" concept of music education and have consistently recommended a greater integration of music in the total life of the classroom. Music activities, therefore, not only contribute to social studies instruction but support the music program itself. The material that follows suggests some possibilities for the use of singing, rhythmic expression, listening, and creative music activities in social studies units.

Singing

For almost any social studies unit, the teacher will find appropriate and related songs for children to sing. One of the chief values of singing is its affective quality; it gives the child a *feeling* for the material not likely to be obtained in any other way. Through singing, the child senses the loneliness of the *voyageur*, the gaiety of a frontier housewarming, or the sadness of a displaced people longing for their homeland. Folksongs can be springboards to the study of a period in history, to the contributions of ethnic groups, to the lifestyles of a group, and/or to many social studies topics. Singing is an experience that can broaden children's appreciation of people everywhere. In the study of communities around the world, the teacher will want to use the songs of various national groups. This provides opportunities to learn more about a culture through the language of music.

Some educators have recognized the rich learning resource folk music provides, and they have promoted the use of folksongs in social studies classrooms.[2] Contemporary folksongs such as "Little Boxes," "We Shall Overcome," "Detroit City," "Sittin' on the Dock of the Bay," convey powerful social messages. Cowboy songs such as "I Ride an Old Paint," "Colorado Trail," "The Night Herding Song," and "Git Along Little Dogie" have both lyrics and melodies that are hauntingly reminiscent of the lonely life of this American folk group. "The Yellow Rose of Texas," "When Johnny Comes Marching Home Again," and "Over There" are associated with significant conflicts of this nation (Texas Independence, Civil War, and World War I, respectively). Teachers interested in learning more about the use of folksongs in the classroom should write to Dr. Laurence I. Seidman, 140 Hill Park Avenue, Great Neck, New York 11021.

Rhythmic Expression

Rhythmic and bodily expression tend to release one from the crust of convention and formality that is built in the normal course of everyday life and provide a means of self-expression. Through

---

[2]Laurence I. Seidman, C. W. Post College; and John Anthony Scott, Rutgers University, have made several presentations at NCSS annual meetings recently: "Elbow Room: The Western Movement through the Songs and Ballads of the Pioneers" (1977); "U.S. Folksong as a Bridge to Youth" (1979); "Folk Song in the Classroom: A Catalyst for Teacher and Student Participation and Education" (1980). They have also initiated a newsletter, *Folksong in the Classroom*, edited by Barabara Yolleck of Rutgers University.

rhythms, bodily expression, and folk dances, the child develops grace and poise and learns the amenities that are characteristic of such social activities. Folk dancing and folk games in themselves are pleasurable and legitimate social activities for children. They provide for teamwork and allow the child to participate in the activity with several other boys and girls. Folk dancing and folk games usually involve eight or more children with a continual shifting of partners. For this reason, folk dancing is well suited for children of elementary-school age.

In social studies, the teacher will want to use the various folk dances and rhythmic activities that are characteristic of many countries, as well as those associated with various periods of our national history. With the present emphasis on ethnic heritage studies, activities of this type can be particularly meaningful. Far from being solely a recreational activity, rhythmic expression provides a wide range of possibilities for social learnings in particular and social studies in general.

Creating

Social studies topics provide many opportunities for the child to create musically. This can be done on an individual basis or as a class

It is not easy to do an ethnic dance, even when one has the appropriate costume! As a part of the ethnic awareness program of this elementary school, pupils are familiarized with the music, dance, and art of several cultures represented by the forebears of pupils who attend the school. Is this social studies education?

328

project, and can be used with almost any topic by any age group. Perhaps it is not used more frequently by teachers because they feel that a considerable amount of technical knowledge of music is necessary. The need for the technical skills of music is greatly overestimated, but if the teacher feels insecure, there will ordinarily be someone available who does have such skills and can be of assistance. This person might be a music supervisor or teacher, the high school music director, or another classroom teacher.

In its simplest form, creative music is a melody or sounds children learn to associate with the topic being studied. For example, the children may make sounds that remind them of a factory, a circus, or a train. Later these sounds can be used in the development of an actual melody. Children commonly produce creative verse to which they may add an appropriate melody. In the middle and upper grades such creative music activities may include the development of words and music for pageants, plays, puppet shows, or simple musicals. These original numbers are frequently of good quality musically and are favorites of the children for years afterward—an indication of the satisfying and long-lasting quality of creative music.

Listening

Although singing, creating, and rhythmic expression involve performing or doing aspects of music, listening places the child in the role of a consumer of music. This role deserves more attention than is usually given it, because it is the type of musical experience that continues throughout life. Long after most persons stop performing musically, they enjoy listening to music. Relating music-listening to the affairs of life and living is, therefore, essential.

Listening to music should be an imaginative experience for children. The teacher can help them learn of mood in music and contrast that which is bright, gay, and lively with music that is quiet and restful. Through listening the child learns to identify the use of music by different groups throughout the world—it provides for another direct cultural contact with people of many lands. The teacher will have no difficulty obtaining recordings for the purposes described.

EXAMPLES OF MUSIC ACTIVITIES

Primary Grades

During a unit on the children of Mexico, Ms. Juarez shared some of her own ethnic background with her class. She was able to teach them a few simple folk dances and folk songs she had learned as a child in Mexico.

After learning the words to the songs in Spanish, the children asked her to teach them other words and expressions in Spanish. By the end of the year, many children had developed a fair speaking vocabulary of greetings and commonly used expressions in Spanish.

329

Intermediate Grades

Mr. Cole's fifth-graders were studying the development of the United States. He thought it was important for them to learn how music reflects the mood of the nation at a particular time. He was able to get examples of popular music from the middle of the 19th century to the present time. The lyrics of these songs were analyzed in terms of national events and concerns of the time. Mr. Cole was also able to get recordings of some of these songs, and without telling the pupils the period from which the song came, asked them to try to determine when the selection was popular.

CREATIVE ART EXPERIENCES

Creative art is widely used in social studies instruction because many topics and activities inspire creative expression. A trip to a farm, airport, zoo, post office, or fire station all give impetus to the desire to create. Observing bulldozers, cranes, demolition crews, as well as going on a hike to a nearby park or stream, are the types of experiences from which come the creative artwork of children. Through an art medium the child may be able to symbolize experiences, express thoughts, or communicate feelings that cannot be done through the use of conventional language. For a young child in the primary grades, a picture or painting is likely to tell a whole story, and all the action is happening in the picture as it is being shared with others. For example, a first-grader's painting may show children playing with a dog while the jet is flying overhead and a police patrol is chasing a speeding motorist. But the action is not stopped at the time the painting was made; it goes on all the time. That is, the children really are playing with the dog and the airplane is actually flying. Children's artwork tells a story; it can be useful in recording social studies experiences.

Many parallels could be drawn between art experiences and music experiences in social studies. Like music, art provides a cultural link with the many peoples of the world, past and present. It also places the child in the roles of creator and consumer as does music. It deals directly with feelings, emotions, appreciations, and creative abilities of children. In addition to the many desirable outcomes associated with any creative endeavor, creative art experiences have much to offer in stimulating and strengthening learning in the social studies.

In the course of the social studies unit, the teacher might use any of the following art activities:

Preparing murals	Poster making
Free painting	Making models
Making illustrations	Making cartoons

It has been said that the arts are the things children like best. If that is true, social studies education should take advantage of this natural interest of children, as the teacher of the child in this photograph has done. Suggest ways art and social studies can be integrated.

Weaving
Block printing
Clay modeling
Potato- or stick printing
Chalk-, charcoal-, and crayon drawing
Pencil sketching

Making booklets and books
Crafts related to some locality or country
Constructing dioramas to illustrate scenes
Planning and preparing exhibits
Sewing

331

Making properties for plays, pageants	Making designs and costumes
Making puppets and mario- nettes	Wood carving
Soap carving	Toy making
Basket making	Finger painting
	Indian sand painting
	Indian bead work

Creative art expression as used in social studies may take two forms. The first of these might be described as *personal* and is performed by the pupil because it expresses an idea or gives personal satisfaction. Having the experience is its own reward, and the child need not share such a piece of art with anyone, although children often want to. Artwork of this type is not evaluated in terms of the product produced but in terms of the satisfactions the experience itself gives the youngster. Any of the art mediums can be used for personal expression.

A second type of creative art expression can be thought of as *functional* in that the product is used in connection with some other activity. It might be a mural to be used as the background for a dramatic activity. It might be a model of something that will be used to illustrate an explanation. It could be a visual aid the child plans to use in making a report to the class. In artwork of this type, the representation has to be reasonably accurate and authentic; consequently, the teacher will need to guard against having the children copy exactly the illustrations they find in reference materials.

The poorest of all art experiences are those that are patterned rather than creative. The teacher might, for example, ditto a diagram of a turkey and have children color certain feathers red, others brown, and others black. Children who follow the directions precisely and who can color within the lines are highly rewarded with teacher praise. Then the 25 turkeys, all alike, are posted on the bulletin board under the caption "We Do Creative Work." Such conspicuous misuse of art may also take the form of black profiles of Lincoln, hatchets and cherries, covered wagons, or Christmas trees. Teaching of this type tends to depress any creative art ability or interest in art expression that an imaginative child may have, and should be avoided.

EXAMPLES OF CREATIVE ART ACTIVITIES

Primary Grades

Third-graders peeled and dried apples to make apple-head dolls. They added yarn hair and formed bodies of wire. Each doll was dressed to resemble some well-known historical figure.

Intermediate Grades

In a study of India, fourth-graders constructed movable rod puppets. They used the puppets to dramatize folk tales from India.

DRAMATIC ACTIVITIES

Dramatic representation in any one of its many forms is a popular activity with children—one in which they have all engaged during their early years. What child has not "been" a fire fighter, a cowhand, a jet pilot, or a doctor during the fanciful and imaginative play of early childhood? Dramatic activities have great value in promoting social studies learnings by helping sharpen the child's power of observation; giving purpose to research activities; giving insight into another's feelings; providing experiences in democratic living; helping create and maintain interest, thereby motivating learning; and affording an excellent opportunity for the teacher to observe the behavior of children.

The most structured dramatic activity is the *dramatization*, which requires a script, staging, rehearsal, and an audience. It may be used to show some historical event, to represent the growth of a movement or idea, or represent life in another period, or to demonstrate some problem of living. Children are usually involved in a considerable amount of creative work in productions of this type. They may plan and prepare costumes, do the artwork necessary for staging and properties, plan a program, send invitations, and make all arrangements attendant to the project. This requires that the children do a great deal of planning, working together, evaluating, and participating.

The least-structured dramatic activity is the spontaneous acting out or reliving of situations from the child's world. It is called *dramatic play*. As this activity is used in social studies, the term *dramatic play* is an unfortunate one because it suggests entertainment. Perhaps the terms *creative dramatic representation* or *representative living* would describe more accurately what is involved in the activity. When kindergarteners and first-graders are playing various roles of mother, father, sister, brother, doctor, and nurse in a corner of the classroom, they are engaging in dramatic play. Free dramatic play is a natural activity for young children, and they participate in it with little or no stimulation from adults. During the periods of free dramatic play, the teacher can learn much about the personalities of individual children—with whom they identify, their attitudes toward others, their willingness to share, and their emotional maturity.

As children move into the second and third grades, there is less evidence of spontaneous dramatic play. At this stage of growth, dramatic play usually requires more suggestion and stimulation from the teacher and may be used profitably to help the child understand or appreciate some phase of human relationships. These slightly more structured dramatic activities are referred to as *role playing, sociodrama,* or *creative dramatics*.

Role playing, sociodrama, or creative dramatics are used to present a specific situation for study and discussion. There is no prepared script, it is unrehearsed, speaking parts are not memorized, and prop-

333

erties, if used at all, are held to a minimum. Some small amount of properties may be used simply to help children remain in role. These activities are used to teach and/or clarify social values, to focus attention on a central idea, to help children organize ideas, to extend vocabulary, and to gain a greater insight into the problems of others by casting themselves in another's role. Because they portray problems in human relationships, they provide an excellent basis for discussion and evaluation. They should be followed by a discussion of questions of this type: "Which character did you like best? Why?" "Which one did you like least? Why?" "How do you suppose the person *felt*?" "If you had been in the wagonmaster's place, what would you have done?" "Have you ever known anyone like that?"

This final discussion and analysis requires that the situation be cut before the problem has been solved and before the outcome is a certainty. Otherwise, there would be little room left for thoughtful consideration of the problem.

Closely related to creative dramatics is the use of *reaction stories*. Reaction stories are brief, narrative accounts dealing with human relations that are used to uncover various attitudes and emotions. They may be written by the teacher or may be passages selected from published works. They deal with a variety of topics such as sharing, teasing, responsibility, peer pressures, respect for property, and intercultural relations. The story is read to the children, and they are asked to tell their feelings about characters, situations, what they would do under similar circumstances, what alternatives were available to the characters, and other comparable reactions. This critique and analysis is similar to the one held at the conclusion of a creative dramatics activity.

EXAMPLES OF DRAMATIC ACTIVITIES

Primary Grades

Mrs. Beatty wanted the children to be able to cope with situations that might arise while they were shopping. She listed situations that could present a problem, such as returning faulty merchandise, knocking over displays, becoming separated from their parent, or inquiring about the location of the restroom. The children added other situations to the list.

Mrs. Beatty asked the children to role-play the situations. These were discussed in terms of possible and responsible responses to such situations.

Intermediate Grades

Miss Hall's pupils had been doing research on the signers of the Declaration of Independence. Each child had been responsible for finding out about at least one of these historical figures.

Miss Hall then asked various groups of children to re-enact the signing of the document. She encouraged them to react as the person they represented might have done.

SIMULATIONS AND INSTRUCTIONAL GAMES

A fifth-grade class was studying the concept of *assembly line production* in its unit on the growth of industry in the United States. In the discussion, the pupils contrasted assembly line production with custom-made, individually built products. The class listed the strengths and limitations of each method of production:

Assembly Line

Strengths

1. it is faster

2. every product is the same

3. can be produced at low cost

4. because of low production cost, more people can afford to buy the product

Weaknesses

1. sameness makes for an uninteresting product

2. production can be slipshod because no one person is responsible for it

3. the sameness of the work makes for a boring job

4. a poor worker, or a breakdown, can stop the whole production

Custom Built

1. "one of a kind" product
2. higher quality because an individual craftsman is responsible for it
3. product can be made to fit the desires of the buyer
4. work is less boring to the workers

1. products are more expensive
2. buyers cannot be sure of the product's quality because each is different
3. fewer people can afford to buy the product
4. it takes longer for workers to become skillful in doing all of the tasks needed to make the product

The teacher pointed out to the class that each of the items they listed could serve as a hypothesis that they might be able to test. "Is it really true," she asked, "that assembly line production is faster? Do workers on an assembly line become bored more quickly than those who make the whole product themselves? Do workers take greater pride in their product if they do it all themselves and sign their name to it? How could we test the truth of the statements?" The teacher and the pupils decided they could test their hypotheses by using a simple simulation involving the manufacture of envelopes. The class was divided into two groups; one would be assembly line

335

workers, the other group would be custom craftsmen. The teacher provided cardboard templates, or patterns of an outline of an envelope, scissors, paste, and used ditto paper that would be needed to manufacture envelopes. By placing the pattern on a piece of paper, its outline could be traced and could then be cut, folded, and pasted to make the finished product. The assembly line was arranged according to a division of labor as follows:

ASSEMBLY LINE

Pattern tracer	Cutters	Folders	Paster	Stacker
Number of workers: 1	Number of workers: 2	Number of workers: 2	Number of workers: 1	Number of workers: 1
Equipment: pattern pencil paper	Equipment: scissors	Equipment: none	Equipment: paste	Equipment: none

Total workers: 7
Supervisor: 1 | SUPERVISOR |

The custom craftsmen consisted of seven individuals (the same number as on the assembly line) and a supervisor. Each of the seven workers had his or her own pattern, paper, pencil, scissors, and paste, and was required to do all of the steps necessary to make an envelope. They would be required to put their own name on each envelope they produced.

CUSTOM CRAFTSMEN

Worker 1	Worker 2	Worker 3	Worker 4	Worker 5	Worker 6	Worker 7

Each worker has:
pattern
paper
pencil | SUPERVISOR |
scissors
paste

All children in both groups took turns and all participated in the activity. The supervisor from each group could make changes and substitutions as needed. Three children served as a quality control panel that would accept or reject finished products in terms of quality of workmanship.

When all preparations were completed, the teacher gave the signal to start, and both groups began manufacturing envelopes. After a half-hour, the production was stopped and the debriefing took place.

Pupils were able to test their hypotheses in terms of the data they generated through the simulation.

We have here an example of a simple simulation. It is a strategy designed to reconstruct as closely as possible some of the essential characteristics of the real thing. Simulations and gaming strategies are enthusiastically accepted by those teachers who pursue innovative approaches to social studies teaching. The simulation may be a simple one devised by the teacher, as the one described here, or it may be one of the growing number of commercially prepared simulations and games now available.

The Nature of Simulations and Games

A *game* may be defined as an activity that involves rules, competition, and players who become winners and losers. The outcome of some games depends entirely on chance, as in the case of tossing dice. In other games, the outcome is determined less by chance and more by the decisions made by the players, as in chess or checkers. Most games involve both elements of chance and skill. It is significant that persons who are involved in a game are called "players." This suggests that games are associated with amusement—they are intended to be enjoyed. When games are used for educational purposes, they are often referred to as *instructional games* in order to avoid creating the impression that they are used only for entertainment. For this reason, too, instructional games frequently are called *simulations*. Instructional games tend to minimize chance and enjoyment aspects, although most contain some elements of chance and most are enjoyed by the participants.

A simulation gives the illusion of reality but removes most of the elements that are irrelevant and those that would be dangerous to the participants. In using simulators in pilot training or driver training, wrong moves by the trainee do not result in disastrous crashes or collisions. Likewise, in educational simulations, errors of judgment or unwise decisions do not produce disastrous social consequences.

Experts do not agree among themselves about the distinction between games and simulations. Not all games are simulations, as, for example, such games as hopscotch, jacks, or jump rope. Similarly, not all simulations are games, as in the case of astronauts working in a simulated weightless environment. However, in education these activities often take on characteristics of both games and simulations. Consequently, they are popularly, although perhaps not altogether precisely, called *simulation games*.

Values of Simulations and Instructional Games

The values of simulations and instructional games for use with elementary school-age children are not firmly established. Research evidence concerning the effects of simulations and games at the elemen-

337

tary school level is sparse. Nonetheless, the following points seem to be well grounded on the basis of research and practice.

1. Simulations and games are highly motivating to pupils. Pupils enjoy participating in these activities and do so without much urging from the teacher. The fact that pupils show increased interest in the subject when they are involved in simulation games is well documented. One can assume that part of this interest is generated by the reality created by the simulation, by the competitive, gaming aspects of it, and by the fact that there are clearly defined goals to be achieved. Because of their motivating power, it is easy to get children involved in simulation games. Even children who are typically on the fringes of most class activities often become enthusiastically engaged in instructional games and simulations. These activities seem to appeal to the natural inclinations of children to be involved in imaginative play, make-believe, and role playing.

2. Simulations and games have been used successfully for instructional purposes outside of school. They have been used in teaching military operations for many years. They are used in training programs in business and industry, in teaching management skills, in the space program, in medicine, law, political science, and many other fields. Computer science has made it possible to develop these simulations and games at a sophisticated level. Because they have proven their usefulness in instructional settings outside of school, it is fair to assume they would have value for in-school instruction as well.

3. There seems to be evidence that simulations and games are effective in dealing with learner attitudes. Wentworth and Lewis cite several studies that report positive learner response after participating in a simulation or game.[3] Many of these studies have been criticized on technical grounds, making it difficult to generalize their findings. Nevertheless, the impact of games and simulations on learner attitudes is widely reported.

4. There seems to be considerable doubt about the effects of simulations and games on cognitive gain. The research to date does not show that these devices have a clear advantage over other learning resources and procedures in promoting cognitive learning. Perhaps this is because the learners must have the prerequisite skills and must understand the basic concepts before the game is played. That is, the simulation game provides opportunities for the application of knowledge and skills rather than breaking new cognitive ground. This might explain, also, why researchers rather consistently report gains in the affective but not the cognitive area.

5. Almost without exception authors and researchers speak to the importance of the postgame or "debriefing" session. It is in these critiques that the major learnings can be identified and discussed.

---

[3]Donald R. Wentworth and Darrell R. Lewis, "A Review of Research on Instructional Games and Simulations in Social Studies Education," *Social Education*, 37 (May 1973), pp. 437–438.

338

These sessions allow the participants to explore in some detail what choices were available to the players, what decisions were made, and how those decisions contributed to the outcome. In this way, the simulation or game provides the group with a common and shared experience that can be used to extend and enrich learning. From an instructional point of view, the debriefing session must be considered an integral part of the game itself.

Using Commercially Prepared Simulation Games

Presently there are many commercially prepared simulation games available for elementary school use, most being designed for the middle and upper grades. In the January 1980 issue of *Social Education*, Sharon Pray Muir provides an annotated list of 88 simulation games for elementary school social studies.[4] In preparing this list, she made a thorough search of the field and included only those that are appropriate for use in grades K-6 and that deal directly with social studies concepts and processes. The list includes the title, recommended grade levels, amount of time needed to play the game, number of players, and the cost. She also indicates the social science discipline with which the simulation is associated. For example:

Economics   IMPORT, grs. 4-5, 2-4 weeks, 18-35 players, $10. Simulates activities of 6 importing firms in various parts of the world. Each firm buys from several countries. To win, a firm must buy 8 products from 3 countries and sell them at a profit. Simile II; SSSS; EMI

Economics   ROARING CAMP, grs. 4-7, five 10-minute periods, 18-35 players,
History $10. Players are given a $600 grubstake with which to file a mining claim and try their luck as prospectors. Each person pays $400 for initial tools, supplies, and equipment and $200 a year thereafter to keep him or her going. Chance selection of plots on which to file claims controls those who hit pay dirt and those who "lose their shirts." Simile II; EMI[5]

A teacher may use a simulation game strictly in accordance with the instructions provided or may adapt it to suit local needs, pupil abilities and interests, and instructional objectives. In her book, *Games for Growth*, Alice Kaplan Gordon makes the following suggestions to teachers using simulations and games:

1. If possible, play the game through with other teachers or friends.
2. Become acquainted with the physical components of the game.
3. Thoroughly read the materials provided for the teacher's use.
4. Modify the game, if necessary, to meet particular needs of the class.

[4] Sharon Pray Muir, "Simulation Games for Elementary Social Studies," *Social Education*, 44 (January 1980), pp. 35-39+.
[5] *Ibid.*, pp. 37, 38.

5. Decide the basis on which roles will be assigned. Try to include bright and slow students on the same teams.
6. Distribute copies of the rules, and profiles and scenarios where they are used, to each student the day before play.
7. Arrange the components of the game in the classroom.
8. Brief students on
   a. the purpose of the game
   b. the roles of individuals or teams, and objectives
   c. the physical layout of room
   d. the first move
   This phase should not exceed fifteen minutes.
9. During play, circulate among groups or individuals and offer suggestions where desirable, answer questions when necessary. Try to involve the student in answering his own questions and arriving at solutions.[6]

Preparing Your Own Game

After some knowledge of, and experience with, simulation games, some teachers have been encouraged to prepare their own games. This is a formidable task, and the teacher may wish to collaborate in such an effort with a colleague. Also, pupils themselves in the middle and upper grades can assist in creating a simulation game. In any case, the teacher may find the following questions to be of help in constructing a simulation game.

1. What instructional purpose is to be served by the game? That is, what objective or objectives are to be achieved through the use of the simulation game?
2. What real-life situations can be used to illustrate or dramatize the objectives? In most cases, this will call for the preparation of a narrative (referred to as a *scenario*) that establishes the situation and makes explicit the problem, conflict, issue, or process to be simulated.
3. What is to be the sequence of events and how much time will be required and/or allowed for each?
4. What players will be involved? How many are there to be? How are they to be grouped?
5. What are the specific objectives of individual or group players? How are success and/or failure experiences to be recognized and recorded? What resources (votes, play money, political support, food, and so forth) will players have for trade-offs and bargaining?
6. How do individuals or groups interact in order to register wins or losses?
7. What is the role of the teacher to be?

[6]Alice Kaplan Gordon, *Games for Growth*, Palo Alto, Calif.: Science Research Associates, Inc., College Division, 1970, p. 112.

SOCIAL ACTION

The real test of a social studies program comes in the out-of-school lives of pupils. If the school has provided the children with new insights, improved skills, or increased awareness and sensitivity to social affairs, such learning should be apparent in their out-of-school behavior as children, and later as adults. The objectives of social studies education, in other words, are tested in the way that learners apply them to social reality in and out of school. In its statement of curriculum guidelines, the National Council for the Social Studies speaks

A third grade class "adopted" the residents of a convalescent center and are shown here presenting a bowling ball and pins to them. The pupils used money they earned by recycling aluminum cans to buy the gift. They maintain a continuing contact with the residents during the year. Children's drawings, mainly on the subject "happiness is," brighten the center's walls. What social studies outcomes do you identify with an activity of this kind?

341

of social participation as one of the four essential components of social studies education.[7]

To be socially active does not mean that young children have to be concerned with the great social issues of our time. But they can and should be involved in experiences that bridge the gap between what is learned in school and the real world in which they live. They can and should practice skills and apply knowledge that prepares them for intelligent and responsible involvement in social affairs of the society of which they are a part.

Of course, children are not going to be able to be socially active without some help and encouragement from their teacher. The following are a few examples of activities that teachers have used successfully with elementary school-age pupils.

1. Middle-grade pupils formed a volunteer Good Neighbor Club to help elderly residents in the neighborhood with yard work, errands, and other assistance as needed.
2. A class interviewed parents, school personnel, and adult friends and neighbors to determine the ethnic background of people living in the area. They used the data to prepare an exhibit entitled "Living and Working Together—Our Ethnic Heritages" to be displayed in a local store window. This included maps, photographs, and artifacts secured from the neighborhood.
3. A group organized a food gathering campaign for the Neighbors in Need Program.
4. On a walk around the school neighborhood, a second-grade class noticed that a main sidewalk was so badly damaged that children on their way to and from school had to walk into the street to avoid it. The class wrote a letter to the City Council asking that the sidewalk be repaired. They received a letter from the president of the City Council thanking them for their concern and assuring them that it would be repaired. He also commended them for their display of civic responsibility. The sidewalk was repaired.
5. A group in a rural area organized a "Clean Up Our Hill Saturday," during which time the children picked up litter in the public areas of the neighborhood. They encouraged and assisted adult residents to do the same. Children were able to secure litter bags, decals for trash cans, litter bags for cars, antilitter bumper stickers, and antilitter literature from the local Department of Ecology. These materials were distributed by the children to the local residents.
6. A class developed a working relationship with a nearby retirement home. Residents who were able to were invited and came to school activities. The children also put on programs for the

[7]National Council for the Social Studies, "Revision of the Social Studies Curriculum Guidelines," *Social Education*, 43 (April 1979), p. 266.

retirees at the home. As the project developed, parents of the children also became involved. Some of the parents invited residents to their homes for dinner, took them to church, and for Sunday drives. The senior citizens had skills and hobbies that they shared with the children.

7. Elementary schoolchildren made tray favors for a local convalescent home for each of the major holidays during the school year.
8. Sixth graders collected and refurbished used toys and donated them to Goodwill Industries for redistribution.
9. Pupils collected books in the neighborhood for the local library's used-book sale.
10. A class made a survey of their homes to look for safety hazards or fire dangers and corrected them.
11. A social studies class sponsored a bicycle safety program in the school.
12. Upper graders volunteered to do free baby sitting for mothers on Election Day.

DISCUSSION QUESTIONS AND SUGGESTED ACTIVITIES

1. Select a unit topic for a grade in which you have a special interest. Suggest ways that the activities discussed in this chapter could be incorporated in such a unit.
2. Criticize or defend the following statement: Social studies for young children should be more activity oriented than subject-matter centered.
3. When you visit an elementary school classroom, observe the type of construction activities underway. Are they accurate and authentic representations? What purposes was the teacher hoping to accomplish through the use of construction?
4. Demonstrate to your peers how you would proceed with a processing activity of some type (i.e. making butter, dipping candles, weaving a basket, and so forth). Indicate the concepts being developed in the activity.
5. Obtain or write an unfinished, open-ended story that could be used as a role-playing activity for children. Put the characters in a social problem situation. What alternatives are open to the major characters in the story?
6. Suggest situations that might be developed into a simulation game. With the help of two or three peers, develop a simple simulation game.
7. Develop plans for a social action project for a grade of your choice. Have your plans critiqued by your peers.
8. The use of song lyrics was not discussed in the text. What possibilities can you suggest for the use of song lyrics in learning about the period in which a song was written?

343

SELECTED REFERENCES

Allen, Elizabeth G. and Jone P. Wright. "Just for Fun: Creative Dramatics Learning Center," *Childhood Education*, 54 (February 1978), pp. 169–175.

Caldwell, Bettye and Robert Yowell. "Action Dramatics," *Instructor*, 86 (January 1977), pp. 118–124.

Duecek, Kathryn G. "Social Action in Elementary Social Studies," *The History and Social Science Teacher*, 15 (Summer 1980), pp. 245–251.

Furness, Pauline. *Role Play in the Elementary School: A Handbook for Teachers*. New York: Hart Publishing Co., Inc., 1976.

Gilbert, Anne Green. *Teaching the Three Rs Through Movement Experiences*. Minneapolis, Minnesota: Burgess Publishing Company, 1977.

Joyce, William W. and Janet E. Alleman-Brooks. *Teaching Social Studies in the Elementary and Middle Schools*. New York: Holt, Rinehart and Winston, Inc., 1979. Chapter 4.

Keach, Everett T. "Simulation Games and the Elementary School," *Social Education*, 38 (March 1974), pp. 284–285. (This article, plus four others dealing with simulation games, is included in the Elementary Education Section of this issue.)

LeClerc, Daniel C. "Architecture as a Primary Source for Social Studies," *How To Do It Series* 2, No. 5, National Council for the Social Studies. Washington, D.C.: The Council, 1978.

Lopez, John Jr. "The 'Real Thing': Social Action," *The Social Studies*, 68 (January-February 1977), pp. 38–41.

McNamara, Shelly G. "Naive Mural Art as a Vehicle for Teaching Elementary Social Studies," *Social Education*, 43 (October 1979), pp. 473–476.

Muir, Sharon Pray. "Simulation Games for Elementary Social Studies," *Social Education*, 44 (January 1980), pp. 35–39.

Reese, Jay. *Simulation Games and Learning Activities Kit for the Elementary School*. West Nyack, N.J.: Parker Publishing Company, Inc., 1977.

Samples, Bob, Cheryl Charles, and Dick Barnhart. *The Wholeschool Book*. Reading, Mass.: Addison-Wesley Publishing Co., 1977.

Sorgman, Margo, Marylou Sorensen, and Marilyn Johnston. "What Sounds Do I Make When I'm Old? A Hands-On Approach to Ageism," *Social Education* 43 (February 1979), pp. 135–139. (Imaginative activities suggested for the middle grades, plus list of learning resources related to this topic.)

Turner, Thomas N. "Using Popular Culture in the Social Studies," *How To Do It Series* 2, No. 9, National Council for the Social Studies. Washington, D.C. The Council, 1979.

Turner, Thomas N. *Creative Activities Resource Book for Elementary School Teachers*. Reston, Va.: Reston Publishing Company, 1978.

IV
Evaluation

13

Evaluating Pupil Achievement in Social Studies

Evaluating pupil learning is an indispensable part of teaching because (1) it helps clarify objectives for learners—it helps them know what is important to learn; (2) it provides feedback to the learners, thereby keeping them informed about their progress or lack of it; (3) it informs learners if and how they are deficient in order that they can improve; and (4) it informs the teacher of the extent to which pupils have achieved desired outcomes. Additionally, evaluation is essential in reporting pupil progress to parents and informing the public about the effectiveness of school programs.

Assessing pupil learning involves comparing outcomes ·of instruction with the anticipated or stated objectives. For this reason, the statement of objectives has to be done with a degree of precision. Unless we can define what we want children to learn and can devise ways of determining whether or not they have learned it, we really cannot make well-grounded value judgments about the effectiveness of the teaching or about the extent to which desired learning has occurred. Assessment of achievement, therefore, always involves identifying the objectives that are sought.

Throughout this book the importance of formative evaluation as an essential part of the teaching-learning process has been stressed. A threefold relationship exists among objectives, teaching procedures, and evaluation; compatibility must be maintained in the relationship. It is inconsistent, for example, to state objectives dealing with the development of inquiry skills, group-work skills, and valuing, and at the same time use teaching procedures that are wholly expository and evaluate only subject-matter outcomes with a paper-and-pencil test at the end of the unit. Teaching methods and evaluation procedures must be in harmony with the objectives to be achieved.

INFORMAL EVALUATION TECHNIQUES

Much of the evaluation of learning in social studies is done informally by the teacher. Many times each day the teacher observes learners and makes a judgment about the quality of their work. The teacher notices what problems individual children are encountering, or what kind of help they need in order to progress. Teachers find themselves spending a considerable amount of time evaluating, diagnosing, and appraising the status of individual children and groups. The teacher then makes decisions concerning what needs the pupils have, whether the instruction is proceeding too rapidly or too slowly, what materials are required, how· well concepts have been understood, or how proficient children are in their use of skills. Of course, formal tests have a place in this process, but most of the evaluation a teacher does involves informal methods and observation. This means that careful records must be kept if pupil progress is to be reported accurately. Some of the more commonly used evaluative techniques and devices are described on the following pages.

Group Discussion

Group discussion can be used to appraise the progress of the class in terms of plans and standards that were previously established. Discussion will activate thinking along the lines of self-evaluation; it helps clarify and remind children of learning goals; it is useful in establishing an attitude of looking forward to progress and growth. It is recommended that the teacher reserve some time near the end of every social studies period for the class to discuss its progress and to make plans for the next day's work. As was noted earlier, this helps children crystallize their thinking, helps identify concepts needing further study, and reminds them of the things they are learning in social studies. In addition to the daily discussions of the progress of the class, this technique can also be used in a variety of other situations:

1. as a follow-up of a major class activity such as a field trip, a social action project, a dramatization.
2. as a method of evaluating group reports, unit projects, creative dramatics activities.
3. as a means of improving small-group endeavors.
4. as a means of evaluating behavior of the class at a school assembly, in the lunchroom, or on the playground.
5. as a method of working out some problem of human relations within the classroom.
6. as a means of bringing to light attitudes that may be held by pupils.

348

7. as a means of verifying information obtained through individual study.

The use of discussion as a technique of evaluation necessitates the identification of standards to be attained and a knowledge of what is expected on the part of the pupils. This means that in most cases the teacher and the class will have to decide on standards that apply in a given situation. For example, if a class is about to engage in an activity calling for small committees, the following standards may be agreed on:

1. Work quietly, so that others may work, too.
2. Know where the materials are.
3. Arrange with other groups to borrow materials.
4. Speak quietly to other committee members.
5. Stop work as soon as the bell rings.
6. Arrange and clean up the area after work.

Specific work standards of the type just described should be posted on a chart and referred to when the work of the class is being evaluated through discussion. Verbal agreement on standards is not sufficient for young children—they forget from day to day just what the standards are. Posting the standards and discussing them without "harping" on them helps remind children of their responsibilities and enhances their learning. Knowledge of progress is a strong force in the motivation of learning, and a knowledge of areas in which improvement is needed helps give direction to learning. The use of class discussion as an evaluative technique can serve both of these purposes.

Observation

Observation is among the best techniques available to the teacher in learning about children, appraising their growth, and sensing their needs. Although all teachers use this method of pupil appraisal, not all teachers are equally skillful in its application. Much of what is called observation of pupils might properly be described as a disorganized set of impressions the teacher obtains during the course of instruction, essentially on a catch-as-catch-can basis. The teacher who makes the most of observation knows what he or she is looking for, systematizes observations, and makes an attempt to objectify the data so obtained. To this end it is suggested that the teacher:

. Spell out exactly the traits to be evaluated and state evidences of these traits in terms of child behavior. For example, if the teacher desires to observe whether or not there is evidence of progress in

349

consideration of others, such things as the following would be appropriate:

Does the child

    a. Show respect for the ideas and feelings of classmates?
    b. Abstain from causing disturbances that make it impossible for others to do their best work?
    c. Carry a fair share of the work load in a small group?
    d. Enjoy giving a classmate an "assist" when needed?
    e. Display sensitivity to injustices that may occur in the course of life in and out of the classroom?
    f. Return borrowed materials? Obtain permission to use materials that belong to others?
    g. Observe rules established by the group?
    h. Fulfill responsibilities on time? Avoid doing things that hold up the progress of the class?

2. Select certain pupils for intensive observation and study rather than observing "in general." This intensive observation might be limited to certain specific situations. For example, just what happens to David when he is placed on a committee to do some project in connection with a social studies unit? How can the situation be changed to help him develop more responsible habits of work in a group situation? The purpose of observations of this type, of course, is to gain insight into the child's behavior in the context of a specific set of circumstances.
3. Not depend on memory as a device to record observations. Keep a written record of data obtained through observation and maintain this record over a period of time to establish a definite pattern in the child's behavior. At best, observation is a highly unreliable method of appraising pupil progress, and without a record of the observations, it is of little value indeed. The written record may take the form of anecdotal accounts, a checklist system, or a rating device. Data of this type are necessary in interpreting and reporting the progress and growth of children to their parents.

Checklists

Checklists may be constructed from previously established specific objectives and can be used either by the teacher or by the children themselves in evaluating progress. It is a good practice for classes to work out short checklists cooperatively and apply them to their work individually. The checklists may be used when children are giving reports or short talks to call attention to clarity of speaking, new information presented, use of visual material, extent of preparedness, and other responsibilities of the speaker. A similar checklist can be devised to cover the responsibilities of the audience. An example of a self-evaluation sheet developed by a teacher with a class is reproduced in part in Figure 18.

DATE _____ NAME _____				
In this unit I was able to	super-well	good	okay	needed more help
choose appropriate activities				
use my work-time efficiently				
work cooperatively with another person				
use materials from the Resource Center				
keep my work area clean				
use the suggestions that others gave me				
Remarks:				

FIGURE 18. Pupil self-evaluation form.

In addition to the checklists developed and used by the pupils for self-appraisal, the teacher can devise similar checklists for use in recording the behavior of children. As previously noted, this procedure adds objectivity and reliability to the teacher's observation of the class. The specific points to be checked would be the behavior characteristics that provide evidence either of the presence or absence of the trait under study. Commercially prepared behavior-rating scales may be used for the same purpose.

Conferences

Conferences with pupils should teach them how to evaluate their own work, thereby leading to increasing self-direction. The teacher-pupil conference can be of help in discovering particular learning problems and difficulties that children may be having, gaining insight into their feelings about schoolwork, and becoming aware of special personal-social problems the children may be having, as well as a method of assisting every child individually in a personal way. The quality of instruction in the elementary school would unquestionably be markedly improved if the teacher could spend an hour each day in ten-minute individual conferences with pupils. Currently, teachers find little time that can be used for such purposes. But, for the children who appear to need the personal contact with their teacher that a conference can give, time should be found.

A conference will be of little value if the teacher does all the talking and the child all the listening. A friendly helpful approach is

351

needed, one that results in greater feelings of personal worth on the part of the child along with some constructive and concrete helps for improvement. This close working relationship with pupils is critical to good elementary education, especially in the social studies.

Anecdotal Records

An *anecdotal record* is a description of some incident or situation in the life of the child. A collection of such descriptions of pupil behavior kept over a period of time, therefore, provides the teacher with a documentary account of changes of behavior that have occurred or are in progress. It is another way of systematically recording observations. Anecdotal records should indicate the data and time of the incident, the circumstances under which it occurred, and an objective description of the situation. If an interpretation is made of the incident, it should be kept separate from the description of the actual happening. The following are six entries in one teacher's anecdotal record on a child.

ANECDOTAL RECORD

Sara Larsen

9/24   Difficulty in getting going in independent choice work; ignored all suggestions of activities. . . . "It's boring."

9/26   Found a fiction book related to unit for Sara. Read during work time. Took it home today.

9/27   Finished book . . . took suggestion to make a poster showing main characters.

10/1   Asked for time to show class the poster and to tell about the story.

10/2   Showed work. Talented artist. Received lots of compliments/support from classmates.

10/3   Sara asked for another book; suggested biography to her, plus suggested she do a map showing the area in which the person lived.

Work Samples

The practice of saving samples of pupils' work by the teacher is similar to the parent who cuts notches on the inside of a closet door recording the height of a child at various ages. Both the parent and the teacher know that growth is occurring but because of their continuous contact with the child on a day-to-day basis, growth and progress are imperceptible. They need, therefore, a specific example of the child's status at one point in time in order to judge growth or progress at a subsequent time. The greater the time interval between the two samples, the greater should be the evidence of change.

Work samples that are saved for this purpose are usually written material and may include a report, a story, a classroom test, an explanation, a booklet, or a research project. The teacher might also want to save a pupil's map work, artwork done in connection with the social studies, or a small construction project. The tape recorder can also be used to obtain a sample of the child's oral language. For example, children find it revealing and profitable to hear reports privately that they have made to the class at various times during the school year. The same device can be used by the entire class to evaluate their progress in discussions, dramatizations, and similar speaking situations. Care must be taken, however, to ensure that such procedures do not call attention to speech disorders of specific children.

Experience Summaries

Experience summaries placed on charts are used to abstract learnings and to record a particular learning experience. They are ordinarily constructed cooperatively by the teacher and the class and are used to record and evaluate a single or specific experience rather than a series of experiences. For example, when the group returns from its trip to the airport, the children can summarize some of the important things they have learned as a result of the trip and place these on a chart. The chart may then be used to evaluate the extent to which they found out the things they set out to learn. The following is an example of an experience summary.

What We Learned at the Food Distribution Center:

1. How food is sent to grocery stores.
2. That food we eat comes from all over the world.
3. Certain foods must be kept in temperature controlled rooms so they do not spoil.
4. It takes many people to handle the food before we see it in our stores.
5. Food is sent by railroad cars, ships, trucks, and sometimes planes before it reaches the store.
6. Grocery stores order the amounts they need each week before it is sent to them.

Diaries and Logs

Diaries and logs are similar to experience summaries except that they are kept on a continuing basis. Each day the class can summarize its progress and record it on a chart or in a notebook. This provides a running account of work in the unit and can be used to review and check on previous plans and decisions as the unit progresses. In the final phases of the unit, the class, by referring to its log, can recall many details of its work that would otherwise be overlooked or forgotten. In the primary grades, the teacher will have to assume much of the responsibility for recording the material to be placed in the log, although children can and should assist in deciding *what* is to

353

be recorded. In the middle and upper grades, individual children or committees can assume this responsibility if they are given some help and guidance by the teacher. A form such as the following can be used to record diary or log entries.

DIARY/LOG

Date _____   Name _____

Today:

I learned a new fact: _____

I tried something new: _____

I worked with: _____

I was best at: _____

I spent most of my time: _____

Sociometric Devices

Sociometric devices are used to evaluate growth in social relations, and/or to observe changes in the social structure of a group. In order to be used effectively for either purpose, they should be applied more than once to the group. Data collected in this way indicate the structure of the group at the time the data were obtained in terms of the reason for which the children made their choices. Social relationships change, and with young children these changes occur frequently. The younger the children are, the less stable their friendships are. As an example, a first-grader's "best pal" one day may be ignored the next; the third day they may be best pals again. Such unpredictability of friendship patterns would have a devastating effect on a sixth-grader. Sociometric devices are, therefore, less reliable at lower levels than when the children are older and more consistent in their choices of children with whom they wish to work or to play.

Carefully administered, sociometric devices will be helpful to the teacher in appraising the extent to which (1) peripheral children have won greater acceptance by the group, (2) leadership roles have shifted, (3) preferences of children for one another have changed, and (4) strong in-groups have become more flexible. Specific directions for the application of sociometric devices can be found in most standard texts on measurement and evaluation.

TEACHER-MADE TESTS

Classroom tests constructed by the teacher usually are used to appraise the child's progress in the more factual outcomes of social studies instruction. Even though paper-and-pencil tests can be used successfully with primary-grade children, their value increases as the child moves into the middle and upper grades. These tests are of maximum value when they are constructed to test basic understandings, concepts, and knowledge rather than only the facts related to the topics under study. Too frequently questions dealing with *who, what, when, where,* and *how many* take precedence over more reflective and penetrating items such as those that call for knowing *why, for what reason,* and *how we know.* An important requirement of any good test is that it should enhance and encourage desirable study habits. Overemphasis on recall of minutiae and inconsequential details inevitably leads to rote memory of facts without understanding their significance or without relating them to the basic and underlying key ideas. When conventional objective-type test items such as multiple choice, alternate response, completion, recall, and matching, are used their construction should be technically correct. Many of the standard works on measurement and evaluation discuss in detail the advantages and limitations of various objective-type test items and offer suggestions for their construction.

Teacher-made tests are essential in evaluating the children's growth in certain social studies skills. Tests designed to measure the child's skill in using a map—locating places, identifying map symbols, reading the legend, understanding scale, interpreting map data, recognizing land forms—are a necessary part of instruction in the use of maps. An example of this type of teacher-made test appears in Figure 20. Similarly, short tests can be designed to evaluate the child's ability to use reference material, to read social studies materials, to understand the vocabulary of social studies, to evaluate news stories, to distinguish between fact and opinion, and other social studies skills. Examples of teacher-made tests are provided on pages 356–360.

In constructing specific items to evaluate certain kinds of learnings, the teacher may find the suggestions of Maxine Dunfee helpful as presented in the Thirty-fifth Yearbook of the National Council for the Social Studies. A few examples of the types of items she suggests are these:

To test for *factual information*—
  Arranging in order the steps in a process
  Matching events with periods of time
  Supplying key words missing in statements of essential facts
  Matching vocabulary and definition
  Placing events or persons on a time line
To test for *understandings*—
  Matching causes and effects
  Supplying a generalization to be drawn from a given set of facts
  Stating the most important ideas learned
  Selecting a conclusion to be drawn from a chart, diagram, or graph
To obtain insights into *attitudes* of pupils—
  Responding to statements in terms of strength of belief, feeling,
    or opinion by indicating degree—always, sometimes, never

355

Responding to statements that imply prejudice or lack of prejudice by indicating state of agreement—I agree, I disagree, I am uncertain

Matching attitudes with likely resultant actions

Writing endings to stories that describe problem situations

To test for *skills*—

Interpreting an imaginary map, locating physical and cultural features and answering questions calling for interpretation of information provided

Supplying a missing step in directions for doing something that involves a skill

Demonstrating how to conduct a meeting, how to give a good report, and so on

Using a table of contents or index to locate specified information[1]

The following are a few examples of teacher-made tests that could be used for evaluating social studies outcomes:

WHAT'S GOING ON HERE?

Directions: Read each paragraph carefully, then write a sentence telling what the paragraph is describing.

Situation 1. It was the first Tuesday in November. On this day the fire station had the United States flag flying just outside the entrance. All day long people were going in and coming out of the fire station. A sign in the window said, "Polling Place."

What was going on at the fire station?

_____

Situation 2. A large number of people are in the room. At the front of the room, sitting behind a large desk up on a platform, is a man dressed in a black robe who seems to be in charge of things. As we watch, two men face each other in front of the man in the black robe. One man seems to be holding a Bible. He says to the other man, "Raise your right hand. Do you swear to tell the truth, the whole truth, and nothing but the truth, so help you God?"

What is going on in this room?

_____

Situation 3. A large crowd of people is in this huge room. There are signs and banners all over the place. There is much noise and confusion. People speak to the crowd, but many are not listening. The person who is now speaking has just said, "I yield five minutes to the delegate from the great state of Virginia."

What is going on here?

_____

Situation 4. People are scurrying around all over the place. Everyone seems to be in a hurry. Over the loud speaker, a voice is saying, "The East Concourse is now open."

Where is all this taking place?

_____

FIGURE 19.

[1]Maxine Dunfee, "Evaluating Understandings, Attitudes, Skills, and Behaviors in Elementary School Social Studies," *Evaluation in Social Studies*, 35th Yearbook, Chap. 8 Washington, D.C.: National Council for the Social Studies, 1965, pp. 165-167.

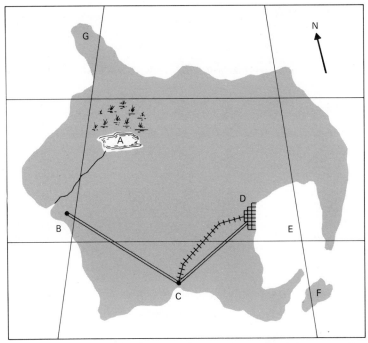

FIGURE 20. Teachers can devise tests of this type to evaluate growth in map-reading skills:

Underline the correct answer:

1. The land north of A is (a swamp), (a desert), (mountainous).
2. The mouth of a river is located near letter (A), (B), (C).
3. The city at D is perhaps a (capital), (seaport), (mining town).
4. The river flows (from southwest to northeast), (from northeast to southwest), (from east to west).
5. An island is marked by the letter (A), (B), (F).
6. A railroad runs between (B and C), (D and B), (D and C).
7. The letter E marks (a bay), (a peninsula), (an island).
8. A peninsula is shown on this map at (B), (G), (C).
9. A delta might be found just north of (C), (A), (B).
10. The letter G is due north of (C), (A), (B).

DO-IT-YOURSELF MAP

Directions:

1. On a clean sheet of paper, draw an outline map of an imaginary continent. You may make it any shape you wish, but you must include at least one peninsula and one bay.
2. Show a scale of miles in your legend for the map.
3. Draw east-west and north-south lines on your map.
4. Draw a mountain range running east and west across your continent but include at least one mountain pass. Place the symbol you use for your mountain range in your legend.
5. Show a city in the northern half of your continent and one in the southern half. Make each one a seaport.

FIGURE 21.

6. Show a railway joining the two cities.
7. Show three rivers on your continent; show a lake and a swamp. Place all the symbols you use for cities, rivers, lakes, and swamps in the legend.
8. Place a third city somewhere on your map where you think a city should be. On the bottom of your map tell why you think a city should be where you have placed it.
9. Show boundary lines that divide your continent into three large countries and one small country.

FIGURE 21. (*Continued*)

KNOWING THEIR MEANING

Directions: The phrases in the right-hand column explain the words or terms listed in the left-hand column. In the space to the left of each phrase, place the letter of the word or term that matches the description.

a. Blimp
b. Drill
c. Mohair
d. Derrick
e. Raw Sugar
f. Helium
g. Gusher
h. Sulphur
i. Refinery
j. Flowing well

_____ 1. An oil well from which the oil shoots high into the air.

_____ 2. A building in which raw materials are changed into finished products.

_____ 3. The brown crystals that form when the juice of sugar cane is boiled and allowed to cool.

_____ 4. The framework that supports the machinery used to drill an oil well.

_____ 5. The tool used to bore holes into the earth.

_____ 6. An airship that floats in the air when filled with a light gas.

_____ 7. Cloth made from goat hair.

_____ 8. A very light gas.

_____ 9. A well from which a steady stream of oil flows without having to be pumped.

_____ 10. A yellow mineral.

FIGURE 22.

WHAT DID YOU LIKE BEST?

Directions: In the space to the left of each activity, write a letter "L" if you liked it and a "D" if you did not like it. Place a star (*) next to the two you liked best of all.

_____ 1. Making individual booklets on the unit.

_____ 2. Working in committees.

_____ 3. Dramatizing important events.

_____ 4. Writing summaries.

_____ 5. Doing map work.

_____ 6. Seeing films and filmstrips.

_____ 7. Reading different books.

_____ 8. Collecting pictures.

_____ 9. Taking the field trip.

_____ 10. Hearing the resource people.

_____ 11. Making a mural.

_____ 12. Preparing the exhibit.

_____ 13. Preparing the report.

_____ 14. Doing the simulation.

_____ 15. Working in the learning center.

FIGURE 23.

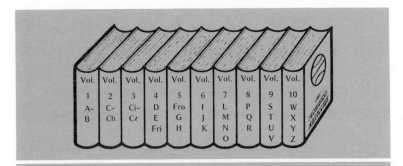

USING THE ENCYCLOPEDIA

Directions: Using the ten-volume *Our Own Encyclopedia* shown in this diagram, select the number of the volume in which you would find information about each of the items listed below. Write the number of the volume you select in the spaces on the left side of the sheet. Then list the volume number of *World Book* in which the same items are found in the spaces on the right side of the sheet.

Our Own   *World Book*

                1. Earthquakes in Guatemala   1. _____

                2. The French writer Crévecoeur   2. _____

                3. The history of rocketry   3. _____

                4. The Peoples Republic of China   4. _____

                5. Russia   5. _____

                6. Apple growing in Washington state   6. _____

                7. Jet aircraft   7. _____

                8. Countries that are members of the   8. _____
                      United Nations

                9. Unidentified flying objects   9. _____

               10. The history of Czechoslovakia   10. _____

FIGURE 24.

TRUE OR FALSE?

Directions: The following list contains some statements that are true and some that are not true. Read each one and decide whether it is or is not true. If it is true, place a "T" in the space just to the left of the statement. If it is false, place an "F" in the space and *rewrite* the statement on the line below it to make it true.

_____ 1. Some of the dry land in Arizona and New Mexico is irrigated and produces fine crops.

_____

_____ 2. Colorado and Nevada were settled by people rushing east.

_____

_____ 3. The Mormons settled at Great Salt Lake in a region then owned by California.

_____

FIGURE 25.

_____ 4. Gold was discovered in the Comstock Lode in the state of Nevada.

_____ 5. The large area in the Rockies that is lower than the surrounding mountains is called the Continental Divide.

_____ 6. The Indian house used by the Navajos is called a hogan.

_____ 7. The Plains Indians lived in villages called pueblos.

_____ 8. An early mission was established in what is now the state of Arizona by Father Kino.

FIGURE 25. (*Continued*)

MATCHING CAUSE AND EFFECT

Directions: Each of the events listed in the first column was the cause of an event listed in the second column. In the space provided at the left, place the letter of the result that matches each cause.

_____ 1. Expanding factories needed many workers.

_____ 2. Automobiles were mass produced at low cost.

_____ 3. Trains and trolleys were built to take people to their jobs.

_____ 4. Workers needed to live close to their jobs.

a. People with average income could buy their own cars.

b. Immigrant workers came in large numbers.

c. Workers lived in crowded and congested conditions.

d. People could have their homes farther from where they worked.

FIGURE 26.

Checklist for Discussion (Middle Grades)	Always	Usually	Seldom	Rarely
1. States problems clearly				
2. Sticks to the point				
3. Shows respect for ideas of others				
4. Contributes regularly				
5. Raises questions on issues				
6. Helps in making decisions				
7. Uses evidence to back up points				
8. Helps in summarizing				

Chart 7.

Checklist for Discussion (Primary Grades)			
	Always	Sometimes	Not Often
1. Helps make plans			
2. Listens to what is said			
3. Takes turns			
4. Gives own ideas			
5. Considers what others have said			

Chart 8.

STANDARDIZED TESTS

Standardized tests are helpful in obtaining an objective measure of progress in the more tangible outcomes of social studies instruction. They can also be used to establish the achievement status of a class or of individual pupils. Standardized tests ordinarily do not evaluate many of the broader goals of social studies instruction, because they usually focus on the measurement of subject-matter knowledge or study skills. Standardized tests can make an important contribution to the program of evaluation in social studies.

Standardized tests are called *norm-referenced* tests. That is, a child's performance is evaluated in terms of the performance of a large sample of other children of the same age and grade, i.e., the norming population. This is different from *criterion-referenced* tests, in which the child is evaluated in terms of the degree of progress toward the attainment of specific objectives. Criterion-referenced tests often are associated with the "mastery" of certain learnings, meaning that the child continues to work on the material until a certain expected level of competence (*criterion level*) has been achieved. Criterion-referenced tests have gained considerable attention in recent years because of the emphasis on individualized learning and the use of behavioral objectives.

Standardized tests provide the teacher with an objective yardstick to measure progress in learning. Furthermore, the teacher can compare the achievement of the group or of any child with other children of the same age and grade. The chief obstacle to wise use of these tests, however, is that teachers have a tendency to regard the grade norm as a standard that all must achieve if their progress is to be regarded as satisfactory. In other words, teachers believe that all children must attain a grade score on the test equal to their present grade status. *This is an erroneous approach to the use of standardized tests* because the grade norm represents an average performance. For many children this level of achievement expectation will be too low;

361

for others it will be too high. The teacher can reasonably expect the range of achievement of groups in which children have been randomly selected to range from two to four grades below, to two to four grades above the grade norm. This range will be less in the lower grades but becomes wider as the children move into the higher grades. Just what constitutes an adequate and satisfactory performance on the test will depend on individual children. Standards or levels of achievement expectation, therefore, should properly be established in terms of the capabilities of individual children and should not be dictated by the norms of a standardized test.

Knowing the results of a standardized achievement test, the teacher may set limited achievement expectations for a child, thus producing the effect of a self-fulfilling prophecy. There is no way of overcoming this problem entirely except to sensitize teachers to it, and to stress the need for data from a variety of sources before making a judgment about an appropriate level of achievement expectation for individual children. Because social studies achievement tests are so closely related to reading ability, the teacher should be especially suspicious of the validity of social studies test scores of pupils who are poor readers.

Published tests in the social studies differ in the extent to which they emphasize various social studies outcomes. Some are almost entirely subject-matter tests. These tests can be of value only if the content of the test and the content of the social studies curriculum are consistent. The test will lack validity to the extent that it lacks congruity with the curriculum. For example, if the teacher were administering a test that was heavily loaded with items about life in early America, the children would not do well on it unless the material had actually been taught. It would be inconsistent and improper to use such a test if the class had studied a series of units dealing with their home state that year. It should be emphasized that decisions on the curriculum content should come first and that the selection of the test should come second although that is often difficult to do. In selecting a test, the person making the selection should ascertain that its content is compatible with the curriculum in the particular school in which it is to be used.

To sidestep the issue of building a social studies test to fit the diverse programs operating throughout the country, some testmakers have placed emphasis on skills rather than on subject matter. Somewhat the same social studies skills should be developed in the grades irrespective of the topics studied. Children should be learning to read maps, to use basic reference materials, to read social studies material with understanding, and so on. Moreover, many of the subject-matter outcomes tend to be somewhat short-lived, because the rate of forgetting factual material is high, whereas mastery of the skills tends to be more long-lasting. Some teachers believe that standardized tests in the social studies are most useful for the measurement of more permanent learnings such as skills and prefer to evaluate subject-matter outcomes through the use of tests they themselves construct.

The following is a partial list of standardized tests that contain sections dealing with elements of social studies or that are entirely devoted to the measurement of social studies outcomes.

1. Stanford Achievement Test, Harcourt Brace Jovanovich, Inc., New York, N.Y.
2. Metropolitan Achievement Tests, Harcourt Brace Jovanovich, Inc., New York, N.Y.
3. SRA Achievement Series, Science Research Associates, Chicago, Ill.
4. Sequential Tests of Educational Progress: Social Studies, Level 4, Grades 4–6, Educational Testing Service, Princeton, N.J.
5. Iowa Every-Pupil Test of Basic Skills, Houghton Mifflin Company, Boston, Mass.

It follows logically that if varied outcomes are expected from social studies instruction, a broad basis of evaluation must be used as well. Effective evaluation depends in no small measure on the teacher's ability to select the appropriate means of appraising pupil growth in accordance with the established goals. The teacher should constantly look for evidences of growth in the child's ability to enter into class discussion, plan, lead, answer questions, assume responsibility, show consideration for others, share, take part in group endeavors, and apply learning to everyday living. The primary goal is continuous progress and growth in the many dimensions of human relationships for each child.

DISCUSSION QUESTIONS AND SUGGESTED ACTIVITIES

1. Why is evaluation essential to good social studies instruction?
2. Select a unit for a grade of your choice and write three objectives that would be appropriate for such a unit. Then prepare evaluative devices that could be used to determine how well those objectives have been achieved.
3. Do you think that it is a good idea to evaluate teacher effectiveness by the amount of pupil gain in achievement during a year? What do you see as the relationship between teacher effectiveness and pupil achievement?
4. The text mentions that a teacher's knowledge of scores on achievement tests may produce the effects of a self-fulfilling prophecy. Explain how this could happen. What other teaching

363

practices in social studies might also result in a self-fulfilling prophecy?

5. Refer to the list of major goals for the social studies on pages 6–8 in Chapter 1. Which goals lend themselves to formal evaluation through paper-and-pencil tests? Which goals require the use of other techniques? Which goals require the evaluator to observe the behavior of the learner on a firsthand basis? Which goals are most frequently evaluated? Why?

6. What advantages and disadvantages can you see in using state-wide or even nationwide achievement examinations in social studies?

7. Is evaluation the same as testing? Explain.

8. Secure a basic social studies textbook for a grade in which you have a special interest and examine the methods of evaluation it suggests and recommends. Do you regard these methods as soundly based? Why or why not? Is there a good balance in emphasis given to the evaluation of knowledge, values and attitudes, and skills objectives?

9. Suggest specific techniques you might use to evaluate each of the following:
   a. ability to apply knowledge or a skill.
   b. ability to generalize.
   c. ability to detect bias in a news story.
   d. knowing where to look for something in a reference book.
   e. degree of acceptance of a child by other children in the class.
   f. ability to detect sex-role or racial stereotyping.

10. What different purposes are served by diagnostic, formative, and summative evaluations?

SELECTED REFERENCES

Berg, Harry D., ed. *Evaluation in Social Studies*, 35th Yearbook. National Council for the Social Studies. Washington, D.C.: The Council, 1965.

Brown, Lena Boyd. "What Teachers Should Know about Standardized Tests," *Social Education*, 40 (November–December 1976), pp. 509–511+.

Chase, W. Linwood and Martha Tyler John. *A Guide for the Elementary Social Studies Teacher*, 3rd ed. Boston: Allyn & Bacon Books, Inc., 1978.

Ellis, Arthur and Janet Alleman-Brooks. "How to Evaluate Problem-Solving-Oriented Social Studies," *The Social Studies*, 68 (May–June 1977), pp. 99–103.

Gronlund, Norman E. *Stating Objectives for Classroom Instruction*, 2nd ed. New York: Macmillan Publishing Company, Inc., 1978. Chapters 8, 9, 10.

Haney, Walt. "Trouble Over Testing," *Educational Leadership*, 37 (May 1980), pp. 640–650.

Hunkins, Francis P. "Rationale for Testing in the Social Studies," *Social Education*, 40 (November–December 1976), pp. 504–508.

National Council for the Social Studies Position Statement. "Revision of the NCSS Social Studies Curriculum Guidelines," *Social Education*, 43 (April 1979), pp. 261–278.

Popham, W. James. "Well-Crafted Criterion-Referenced Tests," *Educational Leadership*, 36 (November 1978), pp. 91–95.

Index